POVERTY AND
WELFARE IN ENGLAND,
1700–1850

MANCHESTER
UNIVERTY PRESS

POVERTY AND WELFARE IN ENGLAND, 1700–1850

A REGIONAL PERSPECTIVE

Steven King

MANCHESTER
UNIVERSITY PRESS
Manchester and New York

distributed exclusively in the United States by St Martin's Press

Copyright © Steven King 2000

The right of Steven King to be identified as the author of this work has been asserted
by him in accordance with the Copyright, Designs and Patents Act 1988.

Published by Manchester University Press
Oxford Road, Manchester M13 9NR, UK
and Room 400, 175 Fifth Avenue, New York, NY 10010, USA
http://www.man.ac.uk/mup

Distributed exclusively in the USA by
St. Martin's Press, Inc., 175 Fifth Avenue, New York,
NY 10010, USA

Distributed exclusively in Canada by
UBC Press, University of British Columbia, 2029 West Mall,
Vancouver, BC, Canada V6T 1ZS

British Library Cataloguing-in-Publication Data
A catalogue record for this book is available from the British Library

Library of Congress Cataloging-in-Publication Data applied for

ISBN 0 7190 4939 3 *hardback*
ISBN 0 7190 4940 7 *paperback*

First published 2000

06 05 04 03 02 01 00   10 9 8 7 6 5 4 3 2 1

Typeset in Sabon
by Servis Filmsetting Limited

Printed in Great Britian
by Biddles Ltd, Guildford and King's Lynn

CONTENTS

FIGURES, TABLES AND MAPS

Figures

List of figures, tables and maps

Tables

Maps

For Marge and Irene

PREFACE

This book has been very long in the making. Some of the data used in the chapters which follow were collected as long ago as 1987, when I was still an undergraduate at the University of Kent and under the direction of historians such as Gordon Mingay, Alan Armstrong, Roger Scola and Sean Glynn. Indeed, had it not been for the way that they collectively enlivened history, there is no doubt that I would have been a bank manager today and this book would never have been written. Since 1987 I have been accumulating more data on poverty and welfare from archives, private collections, libraries and a variety of weird and wonderful places. One of my enduring memories is standing with James Morris in a Kettering shoe factory looking at a case of nineteenth-century account books as the wrecking balls were knocking down the building next door. In 1994, a number of people responded to an advertisement I published asking for help in finding poor law and other documentation in attics and other private collections. Their names can be found in the Bibliography, and to them I owe a considerable debt.

When Manchester University Press offered me the chance to write this book, therefore, I accepted with considerable enthusiasm. Enthusiasm, however, was not enough to get quick results. The hard lessons of the University of Central Lancashire and then a move to Oxford Brookes set back progress considerably, and Vanessa Graham at Manchester University Press must have the patience of a saint to have put up with my failure to meet deadlines. However, now that the book is complete, I owe many debts. Richard Smith and Pat Hudson got me interested in poverty and have been valuable colleagues. Geoff Timmins and Margaret Hanly have often kept me at least a little sane. Pam Sharpe has been a valuable but friendly critic, and numerous seminars and conferences have provided opportunities to explore ideas developed here. In particular, the Cambridge Group has provided a lively forum for discussing the work of chapters five to seven. Others – too many – who have contributed explicitly or implicitly to this book have died during its making. Jack, Marge, Irene, John, James and Dave should have been here to see this but are not. To them and to Catherine, thanks.

Ultimately, this book represents an attempt to do two very different things. On the one hand it tries to synthesise – for undergraduates and others – the literature that tells us where welfare historians have got to in their attempts to distil the essential character of the poor laws old and new and to locate the role of the community in the welfare patterns of ordinary people. For this reason there are places where the experienced welfare historian might wish for more conceptual rigour or a more complex interpretation of data. On the other hand, the book uses extensive new datasets to try to take forward the debate over welfare, drawing out regional, and ultimately also sub-regional, patterns in the character of the poor law and its role in ordinary lives. Inevitably undergraduate readers will find these sections of the book more demanding than they might wish. A dual strategy like this risks much, but it seems to me that a book which brings together, for the first time in the 1990s, the wide body of published and unpublished research on the poor law – *and* asks new questions of new data to suggest ways in which the debate might be taken forward – is long overdue. Against this backdrop, I have tried to make the book as open and accessible as possible – others may use my data in different ways and for their own purposes – and in this task I was helped by the invaluable comments of the publisher's reader of this volume who suggested sophisticated ways to reduce the tensions which my writing strategy might have otherwise generated. I am grateful to this reader and to the others who have contributed to the making of this book.

CHAPTER ONE

INTRODUCTION

In June 1823, the overseer of the Lancashire town of Billington received the following letter from a woman living in the nearby town of Blackburn,

> To the Select Vestry of Billington.
> Gentlemen,
> I am under the necessity to solicit your aid at this time for I am in great distress having no bed to lie on but obliged to lie on the bare ground this gentlemen is a bad case But Gentlemen I hope you will seriously consider my case and allow me a bed and some money I have some money to pay and I want a little money to pay my debt and some while I can set up my looms But Gentlemen I want a pair of stays and a shuttle If I get these things I shall want little of you for I do not like coming to crave your assistance If I can help it now. Gentlemen I have an heart rending case to mention to you the Child and me has not been in a bed this fortnight this is a shocking circumstance the Child is in work but he has not drawn anything yet.
>
> Do Gentlemen let humanity have a place in your hearts consider if you were placed in similar circumstances reason this way and let things come home to your hearts how unpleasant it would appear to you and no person is certain but it may be his case if he has riches – riches sometimes make themselves wings and fly away.
>
> I have my case in your hands and patiently wait your decision on the subject and remain your poor affectionate servant.
> Mary Dewhurst.[1]

Throughout the period 1700–1850, the issue of how poor people like Mary Dewhurst should secure their weekly, monthly and yearly welfare manifested itself as *the* single most important social issue at local and national level. In particular, the question of what role the community (via the poor laws) should and did play in relieving those in need was a source of contemporary debate, and has subsequently been laid at the heart of discussions over welfare amongst modern historians.[2] Did communal welfare provide allowances which were sufficient to allow people a reasonable standard of living? Was communal welfare wide in scope and orientated to the needs of the poor? Or was communal welfare harsh, inflexible and orientated towards the needs of the ratepayer? Would the plight of people like Mary Dewhurst foster compassion or contempt in the minds of the men who usually administered communal relief at local level? Would she be treated differently if she lived in Essex or Kent as opposed to Lancashire? Would her appeal have been better received in a rural area as opposed to this urban one? What does the language in Mary Dewhurst's appeal tell us about the experience of being poor on the one hand, and the nature of the decision-making process in the communal welfare system on the other? More widely, how had Mary Dewhurst got to a position where she had to lie on the 'bare ground'? Using a combination of primary and secondary material, this book attempts to offer answers to questions such as these in the English context, and also to highlight and explore other questions about welfare, communal relief and poverty which are more rarely asked of historical populations.[3] For instance, what did 'poverty' mean in a historical context? How much poverty was there? How did people conceive of their welfare needs? And what avenues did people pursue besides those (borrowing, work and communal relief) indicated in Mary Dewhurst's letter?

In the process of asking and answering these questions, the book will attempt to accomplish the delicate balancing act between providing a synthesis of current and historical thinking on poverty, poor relief and welfare *and* taking the debate forward using new data presented in new ways. There is inevitably a tension between these two aspirations, and yet the need for a book which begins at the beginning in order to understand the experiences of people like Dewhurst seems long overdue. For those who might prefer a more refined treatment of the original data used here, chapter nine offers some provocative suggestions. For undergraduate readers, the overview at the start of each chapter and the conclusion at the end of each chapter provides a quick reference point to the essential arguments of this book. More than other books on poverty or social issues, however, this one must be read as a whole and with an eye for the incremental development of perspectives which may carry the welfare debate forward.

The tasks in hand are clearly considerable and complex, and consequently it is important to develop right at the start an 'approach' to poverty and welfare which will provide the analytical framework for this study. Previous literature on the English welfare system provides a rich tapestry of 'approaches' from which we could choose. Some of the earliest analyses eschewed study of the poor themselves and preferred to investigate the legislative framework which surrounded the poor law and the activities of other agencies that furthered welfare, such as friendly societies, charities, unions, and boot and shoe clubs.[4] As we will see in the next chapter, from the codification in 1601 of formal national obligations for parishes and townships to care for their deserving poor to the creation (between 1846 and 1869) of the rounded legal frame-work necessary to enforce the provisions of the 1834 New Poor Law, parliament considered a bewildering variety of legislative measures related to the poor.[5] This has proved a rich picking ground for *legalistic* approaches, though such studies have yet to provide clear guidance as to what the nuances of the law really meant for welfare on the ground. Other commentators have preferred an essentially *administrative* approach to welfare, concentrating on local, county and national administrations and the question of how these bodies formed and implemented policy initiatives. For those taking this approach, ques-tions about how unions were formed and staffed under the new poor law, how vestries related to overseers under the old poor law, how over-seers interacted with ratepayers, and what role magistrates and politi-cians played in the welfare process under the old poor law, are important issues.[6] Analysis of the careers of prominent welfare reform-ers forms a separate sub-strand of this administrative approach.[7]

Another common way to reach an understanding of the character and role of the poor laws and the experiences of poverty and welfare has been to write *institutional* histories, particularly histories of the workhouse and its inmates.[8] Of course, it is not difficult to see why the workhouse has figured so prominently in the deep psyche of poor law research. A national survey of the poor law for the financial year 1802/3 revealed 3,765 workhouse institutions.[9] The Webbs believed that this figure had risen to 4,000 institutions by 1815, with a resident pauper population of 100,000.[10] By 1831, there were almost 4,800 institutions and while the number fell under the new poor law, workhouses became progressively larger and more grandly constructed.[11] The workhouse, then, appears as a central component of the poor law and welfare system, and where records survive its inmates have proved easier and more interesting to study than the anonymous mass of the poor whose histories are concealed in outdoor relief lists under both the old and the new poor laws or whose poverty went unrecognised and untreated by the communal welfare system. The study of other welfare-related institutions, such as asylums and hospitals, brings a more rounded feel to the institutional approach.[12]

Many of these sorts of 'approaches' have been followed in isolation. Integrated discussions of poor law history – considering the legal and administrative framework alongside the institutional histories and the individual experiences – are by and large relatively elderly, and detailed local studies of poverty and the operation of the poor laws have been notable for their absence. To some extent a sustained 1990s interest in the poor themselves, their experiences and their tactics has begun to rectify this shortcoming.[13] Nonetheless, the systematic local study (particularly for the period between 1700 and the 1790s) still remains a rare animal in welfare historiography. Other potential approaches, for instance investigating the welfare system from the standpoint of local *administrators*, or trying to reconstruct the total *economy of makeshifts* at local level, have been even more completely sidelined.[14]

This book will do little to correct the enormous generalisations used to characterise local administrators under the old and new poor law, but it may help to place more emphasis on the local study as a primary way of grappling with poverty and welfare between 1700 and 1850. It will also help to refocus attention away from the poor law and towards the wider economy of makeshifts as a way of understanding individual and community responses to poverty and marginality. It adopts a different approach from most studies in welfare historiography. The chapters which follow consider the law, the nature of administration and the character of institutional provision, but the book is not a legal, administrative or institutional history. The poor and their detailed experiences are a central part of the analysis from chapter six, but this book is not a 'history from below'. It uses intensive mining of local sources to understand the *real* manifestations of poverty and welfare, but it is something more than a simple local study. It tries to draw national conclusions, but implicitly questions whether we can ever write a 'national' history of poverty, welfare and the poor laws. Rather, the approach is something quite new, an initial attempt (for the period 1700–1850) to draw a systematic *regional* picture of poverty, the character and role of the communal welfare system and the nature of the wider economy of makeshifts deployed by ordinary people.

This is no easy proposition, and three problems initially manifest themselves and need to be confronted:

1 Writing a 'regional' history of poverty and welfare involves drawing regional and sub-regional boundaries on a map and this is an endeavour full of pitfalls. A number of different indicators could be

used to draw these boundaries – density of friendly-society member-ship, degree of urbanisation, poor relief spending per head of popula-tion, percentage of county populations on relief or even the spatial distribution of wage levels in agriculture – and each would identify subtly different 'regions'. Deciding between competing regional bound-aries of this sort is an unenviable task. It is also a task that yields poten-tially uncertain results. Thus, while broad spatial divisions classified on the basis of poor relief expenditure or wages might adequately pick up variations in the scale of poverty, they would not necessarily pick up variations in the character and role of the communal welfare system or in the composition of the economy of makeshifts. Nor could they. The short-term and reactive nature of much welfare provision and the considerable variety of local welfare practices that could be observed over even very short distances in eighteenth- and nineteenth-century England, themes to which we return in later chapters, cloud our ability to search out consistent spatial patterns. Even if our sources were more obligingly homogeneous, any regional analysis involves drawing boundaries that appear as notionally concrete but which in practice were often wide and fuzzy. And we might add a further problem to the melting pot, for in a study such as this space constraints mean that our regional boundaries must stay fixed, whereas those traceable on the ground using any of our potential indicators could change markedly over time.

Many of these problems are intractable. Yet, when parliament started collecting county-level poor law statistics with more regularity and pre-cision in the early nineteenth century, broad spatial patterns in the scale of relief expenditure and the numbers dependent on the communal welfare system *did* manifest themselves and these *can* be used to create a broad if static regional framework for the current analysis. Crudely put, areas to the east of a line running north to south from the East Riding, through Lincolnshire, central and east Leicestershire, south Warwickshire, Wiltshire, east Somerset and then to Exeter apparently devoted more welfare resources to more poor people than did areas to the west of this line. These spatial divisions (which we might broadly label 'south and east' versus 'north and west') are followed up more fully in later chapters. They are, of course, simply a crude shorthand but chapter nine offers some more sophisticated thoughts on the nature of the sub-regional divisions which underpinned these broad spatial units.

This caveat notwithstanding, it is important to recognise that broad north and west/east and south divisions represent more than simple abstract lines on a map. They do have a wider logic in economic and social history. The attempt by Hobsbawn and Rudé to map the geography of machine breaking and incendiarism in the 1830s marks out the area to the east of a line drawn between the East Riding and Devon as having particular problems and gives the 'south and east' region as it is defined here a unity independent of poor law statistics.[15] More widely, broad north and west/east and south divisions reflect distinctions between topography and community types which we might broadly label 'highland' and 'lowland'. The 'highland' communities of the north, west and southwest tended to be engaged in pastoral agriculture, were often in larger parishes than the communities of the 'lowland' east and south, and were themselves less likely to take the form of nucleated settlements than villages in, say, Oxfordshire and Buckinghamshire. Considered as a whole, the 'highland' west and north was more urbanised than the 'lowland' south and east, and it was certainly more industrialised. If we accept that a line running from the East Riding to south Devon marks out the lowlands for the purpose of this book, then almost all of the dynamic proto-industrial development occurring in metalware, hosiery, woollen cloth and cotton from the 1740s and 1750s occurred in the north and west. Leicestershire, Nottinghamshire, the West Country and above all Lancashire and the West Riding came to dominate proto-industrial production by 1800. Moreover, the 'highland' north and west was also home to the English gunpowder industry (in Cumberland and Westmorland), the English coalmining industry (in Nottinghamshire, the northeast and Lancashire) the English pottery industry (in Staffordshire) and the English gun-making industry (around Birmingham). By contrast the 'lowland' south and east was disproportionately characterised by small parishes where people were engaged in arable production or mixed farming, and de-industrialisation rather than industrialisation was a core feature of the economy. The geography of parliamentary enclosure of common fields was heavily concentrated into the broad swathe of 'lowland' counties identified here, and commentators on the rural economy such as Snell, Neeson and Kussmaul have suggested persuasively that the 'lowland' counties are given a unity by the disappearance of female labour opportunities, persistently low wages amongst rural workers, and rural labour markets which time and again failed to reach an acceptable equilibrium as they appear to have done in many parts of the north and west. Of course, these are crude characterisations and for this reason we will revisit the socio-economic character of our broad macro-regions several times during the chapters which follow. However, they are sufficient to suggest that there may be some mileage in the general-ised south/east and north/west framework adopted to organise this book.

2 Yet, even if these divisions are acceptable, drawing boundaries is just the first step in understanding 'regional' structures of poverty and welfare. Aggregate statistics garnered from returns to parliament can take us only so far in characterising the broad poverty and welfare expe-riences within each region. What we also ideally need are more detailed community studies. But how many local studies are 'enough' to characterise an entire region? By the third decade of the nineteenth century there were 15,535 parishes, townships, local incorporations and other bodies responsible for administering poor relief, and an accept-able statistical sample would be both considerable and beyond the scope of an individual researcher. We thus have to assemble a smaller range of community studies to underpin the writing of regional history but this in turn stimulates further questions over representativeness. The area that we have provisionally labelled 'south and east' was predominantly rural, but it also included old charter towns, rapidly growing London hinterlands, market towns, areas of rural industry, ports and seaside resorts. The 'north and west' combined heavy and rural industry with ports, rapidly growing cities, market towns, seaside resorts and areas of commercial agriculture. Searching out a 'representative' mix of com-munities of different socio-economic type is thus complicated. So is getting the right size balance. Of the 15,535 bodies responsible for poor relief, 737 dealt with poverty in a population of fewer than 50 people, 1,907 dealt with 50–100 people, 6,681 dealt with 100–300 people and 5,353 dealt with 300–800 people. In other words just 1,521 places com-prised populations of 800 people or more, and these were biased towards urban areas and to the parishes and townships of the north which tended to have bigger spatial areas and population densities than the south and east.[16]

How to choose 'representative' communities in either macro-region is thus a very difficult question. The tendency for the incredible local diversity in poor law and welfare practice to manifest itself even as between similar communities does not help in this endeavour. Indeed, some may question whether we are yet in a position to write regional histories, or even whether we will ever be in a position to write regional histories. Like the old story of whether a glass is half full or half empty, the answer to this question will always be a subjective matter. For the purposes of this book the solution to questions of representativeness (like the solution to the problem of defining regions in the first place) is not a pretty one. Map 1.1 plots the location of the communities whose poor law and other documentation underpin this analysis. Appendix one records the names and county locations of these communities. When we combine the experiences of the communities represented here with the extant secondary literature (published and unpublished) on the operation of the old poor law in other localities, then writing a regional history of poverty and welfare prior to 1834 relies on under 150 detailed examples. Compared to the 15,535 bodies that administered welfare in nineteenth-century England this is small beer. Even if the detailed studies available to us were evenly distributed on a spatial basis, then we would have just 2–3 studies per county to begin to characterise broad regional patterns. They are not, of course, randomly distributed. The west is under-represented, as is the northeast and the southwest. To some extent this reflects the sheer logistics of collecting poor law data, but it is also partly a conscious strategy. Chapter nine offers a synthesis of the data from the communities recorded here and the published and unpublished studies on poor relief systems undertaken by other historians, in order to look at the sub-regional dynamics of communal welfare. Studies of Devon, Shropshire and other counties which fall into the blank areas of map 1.1 are relatively common and afford a rather better spatial spread when combined with the data offered here, as map 9.1 (p. 261) shows.

Unsurprisingly, these communities do not represent a random socio-economic sample either. Large towns and cities are not considered for logistical reasons, while ports, coastal towns, mining communities and market towns are under-represented. Rural areas, and particularly arable rural areas, by contrast are over-represented. Paradoxically, it becomes no easier to select a representative sample of new poor law unions for the period after 1834, given the way in which parishes were combined into unions. This issue is explored in much more depth in chapter eight. For now, though, while these observations suggest that we must proceed with caution, they do not, as subsequent chapters will show, invalidate a regional approach to the issues of poverty and welfare, especially when combined with the work of other welfare historians on different types of community.

3 The final problem with trying to draw a regional picture is the perennial bugbear of welfare historians – whether, and if so how, to meld urban (in this case smaller urban areas; Manchester, York and other large towns pose an alternative research agenda) and rural experiences of poverty and welfare. For the 'south and east' as we have defined it, the gulf between the scale of poverty and the complexity of poor law

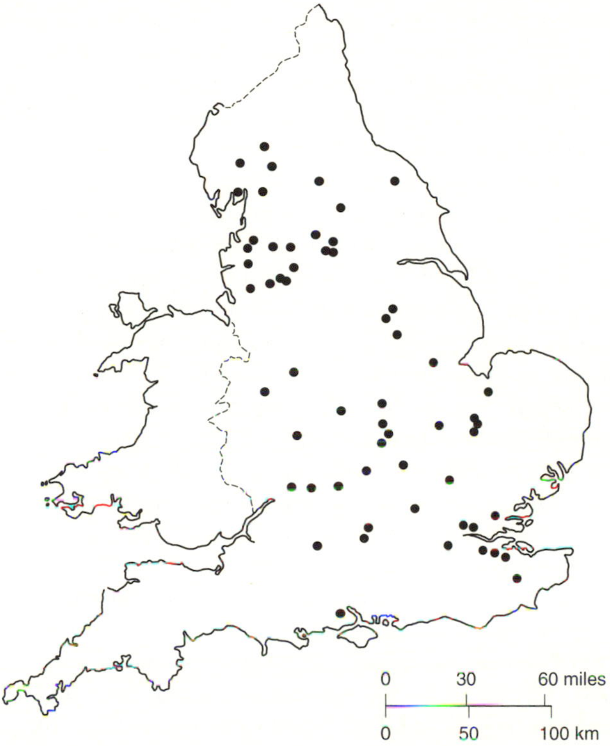

Map 1.1 Major collections of poor law documentation used in this book

practice in urban areas (in many of which individual parishes had been united by a private act of incorporation by the early nineteenth century) and those in predominantly small rural parishes was apparently wide and deep.[17] For the 'north and west' similar divisions might be observed in Cumberland and Westmorland or the North Riding, but on balance the connection between the towns and cities and surrounding rural and rural industrial areas was much more intimate, reflecting a substantial interdependency of their respective poverty problems. It is thus rather easier to incorporate urban areas seamlessly into a regional discussion of poverty and welfare in the north than in the south. Nonetheless, we should beware of thinking that somehow the towns and cities of the south form their own distinct welfare enclaves. They were no more likely to stick to a consistent poor law policy than their rural counterparts, and while they may have had more vagrants the towns suffered the same basic structures of dependency as did rural areas. Their aggregate poor relief bills went in the same direction as, and in many cases grew by similar magnitudes to, those in rural areas. And while southern towns were more likely to use workhouses for their poor than southern rural areas, in both types of place the outdoor dole remained at the heart of communal welfare policy. By the 1840s many towns and rural communities in the north and west and the south and east had in any case been combined by the new poor law into single unions. For these reasons, chapters six to eight make no real distinction between smaller towns like Kettering, Colne or Chipping Sodbury and other types of community, treating them as part of the same regional picture.

The problems with trying to take a regional approach are clearly significant and complex, and the solutions offered here are far from complete or scientific. In this sense it is important to avoid making wide and ambitious claims for the arguments and observations which emerge from this book. Nonetheless, collectively the chapters which follow confirm that we can and that we should write regional rather than national, administrative or legislative histories of poverty and welfare. They begin a process of rethinking the character and role of the old and new poor laws in which it may eventually become apparent (when we have many more local studies available) that England did not have a *single* welfare system but a number of *coalescing regional welfare systems* underpinned by deeply ingrained cultural attitudes towards poverty, communal relief and the economy of makeshifts on the part of both the poor and the wider population. Others may choose to get to grips with this idea; if so they should do so with confidence and purpose rather than having to 'make a virtue out of necessity . . . and celebrate diversity, improvisation and local autonomy as primary themes'.[18]

In the meantime there are two parts to the process of writing this regional history. Chapters two to five, when considered as an integrated whole, offer an interpretation and reinterpretation of the framework within which welfare historians should consider the issue of local and regional welfare practices. Along with the opening 'overview' sections of later chapters, they provide a statement about where we have been and where we are in welfare history. Chapter two will draw out the nuances of the national legal framework and suggest that welfare historians have inadequately appreciated the complex process by which these national laws filtered through to real welfare practices at local and regional level. It will suggest that there were alternative legal and practical realities which constrained the implementation of statute law by local officials, and that it is therefore difficult to reconstruct *the* law on communal welfare. Chapter three will offer a new framework for making sense of a voluminous and contradictory historiographical literature on poverty and welfare which over the course of the last century appears to have come full circle while getting no nearer to offering definitive answers to the question of how we should characterise welfare experiences after 1700. Chapter four will suggest that historians have tended to talk superficially about the 'problem of poverty' and that analysing solutions to poverty has proved a rather more attractive avenue for the energy of commentators than defining and measuring the problem to be solved in the first place. This chapter will offer a review of the different potential approaches towards the definition and measurement of the poverty problem in the absence of formally constructed poverty lines. It will suggest that accepted generalisations on the scale and spatial dimensions of the poverty problem between 1700 and 1850 derived from poor law statistics can easily be turned on their head with a little imagination. Chapter five builds on this analysis and completes the first half of the book. It takes a more detailed look at alternative approaches to conceptualising the nature of poverty. In particular, it suggests that welfare historians must move away from thinking about the extent and causes of poverty at given points in time, and towards thinking about poverty as a life cycle phenomenon demanding subtly different solutions depending upon where in the life-cycle poverty manifested itself. Moreover, the chapter will argue that we can see an increasing polarity in life-cycle experiences between those who were never or rarely poor and those who were always or often poor, resulting in the formation of a distinct poor underclass in both rural and urban areas that had not existed in the seventeenth century. It is against this backdrop that we must interpret the poverty solutions deployed by communities and individuals in the century and a half covered by this book.

The second part of the book, comprising chapters six to eight, takes a new and detailed look at the 'poverty solutions' using the regional approach outlined above. Chapters six and seven investigate the 'regional' characteristics of poor relief and the economy of makeshifts under the old poor law in the broadly defined 'south and east' (chapter six) and 'north and west' (chapter seven) and begin to suggest some sub-regional distinctions. They ask common questions about the supply of, and demand for, welfare. Did the poor law provide allowances that were sufficient to live on? Did it need to? What were the age and gender characteristics of those who managed to obtain relief? How did the character of poor relief change over time? What were the similarities and differences between urban and rural, rural and proto-industrial, and rural and town hinterland areas? What role was there for institutions like the workhouse in each region? Were the poor accepted or marginalised? What role did the poor law play in the economy of makeshifts in the areas considered? Can we trace the sentiment of poor relief in different areas and regions? The answers to these questions, it will be argued, point to a heavily regionalised set of welfare experiences. Chapter eight takes the chronological picture forward, tracing the detailed local and regional welfare patterns that manifest themselves in the change from the old to the new poor law between 1821 and 1850. It asks the same sorts of questions about welfare that were asked of the old poor law and argues that the regional welfare systems we can detect up to 1821 were accentuated and formalised rather than undermined by the new poor law. Chapter nine provides an accessible summary of the main themes of the book but then tries to take the picture forward, offering an initial analysis of the sub-regional dynamics of welfare and some preliminary thoughts on why regional and sub-regional patterns may have manifested themselves.

It should be clear from this description that there are several things this book is not. First, it is *not* a guide to the development of the welfare state. Such reviews have been written by others, and in any case the basic premise of what follows is that the welfare system in force between 1700 and 1850 was not a staging post on the road to the welfare state, but a distinctive and freestanding package of measures which could uniquely influence the lives of the poor.[19] The welfare state, whatever its relationship to the new poor law, belongs to a later period and as a theme is taken up by others.[20] Second, this book is *not* a concerted attempt to write a general overview of the history of the poor law new and old. Now aged, but nonetheless comprehensive, works can be drawn on for a narrative history of both institutions.[21] They can also help to fill in some of the subjects which might be of interest to students of welfare but which are missing here. The book does not, for instance, discuss the issue of settlement and removal in any depth, and it reviews in only a cursory manner the recent acrimonious debate about the meaning and function of the English settlement laws.[22] In part this reflects the pressures of space, but in larger part it reflects the limited importance of the issue notwithstanding Snell's view that a settlement was like currency. With many parishes willing to pay towards the upkeep of paupers who had moved elsewhere, it is a basic truth that most of the people on relief lists or on the margins of poverty never were removed.[23] Nor will this book consider potentially very interesting topics such as vagrancy, which was rife in urban areas, the arable southeast and the far northwest.[24] Again, this partly reflects lack of space, but also the fact that in terms of the poor law as a whole vagrancy (narrowly defined) simply was not that important.[25] Other issues are ignored because of space constraints. Pauper education, the poor law apprenticeship system and the English bastardy problem are all regrettably given little emphasis in the chapters which follow.

Third, this book is *not* about personalities in English welfare history. The lives of Gilbert, Coram, Chadwick, Malthus, Knatchbull or Sturges Bourne will not be central to this regional history.[26] Fourth, this book will say *nothing at all* about London, though it will consider briefly some of the other urban centres. The poor law history of the 'Great Wen' has been well documented, but this is not the reason it is ignored here. Rather, London appears in poor law terms almost as a nation in itself. It had more charitable resources than the sum expended on communal poor relief for the entire country in the nineteenth century.[27] It was the focus of a vast range of private acts and institutions which dealt directly or indirectly with relief and welfare. It had a complex array of alternative welfare avenues, including the densest pawnbroking network in the country.[28] And London had a poverty problem which was so fluid and so unlike that even in other major cities that we must regard it as something of an oddity.[29] Finally, this book is *decidedly not* a final statement on poverty and welfare in England between 1700 and 1850. Just as the historiographical debates on the character and role of the poor laws have proved so enduring because of differing interpretations of material which has many faces, so this book is based upon interpretation of data which, combined with other material yet to be assembled, might lend themselves to a very different interpretation later on. More sophisticated questions about the supply of, and demand for, welfare could be asked, and they could be asked of communities with a different spatial or socio-economic focus from that offered here. After one hundred years of more or less professional research on the English welfare system, welfare history remains still very much in its infancy.

For these omissions of detail and focus, and perhaps for the conflicting aims of the book itself, I expect to be criticised. Perhaps a further potential criticism might be cleared up by way of conclusion. The study is unbalanced in two ways. First, more attention is devoted to the north and midlands than the south in terms of detailed contextualised analysis of both poverty and welfare structures. In large part this helps to correct current biases in the empirical focus of the poor law debate. It is a deliberate strategy. The study is also unbalanced in the sense of giving more attention to the old than the new poor law.

Indeed, it might have seemed logical to finish this book in 1834. However, this would have been folly. The historiography of the new poor law frequently portrays the mid-nineteenth century as a watershed. Michael Rose, for instance, characterises the period 1850–90 as the 'crisis' of poor relief.[30] The Webbs label the post-1848 period as the 'administrative hierarchy', to reflect the fact that it was only after this date that the legal mechanisms were in force to implement the letter and spirit of the new poor law.[31] There are, then, theoretical reasons for continuing the story to 1850. And there are also pragmatic reasons. We can only really begin to judge the role and character of the new poor law after its initial teething troubles and the knee-jerk reactions associated with its implementation had passed, and this means analysis of the 1840s. Certainly by 1850 the stage was set for a new departure, but the history of the new poor law in most practical senses was also the continuing history of the old poor law up to 1850. Thus, while this book makes a nominal distinction between the new poor law and the old, it does not represent the period from the 1830s to the 1850s as a station stop on the train of welfare evolution in the same way that Finlayson does, arguing instead that the new poor law represents the tail end of the creation of regional welfare cultures that stretches back to at least 1600.[32]

Despite these flaws of balance, coverage and focus, I hope that this book offers something new, something interesting and something provocative. When Dorothy Marshall noted that 'awash, above the waves, lie the wrecked hulls of past experiments proclaiming their mute warning, "Here danger lurks. Beware"',[33] she was highlighting the need for sensitive and innovative study of the complex issues of poverty and welfare. As well as providing an accessible synthesis of where we are, this book tries to offer just such a sensitive and innovative approach to edge us forward.

Notes

1 Lancashire Record Office PR2391/46, 'Letter'.
2 For a review of the scale of contemporary writing, see J. Innes, 'The "mixed economy of welfare" in early modern England: assessments of the options from Hale to Malthus (c. 1683–1803', in M. Daunton (ed.), *Charity, self-interest and welfare in the English past* (London, UCL Press, 1996), pp. 139–80. For nineteenth-century contemporary thought, see A. J. Kidd, *State, society and the poor in nineteenth century England* (Basingstoke, Macmillan, 1999).
3 This study does not encompass the poverty and welfare experiences of

Scotland and Ireland. A different legislative framework was in place in these countries, but more importantly the underlying variables which help to characterise communal welfare and locate its role – the extent of kinship, the depth of charitable resources or the nature of the social structure to name but three – looked radically different to those in England. I hope to follow up this theme in joint work with John Stewart of Oxford Brookes University. Wales is excluded for logistical and practical reasons detailed in my unpublished paper 'Grinding out poverty histories: linking poor law records in Wales', available from me on request or at Oxford Brookes University library.

4 See for instance J. D. Marshall, *The old poor law 1795–1834* (Basingstoke, Macmillan, 1973), or for a rather wider interpretation M. E. Rose, *The relief of poverty 1834–1914* (Basingstoke, Macmillan, 1986 reprint).

5 Not all of them successful. On failed legislation, see Innes, 'The "mixed economy of welfare"', and J. Hoppit (ed.), *Failed legislation 1660–1800* (London, Hambledon Press, 1997).

6 See, for instance, M. Blaug, 'The myth of the old poor law and the making of the new', *Journal of Economic History*, 23 (1963) 151–84. Also S. Webb and B. Webb, *English poor law history part II: the last hundred years* (London, Cass, 1963 reprint), and A. Brundage, *The making of the new poor law: the politics of inquiry, enactment and implementation* (London, Hutchinson, 1978). Also P. Harling, 'The power of persuasion: central authority, local bureaucracy and the new poor law', *English Historical Review*, 107 (1992) 30–53.

7 See C. Hamlin, *Public health and social justice in the age of Chadwick: Britain 1800–1854* (Cambridge, Cambridge University Press, 1998). Also A. N. Newman (ed.), *The parliamentary diary of Sir Edward Knatchbull 1722–1730* (London, Royal Historical Society, 1963).

8 See for instance F. Crompton, *Workhouse children* (Stroud, Sutton, 1997), and F. Driver, *Power and pauperism: the workhouse system 1834–1884* (Cambridge, Cambridge University Press, 1993).

9 James Taylor's best guess is that workhouse provision had expanded by 22 per cent between 1776 and 1803. See J. S. Taylor, 'The unreformed workhouse, 1776–1834', in E. W. Martin (ed.), *Comparative developments in social welfare* (London, Croom Helm, 1978), p. 57–84.

10 S. Webb and B. Webb, *English poor law history part I: the old poor law* (London, Cass, 1963 reprint), p. 215.

11 For a recent perspective on workhouse populations under the new poor law, see N. Goose, 'Workhouse populations in the mid nineteenth century: the case of Hertfordshire', *Local Population Studies*, 62 (1999) 52–69.

12 The literature is substantial. For three important examples, see R. Adair, J. Melling and B. Forsythe, 'Migration, family structure and pauper lunacy in Victorian England: admissions to the Devon county pauper lunatic asylum 1845–1900', *Continuity and Change*, 12 (1997) 373–402, D. Wright and A. Digby (eds), *From idiocy to mental deficiency: historical perspectives on*

people with learning disabilities (London, Routledge, 1996), and J. Woodward, *To do the sick no harm: a study of the British voluntary hospital system to 1875* (London, Routledge, 1974).

13 See the different essays in T. Hitchcock, P. King and P. Sharpe (eds), *Chronicling poverty: the voices and strategies of the English poor, 1640–1840* (Basingstoke, Macmillan, 1997).

14 For a recent local study, see L. Botelho, 'Aged and impotent: parish relief of the aged poor in early modern Suffolk', in M. J. Daunton (ed.), *Charity, self-interest and welfare in the English past* (London, UCL Press, 1996), pp. 91–112. On welfare administrators in Devon, see J. S. Taylor, 'Poverty in rural Devon 1785–1840' (unpublished Ph.D. thesis, Stanford University, 1966).

15 E. J. Hobsbawn and G. Rudé, *Captain Swing* (London, Penguin, 1969 reprint), pp. 167–70.

16 S. Mencher, 'Introduction to the poor law reports of 1834 and 1909', in R. Lubove (ed.), *Social welfare in transition: selected English documents 1834–1909* (Pittsburgh, University of Pittsburgh Press, 1982), p. 90.

17 See J. M. Shaw, 'The development of the local poor law acts, 1696–1833, with particular reference to the incorporated hundreds of east anglia' (unpublished Ph.D. thesis, University of East Anglia, 1989), and A. Tomkins, 'The experience of urban poverty: a comparison of Oxford and Shrewsbury 1740–70' (unpublished Ph.D. thesis, University of Oxford, 1994).

18 K. Williams, *From pauperism to poverty* (London, Routledge and Kegan Paul, 1981), p. 35.

19 For the welfare state, see D. Fraser, *The evolution of the British welfare state* (Basingstoke, Macmillan, 1973), and P. Thane, *The origins of British social policy* (London, Croom Helm, 1978).

20 See Fraser, *The evolution*, and S. A. King, 'A model of vision and benevolence: Mary Haslam and the Bolton poor law union 1880–1914', in A. Digby, S. A. King and R. M. Smith (eds), *Poverty, poor relief and welfare in England from the seventeenth to twentieth centuries* (Cambridge, Cambridge University Press, forthcoming). Also Kidd, *State*.

21 Webb and Webb, *English part I*, and G. Oxley, *Poor relief in England and Wales 1601–1834* (Newton Abbot, David and Charles, 1974).

22 K. D. M. Snell, 'Pauper settlement and the right to poor relief in England and Wales', *Continuity and Change*, 6 (1991) 375–415, N. Landau, 'The laws of settlement and surveillance of immigration in eighteenth-century Kent', *Continuity and Change*, 3 (1988) 391–420, and N. Landau, 'The regulation of immigration, economic structures and definitions of the poor in eighteenth century England', *Historical Journal*, 33 (1990) 541–72. Also N. Landau, 'The eighteenth-century context of the laws of settlement', *Continuity and Change*, 6 (1991) 417–39.

23 See J. S. Taylor, 'A different kind of Speenhamland: nonresident relief in the industrial revolution', *Journal of British Studies*, 30 (1991) 183–208, and R.

Wells, 'Migration, the law and parochial policy in eighteenth and early nineteenth century southern England', *Southern History*, 15 (1993) 86–139. This is not to deny that the fear of removal may have influenced behaviour, but on this issue see J. S. Taylor, *Poverty, migration and settlement in the industrial revolution: sojourners' narratives* (Palo Alto, SPSS, 1989). By 1845, just 3 per cent of potential relief recipients nationally were removed.

24 See G. B. Hindle, *Provision for the relief of the poor in Manchester 1754–1826* (Manchester, Manchester University Press, 1975), and L. Rose, *Rogues and vagabonds: the vagrant underworld in Britain 1815–1985* (London, Routledge, 1988).

25 But see A. Rogers, *The state of the poor: a history of the labouring classes in England with parochial reports by Sir Frederick Morton Eden* (London, Routledge, 1928 reprint), p. 56, for a review of the elastic nature of the term 'vagrancy'.

26 But for one example of work in this area, see R. K. McClure, *Coram's children: the London foundling hospital in the eighteenth century* (New Haven, Yale University Press, 1981).

27 J. Imray, *The charity of Richard Whittington* (London, London University Press, 1968).

28 M. D. George, *London life in the eighteenth century* (London, Kegan Paul, 1930), p. 320.

29 See L. Hollen-Lees, *The solidarities of strangers: the English poor laws and the people, 1700–1948* (Cambridge, Cambridge University Press, 1998), and D. R. Green, *From artisans to paupers: economic change and poverty in London 1790–1870* (Aldershot, Scolar Press, 1995). Also A. Tanner, 'The casual poor and the city of London poor law union 1837–1869', *Historical Journal*, 42 (1999) 183–206, and A. Tanner, 'The city of London poor law union 1837–1869' (unpublished Ph.D. thesis, University of London, 1995). F. H. W. Sheppard, *Local government in St. Marylebone 1688–1835* (London, Athlone Press, 1958), provides an excellent local study.

30 M. E. Rose, 'The crisis of poor relief in England, 1850–90', in W. J. Mommsen (ed.), *The emergence of the welfare state in Britain and Germany, 1850–1950* (London, Longman, 1981), pp. 64–93.

31 Webb and Webb, *English part I*.

32 F. G. Finlayson, *Citizen, state and social welfare in Britain 1830–1914* (Oxford, Clarendon Press, 1994).

33 D. Marshall, *The English poor in the eighteenth century* (New York, Routledge, 1969 reprint), p. 254.

CHAPTER TWO

POVERTY AND WELFARE:
THE LEGAL FRAMEWORK

Introduction

Of all the ways to start a study of welfare in the English past, looking at what the law theoretically did and did not allow and how the law came to be interpreted by local administrators might seem to be the least satisfactory. This is an old potato, and one which has been covered in a variety of other works.[1] There are two defences against such a claim. In the first place, it seems desirable to try and understand what the state *thought* should happen in terms of welfare provision, before launching into detailed discussion of what actually did happen. This is a task which cannot simply be brushed under the carpet or added to the end of another chapter. The legal baggage of the English welfare system prior to 1850 was very voluminous. In total 264 general acts and more than 100 local acts impinged *directly* upon the poor and the administration of their communal relief between 1601 and 1850.[2] Other legal changes had an indirect impact on poverty and communal relief, as we will see towards the end of this chapter. Appendix two details the core general acts and provides a commentary on their main provisions. These acts deserve their own review and this review is important for establishing the framework for the rest of the book.

In the second place, the law was not only voluminous but highly complex and it is appropriate to spend some time unpicking it. We will return in more depth to these complexities in later sections. Briefly, however, acts of parliament often simply 'enabled' changes rather than introducing compulsion, and they usually introduced a whole raft of measures rather than concentrating on just one aspect of the welfare system. What is more, it was usual for new acts to amend existing legislation rather than replace or repeal it. This meant an accumulating set of overlapping and potentially contradictory rules for paupers and poor law administrators to understand. Case law supported, modified or invalidated statute law, adding to the difficulty of understanding

18

what the exact legal position of official poor relief actually was. Some contributors to welfare historiography have not been altogether successful in understanding the law, and recent attempts (and failures) to untangle what the law said about the duties of kin to help poor relatives bring its complexity into sharp focus.[3] Contemporaries were no more certain about how to interpret the law. At one extreme, communities like Eaton Socon or Paxton in Cambridgeshire can be found buying printed guidelines for local poor law officials. Administrators in these communities seem to have tried to follow the letter and sentiment of the law and the amount of money that they spent on seeking legal opinions and clarifications increased throughout the eighteenth century. At another extreme, administrators in towns such as Whalley in Lancashire never even instituted a poor rate until the 1780s, choosing to misunderstand or simply ignore their legal duty to provide for the impotent poor from the proceeds of a rate levied on property.

For these reasons, then, it is appropriate to begin this book by looking at the legal framework of welfare even if this might look a little odd to the experienced welfare historian. This chapter thus offers an outline of the statute law on communal welfare between 1700 and 1850, suggests some of the problems with the laws themselves and traces the process by which national legislation was translated into local policy. It also offers a brief review of the ways in which an intertwining of changing statute law and local practice with respect to issues such as gleaning or poaching influenced the interpretation of the legal duties which changes in statute law seemed to impose on local poor law administrators. Thus, the chapter forms a vital foundation for interpreting the theoretical and empirical material which follows. However, given that the legal framework represented an accumulation of overlapping acts we cannot simply begin in 1700, and the rest of this section is devoted to tracing the chronological roots of the eighteenth- and nineteenth-century poor laws.

Hence, the so called 'Old Poor Law', which embodied official attitudes to communal welfare from the start of our period until 1834, was instituted as a series of individual acts between 1572 and 1600, and formally codified (in what was expected to be temporary legislation) in 1601. The act of that year framed what the Webbs called a 'comprehensive poor law, nominally extending to every part of the Kingdom, aiming at a complete and systematic maintenance in the parishes to which they belonged for all sections of the indigent needing relief'.[4] As we will see in the next chapter, the view that England had a comprehensive poor law *system* has shaped much subsequent commentary on the role of the poor law in the welfare strategies of the poor and on the role of the poor law in the wider sweep of English economic development. But what did the 1601 act really say? It had four central principles:

1 That each parish (and from 1662 some individual townships in large parishes) had a duty to provide outdoor relief for those who were 'impotent' (the so-called 'deserving poor' comprising the old, the sick and children), work for those who could not find it, and punishment for those who were able-bodied and unwilling to work – the so-called 'vagrants' (collectively, the 'undeserving poor').[5]

2 That local relief needs were to be met by a local tax called the poor rate, based upon property.

3 That since poverty was a local phenomenon, its relief should be tackled at local level and the relief process should be largely unfettered by national and regional government.[6] In effect the act turned the spotlight on to an amateur administration with the local overseer as the figurehead. However, it instituted no system of payment for overseers and did not set out unambiguously the liability of local people to serve in the office. In most places the task moved, more or less systematically, between ratepayers unless a substitute could be found or until the virtue of paid overseers became apparent, usually in the early nineteenth century. Many parishes adopted a clause allowing ratepayers to buy themselves out of the duty temporarily or permanently. It is not surprising that (where we have detailed records) ratepayers were increasingly likely to choose this option. The task of the overseer was an unenviable one. It was this functionary who had to receive and deal with applications for relief, and to pay allowances from money assembled via the poor rate. In the absence of a select vestry he (there were almost no female overseers) was responsible for deciding who was deserving, what relief should be dispensed to them, and whether they should be relieved in their own homes or in an institution. This role had the potential to pit neighbours against each other and to generate a considerable financial loss for the overseer.[7]

4 That communal relief was to be the court of last resort, to be applied for and dispensed only where private philanthropy, help from kin and individual self-help had been exhausted. The necessity for kin to offer help to poor relatives was given legal force, allowing magistrates to compel relatives such as parents, children, grandchildren and grandparents (though not brothers and sisters) to offer *monetary help* to destitute kin *when able to do so*.[8]

With remarkably little modification, these were the basic principles which underpinned the legislative view on welfare up to and past the reforms of 1834. On the face of it, the interpretation offered by the

Webbs would appear to be accurate. In conception this was a national, rate-based *system* of relief which had the potential to guarantee minimum levels of welfare to those who were discerned to be deserving. Joanna Innes, Robert Jutte and others have drawn excellent contrasts between this English situation and the more disjointed, charity-based provision of welfare resources in most continental countries.[9] However, we should perhaps beware of adopting an overly positive view of the 1601 act. The degree to which conception matched up to reality is the subject of the next sections and the rest of the book, but there is also a further cautionary note to be sounded here. As well as introducing the central pillars of official English welfare, the 1601 act also framed its four key weaknesses:

1 It imposed no restraint on local administrators in the process of defining who was and was not 'deserving', so that potentially someone could be classed as deserving in one parish but not in the next 2 miles up the road. Officials could also construct different grades of 'deservingness'.[10] A 1674 listing of poor people made by the authorities in the Lancashire town of Bolton 'to keep them from starving' divided the poor into three distinct categories. The blind, aged and decayed, and sick formed the neediest category and received the largest payments; widows, orphans and those overburdened with large families formed the second category; those relieved occasionally at the doors of the principal ratepayers in the town formed the third category. There was no legal basis for this sort of categorization, and in other places widows and orphans would have been included in the 'impotent' category while some of the old would not.[11]

2 While parishes were saddled with a duty to relieve the deserving (however defined), the 1601 legislation did not attempt to specify the level and form of such relief, or its regularity. As later chapters will show, this meant that some parishes within a locality would be giving generous money doles while others would be giving relief at low levels, and in kind rather than cash.[12] In turn, it is this freedom of local officials to tailor entitlement and treatment to local conditions of demand for and supply of welfare which makes it difficult to ask really sophisticated questions about the nature and role of the English poor law system.

3 The act, like most subsequent legislation, was overly concerned with the able-bodied poor. This is perfectly understandable in a situation where the threat of public disorder loomed large in the elite psyche, but such a concentration meant that the old poor law was always geared to confronting pauperism rather than treating and preventing poverty and destitution.

4 In making the parish the centre of poor law adminstration, the 1601 act generated two headaches for towns which rapidly became acute in some places. On the one hand the relatively small parishes of towns like York and London became very densely populated during the eighteenth and nineteenth centuries, and the amateur administration imposed in 1601 often lost control of the relief process in such parishes. This could also be a problem in the smaller towns with which we will engage in this book. On the other hand, as towns grew so existing spatial divisions between rich and poor areas were accentuated. One urban parish might thus have lots of wealth and no poverty while others might have lots of poverty and no wealth to deal with it.[13] Since both large and small towns often had an identity over and above the parish itself, relief was often potentially better administered for the whole town and not the individual parish. It is in part for this reason that many major towns took out private acts of parliament to reorganise the way in which relief was administered. Bristol, for instance, obtained a 'Corporation of the poor' in 1696, Gloucester in 1702 and Norwich in 1712.[14]

These fault lines in the 1601 legislation are important and should be kept at the forefront of our minds, for at base they lie behind many of the problems which subsequent chapters of this book will have to grapple with.

Meanwhile, the seventeenth century saw the passage of twenty-three further acts which had a direct bearing on the local relief system. None was more important than the Settlement Act of 1662. This dictated that while local ratepayers had a duty to relieve the deserving poor, they need only relieve those who could prove entitlement by settlement. The parameters for gaining settlement were remarkably fluid and changed with almost every piece of major case law or formal piece of legislation. In general, all children gained the settlement of their father or (in the case of bastard children) their birth. The place of settlement could change through marriage (women took the settlement of their husbands), renting freehold property worth £10 per year or more in a parish (though this gave settlement only for the term of payment), serving a full apprenticeship somewhere else, paying local taxes in another place, employment for a whole year in another place, or living in a place for forty days without being removed provided that notice of residence had been given to the local overseer. Initially, anyone who was, or looked like becoming, dependent on parish relief could be examined to establish parish of settlement and where this was elsewhere they could be 'removed' at the expense of the parish of settlement.[15] From 1697, parishes were allowed to provide a 'settlement certificate' to members of their settled population who wished to leave the area to search for work. This acted as a promise to pay (and potentially a mark of citizenship) should that person and their dependents become needy in a place where they had no legal entitlement to relief.

Such laws were incredibly complicated,[16] and the nature of their application has, as chapter one hinted, generated fierce debate amongst historians. In particular, Keith Snell, Norma Landau and Roger Wells have debated the significance of trends in examinations and removals, arguing respectively that such trends reflected the real burden of chargeability, that examination and removal were essentially a precaution to protect communal property and that examination was simply an attempt to obtain an acknowledgement of liability from the parish of settlement.[17] But as the last chapter suggested, in some respects the whole issue of settlement is a red herring within the wider poor law historiography. It is certainly true that questions of settlement took up increasing amounts of time and money from the 1750s. However, few parishes followed any consistent policy on settlement and removal, generally turning to the settlement laws when worries over spiralling costs briefly called for radical action.[18] By concentrating on those examined and removed, we divert attention from more widely practised means of getting rid of problem paupers (such as paying small amounts or nothing at all and getting the poor to move on of their own accord) and from the vast bulk of the settled poor. The welfare of this group had by 1700, according to the Webbs, been marked by 'almost half a century of centralised inaction'.[19]

So much for the chronological underpinnings of later poor law legislation. The next section provides a broadly narrative history of the major alterations to this legal fabric after 1700. Unfortunately and inevitably many of the more minor pieces of legislation which directly affected the administration of communal welfare, as well as a range of legislative changes which had a more indirect impact on the communal welfare system, are glossed over. Despite Pam Sharpe's call for more attention to be paid to pauper apprentices and the legal framework which surrounded them, they do not figure here.[20] Legislation in 1793, and again in 1803, to ensure that the families of soldiers and militiamen were given regular allowances funded from the county rate has had to be glossed over. So have the thirty-seven acts dealing directly or indirectly with poor relief between 1803 and 1823. Peripheral legislation such as the 1832 Anatomy Act, which allowed the unclaimed bodies of people dying in the workhouse to be sold for dissection, is also ignored.[21] These omissions demonstrate some of the problems which dog attempts to reconstruct 'the law' on communal welfare, and highlight the pressing need for modern welfare historians to engage more purposefully with the nuances of legislation.

'The law', 1700–1850: a narrative history

The first major formal amendment to the seventeenth-century legal fabric was Knatchbull's Workhouse Act of 1722/23. This *enabling* act must be viewed against the backdrop of a perceived rise in both the numbers of paupers and the scale of expenditure upon them, which stimulated a vigorous pamphlet literature on the 'problem' of the poor. Contributors suggested a bewildering variety of schemes for reforming the moral values of the poor and controlling the costs of their relief.[22] The central contradiction of the English poor law framework – the need to care for the impotent *and* to discourage the able-bodied scrounger – was exposed in this debate, and the contemporary view which proposed economy and harshness prevailed.[23] Knatchbull's act gave overseers the power to insist that relief only be given within a workhouse and only in return for labour where the person concerned was remotely able-bodied. A parish might build a workhouse individually under act of parliament, or it might share workhouse facilities located in other parishes. This retained the principle of 'local poverty – local relief', but offered the prospect (often unrealised by parishes sending paupers to workhouses, given the higher per capita costs of indoor as opposed to outdoor relief) of considerable cost savings.[24] The potential of such savings was magnified by a provision in the act that allowed those in charge of local poor relief to contract out care of their poor to 'farmers', individuals who would provide food, clothing, accommodation and even cash doles in return for a fixed price per pauper per week. Profits were theoretically to be made by the 'farmer' pocketing the difference between the per capita contract price and the costs of maintenance, and through sale of work done by the able-bodied in the workhouse. The green light to 'farming' is often seen as the most important component of the Knatchbull act, but perhaps more so is that (even if accidentally) this was the first piece of legislation to enable parishes to apply a test (a workhouse test) of need to those seeking communal welfare.

The second major piece of eighteenth-century legislation – Gilbert's Act of 1782 – was more sensitively framed. Cowherd locates the act firmly within a tide of sentiment against the harshness of the poor law embodied in 1722/23.[25] A study of the tone of wider pamphlet literature suggests that support for the terms of the act was nowhere near so clear-cut in the popular imagination, but it did at least make the statute books where other measures failed. The central provision of this *enabling* act was to allow parishes and townships to come together as a 'union' and to build a common workhouse at joint expense. This was the first real breach of the 1601 principle of 'local poverty – local relief'. The act also set out the accounting, organisation and administration methods which had to be followed by places taking this path. The formation of unions required the consent of two-thirds of major ratepayers prior to seeking a private act, and the size of unions was strictly controlled by the requirement that all component parishes had to lie within a 10-mile radius of the communal workhouse. Institutional provision was to be for the impotent poor only (and thus a source of care, not deterrence) and the costs were to be borne by individual parishes according to the number of their paupers using the workhouse. Crucially, the act also gave sanction to the payment of outdoor relief for those who were not given institutional care.[26] Such measures encompassed considerable potential for humane treatment of the poor and by 1834 there were sixty-seven 'Gilbert' unions incorporating 924 parishes. However, this is hardly testimony to momentous change at a time when there were 15,535 different units responsible for administering poor relief. Flaws in the drafting of the enabling legislation – parishes were free to leave a union at will, fostering instability, there were no rules for the arbitration of the frequent disputes between parishes, and capped rates were usually written into the constitution of the union, making it financially fragile – may help to explain this lack of take-up. Nonetheless, it is important to acknowledge that many of these Gilbert unions were to outlast the old poor law system from which they were carved.[27]

Further change to the basic legal framework was to be heralded by a series of acts between 1793 and 1796. While many early commentators thought that the practice of farming the poor had been revoked under Gilbert's Act, in practice it was not until an act of 1796 that the law really started to undermine contracting, in this case allowing two magistrates to grant casual outdoor relief at times of sickness or temporary distress on the part of any applicant to them. These provisions applied even where the poor had been contracted by local administrators.[28] The central principle of 'local problem – local treatment' which had been breached in 1782 was thus subjected to additional pressure as magistrates were given more power in the relief process. Further 1790s amendments to settlement legislation ensured that only those who were actually chargeable could be removed and introduced the suspended removal order for those too old or ill to be moved, another breach in the principle of local autonomy. This trend was to continue with further legislation in the first decade of the nineteenth century, allowing a single magistrate to overturn the decision of local overseers.

The sentiment of relief legislation apparently changed once more in response to the stresses and strains of war. From the late 1790s relief expenditure was again a source of concern, and the humanitarian ideals of the 1780s were replaced by a situation in which 'contemporaries came to see the needs of the poor as a threat to their own prosperity' and 'Not only their immorality, but also their inadequate performance as workers and consumer justified harsher treatment.'[29] In the immediate aftermath of the Napoleonic Wars 'the destitute had lost much of the legitimacy that they had earlier enjoyed in communal eyes', and the idea that relief bills had risen because the administration of relief and the determination of local relief policy had become divorced from the people who were paying most of the bills was a powerful rationale for further reform.[30] The Sturges Bourne Acts of 1818 and 1819 attempted to correct these apparent abuses.[31] The first act changed the voting system by which ratepayers determined local policy in an open meeting. Those who paid no rates were to have no vote, and thereafter the number of votes an individual could cast was related to the extent of their property. Individuals with property worth less than £50 were afforded one vote, while those with property worth £150 or more were afforded the maximum six votes. The second act allowed the open vestry to transfer its poor law functions – oversight of applications for relief and monitoring the activities of the overseer – to a much smaller elected body called a select vestry. These 'statutory' select vestries were established alongside select vestries which had emerged by a process of agreement or custom in a wide range of communities during the seventeenth and eighteenth centuries. Where both enabling acts were taken up they had potentially fundamental consequences for the experience of being poor, as will become apparent in later chapters.[32]

Little work has been done on the geography of statutory and other select vestries, but the Webbs suggest that by 1823 there were 2,452 statutory select vestries in England, with a broad division between the north and west and the south and east as these were defined in chapter one. Three northern counties (Cheshire, west Yorkshire and Lancashire) accounted for one-quarter of this total while the eight poorest southern counties defined on the basis of per capita poor relief bills accounted for just 6 per cent.[33] In a survey conducted for the purposes of this book, it emerged that around 1,700 other communities had supported select vestries by custom or agreement at some point during the eighteenth century, and that there was an equally stark division between the north and west and the south and east in these alternative forms of vestry.

These acts represent the last major roll of the reform dice under the old poor law, but taking a collective overview of the totality of old poor law legislation is difficult. One commentator has likened the legal framework of the old poor law to 'a threadbare and much-mended patchwork of additions, amendments and corollaries'.[34] By contrast welfare historians have often seen a whole new legislative broom from the 1830s. Although informal initiatives for reform of the old poor law had been common from 1810 onwards, it was not until 1832 that both parliamentary conditions and public opinion allowed for substantial reform. A commission of inquiry was established to collect information on the state of the old poor law, sending out questionnaires to most parishes and calling witnesses engaged in all aspects of the communal welfare conundrum.[35] The personalities and ideological positions of those comprising the commission have been explored elsewhere and will not figure in this chapter.[36] Briefly, however, much of the current literature on the process which resulted in the advent of the new poor law in 1834 has been highly critical, suggesting that the commissioners used limited evidence very partially, that they entered the inquiry determined to find chaos in the old poor law and that they were driven by a preexisting agenda for reform.[37] Such positions almost certainly understate the complexity of the bargaining and concessions process which surrounded both the initial movement for reform and the whole process of converting the report of the commission into formal legislation.[38] They also fail to do justice to the intensity of public debate on the issue of poor law reform, and to the range of alternative measures which were on the table in the early 1830s.[39] However, these issues are not central to the agenda pursued here.

Whether the 1834 legislation was the artificial product of a paper exercise in consultation or not, on the face of it the provisions appear both voluminous and fundamental. They were also compulsory rather than simply enabling and they hit at the heart of some of the basic principles embodied in the 1601 act as well addressing some of its flaws.[40] The core changes can be simply listed:

1 In *administrative* terms, the 1834 legislation appeared to break asunder the already weakened link between local poverty and local administration of relief. It attacked this basic 1601 provision on two fronts. First, through unionisation. Assistant commissioners were

employed to group parishes into unions, and while the grouping process was supposed to have a local input, in practice (as chapter eight will show) the prevalence of consultation was very patchy and appears to have been determined by the timing of unionisation and the presence or absence of large landowners in the places being unionised.[41] By 1839, 13,691 parishes had been unionised, with a particular lead in the south and east, where the Webbs portrayed rural parishes as falling over themselves to shift the burden of relief administration away from the parish. In turn decision making in the union rested not with local administrators but with a board of elected guardians whose theoretical job was to think of the interest of the union ahead of its constituent parishes. The second strategy was to put union decision making into a straightjacket of accounting and procedural rules administered by a central body of Poor Law Commissioners up to 1847, and by the Poor Law Board thereafter. We return to these issues in chapter eight, but for now it is easy to see why some commentators have suggested that we should think of the new poor law as imposing a new system of administration rather than a new system of legislation.[42]

2 In *personnel* terms, the 1834 act represented a move away from the unpaid and amateur administrations imposed in 1601. While guardians were unpaid, they were assisted in their responsibilities by a core of more professional and paid staff including the workhouse master, relieving officers, clerks and purchasing officers. Of course, guardians in many unions tried to cut corners in terms of staff numbers or staff pay. Moreover, as we will see, many of the staff of old poor law institutions moved remarkably seamlessly to the new poor law. However, in conception the provision in the 1834 act for paid staff represents one of the most fundamental breaches in traditional welfare policy.

3 In *conceptual* terms, the new poor law introduced the first deliberate test of need for any group of paupers, requiring relief for the able-bodied to be given only to those entering a workhouse. Each union was encouraged to provide sufficient institutional space, with inspectors after 1834 pressing for wholesale closure of existing small workhouses and the construction of much larger institutional locations. Once inside, paupers were to be classified by age and sex, and families split up in a physical sense and distributed in different 'wards'.[43] The commissioners had no powers of compulsion in terms of workhouse building, but another part of the act dictated that 'parish houses' were to be sold which placed considerable pressure on the guardians to relocate those previously maintained in this way. In Long Itchington, in Dorset, for instance, fifteen cottages were sold in 1837 and long-term

pensioners were evicted. Other parishes in Poole union had the same experience, and the financial and practical strains of boarding out fifty pensioners nudged the union into borrowing for workhouse building where the previous admonitions of the inspectors had failed.[44] Certainly by the end of our period workhouses meant, in theory at least, for the able-bodied were springing up in considerable numbers. What the 1834 act did not do, however, was to specify a test of need for the traditional poor – the old, children, the sick, widows or the disabled. Despite a deeply ingrained view that the test of institutional relief was to be applied to all people, even the traditional 'deserving' poor, a careful reading of the original report suggests that reformers never envisaged the end of outdoor relief for the old and sick.

4 Finally, the 1834 act introduced the first positive guidelines on the *form and level of relief*. It linked welfare for the able-bodied not only to the workhouse but also to the principle of 'less eligibility', dictating that the standard of welfare offered in the workhouse was to be lower than the standard of welfare which could be obtained by taking the lowest paid job outside. In practice this proved impossible in many southern areas, given structural low wages, and so less eligibility rapidly came to be associated with a regular but monotonous diet, the provision of work for those able to do it, the imposition of a system of classification, rigid time management, and the control of visiting and leaving the workhouse.

Further meaningful change to the legislative framework had to wait until unionisation was as complete as it could be, in the early 1840s. Then we see wide-ranging legislative action on issues as varied as union finance and the chargeability of different types of paupers (1842, 1846 and 1848), auditing districts (1844), the powers and permanence of the central commission (1841, 1844, 1846, 1848, 1850) and classification within workhouses (1844, 1847 and 1852).

From statute to local practice: problems and perspectives

The last section provides a somewhat tedious but very necessary narrative of the broad outlines of statute law. We must first understand the letter and sentiment of the 'threadbare and much-mended patchwork' of national statutes before we can go on to assess the extent to which the provisions of 'the law' filtered through to local practice. This issue has excited strong commentary in welfare historiography. On the nature of the relationship between law and practice under the old poor law the Webbs were clear, suggesting that,

> Between the statute book and the actual administration of the parish officers there was, in the eighteenth century, normally only a casual connection . . . the two were separated by . . . ignorance and indifference, amid the assumption of unfettered local autonomy that characterised English local government.[45]

Commentators on the new poor law have been no less severe, suggesting that after an initial honeymoon period the basic principles of 1834 were contravened systematically by unions in the north and midlands in particular and that regional and sub-regional variation in the level of, and entitlement to, relief remained at least as marked as it had been under the old poor law. Alan Kidd suggests that 'There was no entirely consistent or uniform *national poor law*.'[46] How far these sorts of views are correct or incorrect is one of the sub-texts of this book. In some respects, however, simply contrasting local practice with what ought to have happened according to prevailing legislation starts in the middle of the story. What we initially need to understand if we are to characterise the English poor laws and locate their role in the overall welfare patchwork is less the extent of local diversity than the nature of the process which distorted, reshaped and misinterpreted statute law to give us this diversity. In practice, those charged with implementing 'the law' read it through thick spectacles, and five of the key influences shaping what they saw and what they did with what they saw are worthy of consideration in some detail:

1 As we saw earlier in this chapter, new laws were superimposed on the administrative baggage of the past. A long and voluminous history of enabling rather than compulsory legislation had, by the opening decades of the nineteenth century, delivered an inheritance of a huge variety of administrative forms within any county. Kent in 1830, for instance, had 13 Gilbert unions (incorporating fifty parishes), 1 union by local act (the fourteen parishes of Canterbury), 28 statutory select vestries, 9 other select vestries and a range of parishes where relief was organised and dispensed by overseers and open vestries. In the west, Shropshire in 1821 had 7 private incorporations, 4 Gilbert unions, 49 statutory select vestries and over 100 overseer-centred administrations. Whatever the law directed or enabled, the baggage of prior forms of organisation at local level created inertia in poor law policy in a way which is rarely appreciated in current poor law historiography.[47] Once we allow for the fact that legislation was also superimposed upon communities with radically different cultural traditions and poverty problems, then it is clear that even the new broom of the poor law after 1834 must necessarily have been incapable of eliminating local diversity.

2 The translation of national laws to local poor law practice was also influenced by the fact that local administrators under both the old and the new poor laws had to balance the instructions of 'the law' against a range of competing and conflicting restrictions on their actions in the working out of local poor law policy. One restriction was affordability. Poor law legislation dealt largely with the demand side of the poor relief equation – the needs of paupers – but overseers under the old poor law and guardians under the new had to devote attention to the supply side of the welfare equation, pacifying ratepayers concerned at spiralling costs which could sometimes put them on the verge of pauperism. It is not at all clear to me that 'during the eighteenth century, the poor laws continued to enjoy legitimacy, if not popularity, among ratepayers', a view challenged by rate strikes and massive splits in eighteenth-century vestries.[48] In turn, the unstable equilibrium between demand and supply side factors is what we see being played out in frequent policy changes in most communities during the eighteenth and nineteenth centuries. Another restriction was the customary 'rights' of the poor legitimated by the local community. In some areas 'custom' appears to have dictated that certain groups – the old and the sick for instance – should automatically be given outdoor relief, whatever the changing strictures of the law on eligibility for, and the form of, relief.[49] In other places it was 'customary' to give relief to even the most feckless poor. Robert Sharp of South Cave in East Yorkshire noted the case of two such paupers:

> Joseph Barratt applied to the overseers for relief, they have allowed him 5s. per week which amounts to the same thing as if he had put out £250 to interest. Geo Dunn, after all his spending and extravagance and running into debt has likewise applied for relief and has had some money given him.[50]

The indignation in this text is palpable. Many vestries were imbued with a narrower view of entitlement, and they instigated periodic attempts to cut back the scale of expenditure and the length of local relief lists. Nonetheless, in face-to-face relations between overseer and pauper the issue of custom was a powerful one and there were often riots when customary notions of entitlement were breached by local officials. This was as true of the new poor law as it was of the old. Meanwhile, a third restriction on local action was the need to ensure social order. In a situation where poverty might affect well over half of the local population at some point in their lives, the way in which communal relief was organised was an important factor shaping the degree of social tension. Magistrates appear to have been particularly aware of this point and to have used their supervisory power over local poor law administration to mitigate potential sources of stress. For the southeast, Peter Dunkley sees the magistrates as a restraining influence, softening some of the harshest decision making of local officials during the crisis of the old poor law after 1795 and effectively setting a floor to how far relief levels could fall even in the strongest of cutbacks.[51] The activity of the magistracy on poor law issues in other areas was not nearly so important or continuous, especially in the north and midlands. However, it is now widely accepted that the spectre of magistrate inter-ference rather than its practical manifestation lead some overseers to anticipate their decisions by the 1820s, giving relief to some groups who in a theoretical legal sense did not have a right to it. It is thus no sur-prise to see Robert Sharp concluding that 'These country justices are the masters in general.'[52]

3 It is also important to acknowledge that statute law probably had a three-strand 'legitimacy problem' in the eyes of local administrators which complicated the way they viewed 'the' law. First, as we have seen already alternative practical and ideological models for the treatment of the poor and the administration of relief were published in the form of pamphlets, letters and books throughout the period 1700–1850. The volume of this literature was substantial. Writing in 1795, Frederick Morton Eden listed thirty pamphlets concerned directly with poor law reform.[53] Joanna Innes has likewise drawn attention to the large numbers of such tracts, while research for this book has revealed 249 pamphlets or open letters in the public forum between 1700 and 1820. Local policy could not have been entirely insulated from this sort of public debate, and the fact that poor law archives such as those for Bolton in Lancashire preserve some of these tracts is ample confirma-tion that this was so. For those who missed the tracts, public reporting of parliamentary business offered similarly diverse information.[54] And even if they took no interest in parliamentary business local adminis-trators were unlikely to be able to escape the clutches of the local parson, who, like those in the diocese of Chester, may have been active in channelling information on alternative models of welfare provision.[55] Overseers and guardians were well aware, then, that there were viable alternatives to the prescriptions of statute law.

It also seems likely that local administrators were aware of the raft of failed and modified legislation which cluttered the welfare field, and that this potentially provided a second legitimacy problem. In parlia-ment during the period 1700–1850 there were almost as many failed leg-islative initiatives on welfare as made it to the statute books. Indeed, there were at least seven (failed) parliamentary moves for wholesale change in welfare provision between 1750 and 1850 alone. Such moves should suggest to the modern welfare historian that sentiment on welfare and the law on welfare could be substantially out of touch for considerable periods. In an age where parliamentary business was widely reported, why should the same thing not be obvious to local administrators? It is important also to realise that most of the measures which did eventually become 'law' were considerably modified between the proposal and the statute book. Right from its inception the new poor law was a compromise between those who wanted no reform at all and those who wanted a national system of relief financed by a single tax. Moreover, as Crowther points out, and as many of the stories of workhouse horrors invented by the press show, right from the very start the theory and practice of the act was subject to niggling and persistent criticism in public forums from parliament downwards.[56] These facts may, as chapter eight will show, have had a direct effect on how law was translated to practice in the sense of encouraging contempt among local guardians. More importantly, because it was a compromise between so many interest groups the drafting of the 1834 legislation was ambiguous, contained structural loopholes, and embodied only some of the powers of compulsion that the Poor Law Commission would need to carry the new poor law fully and permanently into effect. While it is tempting to think of the barely literate and insular local overseer or the self-interested and petty-minded guardian at the centre of local poor law policy, it is inconceivable that these features of the law did not raise legitimacy questions in their minds.

Finally, statute law had a legitimacy problem in the sense that it usually lagged behind local practice anyway. Before 1834 there was no explicit legal justification for the overseers to provide medical relief, and yet large provincial towns had appointed dedicated poor law surgeons by the 1790s and most other parishes had at least an informal contract with a medical practitioner of some sort by the 1820s.[57] Moreover, select vestries, settlement certificates, the contracting system, workhouse building and the payment of poor law officers, can all be found in local records well before the law formerly sanctioned or enabled them. And almost every provision of the new poor law had been extensively tested at local level over the previous century. It would thus seem unlikely that many statutes had anything new or useful to say to some local administrators.

4 A fourth influence operating on local administrators in their reading of changes in the statute law was that such changes were played

out against the backdrop of often well-entrenched 'extra-legal' relief strategies. Magistrates in particular often stepped outside the law in their directions to local overseers, effectively creating an alternative legal version of what relief was all about which might have considerable resilience in the face of notional changes in national statutes. Innes labels this 'supplementary law'.[58] Nowhere is this supplementary law more visible than in the response of the justices to growing pressure on wages and employment regularity in late eighteenth-century rural southern England. The Speenhamland system remains the most (in)famous mechanism to deal with such problems, but one which was never given formal legal sanction. The story of the development of a sliding scale of relief rates by a group of Berkshire magistrates, relating relief to the price of bread and the size of family, making no distinction between those in work and those out of it, is well known.[59] The most recent research has tended to suggest that many schemes of this sort were very short-lived, that allowances were the subject of rapid downsizing after the extraordinary conditions of the period 1794 to 1814, and that in fact the Speenhamland system was simply an aberration on what was otherwise a fairly consistent poor law policy.[60]

Such perspectives are important but they detract too much from the significance of the presence of magistrate-inspired extra-legal structures for the interpretation of national laws at local level. Speenhamland-type systems of employment subsidy were not new in 1795. They had been enforced by magistrates in Dorset, Norfolk, Buckinghamshire and Oxfordshire well before the Berkshire justices met, and indeed had been developing since the 1750s at the level of individual parishes. Moreover, the systems which were employed from the 1790s onwards demonstrated considerable variety. The number of children at which allowances would 'kick in' varied between counties and localities, as did the ages at which children would stop counting in the relief equation. Price scales also showed considerable variation, with eleven different variants in place in southern coastal counties by the late 1790s. And both family allowances and wage support payments could be and were practised individually rather than being tied together as under the Speenhamland rules. Not only was there an alternate legal reality which local officials had to comprehend, but this legal reality varied between and within counties. Moreover, we might also do well to remember that Speenhamland systems were just one strand of a package of measures, many of them ancient in origin and most of them outside the strict letter of the law, which were deployed to combat unemployment and underemployment in both rural and industrial areas. These have been well explored elsewhere, but included mechanisms such as the labour rate, the subsidy of paupers through other parish accounts in return for public work, and the roundsman system.[61] Whatever the statute law said, pragmatic and often short-term 'extralegal' policies like these were an invaluable coping strategy under both the old and the new poor laws, and they mean that 'the law' would not have been as clear to local administrators as we might assume.

5 Perhaps the most important influences on what local officials did when faced with changes in the statute law on communal welfare were what we might label 'exogenous'. That is, what mattered was less the letter of the law on poor relief than the degree to which prior or simultaneous changes in the legal framework surrounding, or local attitudes to, alternative elements of the welfare patchwork to which ordinary people could turn made the letter of the law relevant to local conditions. Potentially the field of review is wide. Changes in the composition of the factory labour force in response to legislation, social concern and union pressure could hit the welfare strategies of poor people who made ends meet by sending family labour to work in the mills and oblige local administrators to change the focus of their relief policy. Changes in the criminal law – for instance stricter sentencing which might lead to family breakdown and dependency, or attempts to criminalise embezzlement amongst rural industrial workers – could have unforseen local welfare consequences. Railway building might involve the knocking down of low rent housing, forcing the poor into overcrowded and unhealthy areas and thereby obliging overseers to spend more money on the treatment of ill-health. Public health improvements declared a new war on dung in the streets, but this in turn robbed poor people who had collected dung to sell of a significant earning opportunity, increasing dependence on the poor law. A list of this sort could continue for many pages. However, and by way of example rather than comprehensive coverage, we can consider the potential impact of the intertwining of legal and practical changes in two particular areas of the wider welfare patchwork.

First, the privatisation of customary rights. The right to take game and wood from common and waste land was progressively curtailed by law and local restrictions (walls, fences, gamekeepers, etc.) from 1676. Statute and local case law ensured that definitions of poaching were frequently changed so as to encompass more land and more types of game, and to obtain more convictions. Between 1750 and 1799, for instance, there were twenty-three national statutes which impinged in some way on the issue of poaching or other resource stealing, largely attempting to provide clearer guidance on procedures and penalties. By the end of the period considered by this book, more than 1,000 convictions per year were obtained under the game laws alone, and in totem poaching and local resource crime came ninth in a list of the top ten types of crime by 1820.[62] In many ways, however, the direct national law is a red herring in the sphere of 'resource crime'. The work of Landau (reviewed in chapter one) suggests that, certainly in the eighteenth century, overseers and others monitored access to communal resources and where these were threatened they simply used the settlement system to protect those resources. More widely at local level, it was informal agreement on who could and could not take game (enforced by local bylaws) which really impacted upon people trying to construct a welfare patchwork. Rabbits in particular come to be a source of contention in many counties, with warrens increasingly defined as private property by landlords in ways which defied the strict letter of the law but proved extremely effective on the ground.[63] Directly or indirectly, then, customary rights that might previously have helped to diversify an economy of makeshifts were curtailed, and this inevitably fed into the nature of the poverty landscape that local administrators had to grapple with irrespective of what the law said.

We should not of course overstate the decline of customary rights. In the west and north embezzlement of raw materials remained a thorn in the side of rural industrial merchants, and even by the opening decades of the nineteenth century workers were fiercely defending their right to this 'perk'.[64] Nonetheless, the intertwining of statute law, case law and autonomous local practice had served to seriously undermine customary rights by 1800.

Enclosure by custom and statute – the second of our exogenous influences – may have had equally important implications for local overseers faced with changes in welfare law. The extension of the principal of the private act in the south and midlands, particularly to those places where agreement would have been most difficult to get, carried with it considerable consequences for individual and communal welfare strategies. The process of enclosure under these acts, where both fields and waste/common land were to be taken into private ownership, is well known. Once an act was granted, commissioners were appointed to survey the land, lay out private fields (with changes to road and watercourse systems where necessary), establish entitlement to land held in open fields or as waste, establish entitlement to compensation for the loss of common rights and then to divide up the land. Established farmers and others granted small plots in lieu of common rights were obliged to find the cost of putting fences or hedges around the land, and to find a contribution to the costs of the commissioners.

Historians continue to differ on the question of the social impact of this process in terms of the number of people not recognised as having common rights even though they used the commons, and in terms of those given compensation in land for common rights but who were forced to sell because they could not meet the costs of the enclosure. However, one of the most detailed local studies, by Jeannette Neeson, is clear on the subject. Enclosure represented 'individualised agriculture, a new set of smallholders, and a bitter sense of betrayal among commoners'.[65] A link between dispossession and poverty was not inevitable, but Keith Snell provides important evidence that enclosure stripped away a significant plank of the welfare patchwork deployed by many ordinary people, intensifying traditional patterns of seasonal unemployment and preventing the poor from keeping the animals which had been so important prior to enclosure. Thus in the southeast at least, there was a strong positive relationship between the proportion of land enclosed (by statute and by agreement) and the size of per capita poor relief bills.[66] Faced with 'exogenous' influences like these local officials may have been obliged to do what was right and expedient in the short term rather than what was legal.

Clearly, the 'process' by which national legislation was translated into local practice was long and winding. It was also very uncertain, and if we were to take a snapshot of local communal welfare provision at any point between 1700 and 1850 the Webbs' characterisation of the loose relationship between 'the law' and local practice would probably seem to be correct. Spatially the poor law (old and new) appeared to be a chaotic mixture of parishes and regions where poor law practice was located between the two extremes highlighted earlier – those that followed the letter of the law with considerable rigour, and those that ignored the letter and spirit of the law entirely. However, there were also considerable variations in poor law policy within the same place over time. As chapter one began to suggest, over time few parishes followed a consistent poor law policy in relation to the form of relief, eligibility of different types of pauper or the level of relief. On the ground, the poor could experience four or five different types of poor law regime within a single lifetime of need. In the Westmorland parish of Troutbeck, for instance, the poor coming into contact with the poor law between 1750 and 1790 would have been able to enjoy generous weekly allowances until 1759. After that they would have been sent to a workhouse in the parish of Ambleside (8 miles away) with which the poor law had contracted. Allowances were slashed for those remaining on outdoor relief. From 1765 the same poor people would have been contracted to a farmer, and the farmer was in turn replaced in 1779 by an 'undertaker'; a middleman who arranged the boarding out of individuals to private houses in the parish, charging the parish a fixed price and making a profit out of the difference between the fixed price and that agreed with individual householders. The poor would again have enjoyed generous weekly outdoor allowances by 1785, before once more being largely institutionalised on the opening of a new workhouse in 1788.[67]

Local practice was diverse then. The opposite side of the coin was the patchy take-up of enabling legislation. Responses to Knatchbull's act provide a good example. The poor of St Marylebone were contracted out between 1736–52 at the rate of 2s. per head per week. Most parishes in east Kent contracted their poor from around the 1750s, usually at the rate of 2s., while 80 per cent of Cambridgeshire parishes contracted for their poor between 1752 and 1768 at rates ranging from 1s. 9d. to 3s. 6d.[68] The Webbs' early survey of farming practices suggested that the larger urban areas and most areas north of the Humber river did not adopt the practice of farming, but a new review of poor law materials for this book suggests that even northern counties such as Cumberland and Westmorland had more than half of their parishes contracting some aspects of poor relief by the 1760s.[69] However, many of these experiments were short-lived. It often proved impossible for 'farmers' to make a profit from fixed rates, and it was normal for them to seek to vary the terms of the contract at least once during its term. Even those schemes which were in force for a number of years might have to issue several contracts to different farmers. Such was the case in the Cambridgeshire village of Linton, which managed to hire and fire eight contractors in ten years.[70] Nor was workhouse provision under the act much more successful, as the introduction to this chapter implied.[71] By 1776 there were more than 1,900 workhouses in England, rising to almost 2,100 where we also include institutions established under individual acts of parliament. This absolute number seems impressive, and certainly Paul Slack believes that by 1782 one-third of the 13,000 English poor law administration units would have had access to a workhouse (their own or that of another parish).[72] How many places would have tried out the workhouse irrespective of whether it was legal is of course a different matter. Moreover, it is important to be aware that most of these institutions were small and under-resourced. In 1776, less than 200 had a capacity of over 100 people, and there were marked regional and sub-regional variations in workhouse provision with Kent and East Anglia embracing workhouses while the North Riding and Lancashire rejected them.[73] We return to this theme in chapters six and seven. Even where workhouses were developed, however, Knatchbull's act gave no lead on how they were to be administered or financed, and provided no rules on how relationships between parishes should be conducted where they shared facilities. Rancorous disputes between parishes sharing workhouse facilities were common, and more generally the fact that parishes claimed to have their own workhouse or access to that of another parish did not mean that the institution was a central or regular feature of local welfare policy.

These are interesting conclusions, and they free us from a potentially complex attempt to discuss legal form and local practice side by side in chapters six to eight. But in many respects the observation of a rich patchwork of local practice, a complex process of local interpretation of national laws leading to a loose relationship between statute and local relief policies, and a range of alternative legal realities, is merely the starting point for a series of other questions. Was there *any* spatial logic to local experiences? How have modern welfare historians interpreted both diverse local practice and the gulf between legal prescription and poor law reality? The question of spatial logic is confronted in chapters six to eight, and the perceptions of modern welfare historians is the subject of the next chapter.

Conclusion

Ultimately the relationship between legislation, the local interpretation of legal directives and the changing ways of making ends meet at individual level lies in hundreds of charity accounts, thousands of parish poor law archives, and millions of individual and family life cycles. The possibility of specifying it with exactness is very slim indeed. However, this chapter has demonstrated three important points that we must bear in mind when trying to construct a regional analysis of poverty and welfare.

First, the strictures of statute law ('the law') in the whole period 1700–1850 were only one version of poor law and welfare reality. Magistrates, custom, the specific characteristics of local need, the size of the local rate base, and the very public nature of debate over the poor law, all influenced the way in which the law filtered through to local poor law practice. Moreover, local administrators could not be immune from the indirect welfare effects of national and local initiatives on gleaning, enclosure, poaching, and use of woodlands. Whatever the national legal directives of poor law legislation, exogenous influences like these could demand both short-term fixes and longer-term tinkering to make communal relief more responsive to local poverty conditions.

Second, irrespective of the filters through which national statutes had to pass in order to feed into local practice, the really significant thing about the operation of the law was its frequent ambiguity and limited coverage. Most acts covering communal welfare were simply enabling acts, and even where regulation and reform were more forceful, the bounds of state interference were carefully drawn. Against this backdrop it is no surprise to see considerable diversity in experiences of communal welfare.

Finally, the sheer volume of the law (widely conceived to take account of statutes, case law and bylaws) in areas that were regulated created a considerable 'welfare baggage' which in turn gave local welfare practices a strong sense of inertia. It is perhaps for this reason that English poor law administrators consistently failed to address the causes rather than consequences of poverty, and in dealing with the latter came back over and over again to a limited field of remedies, some of which had no legal sanction at all.

These conclusions, then, are one step towards the elaboration of the framework within which we must consider the nature of local and regional welfare experiences. The next three chapters take the creation of this framework forward, and the initial focus is on how welfare historians have interpreted and reinterpreted the diverse local practice that stems from the process of interpreting 'the law'.

Notes

1 Classically, S. Webb and B. Webb, *English poor law history part I: the old poor law* (London, Cass, 1963 reprint), and S. Webb and B. Webb, *English poor law history part II: the last hundred years* (London, Cass, 1963 reprint). Also P. Slack, *The English poor law 1531–1782* (Basingstoke, Macmillan, 1992).

2 See J. Innes, 'Parliament and the shaping of eighteenth-century English social policy', *Transactions of the Royal Historical Society*, 40 (1990) 63–92. Local acts were acts obtained privately to reorganise the poor relief structures of groups of parishes, usually in urban areas, to provide an overarching 'corporation' of the poor managed notionally by groups of guardians but with day-to-day administration usually devolved to professional staff. For a discussion of acts in Kent and a reproduction of the text of a local act for Maidstone, see B. Keith-Lucas, *Parish affairs: the government of Kent under George III* (Ashford, Kent County Library Service, 1986).

3 For a discussion of these attempts, see P. Thane, 'Old people and their families in the English past', in M. Daunton (ed.), *Charity, self-interest and
welfare in the English past* (London, UCL Press, 1996), pp. 113–38.

4 Webb and Webb, *English part I*, p. 54.

5 This chapter will not consider vagrancy directly. See J. Innes, 'Prisons for the
poor: English bridewells 1555–1800', in F. Snyder and D. Hay (eds), *Labour,
law and crime: an historical perspective* (London, Longman, 1987), pp.
42–122. Innes argues convincingly that by the early eighteenth century,
Bridewells were seen as a potentially useful instrument for controlling an
emergent industrial and urban population which often developed beyond
the reach of traditional forms of regulation. For a particularly interesting
regional example, see A. Eccles, 'Vagrancy in later eighteenth century
Westmorland: a social profile', *Transactions of the Cumberland and
Westmorland Antiquarian and Archaeological Society*, 189 (1989) 249–62.

6 For wider centre–local relations, see J. Kent, 'The centre and the localities:
state formation and parish government in England 1640–1740', *Historical
Journal*, 38 (1995) 363–404, and M. Braddick, 'State formation and social
change in early modern England: a problem stated and approaches suggested', *Social History*, 16 (1991) 1–17. Also D. Eastwood, *Government and
community in the English provinces, 1700–1870* (Basingstoke, Macmillan,
1997).

7 On this, see S. A. Peyton, *Kettering vestry minutes 1797–1853*
(Northampton, Northamptonshire Records Society, 1933).

8 In addition, the act made provision for a range of other welfare problems,
notably giving overseers and churchwardens the right to apprentice children
where their parents were actually or potentially destitute, or where the children were orphans and foundlings.

9 J. Innes, 'The state and the poor: eighteenth century England in European
perspective', in J. Brewer and E. Hellmuth (eds), *Rethinking leviathan: the
eighteenth century state in Britain and Germany* (Oxford, Oxford
University Press, 1999), pp. 225–80, and R. Jutte, *Poverty and deviance in
early modern Europe* (Cambridge, Cambridge University Press, 1994). Also
C. Lis and H. Soly, *Poverty and capitalism in pre-industrial Europe*
(Brighton, Harvester Press, 1979).

10 On conceptions of entitlement, see L. Hollen-Lees, *The solidarities of
strangers: the English poor laws and the people 1700–1948* (Cambridge,
Cambridge University Press, 1998).

11 Lancashire Record Office (hereafter LRO) DDKe 2/6/2, 'Bolton survey
1674'. I am grateful to R. W. Hoyle for this reference.

12 Nor did the act require officials to keep records of their disbursements,
making it difficult to assess the early years of the English welfare system.
However, see the classic text by P. Slack, *Poverty and policy in Tudor and
Stuart England* (Basingstoke, Macmillan, 1988), and his 'Books of orders:
the making of English social policy 1577–1631', *Transactions of the Royal
Historical Society*, 30 (1980) 1–23. Also P. Slack, *From reformation to*

improvement: public welfare in early modern England (Oxford, Clarendon Press, 1999).

13 For the example of London, see R. A. P. Finlay, *Population and metropolis* (Cambridge, Cambridge University Press, 1981), and D. R. Green, *From artisans to paupers: economic change and poverty in London 1790–1870* (Aldershot, Scolar Press, 1995).

14 For a discussion of Bristol as one of the most famous corporations, see M. E. Fissell, 'Charity universal? Institutions and moral reform in eighteenth century Bristol', in L. Davison, T. Hitchcock, T. Keirn and R. B. Shoemaker (eds), *Stilling the grumbling hive: the response to social and economic problems in England, 1689–1750* (Stroud, Sutton, 1992), pp. 121–44. Also note 2 above.

15 This process generates documents such as settlement examinations which set out the life histories of individuals and families. See use of these in J. S. Taylor, *Poverty, migration and settlement in the industrial revolution: sojourners' narratives* (Palo Alto, SPSS, 1989).

16 J. S. Taylor, 'The impact of pauper settlement 1691–1834', *Past and Present*, 73 (1976) 42–74, argues that the complexity of the settlement laws dragged up background standards of poor law administration. There is, however, little evidence for this idea in the present survey. For a well-written guide to the settlement laws, see N. Landau, 'Who was subjected to the laws of settlement? Procedure under the settlement laws in eighteenth-century England', *Agricultural History Review*, 43 (1996) 139–59.

17 K. D. M. Snell, 'Pauper settlement and the right to poor relief in England and Wales', *Continuity and Change*, 6 (1991) 375–415, N. Landau, 'The laws of settlement and surveillance of immigration in eighteenth-century Kent', *Continuity and Change*, 3 (1988) 391–420, and N. Landau, 'The regulation of immigration, economic structures and definitions of the poor in eighteenth century England', *Historical Journal*, 33 (1990) 541–72. Also R. Wells, 'Migration, the law and parochial policy in eighteenth and early nineteenth century southern England', *Southern History*, 15 (1993) 86–139, and N. Landau, 'The eighteenth-century context of the laws of settlement', *Continuity and Change*, 6 (1991) 417–39.

18 See J. W. Ely, 'The eighteenth century poor laws in the West Riding of Yorkshire', *American Journal of Legal History*, 30 (1986) 1–24.

19 Webb and Webb, *English part I*, pp. 90.

20 P. Sharpe, 'Poor children as apprentices in Colyton, 1798–1830', *Continuity and Change*, 6 (1991) 253–70.

21 For more on this, see T. Laquer, 'Bodies, death and pauper funerals', *Representations*, 1 (1983) 109–31.

22 For a discussion, see J. Innes, 'The "mixed economy of welfare" in early modern England: assessments of the options from Hale to Malthus (c. 1683–1803)', in M. J. Daunton (ed.), *Charity Self-interest and welfare in the English past* (London, UCL Press, 1996), pp. 139–80. Also J. Innes, 'Politics and morals: the reformation of manners movement in later eighteenth

century England', in E. Hellmuth (ed.), *The transformation of political culture in late eighteenth century England and Germany* (Oxford, Berg, 1990), pp. 57–118.

23 See D. Valenze, 'Charity, custom and humanity: changing attitudes to the poor in eighteenth century England', in J. Garnett and C. Matthew (eds), *Revival and religion since 1700: essays for John Walsh* (London, Hambledon, 1993), pp. 59–78. For a discussion of related notions that a substantial sector of poor people was necessary to secure economic prosperity and that in turn measures should be taken to keep the poor poor, see D. A. Baugh, 'Poverty, protestantism, and political economy: English attitudes toward the poor, 1600–1800', in S. B. Baxter (ed.), *England's rise to greatness, 1600–1763* (London, University of California Press, 1983), pp. 63–108.

24 The terms 'poorhouse', 'almshouse' and 'workhouse' theoretically referred to the residences of different types of paupers. In practice however, many overseers made little distinction between these terms and no consistent or useful distinction between workhouses and poorhouses can be drawn.

25 R. G. Cowherd, 'The humanitarian reform of the English poor laws from 1782–1815', *Proceedings of the American Philosophical Society*, 104 (1960) 328–42. See also A. W. Coats, 'The relief of poverty, attitudes to labour and economic change in England 1660–1782', *International Review of Social History*, 21 (1978) 98–121.

26 The act also instituted a system of fines for overseers who undertook sharp practices to get round the settlement laws and introduced stricter supervision of local procedures by magistrates.

27 For a review of the detailed workings of a Gilbert union, see C. Workman, 'The effect of Gilbert's act on poor law administration in north Lancashire: Caton union 1800–1841' (unpublished dissertation for the Diploma in Local History, University of Liverpool, 1989).

28 Following the early work of the Webbs, it has been usual to accept that in any case farming fell into disuse after 1800. In fact, the government was legislating on the residential criteria for contractors who farmed the poor in more than one parish in 1805, and various forms of contracting appear to have been a common response to the rising poor relief bills which characterised the so-called 'crisis of the old poor law' after 1795.

29 Valenze, 'Charity', pp. 78 and 65.

30 Hollen-Lees, *The solidarities*.

31 It is important to note that the government itself did no more than tinker with legislation after 1805. Any significant changes in the law – of which Sturges Bourne is one example – was stimulated by the activities of backbenchers.

32 Though what the acts did not do was to update the sanctions which vestries could apply to overseers who failed to respond to their directions. This is significant, for vestry books in the 1820s are often full of repetitive memoranda to the effect that overseers must follow the policies instituted by the vestry.

33 Webb and Webb, *English part I*.
34 K. Gilbert, *Life in a Hampshire village: the history of Ashley* (Winchester, Pica Press, 1992), p. 134.
35 See S. G. Checkland and E. O. Checkland (eds), *The poor law report of 1834* (London, Penguin, 1974).
36 Webb and Webb, *English*, and D. Fraser, 'Introduction', in D. Fraser (ed.), *The new poor law in the nineteenth century* (Basingstoke, Macmillan, 1976), pp. 1–25.
37 See A. Brundage, *The making of the new poor law: the politics of inquiry, enactment and implementation* (London, Hutchinson, 1978), and P. Mandler, 'Tories and paupers: Christian political economy and the making of the new poor law', *Historical Journal*, 33 (1990) 81–103.
38 There has been very considerable debate over what the new poor law was designed to achieve. David Eastwood, for instance, portrays the passage of the act as an attempt to shift the control of welfare spending from the locality to the region and the centre. Anthony Brundage argues that the new poor law represented a sustained attempt to restore the cohesion of rural society by giving more control to larger landlords. D. Eastwood, 'Rethinking the debates on the poor law in early nineteenth century England', *Utilitas*, 6 (1994) 97–116, and A. Brundage, 'The English poor law of 1834 and the cohesion of agricultural society', *Agricultural History Review*, 22 (1974) 405–17. Also P. Mandler, 'The making of the new poor law redivivus', *Past and Present,* 117 (1987) 131–57.
39 Commentary on the new poor law was as divided as that on the old poor law. See R. G. Cowherd, *Political economists and the English poor laws* (Athens, Ohio, Ohio University Press, 1977).
40 Though the act also generated some new weaknesses. Most notably, union finances were still based upon local rating systems even though the problem to which those rates were applied had theoretically been taken to a higher spatial level. See M. Caplan, 'The new poor law and the struggle for union chargeability', *International Review of Social History*, 23 (1978) 267–300.
41 See A. Digby, 'The rural poor law', in D. Fraser (ed.), *The new poor law in the nineteenth century* (Basingstoke, Macmillan, 1976), pp. 149–70.
42 See E. W. Martin, 'From parish to union: poor law administration 1601–1865', in E. W. Martin (ed.), *Comparative developments in social welfare* (London, Croom Helm, 1978), pp. 25–56. Also U. Henriques, 'Jeremy Bentham and the machinery of social reform', in H. Hearder and H. R. Koyn (eds), *British government and administration: studies presented to S. B. Chrimes* (Cardiff, University of Wales Press, 1974), pp. 68–79.
43 We should realise that this was actually a corruption of the intention of the poor law report and subsequent act. Both envisaged classification over separate sites rather than classification within one general mixed workhouse. This highlights a recurring theme in new poor law historiography, that many of the early criticisms of the act were based on problems arising where assistant commissioners or Boards of Guardians moved away from

the letter of the law. See D. Ashforth, 'The urban poor law', in D. Fraser (ed.), *The new poor law in the nineteenth century* (Basingstoke, Macmillan, 1976), pp. 128–48.

44 A. Payne, *Portrait of a parish* (Kineton, Roundwood Press, 1968).

45 Webb and Webb, *English part I*, p. 149.

46 A. Kidd, *State, society and the poor in nineteenth century England* (Basingstoke, Macmillan, 1999), p. 32. My italics.

47 Keith-Lucas, *Parish affairs*. On Shropshire, see V. J. Walsh, 'Poor law administration in Shropshire 1820–1885' (unpublished Ph.D. thesis, University of Pennsylvania, 1970).

48 Hollen-Lees, *The solidarities*, p. 73.

49 K. Wrightson, 'The politics of the parish in early modern England', in P. Griffiths, A. Fox and S. Hindle (eds), *The experience of authority in early modern England* (Basingstoke, Macmillan, 1996), p. 21, notes the speed with which a given poor law policy could become 'customary'.

50 J. Crowther and P. Crowther (eds), *The diary of Robert Sharp of South Cave: life in a Yorkshire village 1812–1837* (Oxford, Oxford University Press, 1997), p. 241.

51 P. Dunkley, *The crisis of the old poor law in England, 1795–1834: an interpretive essay* (New York, Garland, 1982), and P. Dunkley, 'Paternalism, the magistracy and poor relief in England 1795–1834', *International Review of Social History*, 24 (1979) 371–97.

52 Crowther and Crowther, *The diary*, p. 153.

53 F. M. Eden, *The state of the poor: a history of the labouring classes in England with parochial reports,* 3 vols (London, Cass, 1963 reprint).

54 Discussion was conducted on three essential levels – the philosophical (essentially whether the poor had a right to relief in return for exploitation and the loss of common rights), the parliamentary and the popular. See T. A. Horne, *Property rights and poverty: political argument in Britain 1605–1834* (London, Ohio University Press, 1990). For wider contextualisation of these pamphlets, see A. W. Coats, 'Economic thought and poor law policy in the eighteenth century', *Economic History Review*, 13 (1961) 34–78, and G. Himmelfarb, *The idea of poverty: England in the early industrial age* (London, Faber, 1984).

55 See P. G. Green, 'Charity, morality and social control: clerical attitudes in the diocese of Chester, 1715–1795', *Transactions of the Historic Society of Lancashire and Cheshire*, 141 (1992) 207–33. Also T. V. Hitchcock, 'Paupers and preachers: the SPCK and the parochial workhouse movement', in L. Davison et al., *Stilling the grumbling hive: the response to social and economic problems in England, 1689–1750* (Stroud, Sutton, 1992), pp. 145–66.

56 M. Crowther, *The workhouse system: the history of an English social institution* (London, Methuen, 1981).

57 See E. G. Thomas, 'The old poor law and medicine', *Medical History*, 24 (1980) 1–19. These issues are followed up in much more depth in chapters six and seven.

58 Innes, 'The state'.
59 See M. Blaug, 'The myth of the old poor law and the making of the new', *Journal of Economic History*, 23 (1963) 151–84. The most accessible review of Speenhamland decisions and scales can be found in A. Aspinall and E. A. Smith (eds), *English historical documents 1783–1832* (London, Eyre and Spottiswoode, 1969), pp. 414–15.
60 M. Neuman, *The Speenhamland county: poverty and the poor laws in Berkshire 1782–1834* (New York, Garland, 1982).
61 D. Eastwood, *Governing rural England: tradition and transformation in local government 1780–1840* (Oxford, Oxford University Press, 1994), provides good background material on such schemes.
62 See P. Munsche, *Gentlemen and poachers: the English game laws 1671–1831* (Cambridge, Cambridge University Press, 1981). Of course, much depends on the year of reference; this sort of crime was more prevalent in times of crisis than in times of prosperity, though at the time of the Lancashire trade depression of 1842 magistrates proved notably reluctant to convict for resource-related crime.
63 See LRO DDGa/17/88–9, 'Correspondence regarding trespassing', DDHe/82/18, 'Correspondence regarding the taking of game by unqualified persons, 1804', DDHe/79/104a, 'Memorandum regarding trespassing in Hesketh fisheries, 1821'. Also G. Christian (ed.), *James Hawker's journal: a Victorian poacher* (Oxford, Oxford University Press, 1961).
64 Other customary rights also appear to have been resilient. P. King, 'Legal change, customary right and social conflict in late eighteenth century England: the origins of the great gleaning case of 1788', *Law and History Review*, 10 (1992) 1–31, argues that the right for women and children to enter arable fields after harvest and collect dropped grain (something which he believes could add significantly to family incomes for some sections of local society) survived for well over fifty years after it was theoretically outlawed in 1788.
65 J. M. Neeson, *Commoners: common right, enclosure and social change in England 1700–1820* (Cambridge, Cambridge University Press, 1993), p. 18.
66 K. D. M. Snell, *Annals of the labouring poor: social change and agrarian England 1660–1900* (Cambridge, Cambridge University Press, 1985).
67 M. A. Parsons, 'Poor relief in Troutbeck 1640–1836', *Transactions of the Cumberland and Westmorland Antiquarian and Archaeological Society*, 95 (1995) 169–86.
68 See F. W. Sheppard, *Local government in St Marylebone, 1688–1835* (London, Athlone Press, 1958), and E. M. Hampson, *The treatment of poverty in Cambridgeshire, 1597–1834* (Cambridge, Cambridge University Press, 1934). For Kent, see A. E. Newman, 'The old poor law in east Kent, 1606–1834: a social and demographic analysis' (unpublished Ph.D. thesis, University of Kent, 1979).
69 Webb and Webb, *English part I*.
70 Hampson, *The treatment*.

71 Parishes could choose to implement just parts of the act, so that it was possible to have a workhouse but not to farm the poor, though the two usually went hand in hand.

72 Slack, *English*.

73 See G. Oxley, 'The permanent poor in south west Lancashire under the old poor law', in J. R. Harris (ed.), *Liverpool and Merseyside* (London, Allen and Unwin, 1968), pp. 16–49.

CHAPTER THREE

THE WELFARE DEBATE

Overview

Chapter two suggested that the local internalisation of national welfare legislation was a process characterised by numerous intricate twists and turns. The result was diversity of local practice within and between counties. This very diversity represents a major stumbling block for modern welfare historians seeking to characterise the old and new poor laws. Crudely, where and when we look has the potential to shape the conclusions we draw even more than is usual in historical analysis. However, there is also a more central stumbling block, and that is the question of how to interpret the local experiences of poverty and welfare which we *can* reconstruct through detailed micro-research. A brief example will highlight the nature of the problem. In the west Yorkshire proto-industrial town of Calverley, regular payments to the 'deserving poor' during the period 1750–80 fluctuated between 6d. and 2s. per week. Small allowances were also made for clothes and coal, but at no point did the community provide in welfare terms more than the equivalent of 30 per cent of individual male weekly earnings. Nor did it guarantee stable income; a reconstruction of pension life cycles reveals considerable volatility for people on long-term relief. Those who appeared in the poor law accounts were disproportionately likely to be either migrants or those without kin, suggesting that those who had kin were either less likely to fall into poverty, or more likely to call on kin rather than communal welfare when they did. Opportunities for work in rural industry offered a further alternative welfare avenue, as did recourse to charity and provision of goods and services for the poor law itself. Nonetheless, for those least able to exploit these other opportunities, the poor law prevented absolute destitution and starvation. How should we regard the character and role of the poor law in the town? Was it humane and generous? Was it just a safety net to be resorted to at the last? Or was the poor law in Calverley meagre, insensitive and discriminatory? Who was and was not entitled to relief (meagre or not), and how was their entitlement established? What role did communal relief play in the overall welfare patchwork? Was it central or was it peripheral, and how did this vary by the age or sex of the recipient? How did the poor themselves think of the poor law? The data for the town are capable of supporting a range of optimistic and pessimistic interpretations depending on the standpoint of the welfare historian who is looking at them.[1]

It is little wonder that, faced with this sort of ambiguous local data (plus a patchwork of local experiences, chronological turmoil in poor law policy at local level and a general lack of detailed empirical studies of either poor relief or the economy of makeshifts), historians have adopted a range of overlapping and contradictory perspectives on the character of the poor laws old and new and on the relationship between communal welfare and alternative welfare strategies. This chapter will attempt to impose some structure on these views. It will suggest that modern welfare historiography forms a complete spectrum from positive to pessimistic interpretations of the character and role of the communal welfare system before 1830, but that three broad and subtly different 'camps' can be observed. A similar breakdown of the historiographical literature on the nature of communal welfare after 1834 will also be noted. The chapter will conclude that coming to a better understanding of welfare in early modern England is a function of a three-stage process involving a reconsideration of definitions and measurements of poverty, more precision in the conceptualisation and theorisation of poverty and welfare, and a greater awareness of the spatial continuities of relief experiences – what Alan Kidd has labelled the 'organised diversity of practice'.[2] Much of the focus will be on historiographical interpretations of the communal welfare system. This is deliberate, for by implication establishing the character and role of communal welfare generates a research agenda for alternative welfare strategies.

Welfare in the era of the old poor law

Writing in the early twentieth century, the Webbs were scathing on the topic of the old poor law. To borrow a quote that was used in the last chapter, they concluded that,

> Between the statute book and the actual administration of the parish officers there was, in the eighteenth century, normally only a casual connection . . . the two were separated by . . . ignorance and indifference, amid the assumption of unfettered local autonomy.[3]

The truth of this statement has already been established. Moreover, they went on to engage with the question of relief entitlement, suggesting that,

> The English poor law at no time gave the destitute a personal 'right' to relief . . . what was enacted was not a right at all, but an obligation . . . the obligation to relieve the impotent poor and to provide the able-bodied with the means of earning their livelihood by work . . . the amount of relief and the manner of relief were left to the discretion of the parish officers.[4]

In practice this meant inflexible and harsh treatment meted out by incompetent or corrupt amateur administrators who 'thought of the poor in the lump' and varied their policy so frequently that there was little certainty of entitlement or continuity of relief. Ultimately, 'The inference cannot be escaped that there was a great amount of sheer inhumanity about the system which individual justices spasmodically tried to check.'[5] Anecdotal evidence from localities could certainly be marshalled to support such a view. Henry Smith, the overseer for the Essex town of Wivenhoe was investigated twice in the same year after claims that paupers to whom he had refused relief starved to death. Just down the road, the Colchester workhouse saw the appointment and dismissal of three workhouse masters in as many years in the late eighteenth century, for misdemeanours ranging from being drunk on duty to abusing the inmates of the workhouse. In Westmorland the overseer of Kirkby Lonsdale had a long record of dissembling over, or denials of, relief applications, to the considerable detriment of paupers.[6]

However, the Webbs themselves have been targeted for criticism of their work on both the old and new poor law. Alan Kidd has suggested that their research was second-hand, informed by a deep ideological commitment to state centralisation, and over-hasty.[7] True or not, there are certainly alternative and less severe views of the old poor law amongst other early commentators. Dorothy Marshall was scathing in her criticism of the administration of relief, claiming that 'a careless, lazy administration was the utmost that could be expected' from amateur administrators[8] and that, 'law, custom and training alike conspired to make the administration of the poor law at best careless and extravagant, and at worst full of loopholes for personal profit'.[9] The consequences of such 'inefficiency, stupidity and brutality' for the morals and self-respect of the poor were fundamental. Marshall also regretted attempts by eighteenth-century local elites to break from seventeenth-century traditions and recreate the poor as a 'distinctive species, a sect apart'.[10] Despite these misgivings, however, there was much that was positive in the relief system as it was worked out in practice, and there was strength rather than weakness in the gulf between law and practice. She concluded that, 'Only a very considerable measure of poverty, and not destitution, was required of applicants for relief. In other words the parish was not only a relieving, but, in some cases, a preventative agent', and that 'in the field of out-door relief the overseers achieved a qualified success'.[11] Indeed, 'the standard of life enjoyed by those who received the highest amounts [of pensions] cannot have been markedly lower than that of the ordinary labouring part of the country'.[12] This was a flexible and generous system in which the borderline between entitlement and non-entitlement was visible and well specified.

Two practical developments in the 'science' of studying historical welfare patterns stemming from the 1970s have apparently constrained our ability to make either positive or negative statements as definitively as was the case in the early twentieth century. First, accessability to records has improved. Records remain in private hands. However, the advent of record office collections on the theme of welfare has facilitated larger-scale, more intensive and more systematic studies of the poor, the poor law and poor law administrators. Substantive results (set out in much more detail in chapters six and seven) have begun to demonstrate, even more clearly than the Webbs could appreciate, the depth of intra- and inter-regional variety in the demand for, and supply of, communal welfare. Recent poor law historiography has been a long way from even obtaining an overview, let alone explaining the variety in the broad overarching terms of the Webbs. The second development lies in the fact that modern studies have increasingly shown that both the manipulation and interpretation of poor law sources throw up treacherous problems to which the Webbs devoted scant attention.[13] As we shall see in the next chapter, even something as ostensibly clear as the lessons to be drawn from rising poor law expenditure in the eighteenth century needs to be approached with considerable caution. In the light of these developments, most recent commentary on the old poor law has not been so comprehensively pessimistic as that afforded by the Webbs. That local practice was highly variable is something which has been acknowledged consistently in poor law historiography. However, while the Webbs saw local autonomy as a weakness, more recent writers have viewed it as a strength. And here lies the key lesson of this chapter. To restate the point with which this chapter opened, assessing the character of the old poor law rests not just upon where and when we look, but how we interpret records which have many potential meanings when placed in their local context. Only the standard-of-living debate has more nuances in English historiography.

Three sets of perspectives can be distilled from the recent literature. They can only be unpicked in general terms here, but the themes recur again in the chapters which follow. In the most *optimistic* perspectives, the old poor law has become a flexible and pragmatic institution, financed and administered at the local level, and with a deep commitment to the poor.[14] From this standpoint, entitlement to welfare was wide and relatively certain. A majority of people would expect to come into contact with communal relief at some point in their life cycle, and even criminals, debtors and the morally disreputable might reasonably apply for relief. One case considered by the Wimbledon vestry highlights this idea well.

> Ri Edmons [sic] to be admitted to come home to his wife and family on condition that he pays the rent he left unpaid to Jo Paterson. The parish then agrees to lend the goods to him during the time they live together in peace and quietness . . . and they are to be returned to the parish on the first offence.[15]

In principle, local people were familiar with local poverty problems, and administrators had to tread a fine line between the demand of the poor for welfare and the ability and willingness of ratepayers to supply the funds to meet this demand. As we saw in chapter one, however, the majority of poor law administrators were dealing with small numbers of people right up to 1834, while in a substantial core of other parishes the numbers needing help rose so much and so fast that local administrators lost control of the relief process and gave indiscriminate doles. Only in perhaps 25 per cent of parishes was the fine line really fine. In the rest, the long-term balance in the poor versus ratepayer equation may have been heavily in favour of recipients. Certainly in the majority of smaller parishes there was plenty of scope for custom to do what the law had not, and for an obligation to relieve on the part of poor law administrators to become a right to relief on the part of certain categories of poor people such as the old and sick. The fact that there is a well-documented history of the poor using the threat or practice of violence where customary notions of entitlement were threatened or contravened demonstrates the validity of this point. Thus, a survey of poor law accounts in Westmorland for this book revealed thirty-eight cases of unrest among the poor during the eighteenth century, often in response to attempts to cut pensions or to the poor conditions implicit in the contracting out of the poor. Riots and abuse of institution staff in response to attempts to peel back the boundaries of entitlement were also common elsewhere, with the poor law accounts of the Lancashire township of Lund recording three prosecutions of workhouse inmates for riot in the late 1810s.[16] In some parishes, entitlement had been extended to a 'going rate' for different types of pauper by the mid-eighteenth century.

This set of optimistic interpretations also suggests that once the poor got their communal benefits, they were considered an integral part of local society, rather than a collective body of 'others' as the Webbs or Marshall thought. A heady mix of statutorily defined provision, custom, and the active engagement of paupers with poor law administrators, may have left little scope for the poor law to become a source of class or societal tension. Mitchison argues forcefully that the poor and the elites who shaped the local system shared 'a basic social unity of values and purpose' and that the poor law 'was a system of social security in which the mass of people had rights ... and the poor had dignity as well as aid'.[17] Hollen-Lees also suggests that 'whatever the motivations of the parties involved, the result of welfare transactions was unavoidably a reinforcement of social solidarity on the communal level'.[18] Martin Daunton agrees, doubting the existence of a poor underclass.[19] The communal welfare system was not just a welfare safety net to deal with emergencies, but a proto-welfare state which reflected, and reacted to, the wide risks of poverty at any point in time and over the life cycle. Such views support the earlier perspective of Geoffrey Taylor, who argued that meaningful care of the poor was one of the props of rural society in the eighteenth and nineteenth centuries,[20] and find resonance in recent textbooks such as that from Martin Daunton.[21] Certainly, there is empirical support for the idea that the poor law constituted a meeting point for the poor and elites rather than a forum for conflict. In the Lancashire township of Cowpe, for instance, the machine breaking and mill burning of 1826 brought the families of rioters to the poor law, and these were relieved without question. More surprisingly, the poor law also paid the defence costs of some of the female rioters. This despite the fact that one millowner was an overseer and that the poor rate was already substantially mortgaged to the local millowners who had advanced the money to meet yearly shortfalls in rate collections and had never been repaid.[22]

The most optimistic observers also go further, portraying the poor law not only as having wide and accepted entitlement, but also as offering what is sometimes styled 'generous' and 'humane' treatment. Of course, these are crude labels with which to try and characterise the allowances given by the poor law. The term 'generosity' is an ambiguous one. It assumes that we have some yardstick against which to measure poor law payouts and it implies that communities could choose to be generous or not. The latter assumption is clearly problematic – magistrates could and did enforce 'generosity' in many southern and eastern rural parishes. In this case, though pensions might be 'generous' the meaning that we must attach to this generosity is very different from that in parishes which had chosen to give 'generous' pensions of their own accord. In the same vein, we must also acknowledge that the relationship between the ability of ratepayers to pay poor rates and the scale of relief allowances is by no means well researched. There is ample evidence of parishes being too poor to pay extensive relief and in places where this was so the failure to pay 'generous' allowances has to be read very differently from cases where parish elites refused to pay generous allowances. Nor, meanwhile, do we have a cast-iron yardstick against which to measure 'generosity'. We might compare relief rates to wages, to published household budgets, to the cost of maintenance by a farmer of the poor or even to charity payments. Invariably poor relief provides only a fraction of yardsticks such as wages, but allowances may nonetheless have been 'generous' (even if they seemed relatively small) where poor law payouts were meant to provide subsistence for the individual whereas our comparators were supposed to provide welfare for families. The opposite side of the coin is that even if relief payments constituted a substantial proportion of the local male day wage, this is illusory generosity where wages were in general at or below subsistence level. Using simple labels might also compromise comparability of experiences over time within the same community (where the background standard of living could change rapidly thus making the poor law more or less generous even if allowances were stable) and comparability between areas and regions with very different background living standards. Thus, if allowances under the old poor law were set at 50 per cent of the mean wages in textile communities (about 14s. per week in the 1780s) then this would yield a level of relief greater than the weekly wage of a male rural labourer in the south. Allowances at 50 per cent of wages in the south might yield just 4s. per week. Concentrating simply on indicators such as wages might thus be potentially misleading. As in many areas of poor law history, the terms which we tend to use casually are in fact loaded with meaning in subtle ways.

Chapters six and seven engage further with these tricky terminological problems as they were played out in real poor law data. Yet, while we must acknowledge problems like those reviewed above, this book *will* use the term 'generosity' as a convenient shorthand for the value of allowances in relation to broadly defined background levels of living standards amongst the wider population. This is because other welfare historians have used the term and because, as so often in welfare history, there is a danger of not seeing the wood for the trees if we do not use some conceptual simplifications to unpick data which by their very volume frustrate historical research. Against this backdrop, it is important to recognise that even the most optimistic of welfare historians differ in their interpretation of the scale of 'generosity' and its timing. Dunkley, for instance, detected more generosity from 1795.[23] Cowherd believed that the old poor law became more humane from the mid-1780s, while Blaug believed that a 'humane concern over the plight of the poor' manifested itself most strongly in the early nineteenth century.[24] In contrast, Keith Snell and Richard Smith have both suggested that the poor law was more 'generous' in the early part of the eighteenth century, before inflation eroded largely static payments.[25]

Whatever the exact timing, the Webbs conclusion that relief payments were meagre, even by the turn of the nineteenth century, has been re-evaluated by optimistic commentators and 'pension' payments have been related to local wage levels in a way which the Webbs did not do. During the overlapping period between the old and new poor laws Thomson's research on Bedfordshire parishes has suggested that old people in receipt of relief would be receiving a minimum of 70 per cent of the spending power of young adults in the same community. Alternative income strands such as war pensions helped to secure welfare, but other obvious sources, such as kin, were not exploited to bring down the contribution of the poor law to yearly welfare. Indeed in Bedfordshire, and for optimistic commentators more widely, it is clear that the poor law had become *the* central source of welfare for the old by the nineteenth century. The same optimistic conclusions might be drawn for other marginal groups such as the sick, widowed and underemployed.[26] At the other end of our period, Richard Smith undertakes a tentative exercise in linking poor law and family reconstitution data for various locations, suggesting that,

> 40 to 45 per cent [of old people] were in receipt of a regular weekly pension paid at a level in the south equivalent to a labourers weekly wage. In this finding we observe patterns that are strongly reminiscent of Thomson's work.[27]

Other old people would have obtained irregular monetary relief or payment in kind, reinforcing the centrality of the poor law to the welfare of the old even at this early date. Moreover, it is clear that in some areas the old poor law could be incredibly sensitive to the changing circumstances of the elderly poor, paying, for instance, larger pensions as old paupers were forced to abandon their alternative welfare avenues or incurred extra costs associated with their condition. More widely, Daunton claims that, 'there was no great discrepancy between the standard of living of those receiving welfare and those dependent on earnings from the late seventeenth century to the early nineteenth century.'[28] Keith Snell agrees, suggesting that the old poor law in the southeast and east midlands bore the brunt of the consequences of declining opportunities for service in agriculture, enclosure and competition for seasonal jobs, providing 'generous terms of relief' and being applied in a 'largely benevolent and sympathetic' manner.[29]

A collective interpretation of this bundle of 'optimistic' views would perhaps suggest that by the early nineteenth century people *expected* to need communal relief at some point in the life cycle, *expected* to get it when they did and *expected* it to provide a substantial portion of their welfare when it came.[30] Law, custom, and sympathy with the poor over a plight which could hit most labouring and ratepaying people with an ill wind, put in place a floor to welfare but only enforced a concomitant ceiling irregularly. For 'deserving' groups such as the old, this ensured very generous treatment indeed.

A second constellation of what we might label *'neutral'* thinking places a different spin on similar evidence. It shares some common ground with the more optimistic views, acknowledging, for instance, that the poor were regarded very much as part of the parish furniture. Nor is there any dispute that communal welfare kicked in progressively as recipients were obliged to withdraw from the labour market. Hunt, for instance, believed that 'pensions' were really disability payments rather than pensions in the modern sense of the word.[31] A gradual expansion in entitlement and generosity over time is also compatible with 'neutral thinking'. However, this second bundle of commentary also diverges from the optimistic views outlined above in three respects.

First, in its characterisation of entitlement. While some optimistic commentators have likened the poor law to a miniature welfare state with a wide remit, this group of historians represents the poor law as a welfare safety net, to which people could turn when all else failed, as the 1601 act envisaged. Peter Solar, for instance, has argued that England had the only national *system* of relief in Europe and that this welfare safety net stimulated both the labouring poor and ratepayers to foster early industrial development.[32] Hollen-Lees has characterised the communal welfare system between 1700 and 1834 as 'residualist' in the sense that the state was 'usually coming in late and with little'. Indeed, she suggests that the old poor law actually became more residualist over time, even if, 'Despite all the problems and the niggling meanness of overseers, the laws offered a shelter in bad times'.[33] The evidence that the poor, poor law administrators and the state recognised this 'insurance' role is persuasive. Manuals for poor law officers explicitly stated that this was the role which they should expect to play or to create for themselves.[34] The safety net was not inflexible. When the old poor law was tested by intense poverty in the rural southeast in the late eighteenth century, local administrations spawned an infinite variety of co-existing wage-support and unemployment-relief mechanisms which have often been lumped together under the term 'Speenhamland'. The judgement on such coping strategies by many contemporaries and some later historians has been severe, as we saw in the last chapter. However, the central point is that when more and more able-bodied men and families needed communal help from the 1790s, the safety net was there – and there on a region-wide basis. This was the 'flexible if never generous' poor law system which Pat Thane placed at the heart of her review of government and society.[35]

The second difference between the two strands of thinking centres on the key question of whether the old poor law was 'generous'. While poor law pensions in parts of Bedfordshire during the final years of the old poor law may have been generous in absolute terms, and when related to average income through the locality, the same was not true in many other areas where different socio-economic conditions and poor law sentiments applied. Hunt has charged Thomson with selective use of evidence, relating high poor law payments to low wage levels to come up with the notion of a generous poor law. In practice, he suggests, the poor law pension provided a third or less of average individual income in most areas.[36] Similar critiques of the positive interpretations of Snell and Smith for the earlier periods might also be offered. In Wivenhoe, Essex, poor law pensions provided just 20 per cent of the average weekly wage of a day labourer by the 1750s, while in Kettering during the 1790s the figure was just 28 per cent. This is slightly misleading. Too much attention in the question of generosity has been devoted to regular money pensions when in some places a majority, and in most others a substantial minority, of spending was on irregular forms of relief or payment in kind, such as rent, clothing or fuel. If we add these items to the equation, then the welfare safety net might seem more generous. On this basis figures would rise to 42 per cent of average male labouring wages in Wivenhoe and 41 per cent in Kettering. However, these figures are still substantially below those found for Bedfordshire. Nor does the evidence end here. Using a census from Corfe Castle in 1790, Richard Wall suggests that the net importance of the poor law could be even lower. It provided the equivalent of less than one-fifth of 'going income' for all poor law recipients combined in this small town, and still provided less than 40 per cent for highly vulnerable groups such as widows or single women.[37] Chapters six and seven do more to set these sorts of figures within a wider context.

By implication, the third issue on which this second bundle of thinking diverges from the optimistic school is in the perceived degree to which the poor law was central to welfare. Thomson, Mitchison and others thought that payments from the poor law were a central part of the welfare patchwork assembled by most families, or even *the* most important element. This idea may have been taken too far.[38] For that core of recipients (usually just 10 per cent of individuals and families on the relief lists) who might absorb up to one-third of all relief spending in a given year, the importance of the poor law cannot be disputed. For the rest, supplements to relief in the form of resource sharing via neighbourhood networks, charity, crime, petty work opportunities, household diversification and kinship may all have been important factors in the overall scheme of making ends meet. Pat Thane concludes that the old poor law was 'overwhelmingly residual in character' and that it helped only a small minority of people at any point in time or over the life course.[39] Local studies provide evidence that this was the case. In the north and midlands the vast majority of old people either did not come to the poor law, or had to assemble a range of other welfare avenues when they did. Even for the southeast Sokoll has shown that many overseers saw the communal welfare system as in a partnership with neighbourhood and kinship networks, showing a willingness to pay minimal relief to old paupers in whatever household conditions they found them. For Essex this contributed to the average pauper household being quite large and complex when compared to the wider population.[40] And if the poor did not co-reside they sometimes crowded together as a means of maximising welfare opportunities outside of, or in addition to, the poor law. In the parish of Calverley, West Yorkshire, the poor crowded on to and around common land, and when good fortune took some families out of poverty their first task was to find new housing in a different part of the village. Proximity to the commons, the ability to create networks among the poor, and perhaps even the opportunity of sharing fuel during an evening attracted poor people who might otherwise be dependent on relief or who might have been more dependent than they actually were.[41] In the 1787 census of Westmorland, 60 per cent of all households ascribed as 'poor' or 'pauper' in most of the parishes were grouped together, also suggesting proximate residence as a coping strategy.[42] It is no surprise, then, to find Horrell and Humphries concluding that their household budget material indicates that only in the lowest wage agricultural and 'casual' households did the poor law play more than the most minor part in generating household income.[43]

More than the optimistic school, this strand of historiography real-ises that all of the welfare avenues explored in Olwen Hufton's classic portrayal of the 'economy of makeshifts' in France were also to be found in an English context.[44] It is unfortunate that this realisation has not lead to integrated historical research which throws light on how these different avenues were utilised over time, region and the life cycle. Charity, for instance, might be used to supplement poor law income or to keep off relief in the first place, but welfare historians have generally failed to discuss charity as a part of the economy of makeshifts.[45] Work has proved equally difficult to place. For ordinary people, revenues from work are extraordinarily difficult to pin down. Even the meaning of the word 'work' is problematic in a welfare sense. Work opportunities involving tasks for the poor law spanned the boundaries between the labour market and welfare, and kept some of those who might other-wise have been fully dependent on relief in a less dependent situation. Nursing, caring for orphan children, midwifery and tailoring were all put out to those who might otherwise be on poor relief. More directly, the poor law actively encouraged and supported employment as part of the welfare patchwork. In the south such activities took the form of Speenhamland and related practices. In the north, labour market support operations were more subtle and have attracted less com-mentary. The strongest evidence comes from Lancashire, where vestry books clearly suggest that overseers were directed to negotiate with employers for employment of people who were, or looked like becom-ing, dependent on relief. Finally, kinship has proved one of the thorni-est elements of the welfare hedge. A renewed interest in kinship during the last five years has demonstrated clearly that kinship densities were much more significant in some places than the earliest commentators allowed. Pat Thane believed that kin networks were functional as well as dense. While there were relatively few prosecutions at national level for kin failing to look after poor relatives, as Thomson contended, the poor law could use a carrot and stick formula to encourage subsidy of communal welfare. The carrot was an incentive payment in the form of a pension which was often inadequate for normal living but which subsidised the full cost of the pauper. The stick was the threat of magistrates where kin did not offer welfare support. If we acknowledge that outside the ambit of the poor law, some groups of paupers such as the old could exert a powerful sense of duty over relatives and friends, it is clear that informal help could form a vital part of the economy of makeshifts.[46] However, help on the welfare front remains very hard to reconstruct, and even detailed local histories such as that for Calverley in West Yorkshire have had to take a circuitous route around this issue.[47]

We return in other chapters to the issue of the 'economy of makeshifts'. In the meantime, the borders of this second strand of historiography are well defined. While the poor law was not always, or perhaps usually, generous (in the sense of providing comfortable allowances sufficient on their own to guarantee welfare), it did provide a basic safety net for those who had exhausted other means. And while it was perhaps not as central to welfare at the individual level as some of the most optimistic commentators have believed, it had the power to provide very substantial help indeed to those with nowhere else to go. Overall, the *sentiment* of the old poor law as it was practised at local level was essentially positive. It was a court of last resort, but people could turn to it with a reasonable expectation of some help and in the knowledge that they retained a vague 'right' to communal help. Faced with the breakdown of the family economy in the rural south and midlands, as well as inexorable population increase, the poor law could hardly have played a different role, it is argued.

Yet, there is also a third bundle of historiographical views on the old poor law which collectively stray rather nearer to the pessimistic interpretations of the Webbs. Starting from the perspective that the empirical basis for debate over the old poor law remains thin and regionally concentrated, it suggests that the sentiment of the poor law in individual communities can usually be seen to be negative, driven by cost and the need to control the supply of welfare resources rather than any perceived duty of care to the poor.[48] Pessimistic commentators also go further, suggesting that the old poor law was in places less 'generous' and less central to the economy of makeshifts than even the more sceptical poor law historiography allows, and that the picture of the poor law as a court of last resort is a false one. Rather than the poor being an integral part of a cosy, rounded local society with shared values, experiences and risks of becoming poor, this view sees the poor as a focus of conflict and dispute. Robert Sharp of South Cave observed the comments of one of his friends that 'the fellow was very wise who called the lower classes the swinish multitude', and noted that landlords 'think the poor of almost a different species'.[49] For commentators like myself this represents the essence of the old poor law. In the form of this broad perspective the debate has come full circle back to the Webbs, with intra- and inter-regional diversity once again becoming an indicator of weakness rather than strength.

It should be clear from this discussion that the *pessimistic* view differs from those already cited in three core ways. First, over the question of entitlement and the alternative views that the old poor law was a basic safety net or a welfare state in miniature. Cowherd characterised the period after 1723 as one of 'social irresponsibility'. This was the year which ushered in the workhouse and the contracting system, and which gave new incentives to sew distinctive badges on to the clothing of paupers and take inventories of their possessions as a precursor to claiming them on the occasion of the pauper's death. Thereafter, most parishes and townships availed themselves of some of these techniques for controlling the poor in the eighteenth century. The contention of more optimistic welfare historians would presumably be that these were shortlived experiments, but this is more often presumed than proved. An alternative view might be that local poor law administrators were continually trying to suppress spending and thus moved from one scheme to the next with considerable ease, generating selective and discontinuous entitlement. The net effect of such rapid policy changes must surely have been that paupers could not be certain that the poor law would be there as a safety net, let alone a generous one, and that if they moved up the road they might get rather different treatment from that in the place they had left.

An example might help to illustrate the problem of interpretation. In the township of Eaton Socon, near St Neots, administrators alternated between the workhouse, outdoor relief, contracting the poor at a fixed rate per head to a 'farmer' and vestry vetting of applications as the main plank of welfare policy. Individuals 'bouts' of a particular policy rarely lasted more than a few years. The numbers receiving relief went up or down alongside these policy changes, and at the individual level both the scope and generosity of the poor law was rarely consistent. Just up the road in Paxton, the eighteenth- and early nineteenth-century poor law witnessed sixteen major policy changes, and as a rule when Eaton Socon was abandoning one type of policy initiative, Paxton was adopting it at around the same time. In terms of individual pauper life cycles, those who were able to ride out policy changes and to accrue help over the long term were few in number. Rather more representative were the poor who moved on and off poor relief according to the harshness of the retrenchments. For other areas of the south and east Dunkley has suggested that it was only the right of appeal to magistrates, and the complementary willingness of magistrates themselves to intervene in welfare processes, which restrained an inherently harsh attitude amongst ratepayers to their local poor.[50] Such experiences are not definitive proof of anything, but they do raise the spectre of a local poor law which was much less attuned to the needs of the local poor than more optimistic views allow. If we add in the contention, followed up in chapter four, that in some areas of the north and west it was 'normal' to turn down a substantial minority of those who applied for relief in the first place, then we find clear hints that the old poor law might not even have represented a safety net, let alone a welfare state in miniature.[51]

The second point of difference lies in the interpretation of the treatment afforded to those who were successful in getting or keeping relief. That some places were generous (either voluntarily or because local poverty conditions demanded that they had to be) and willing to fund a complex array of welfare arrangements, putting the poor law at the centre of the welfare patchwork and guaranteeing substantial allowances, is not to be denied. However, almost all of the empirical evidence which underpins a more positive view than that advanced by the Webbs has been based upon communities in the east and south. This masks key differences in communal welfare policy between north and south, and east and west. As was suggested in chapter one, when the numbers of poor and the amount spent of them by the poor law start to be systematically recorded from the early nineteenth century, it is the northern rural and industrial counties, and those in the west, that had the lowest levels of per capita poor relief. The picture is not uniform. Apparently generous pensions in the North Riding must be balanced against the fact that in the West Riding, Lancashire, and Cumberland and Westmorland, the poor law relieved fewer people, at lower levels of relief and for shorter periods than almost anywhere else.[52] On balance, however, pension levels were low in the north and it would be hard to disagree with Bonfield and with Rose that communal relief provided only 'paltry sums' to piece together a meagre subsistence.[53]

Such observations of spatial disparity in 'generosity' do not in themselves support the Webbs or compromise a positive view of the old poor law. As was suggested earlier, communities that gave substantial allowances might have done so because they chose to or because they had to, while communities which failed to give substantial allowances might have chosen not to, been unable to or might not have needed to. The exact circumstances influence how we should characterise the welfare system. Thus, Hastings believed that certainly the North Riding did not have a large poverty problem, or at least that poverty was of a different type to that in the south and midlands. Endemic poverty was relatively rare, and life-cycle or cyclical poverty was 'normal', with all this implied for a more intermittent poor law role.[54] A related explanation would be that there were more opportunities for supplementing poor relief in the north than in the south. Wastes and commons were longer-lived than in the south and midlands, rural industry was more resilient, urbanisation was greater, and, as Eden contended in the 1790s, northern families were more imaginative about diets, clothing and housing than their southern counterparts.[55] In other words, lack of generosity and the limited scope in these northern communities reflected the superficial character of local need. Such ideas would be convenient, but it has yet to be proved either that the poverty problem was less in the north than in the south and midlands, or that the communal system was less generous than elsewhere because people had more numerous potential welfare strategies open to them at family level. And even if more had been done in this area, there is a further potential explanation. That is, the northern and western old poor law took a severe view of poverty and poor relief recipients, using a complex series of blocking mechanisms and discouragement tactics to create a body of the background poor who were obliged to scrape a living at the most basic levels outside the ambit of the communal welfare system. Thus, for Lancashire Midwinter believed that paupers were actually better off under the new poor law than they had been under the old because,

> The abiding feeling evoked by a study such as this is a sad awareness of the miseries of Lancashire folk throughout all of the dreary years considered, and of the chilly appraisal of misfortune by those more prosperous and in authority.[56]

Chapter seven returns to this theme in more detail.

A final area of difference springs implicitly from this discussion of the nature and value of relief, and that is on the place of the poor in their wider society. Commentators from Taylor to Hollen-Lees have come to accept that the poor were a large and integral part of the community who could not and would not be shunted into the background and treated as second-class citizens. According to Hollen-Lees, 'The poor laws rested upon common understandings of citizenship and social rights' and it was only in the nineteenth century that we see a concerted move towards the physical and social marginalisation of poor people.[57] While poor law administration could become a focus for conflict between different social groups, the risk of poverty was so ubiquitous that even major landowners and ratepayers could witness their own relatives applying to the community. To hark back to Mitchison, the 'poor had dignity as well as aid'. But this was not the case everywhere. Dorothy Marshall was severe in her characterisation of the attitude of local elites, concluding that, 'The poorer sort took relief as their right while the ratepayers despised them for their indolence, insolence, and even for their very misery.'[58]

Earlier in this chapter we saw some of these very attitudes being played out in early nineteenth-century South Cave. Keith Wrightson also viewed the poor law as a contest between those on the margins, and the elites who were intent on isolating the poor and 'stressing their otherness'.[59] The 'poor' could be marginalised physically and socially, and any lingering attachments to a blanket positive view would be extinguished by a tour around the poor law records of Calverley parish in West Yorkshire. Here, the poor were stoned with 'sods' on their way to Sunday service. In part this is explicable by the fact that a large core of recipients were not natives, but such an observation notwithstanding it is still clear that some village natives were stoning their own grandmothers.[60] In other places, conflict over the siting of workhouses, poorhouses and low-rent housing lead to the poor being consigned to the very edge of population settlements.[61] Moreover, reading vestry minutes from the north in particular betrays the exasperation with which many ratepayers viewed the poverty problem, and certain groups of paupers in particular. Such exasperation took the practical form of turning down relief applications, with the applicant 'to have the workhouse if dissatisfied'. Interestingly, while much is made of the right of appeal to magistrates, where vestry books, poor law accounts and quarter sessions records survive side by side it can be shown that almost none of those turned down appealed to the higher authority. In places like Stone this reflected the fact that the poor law made the pauper pay all the expenses of the appeal. In other places, it reflected ignorance of the processes involved. There is also another interpretation – that the poor did not have the implicit and explicit support of the community and hence could not take the case further, resorting instead to repeated applications, often after a period of reform where the initial plea was declined for moral or other 'curable' reasons. There is, then, at least some support for Jutte's conclusion that, 'In pre-industrial Europe, poverty was more than a certain lack of material goods . . . it was above all seen as a subordinating relation between people.'[62]

A growing interest in the detailed logic and posturing which paupers deployed in order to obtain relief highlights the same issue from another angle. Pauper applicants who could claim respectability and attempts at self-help, and who adopted a respectful stance towards those controlling the relief process, were apparently more likely to get relief, and to get the relief that they asked for, than those who did not.[63] The letter from Mary Dewhurst which opened this book shows what this meant in practical terms.

Making sense of old poor law historiography in the face of such division is difficult. Paradoxically, none of the views on this optimistic–pesimistic continuum is right or wrong. Optimistic, neutral and negative interpretations of the poor law could simply refer to different periods, different areas, or different groups of paupers defined by age, sickness or marital status. The fact that poor law records show us so many faces and offer so many interpretations perpetuates division in the historiography. So does the terminology of the welfare debate which runs the risk of allowing historians to talk past each other. Perhaps the one certainty in the debate over the old poor law is that all of these strands of historiography have been underpinned by a regionally unbalanced and in any case thin empirical base. If we are to understand the character of the communal relief system and to trace its role in the ordinary lives of poor people, we must know more about the local mechanics of poor relief, more about the wider patterns that can be drawn out of local diversity and more about the poverty that the communal welfare system had developed to address. These issues lie at the heart of the rest of this book. For now, what we also need to grapple with are historiographical interpretations of the new poor law.

Welfare in the era of the new poor law

The Webbs were almost as severe on the new poor law as on the old. They traced a large gap between the sentiment of the poor law report, the letter of the law and the poor law practice which followed, claiming that 1834 imposed a 'dogmatically uniform direction to English poor law policy'. A rigorous and narrow concentration on the question of poverty and relief amongst the able-bodied meant that the new poor law was 'lopsided and seriously imperfect', dealing with pauperism where it should have been dealing with destitution amongst more traditional

categories of poor people such as the old and sick.[64] Ambiguous drafting and the lack of clear support for the measure, highlighted in chapter
two, compounded the effect of this overly narrow focus, and the new
poor law rapidly became part of the problem of poverty rather than
part of its alleviation and prevention. While Dorothy Marshall's per-
ceptive analysis allowed the eighteenth-century old poor law at least a
small positive and preventative role, early writing on the new poor law
left no hiding place. The Webbs conclusion that, 'The act itself,
notwithstanding its one hundred and ten long and verbose sections,
contained nothing that can be called a scheme for the relief of destitution, or even any explicit plan of reform',[65] shaped discussion of the
new poor law for much of the twentieth century. Outdoor relief continued in large measure as it had done before, as did a whole variety of
other practices hanging over from the old poor law. Perhaps the only
positive impact was that 'the administration was usually doubtless
improved, the cases were more carefully investigated, and possibly more
regularly watched.'[66] This, in the opinion of the Webbs, was the insubstantial achievement of the new poor law up to 1850.

Such views on the general status of the new poor law have not been
subjected to the same sort of systematic makeover in more recent historiography as have the Webbs' comments on the old poor law. While
the education and training afforded to children under the new poor law,
and some of its health services, have been viewed in a positive light,[67]
there is a strong modern historiographical consensus that in conception
the new poor law was flawed, as the Webbs supposed. It imposed a
'solution' to the waning and never very important problem of the able-
bodied rural unemployed on the whole country. Moreover, as we saw in
chapter two, it was from the beginning a compromise, a compromise
between the aspirations of a new middle class and a traditional county
gentry, a compromise between the needs of major and minor ratepayers, a compromise between industrial and agricultural interests, and a
compromise between locality and centre.[68]

Opinions differ rather more over the issue of how to characterise and
interpret the execution of the law at local level. On the one hand, there
is the notion that the new poor law 'failed' on two levels. First, in an
administrative sense. Underfunded, understaffed and racked by
infighting, the Poor Law Commission was unable to prevent the rapid
dilution of the principles embodied in the 1834 act in favour of a rickety
pragmatism which could do little to enforce common standards and
expenditure. From the outset, many unions were poorly organised,
generating persistent tensions between urban and rural components, or

high and low pauperism parishes.[69] These structural problems did not begin to be rectified until the very end of the period considered by this book. Once organised, the small number of inspectors, combined with the lack of compulsive powers, meant that little could be done to police the running of the new poor law in the 1830s and early 1840s. Laggardly unions like Bolton and Preston refused to cut outdoor relief, to close multiple small workhouses and to renew the fabric of the unionised poor law, and there was little to do but wait. In other unions, the politicisation of the boardroom meant that policy was inconsistent and frequently logjammed. Inspectors had no power here either.[70]

The new poor law is also said to have failed in a second, *practical*, sense with much in the way of continuity between the old and new poor law observable after the initial flush of enthusiasm for the principles of 1834 had waned. In his study of Lancashire, Eric Midwinter concluded perceptively that 'stripped of novel titles and terminology, the humdrum workings of the [the old and new poor laws] were fairly similar'.[71] While Hollen-Lees contends that in London the new poor law and its ideology changed the character of relief completely,[72] there is plenty to suggest that this was not true of other large cities and certainly not of rural areas. The practice of convening local relief committees as sub-committees of the larger Board of Guardians meant that in urban and industrial unions, and even in many northern and midland rural unions, pauper applicants continued to be judged by their local administrators rather than 'outsiders'. For the vast majority of poor law applicants this meant the continuation of traditional outdoor relief practices. Individual unions rarely managed to get more than one-fifth of pauper recipients on indoor relief. At the national level in 1840, just 14.3 per cent of paupers were 'indoor', and this had fallen to 12.2 per cent by 1849.[73] Meanwhile, Boards of Guardians were often loathe to spend money on staffing, and most unions did not get the full complement of recommended paid staff until after 1850. In workhouses in particular, this meant that paupers could avoid supervision, or were obliged to supervise themselves, just as they had done under the old poor law. Since it took many unions outside the southeast and east a number of years to close an assembly of old workhouses and poorhouses, and to build centralised institutions, there was often little change in the fabric of the old poor law either.

Above all, the character of relief under the new poor law remained endearingly riven with intra- and inter-regional differences. Spending per capita varied by as much as 200 per cent between unions, even where they had the same broad urban–rural and socio-economic 'feel', and attitudes to the sick and the insane as well as the able-bodied varied enormously. Within this framework, more research has been revealing the problems with accepting that the new poor law stigmatised relief and relief recipients. Women in particular can be seen to have written the new poor law, and even the workhouse, into their welfare and income generation strategies with apparently little concern for 'stigma'.[74] A new appreciation of the range of ways in which paupers could apply pressure to union policy also highlights the active involvement in poor law processes of those who in the past have been seen in such a powerless light. These were traditions drawn directly from the old poor law. Thus, Anne Digby can conclude 'that the new poor law was merely a continuation of the old was undoubtedly true of many parts of southeastern rural England'.[75] Such 'failure' leaves the new poor law damned in much recent historiography. It was a backward-looking anachronism whose multiple failings could do little to tackle the causes of poverty or ameliorate its symptoms. It was simply a relatively anonymous stage on the way to something else, the formative welfare state after 1906.[76]

An alternative set of historiographical perspectives, coalescing around the idea that the new poor law succeeded, provides a no less harsh judgement. Keith Snell claims that the new poor law was in design and practice an attempt to manufacture a low-wage, submissive labour force. Wages and the aggregate regular relief bill fell (the latter by up to one-half in some parishes) after 1834, and the scope of the relief system in terms of the number of recipients and the range of items for which the poor law took responsibility was savaged. The initial losses were not made up before the close of the period considered here and the new poor law was a 'brutal and superfluous measure'.[77] For those who survived the cutbacks, welfare took a new shape. In badly run new poor law institutions conditions could be dreadful, even if we realise that most of the major scandals were fakes or arose where local boards ignored central guidelines. The discovery of paupers in Bolton workhouse so infested with lice that their skin was hanging off provides ample testimony of just how dreadful these conditions could be. In better-run institutions, the day-to-day life of workhouse inmates involved monotony, drudgery and separation from home, family and neighbourhood. Where indoor relief could be avoided, outdoor allowances were meagre, and Hollen-Lees traces a stagnation of pension levels after 1834.[78] And above all of this hovered the fact that the new poor law actively set out to stigmatise the poor, emphasising the shame in receipt of communal aid as against the 'right' to, and ubiquity of, allowances during the later parts of the old poor law regime. Intentional or not, a convincing case could be made for the claim that badly administered the new poor law had the power to stigmatise and terrorise, making the spectre of poverty something to be dreaded above all else in the uncertain world of the nineteenth century. We return to these important themes later in the book. The key point is that whether the new poor law 'succeeded' or 'failed', the vast majority of recent historiography damns it.

Yet there is also a third way, founded on the disjointed views of opti-mistic contributors in the historiographical woodwork.[79] There are three basic strands to this third way. First, it could be argued that the achievements of the new poor law have been judged against inappropri-ate yardsticks. Given limited resources, poor legislation, a lack of direct representation in parliament, strong local opposition and the fact that poor law reform had to be started from scratch, it might be more real-istic to celebrate the success of the new poor law in the sensitive imple-mentation of measures which were practically possible even if it could do little to narrow local and regional diversity. What the new poor law did above all was to introduce the principle of central administration with remarkably little obstruction given previous sentiment against such structures. The process which Harling labels 'bureaucratic creep' was an undeniable and important feature of localised new poor law experience.[80]

Second, there is also scope for arguing that the degree of continuity between the old and new poor law has been overplayed. In some Bedfordshire unions, newly elected guardians ruthlessly confronted the poor and neither the practice nor the ideology of relief looked remotely like that which underpinned the old poor law.[81] Within the remit of what was practically possible, poor law practice as well as poor law personnel changed considerably in the northeast after 1834 as well.[82]

Finally, Karel Williams has argued for a more 'positive' view of the intentions of the new poor law. He suggests that welfare historians have been too ready to concentrate on the struggle for power between local-ity and centre and that they have been blinded by the provisions of the amendment act on healthy able-bodied males. The importance of this group within the overall roll call of welfare recipients was declining well before the 1834 act, and by placing them centre stage in ways that were never intended, welfare historians remain blind to many of the positive things that the new poor law set out to do.[83] As Martin reminds us, the new poor law had to react to and shape a society in which ever more complex and anonymous interpersonal relationships were reshaping conceptions of need, deservingness and welfare.[84] Against this backdrop, it is significant that new studies of unions in the north-west (supposedly the most reticent of all new poor law bodies) have begun to suggest that the new poor law was a vehicle for improving standards of care, and that (when we locate the new poor law structure within the wider context of local philanthropy, voluntarism, housing, work and the broad institutional picture) it can be seen to have played a key role in directing and shaping changes in local perceptions of, and responses to, need.[85] Through all of this, the new poor law continued to offer a safety net for the vast majority of those who encountered need. These themes are revisited and developed in chapter eight.

Conclusion

The historiography of the poor law old and new can be seen to be a complex beast. The spectrum of opinion is wide, and founded on a thin and ambiguous empirical base, where the licence of interpretation fuels debate. For the new poor law in particular, an enduring historiographical pessimism has prevented the development of a flourishing tradition of detailed local analysis. The legacy of the new poor law to the history books has been of a state venture based on invisible foundations and with the seeds of its own destruction planted in its very fabric. The effect of the new poor law in general, and the workhouse in particular, on the psyche of the poor and potentially poor can be seen, it is argued, in the reminiscences of ordinary people preserved in repositories such as the northwest sound archive. However, there is a lack of balance here. How 'generous' was relief under the new poor law? What was the nature of spatial differences in welfare practice? What did spatial diversity mean for the experience of being poor? How did the new poor law cope with a background of rising relative poverty engendered by rising living standards after 1834? Where did the welfare offered after 1834 fit within the economy of makeshifts?[86] An equally long list of questions about the scope, scale and sentiment of communal relief under the old poor law could also be set down. Who got relief? How long did it last? Was it generous or not? How many applied and were turned down? What was the relationship between work, charity and poor law? How can we widen the focus of the welfare microscope? What were the regional dimensions of welfare?

To get answers to these important questions, and thereby to begin reconciling the different strands of thinking outlined in this chapter, it is tempting to launch straight into detailed regional and local investigation of the nature of relief, relief processes and experiences of being poor. Certainly most recent studies have leapt in this direction before they have looked. Yet, this plan of action is false. Asking the right questions of local data, interpreting the results of local analyses, deciding which part of the historiographical spectrum carries most weight and treading warily around data that have so many faces – all this calls for a detailed appreciation of the nature of the poverty problem that the communal welfare system evolved to confront before we look at the solutions deployed by individuals, families and communities. Chapters four and five, dealing with the definition and measurement of poverty, provide this sort of groundwork.

Notes

1 See S. A. King, 'Reconstructing lives: the poor, the poor law and welfare in rural industrial communities', *Social History*, 22 (1997) 318–38, and West Yorkshire Archive Service (hereafter WYAS) Calverley 84, 'Poor law accounts'.

2 A. J. Kidd, *State, society and the poor in nineteenth century England* (Basingstoke, Macmillan, 1999), pp. 32.

3 S. Webb and B. Webb, *English poor law history part I: the old poor law* (London, Cass, 1963 reprint), p. 149. See also M. Crowther, 'Family responsibility and state responsibility in Britain before the welfare state', *Historical Journal*, 25 (1982) 141.

4 Webb and Webb, *English*, p. 406.

5 *Ibid.*, pp. 169.

6 J. S. Taylor, 'Voices in the crowd: the Kirkby Lonsdale township letters, 1809–36', in T. Hitchcock, P. King and P. Sharpe (eds), *Chronicling poverty: the voices and strategies of the English poor, 1640–1840* (Basingstoke, Macmillan, 1997), pp. 109–26.

7 A. J. Kidd, 'Historians or polemicists? How the Webbs wrote their history of the English poor laws', *Economic History Review*, 50 (1987) 400–17.

8 D. Marshall, *The English poor in the eighteenth century* (New York, Routledge, 1969 reprint), p. 10.

9 *Ibid*, p. 60.

10 *Ibid*, p. 46.

11 *Ibid*, pp. 2 and 161.

12 *Ibid*, p. 101.

13 See S. A. King, 'Power representation and the self: problems with sources for record linkage', *Local Historian*, 24 (1997) 1–11, and D. Eastwood, 'The republic in the village: parish and poor at Bampton 1780–1834', *Journal of Regional and Local Studies*, 12 (1992) 18–28.

14 For positive comments covering the very end of the old poor law period, see D. Thomson, 'The welfare of the elderly in the past: a family or community responsibility', in M. Pelling and R. M. Smith (eds), *Life, death and the*

elderly: historical perspectives (London, Routledge, 1991), pp. 194–221, D. Thomson, 'The decline of social security: falling state support for the elderly since early Victorian times', *Ageing and Society*, 4 (1984) 451–82, and D. Thomson, 'Provision for the elderly in England 1830–1908' (unpublished Ph.D. thesis, University of Cambridge, 1980). Also D. Thomson, 'The elderly in an urban-industrial society: England 1750 to the present', in J. M. Eekelaar and D. Pearl (eds), *An ageing world: dilemmas and challenges for law and social policy* (Oxford, Oxford University Press, 1989), pp. 55–60, and D. Thomson, 'Welfare and the historians', in L. Bonfield, R. M. Smith and K. Wrightson (eds), *The world we have gained* (Oxford, Oxford University Press, 1986), pp. 355–78. For longer-term perspectives, see J. S. Taylor, *Poverty, migration and settlement in the industrial revolution: sojourners' narratives* (Paolo Alto, SPSS, 1989), and J. S. Taylor, 'A different kind of Speenhamland: nonresident relief in the industrial revolution', *Journal of British Studies*, 50 (1991) 183–208. Also the excellent essay by R. M. Smith, 'Charity, self-interest and welfare: reflections from demographic and family history', in M. J. Daunton (ed.), *Charity, self-interest and welfare in the English past* (London, UCL Press, 1996), pp. 23–50.

15 F. M. Cowe (ed.), *Wimbledon vestry minutes 1736, 1743–1788* (Guildford, Surrey Record Society, 1964), p. 3. Edmonds had abandoned his family at an earlier date.

16 I am grateful to Martin Ramsbottom for allowing me access to the Lund material.

17 R. Mitchison, *Coping with destitution: poverty and relief in western Europe* (Toronto, Toronto University Press, 1991), pp. 33 and 48.

18 L. Hollen-Lees, *The solidarities of strangers: the English poor laws and the people 1700–1948* (Cambridge, Cambridge University Press, 1998), p. 7.

19 M. J. Daunton, 'Introduction', in Daunton (ed.), *Charity, self-interest and welfare in the English past* (London, UCL Press, 1996), pp. 2–3. See also K. D. M. Snell, *Annals of the labouring poor: social change and agrarian England 1660–1900* (Cambridge, Cambridge University Press, 1985), p. 104, who argues that agreement and mutual respect were key characteristics of the old poor law.

20 G. Taylor, *The problem of poverty 1660–1834* (London, Longman, 1969).

21 M. J. Daunton, *Progress and poverty: an economic and social history of Britain 1700–1850* (Oxford, Oxford University Press, 1995), p. 452, who claims that 'there was a broad identity between ratepayers and recipients of relief'.

22 Rawtenstall Library, 'Poor law accounts for Cowpe, Lenches, Newhallhey and Hall Carr'.

23 P. Dunkley, 'Paternalism, the magistracy and poor relief in England 1795–1834', *International Review of Social History*, 24 (1979) 371–97. Public expressions from magistrates in the 1790s that the poor had a right to relief was the analogue to the 'custom' deployed by poor people in their

relief negotiations. On magistrates, see also D. Eastwood, *Governing rural England: tradition and transformation in local government 1780–1840* (Oxford, Oxford University Press, 1994).

24 R. G. Cowherd, 'The humanitarian reform of the English poor laws from 1782–1815', *Proceedings of the American Philosophical Society*, 104 (1960) 328–42, and M. Blaug, 'The myth of the old poor law and the making of the new', *Journal of Economic History*, 23 (1963) 151–84, p. 157.

25 Snell, *Annals*, Smith, 'Charity', and R. M. Smith, 'Ageing and well being in early modern England: pension trends and gender preferences under the English old poor law 1650–1800', in P. Johnson and P. Thane (eds), *Old age from antiquity to post-modernity* (London, Routledge, 1998), pp. 64–95.

26 Thomson, 'The welfare'. Also H. J. Wilkins, *The poor book of Westbury on Trym* (London, Calender, 1910).

27 Smith, 'Charity', p. 38.

28 Daunton, *Progress*, p. 450.

29 Snell, *Annals*.

30 Alternative welfare strategies, where they are examined at all by the more optimistic commentators, are often portrayed as ways of keeping off relief altogether, with little focus on how the poor balanced the poor law with other income generation strategies to construct a yearly welfare profile.

31 E. H. Hunt, 'Paupers and pensioners past and present', *Ageing and Society*, 9 (1990) 407–30.

32 P. Solar, 'Poor relief and English economic development before the industrial revolution', *Economic History Review*, 48 (1995) 1–22.

33 Hollen-Lees, *The solidarities*, pp. 19 and 77.

34 See A. W. Coats (ed.), *Poverty in the Victorian age* (Farnborough, Allen and Unwin, 1973), and W. Mackenzie, *The overseer handbook* (London, Peterworth, 1820).

35 P. Thane, 'Government and society in England and Wales 1750–1914', in F. M. L. Thompson, *The Cambridge social history of Britain 1750–1950* (Cambridge, Cambridge University Press, 1990), p. 10.

36 Hunt, 'Paupers'.

37 R. Wall, 'Some implications of the earnings, income and expenditure patterns of married women in populations in the past', in J. Henderson and R. Wall (eds), *Poor women and children in the European past* (London, Routledge, 1994), pp. 312–35. Calculated from table 15.3.

38 See P. Thane, 'Old people and their families in the English past', in M. J. Daunton (ed.), *Charity, self-interest and welfare in the English past* (London, UCL Press, 1996), pp. 113–38.

39 *Ibid.*

40 T. Sokoll, *Household and family among the poor: the case of two Essex communities in the late eighteenth and early nineteenth centuries* (Bochum, Verlaag, 1993).

41 See S. A. King, 'Dying with style: infant death and its context in a rural industrial community', *Social History of Medicine*, 10 (1997) 3–24.

42 L. Ashcroft, *Vital statistics: the Westmorland census of 1787* (Berwick, Curwen Archive Trust, 1992).

43 S. Horrell and J. Humphries, 'Old questions, new data and alternative perspectives: families' living standards in the industrial revolution', *Journal of Economic History*, 42 (1992) 849–80.

44 O. Hufton, *The poor of eighteenth century France 1750–89* (Oxford, Oxford University Press, 1974).

45 See F. K. Prochaska, *Women and philanthropy in C19th England* (Oxford, Oxford University Press, 1980), who argues that much of the money which went into 'charity' came out at the other end in the form of tracts, bibles and soup, rather than resources to really alleviate poverty. Also on changing rules for entitlement to charity, M. J. D. Roberts, 'Head versus heart? Voluntary associations and charity organisation in England 1700–1850', in H. Cunningham and J. Innes (eds), *Charity, philanthropy and reform from the 1690s to 1850* (Basingstoke, Macmillan, 1998), pp. 66–86.

46 Thane, 'Old people', provides an excellent review of the literature on kinship.

47 King, 'Reconstructing'.

48 King, 'Reconstructing', and S. R. Broadbridge, 'The old poor law in the parish of Stone', *North Staffordshire Journal of Field Studies*, 13 (1973) 11–25.

49 J. Crowther and P. Crowther (eds), *The diary of Robert Sharp of South Cave: life in a Yorkshire village 1812–1837* (Oxford, Oxford University Press, 1997), pp. 57 and 64–5.

50 P. Dunkley, *The crisis of the old poor law in England 1795–1834: an interpretive essay* (New York, Garland, 1982). For a perspective of the fluctuating and uncertain entitlement of poor women, see R. Connors, 'Poor women, the parish and the politics of poverty', in H. Barker and E. Chalus (eds), *Gender in eighteenth century England: roles, representations and responsibilities* (London, Longman, 1997), pp. 126–47.

51 Of course, welfare systems always turn down some applicants and it is possible to make a case for ignoring this variable in an analysis of the poor law. However, what is significant for this analysis is not just that people were turned down, but that entitlement to welfare fluctuated over time and area and that in many places the dividing line between entitlement and non-entlement to welfare was narrow and fuzzy. In a modern rule-based welfare system there is less scope for inconsistent entitlement and hence the number turned down is used as a yardstick by which to judge the character and role of the poor law in this analysis.

52 R. P. Hastings, *Poverty and the poor law in the North Riding of Yorkshire 1780–1837* (York, Borthwick Institute, 1982).

53 L. Bonfield, 'Was there a "third age" in the pre-industrial English past? Some evidence from the law', in J. M. Eekelaar and D. Pearl (eds), *An ageing world: dilemmas and challenges for law and social policy* (Oxford University Press, 1989), p. 50. Also S. O. Rose, 'Widowhood and poverty in

nineteenth century Nottinghamshire', in J. Henderson and R. Wall (eds), *Poor women and children in the European past* (London, Routledge, 1994), pp. 269–91.

54 Hastings, *Poverty*.

55 F. M. Eden, *The state of the poor: a history of the labouring classes in England with parochial reports* (London, Cass, 1963 reprint).

56 E. C. Midwinter, *Social administration in Lancashire 1830–1860* (Manchester, Manchester University Press, 1969), p. 62.

57 Hollen-Lees, *The solidarities*, p. 7.

58 Marshall, *English*, p. 252.

59 K. Wrightson, 'The politics of the parish in early modern England', in P. Griffiths, A. Fox and S. Hindle (eds), *The experience of authority in early modern England* (Basingstoke, Macmillan, 1996), p. 21.

60 WYAS Calverley 84, 'Poor law accounts'.

61 For a Cumbrian example, see Cumbria Record Office WD/BIG/1/64/36, 'Plan of encroachments'. In Lancashire, Lancashire Record Office (herefter LRO) DDIn/45/14, 'Report on town cottages, Birkdale 1815', and LRO DDIn/46/37, 'Lease'.

62 R. Jutte, *Poverty and deviance in early modern Europe* (Cambridge, Cambridge University Press, 1994), p. 9.

63 See T. Sokoll, 'Old age in poverty: the record of Essex pauper letters 1780–1834', in T. Hitchcock, P. King and P. Sharpe (eds), *Chronicling poverty: the voices and strategies of the English poor* (Basingstoke, Macmillan, 1997), pp. 127–54. However, see also P. Sharpe, 'The bowels of compation: a labouring family and the law c. 1790–1834', in *ibid.*, pp. 87–108, who shows that even the blatantly dishonest could also get relief.

64 S. Webb and B. Webb, *English poor law history part II: the last hundred years* (London, Cass, 1963 reprint), pp. 1 and 88.

65 *Ibid.*, p. 100.

66 *Ibid.*, p. 145.

67 R. G. Hodgkinson, 'Poor law medical officers of England 1834–1871', *Journal of the History of Medicine*, 11 (1965) 229–38, and R. G. Hodgkinson, *The origins of the National Health Service: the medical services of the new poor law 1834–1871* (London, Wellcome Institute, 1967), and A. Digby, *Making a medical living: doctors and patients in the English market for medicine, 1720–1911* (Cambridge, Cambridge University Press, 1997). However, see also I. Loudon, 'I'd rather have been a parish surgeon than a union one', *Bulletin of the Society for the Social History of Medicine*, 38 (1986) 68–73.

68 For more on this issue, see K. Laybourn, *The evolution of British social policy and the welfare state 1800–1993* (Keele, Keele University Press, 1995).

69 D. Ashforth, 'Settlement and removal in urban areas: Bradford 1834–71', in M. E. Rose (ed.), *The poor and the city: the English poor law in its urban context 1834–1914* (Leicester, Leicester University Press, 1988), pp. 58–91. See also D. Ashforth, 'The urban poor law', in D. Fraser (ed.), *The new poor*

law in the nineteenth century (Basingstoke, Macmillan, 1976), pp. 128–48, who argues that many unions were financially fragile.

70 See D. Fraser, 'Poor law politics in Leeds 1833–55', *Publications of the Thoresby Society*, 15 (1977) 23–49, and D. Fraser (ed.), 'The poor law as a political institution', in Fraser, *The new*, pp. 111–27.

71 E. C. Midwinter, 'State intervention at the local level: the new poor law in Lancashire', *Historical Journal*, 10 (1967) p. 106.

72 See L. Hollen-Lees, *Poverty and pauperism in nineteenth-century London* (Leicester, Leicester University Press, 1988).

73 See K. Williams, *From pauperism to poverty* (London, Routledge and Kegan Paul, 1981).

74 L. Hollen-Lees, 'The survival of the unit: welfare policies and family maintenance in nineteenth century London', in P. Mandler (ed.), *The uses of charity: the poor on relief in the nineteenth century metropolis* (Cambridge, Cambridge University Press, 1990), pp. 68–91.

75 A. Digby, 'The rural poor law', in D. Fraser (ed.), *The new poor law in the nineteenth century* (Basingstoke, Macmillan, 1976), p. 158.

76 See Kidd, *State*. On the testing of 1834 principles before 1834 and the view that there was not much 'new' in the new poor law, see J. D. Marshall, 'The Nottinghamshire reformers and their contribution to the new poor law', *Economic History Review*, 13 (1960/61) 382–96.

77 Snell, *Annals*, pp. 135.

78 Hollen-Lees, *The solidarities*.

79 For a general overview, see D. Roberts, 'How cruel was the Victorian poor law?', *Historical Journal*, 6 (1963) 97–107, p. 104. Also U. Henriques, 'How cruel was the Victorian poor law?', *Historical Journal*, 11 (1968) 365–71.

80 P. Harling, 'The power of persuasion: central authority, local bureaucracy and the new poor law', *English Historical Review*, 107 (1992) 30–53.

81 W. Apfel and P. Dunkley, 'English rural society and the new poor law: Bedfordshire 1834–47', *Social History*, 10 (1985) 41–69.

82 P. Dunkley, 'The hungry forties and the new poor law: a case study', *Historical Journal*, 17 (1974) 329–46.

83 Williams, *From pauperism*.

84 See E. W. Martin, 'From parish to union: poor law administration 1601–1865', in E. W. Martin (ed.), *Comparative developments in social welfare* (London, Croom Helm, 1978), pp. 25–56.

85 See S. A. King, 'A model of vision and benevolence: Mary Haslam and the Bolton poor law union 1880–1914', in A. Digby, S. A. King and R. M. Smith (eds), *Poverty, poor relief and welfare in England from the seventeenth to twentieth centuries* (Cambridge, Cambridge University Press, forthcoming).

86 N. McCord, 'The poor law and philanthropy', in D. Fraser (ed.), *The new poor law in the nineteenth century* (Basingstoke, Macmillan, 1976), pp. 87–110.

CHAPTER FOUR

DEFINING AND MEASURING POVERTY

Overview

The question of how much poverty we find in modern and early modern England is a beguilingly simple one. In fact, exploring this issue involves asking two different but interrelated questions. First, how can poverty be defined, and second, what tools and sources should historians use to measure poverty thus defined? To development economists or social policy analysts, these would be familiar questions, but they have been less often asked in the study of the historical poverty problem.[1] Welfare historians have, as was suggested earlier, devoted much more energy to discussing solutions than they have to considering the nature of the problem in the first place. Where the issue has been considered at all, general perspectives have been preferred to attempts at definite measurement. Thus, welfare historians have been happy to accept the contention that poverty was a constant risk for much of the labouring population, that it almost certainly increased in scale over the course of the eighteenth century and that relatively few labouring people could escape the spectre of communal welfare at some point in their life cycle.

Real and apocryphal stories of wealthy men sinking to beggary, of workhouse masters obliged to apply for relief and of the grinding urban poverty related to the proliferation of casual jobs in nineteenth-century towns give the human backdrop to these basic assumptions.[2] The gloomy diary of William Rowbottom provides a comprehensive litany of such cases. One in particular exemplifies the spectre that poor law historiography assumes to have haunted the great majority of people before 1850; thus 'Jonathan Nield of Oldham died in an advanced age, April 30th 1790. He was formerly a man of property. Died poor.'[3] Pauper letters also provide indications that the margin between independence and poverty was a slim one, as we saw with the example of Mary Dewhurst in chapter one.[4] Even allowing for poetic licence, Dewhurst was poor in the sense that she was destitute. In turn, if we could argue that the granting of communal relief usually reflected poverty of this sort, then studying the numbers in receipt of relief or, more importantly, the expenditure on them would provide (once we take account of changes in the criteria for eligibility set down by the law as discussed in chapter two) at least a minimal quantitative snapshot of the extent of the national landscape of poverty.

Indeed, there is something inherently appealing about a 'fuzzy' approach to the definition and measurement of need. Systematic indicators of absolute and relative poverty were not formulated and applied before the social surveys of the late nineteenth century.[5] Overseers under the old poor law, and guardians under the new, might thus hold very different ideas about what constituted 'poverty' in different parts of the country, or even over time in the same place. Then, as now, it is likely that some 'poverty' was socially constructed as a relative experience – relative to what other people within the community had and what custom dictated was necessary for 'normal' life.[6] Indeed, the tendency for poverty to become more 'relative' might be what we see in the expanding range of goods and services which local studies indicate poor law administrators were expected to provide from the 1780s. It is also likely that those administering relief made a distinction between poverty arising out of inadequate resources and poverty arising out of poorly managed resources.[7] Defining what 'poverty' *was*, and measuring its extent, might thus be potentially very difficult for welfare historians who do not use proxies such as relief spending. Nor is the picture less complex if we try to define 'poverty' from the standpoint of labouring people themselves. Over the lifecycle of individuals and families, periods of economic stress were interspersed with periods of accumulation. Autobiographical accounts leave us in little doubt that people *expected* to accumulate goods and money at some parts of the life cycle and then *expected* to liquidate these 'savings' at other times. Whether the process of liquidation amounted to poverty in their eyes is very uncertain. Indeed, when surveys of the poor became more common from the 1790s, many of the reports which emerge consistently record the tendency for families struggling under life- and trade-cycle stress to be able to point to others worse off than themselves. The temptation to regard poor law statistics as providing quantitative evidence of poverty which was acknowledged by individuals, community administrators and the wider community is thus understandable. Indeed, this 'demand side' definition lies at the heart of most recent overviews of English welfare patterns. Hollen-Lees, for instance, notes that 'it is illegitimate to suppose a direct and tight correlation between changing numbers of people on relief and changing amounts of poverty', but accepts that 'those who received relief were no doubt poor'.[8] Whether such assumptions are accurate or sufficient is an entirely different matter.

This chapter will offer an initial exploration of the chronological and spatial dimensions of 'poverty' which can be observed using poor law data as a proxy measurement. It will then go on to try an unpick what exactly poor law statistics really tell us about need – considering the accuracy of expenditure figures, concepts of absolute and relative poverty and the fluctuating nature of entitlement – and in doing so suggest an alternative framework for interpretation of poor law data. It will conclude that while a general notion that poverty 'increased' is probably correct it is insufficient to use this perspective to frame detailed local and regional analysis of the 'solutions' to poverty. Chapter five will consider how welfare historians might move forward from this general notion to greater precision on magnitudes and a richer appreciation of the changing causal structure of poverty, its life-cycle manifestations and contemporary understanding of the nature of poverty. Only when we have done this will the framework within which we must discuss welfare solutions be complete.

Defining and measuring the poor: the story so far

Prior to 1700, the survival of sources which throw light on the scale of poverty is rare.[9] However, the work of Tom Arkell gives us a broad starting point. Using data from twelve Warwickshire parishes in the late seventeenth century, he argued that equating 'poverty' with just those in receipt of relief provided the narrowest definition of need. Only around 10 per cent of households would be classed as poor on this basis. Equating exemption from the hearth tax and 'poverty' would imply that 35 per cent of households were in need, while this figure would fall to 30 per cent using exemption from local taxes as a proxy for poverty.[10] There is support here for the idea that poor law statistics provide at least a minimal definition of poverty. More importantly, on the basis that the families of 'poor' household heads were also likely to be in need, it might be reasonable to suggest that coming into the eighteenth century perhaps one-third of all local populations *could* be classed as 'poor' in the sense of contemporary definitions. For some parts of England, the seventeenth century also yields up rich life-cycle data to support this general perspective. Newman-Brown linked family reconstitution and poor law data for the Hertfordshire township of Aldenham and found that the poor law was relieving 36 per cent of household heads by 1681.

Tim Wales conducted a similar exercise for seventeenth-century Norfolk parishes, arguing that over two-fifths of all households might be dependent on relief at some life-cycle point.[11] However, the studies on which a picture of substantial poverty might be based are neither so numerous nor so spatially detailed that we can attempt broad general-isations on the likely socio-economic or regional dimensions of the poverty problem coming into the eighteenth century.[12]

Paradoxically the situation is not much better after 1700. Almost no eighteenth-century reconstitution studies have been linked to poor law data, and tax exemption figures as an indicator of poverty have also fallen by the historiographical wayside.[13] The latter observation is perhaps not surprising. The abolition of the hearth tax puts an end to easily accessible national sources on tax exemption, and though sur-viving local tax figures (the poor rate, churchwarden rate or highway rate) become more common for the eighteenth century they raise thorny issues to do with the criteria for exemption over time and place. These are reviewed in chapter five. Meanwhile, the records of friendly societies and charities have been more comprehensively considered, but often outside the context of bigger debates on poverty and welfare. On the other hand, records from the poor law become more voluminous in the eighteenth century. Welfare historians have thus both implicitly and explicitly relied on poor law statistics to say anything meaningful about the scale of poverty in this period.

Against this backdrop it is perhaps expedient, if illusory, to consider the measurement and definition of poverty using poor law data during the period 1700–1850 in three convenient parts: 1700–76, 1776–1834 and 1834–50. Thus, the attempts of welfare historians to define and measure poverty between 1700 and 1776 stumble across a barren source landscape. The pamphlet literature on poverty and relief structures which blossomed in this period contains numerous estimates of the scale of the problem, but we have no adequate yardstick against which to judge their reliability.[14] Aggregate poor law spending, however, pro-vides one way forward. By 1700 welfare expenditure was probably of the order of less than £500,000. This figure had expanded to almost £690,000 by the mid-eighteenth century, at which point Paul Slack has estimated that poor relief absorbed 1 per cent of national income.[15] By 1776, when we get our first really concrete national figures, poor relief expenditure stood at £1,529,780.

While the 1776 figure implies an enormous rise since mid-century, it is actually the 1700–50 increase which is the more significant. After 1750 population was growing rapidly and food prices were on a rising trend.

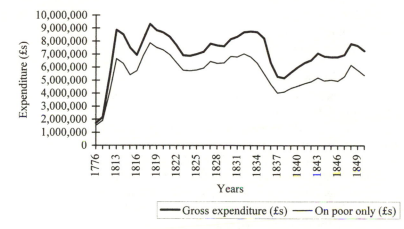

Figure 4.1 National welfare expenditure in England

We would thus expect some increase in the nominal cost of the relief bill whatever was happening to underlying poverty. However, for much of the first half of the eighteenth century food prices in particular fell, while new data from Wrigley et al. confirm that population growth was relatively slow until the 1740s.[16] All other things being equal, poor law expenditure should have fallen in this period. The fact that it did not might, where we equate 'poverty' and poor law expenditure, ostensibly testify to a growing poverty problem. Some local studies provide support for the idea that poverty was growing throughout the period 1700–76, balancing rising expenditure with observation of a long-term rise in numbers of recipients over and above the growth that would have been expected simply because of population increase. Indeed, it would perhaps not be unrealistic to suggest that up to one-third of any birth cohort from the early eighteenth century onwards would expect to come into contact with the poor law at some point in their subsequent life cycle.[17] However, disjointed local studies and national expenditure snapshots offer little scope for tracing the regional picture and can give only the most general perspectives on the scale of poverty.

The second reference period, 1776–1834, ostensibly provides rather more extensive data. The 'national' returns of 1776 were followed up with further enquiries in 1783–85 and 1802–3, before data were collected on a regular basis from 1813. Figure 4.1 plots these data on two curves, one reflecting gross payments and the other allowing for administration costs.[18] The precipitous rise in net expenditure after the high base of 1776 is clear. By 1785 the relief bill had increased to

£2,004,238 and it was to more than double by 1803, to £4,267,965. Increases of this sort were much quoted by contemporary pamphleteers agitating for reform of the old poor law from the late 1780s. Initially, expenditure rose fastest in towns and cities, with densely populated urban parishes in London, Manchester and Liverpool all petitioning parliament between 1776 and 1790 for help in combating the huge poverty problem which they said they faced. Thereafter, the introduction of more systematic wage subsidies and 'make-work' schemes in a wide range of rural areas, from the East Riding to Dorset, fostered fastest expenditure growth rates in rural areas.

Trends in expenditure (and by implication poverty) after 1813 are not so clear.[19] The withdrawal of systematic allowances in aid of wages brought a familiar seasonal 'feel' to rural poor law expenditure. In urban areas, the uniform upward trend in expenditure of the late eighteenth century was replaced by a more diversified experience. Manchester and Liverpool continued to post year-on-year expenditure records, while Leeds, Coventry and older towns such as Kendal or Norwich could post frequent expenditure falls. The net effect on 'national' figures was more wave-like development. A post-war expenditure peak at near £7,000,000 was succeeded in 1815 by a significant fall, which was in turn followed by a depression-led rise in expenditure late in the 1810s. Thereafter, expenditure stabilised, and not until the early 1830s did the net relief bill approach £7,000,000 again. Per capita expenditure figures fluctuated fairly consistently between 9 and 13 shillings per year in the last years of the old poor law, a level which would have been inconceivable fifty years before. The loud complaints of ratepayers became a familiar public spectacle in the later years of the old poor law.[20]

On the face of it, then, equating poverty with poor law spending would seem to point towards a sustained rise in the scale of the poverty problem during the later eighteenth and early nineteenth centuries. Other evidence supports this notion. In the 1802/3 relief year, 1,060,000 people (9 per cent of the population) were receiving relief in some form. By 1813 the relief list had increased by one-half. Allowing for the dependents of those on relief (increasingly large numbers of whom were males with families according to much recent poor law historiography), it might not be unrealistic to suggest that at least one-third of many county and village populations were 'in poverty'. These national figures are, of course, ambiguous. It is not absolutely certain under either the old or new poor law whether the numbers of recorded recipients refers to the number of distinct individuals relieved or whether they actually relate to the number of relief applications made. Equally it is sometimes uncertain whether the 'number' of recipients represents a count throughout the year or some multiplied total based upon counts at just a few points in the year. Again, however, some local studies confirm a substantial poverty problem. For the crisis year of 1796, Thomas Sokoll used a listing of *households* in Ardleigh, Essex, to demonstrate that 41 per cent were pauperised. In Braintree, Essex, in 1821 some 38 per cent of all households were pauperised.[21] For the Hampshire parish of Odiham, Barry Stapleton has been able to link family reconstitution data and charity accounts to demonstrate that those receiving welfare became younger over the course of the eighteenth and early nineteenth centuries, and that perhaps two-fifths of all households would have been 'in poverty' by 1800.[22] Nor would Frederick Eden have found these broad perspectives unusual in his wide survey of poverty throughout England.[23] The stabilisation of spending in the 1820s, and what this implies for poverty, is intriguing, but the key point is that if poor relief expenditure can only provide a partial reflection of the scale of poverty, then a substantial portion of labouring society was firmly embedded in a quagmire of need leading up to reform of the poor law.

Meanwhile, for this second period we can add a further layer to the discussion by mapping the regional dimensions of static data from the national surveys. Undertaking such an exercise for the individual parish-level returns is a potentially massive task, but aggregating parish experiences to provide county-level totals provides an easier way forward. Of course this is an artificial approach. Counties themselves provide illusory boundaries which have no inevitable relevance to constellations of poverty, and nor can such a mapping exercise give us an idea of whether counties and regions were becoming more or less pauperised. Intra-regional diversity in poor law expenditure or numbers on relief is also a problem. Nonetheless, an appreciation of the broad regional lessons to be drawn from these national surveys is implicit in much of the most recent historiography of the poor law and a cursory look at them is necessary.

Map. 4.1 represents per capita relief spending by county in 1802/3. Two features of this map are particularly important. First, the sheer scale of relief spending; almost all counties were spending more than 5s. per capita on relief by 1802/3 and the unweighted average for all counties was nearer 10s. per capita. Second, the regional disparities in spending which marked out the south and east from the north and west and may have equated to considerable differences between these macro-regions in the extent or intensity of poverty. The same divide can be seen

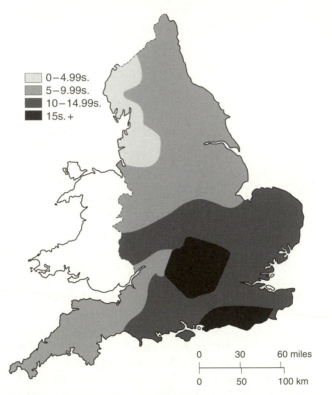

0–4.99s.
5–9.99s.
10–14.99s.
15s.+

0   30   60 miles

0   50   100 km

Map 4.1 Per capita relief spending (shillings) by county, 1802/3
Source V. J. Walsh, 'Poor law administration in Shropshire 1820–1855'
(unpublished Ph.D. thesis, University of Pennsylvania, 1970), p. 57.

even more clearly through the (less comprehensive) 1831 returns to parliament. Map 4.2 (showing county level per capita relief levels for this year) marks out Lancashire as the most distinctive English county but more importantly demonstrates very clearly the dividing line between the 'south and east' and 'north and west' suggested in chapter one.

Map 4.3 takes an alternative approach and represents the county-level figures for proportions of the population defined as poor by the receipt of relief in 1802/3. For the reasons mentioned already such figures are necessarily suspect, but the lessons to be drawn from the map do chime with those which emerge from the expenditure data and are thus worth considering. Thus, two features of map 4.3 are particularly important. First, the fact that in some areas up to one-fifth of all individuals were in receipt of relief. This is a lower figure than that to be

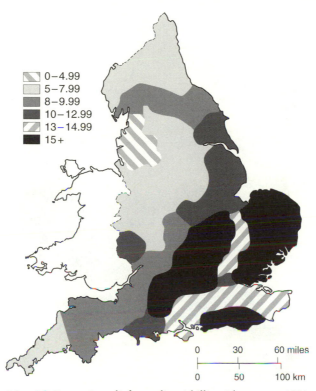

Map 4.2 Per capita relief spending (shillings) by county, 1831
Source Walsh, 'Poor law'.

found in community studies of the crisis years from 1792, but still substantial. We do not know the family circumstances of the individuals
who made up this measure, but we can be sure that at least some of them
would have been supporting families out of their relief income who
could thus also be described as poor. Allowing for this it might be a fair
guess that a minimum of two-fifths of people could be described as
poor in some regions. The second feature is the broad regional disparity in the scale of poverty measured in this way. The north had a broad
uniformity which we might want to class as 'low poverty' while large
areas of the south would have to be classed as 'high poverty'. As chapter
one suggested, many social and economic historians would recognise
these broad 'highland'/'lowland' divisions, and they also find support
in discussion of the spatial dimensions of consumption and historical
demography.[24]

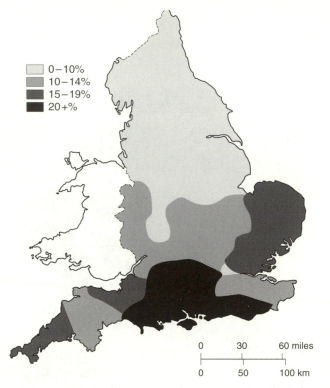

0–10%
10–14%
15–19%
20+%

0   30   60 miles

0   50   100 km

Map 4.3 Proportions of county populations in receipt of relief, 1802/3
Source A. Aspinall and E. A. Smith, *English historical documents 1783–1832*
(London, Eyre and Spottiswoode, 1969), pp. 411–12.

By the time the commission of inquiry into the state of the old poor
law sat in 1832, then, poor law expenditure (and by implication poverty)
had shown a century of substantial rise. The writing of numerous
travellers and itinerant commentators has left us a rich vein of testimony that poverty remained a serious life-cycle and point-in-time
problem for most labouring people and for those charged with creating
a new administration.[25] Moreover, distinct regional patterns of need
seem to have developed. Many of these trends were to continue in the
third period of this analysis, 1834–50. As figure 4.1 shows, the initial
result of the legislation of 1834 was to trigger a precipitous, particularly
southern, fall in relief expenditure. Between 1834 and 1840 there was a
28 per cent reduction in gross expenditure, but in some mainly rural
counties such as Berkshire, the decline was 40 per cent or more. Such

movements could not have reflected the course of underlying poverty, and the rise of expenditure in the early 1840s was testimony not to rising poverty but simply the return to mainstream relief of those whose poverty had been previously disguised. At this point, and to the end of the period considered by this book, the regional differences in the scope and scale of poor law expenditure highlighted during the old poor law period were as strong as ever.[26] Despite improvements in abstract measures of standard of living from at least the 1830s, equating 'poverty' with poor law statistics suggests that at least as many people were 'poor' by 1850 as had been in 1780 or before.[27]

Yet are we right to use poor law data, particularly expenditure statistics, as a proxy for poverty? What does the level of, and trends in, aggregate or local expenditure actually tell us? What factors other than pauper demand might shape the level of relief spending? Moreover, before we even start to think about the message to be drawn from local and national expenditure figures, are they really accurate? The rest of the chapter deals with these issues.

Defining and measuring: the accuracy of expenditure figures

Some of the ambiguities surrounding poor law expenditure figures are familiar and relatively easily dealt with. Gross relief expenditure figures, for instance, mask the fact that both pension payments and payments in kind were influenced by price rises and falls. At times of price inflation such as the 1790s, rising food and fuel prices could add 20 or 30 per cent to the aggregate poor relief bill even if there was no change in the numbers of people relieved or the extent of their poverty. By the same token at times of falling fuel and food prices, such as those after 1814, poor law bodies were sometimes eager to reduce pension payments, irrespective of the scale and trend of underlying poverty.[28] For these reasons, welfare historians have tried to establish 'real' relief costs. At its crudest level, this process involves the assumption that the centrepiece of the household budgets of the poor was bread, so that dividing gross relief by an index of the price of wheat yields a measure of the purchasing power of relief. Using data from a set of rural southeastern parishes, Baugh used this method to suggest that the 'real' cost of relief rose not in the 1790s as is usually assumed (and as figure 4.1 implies), but from 1813 as the post-war boom faded and labour markets became overstocked. Hastings has used similar methods to demonstrate that the 'real' cost of relief was static between 1790 and 1813.[29] Such conclusions potentially put a rather different gloss on our appreciation of the poverty picture, but they are in themselves suspect. Even for the poor, bread became less and less central to the family budget from the 1770s, and as the range of expenditure of ordinary people widened, so did the range of areas in which the poor law intervened.[30] One of these areas was rent, with the poor law north and south coming to pay the rent of more people in the late eighteenth century than it ever had before, and pay those rents in full rather than in part, as had been the case previously. Deflating relief expenditure by a rather wider 'expenditure basket' for the poor might reveal different trends for real relief costs and thus for the measurement of poverty. This process is not attempted here, but it is nonetheless important to bear in mind the need to control for factors such as inflation in reading poor law expenditure statistics.

Other problems with the accuracy of poor law expenditure figures are less obvious and less easily addressed. Most importantly, in *accounting* terms neither gross nor 'real' expenditure figures usually take account of debts. It was surprisingly rare for overseers to balance their books, and almost all poor law units incurred in some years very considerable spending overshoots or rate collection undershoots. These yearly debts had to be balanced by raising more in the following year, by becoming a personal loss to the overseer, or they were converted to a rolling debt of the poor law system with interest paid out of the yearly poor rates. This may seem like an insignificant issue, but take a hypothetical example. The overseer of a good-sized parish in the midlands sets a rate for the year to raise £100. However, £20 worth of rates go uncollected because the ratepayer was an absentee landowner or simply failed to pay. In addition, a bad winter pushes expenditure £30 over budget, so that the total debt of the poor law (or in reality the overseer) is £50. What figure is reported in the parish accounts as income and expenditure – £80, £100 or £150? More importantly, what figures are reported to parliament when returns have to be made? If the yearly debts are converted to rolling debts, what impact do interest payments have on perceived local expenditure? If rolling debts are created, who holds them and what impact does this have on local policies towards entitlement? These are complex and important questions, and they mean that we cannot simply accept the figure at the bottom of parish accounts as representing expenditure on the poor in any given year.

In 'real historical life', these problems could be substantial. Most overseers were no accountants and they were not very good at predicting need and hence raising sufficient money at regular intervals during the year. The result was substantial and often repetitive yearly

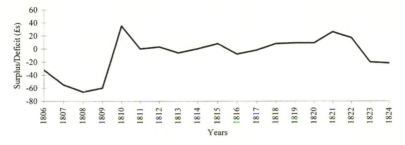

Figure 4.2 Poor law current account surpluses and deficits for Cowpe

debts. Figure 4.2 provides a view of the deficit figures for a collection of four contiguous Lancashire townships. Not only were the debts themselves significant on an individual basis, but they were consistently rolled over as a charge on the poor law, such that by 1826 they amounted to 120 per cent of poor rate yield. In other places too the scale of loans and accruing interest charges was very substantial. At Addingham in the North Riding, for instance, accumulated debts stood at 203 per cent of the annual poor rate yield by 1803. More widely, northern towns in general could assemble only feeble finances to meet the poverty problem and consistently ran into substantial debt.[31] Not everywhere was this bad. Wimbledon parish officers ran into debt to major local figures on a regular basis, but these debts were paid back generally within a year. In Lancashire, miscellaneous notes on the parish of Kirkham reveal that 'May–October 1782 – first time for ages that the overseer owed money'.[32] Some overseers responded to looming debts by simply letting the allowances of the poor fall into arrears, and this practice also has implications for the use of expenditure figures to measure poverty.

However, the wider point is that there was a spectrum of experience at any point in time and over time. Rigorous parishes could become debtor parishes, debtor parishes could make good over time, and parishes with a surplus could sit adjacent to those with substantial year-on-year and rolling debts. This patchwork of experience and our uncertainty about how yearly and rolling debts related to the nominal yearly expenditure figures recorded by parish officials for the consumption of ratepayers, magistrates and parliament mean that we must be very careful indeed in assuming that expenditure figures elaborated from thousands of parish returns to parliament really can tell us what we need to know about poverty between 1700 and 1834. Nor is it necessarily any easier to interpret expenditure curves after 1834. Under the new poor law an audit process controlled current account deficits.

However, unions also faced the continual headache of parish and ratepayer resistance to meeting union bills, which could force temporary borrowing and hidden interest bills in the union accounts. Again we must be cautious in the use of expenditure figures and our interpretation of the lessons they appear to hold.

Defining and measuring: an alternative interpretation of poor law statistics

Even if local and national poor law expenditure statistics were totally accurate, the message to be drawn from them – greater poverty over the eighteenth century, particularly in the south and east – is perhaps more ambiguous than at first it seems. Thus, it is possible to argue that the level of, and trends in, yearly expenditure figures recorded in individual parish accounts (and subsequently reported to parliament) reflect less the scale and intensity of local poverty than the outcome of a yearly negotiation process in which 'absolute need' was just one of the variables shaping the expenditure agenda. Crudely, this negotiation process might be seen to have four interrelated and overlapping levels,

1 In any year the 'supply' of welfare in the form of the maximum yield of the parish poor rate was something that had to be negotiated between ratepayers and the parish in the guise of the vestry or the overseer. As we have seen, it was common for parishes to go into debt to fund overspends, but ultimately the size of the rate yield rather than the scale of poverty underpinned the level of and trends in local expenditure.

2 Overseers, ratepayers and prominent local figures had to negotiate a 'parish policy' on the general parameters for grading 'need' or poverty. In particular, where the parish was to fall on the spectrum between relieving only total destitution and relieving anybody who fell below the basic living standards of the wider community had to be subjected to constant yearly renegotiation.

3 Often simultaneously the outlines of the 'demand' for welfare had to be negotiated between those who felt poor enough to apply and the overseer in a process of establishing entitlement. As well as 'parish policy' on relieving relative poverty, notions of custom, personal relationships and moral considerations might form important yardsticks against which applications were judged.

4 The available supply of welfare had to be matched to legitimate demand by the overseer who might recognise different grades of poverty and had to determine the level of allowances appropriate to each grade. A range of personal, political and cultural factors may have influenced

this last stage of the process by which need was recognised and amelio-
rated.

Of course, the process by which supply and demand reached equilibrium was infinitely more complex and painful than this simple model
allows. The mechanism of supplementary rates meant that demand and
supply were not conveniently separate as they appear here. Similarly, the
processes of establishing entitlement and the overseer allocating money
might be linked where parishes had predefined allowances for certain
types of paupers such as the old or widows. Nonetheless, this very crude
model does at least have the advantage of making plain the ambiguous
relationship between 'poverty' and expenditure and of suggesting the
scope for parish welfare systems to effectively 'write off' much that we
might regard as true poverty. A more detailed analysis of three of these
levels (allowances are considered in chapters six to eight) may go a
considerable way to clarifying the messages we should read from poor
law statistics.

The 'supply' of welfare

On the face of it, ensuring a good 'supply' of welfare funds was a simple
process. The overseer had to get a rate list (either recycled in totem from
the previous year or updated during a tour of the parish), make an estimate of likely need, set a rate in the pound, notify the parish of the rate
and then collect it monthly, quarterly or annually. If it were this simple,
then we would expect a strong correlation between movements in the
level of need recognised by the community and the cost of local relief.
And if such a responsive link between demand and supply did exist it
would be easy to imagine at the aggregate level a scenario in which the
rising expenditure curve outlined in figure 4.1 reflected less the changing scale and intensity of poverty than a cumulative advance in the
ability and willingness of ratepayers to pay for more generous treatment
and wider recognition of entitlement. There is certainly good reason to
think that the increasing ability was there. Rising land values in both
agricultural and industrial areas, rising rents, low and stagnant wages
in most of the rural south and east, and the income to be garnered first
from rural industry and then mining and factory industry must have left
the central core of ratepayers in many communities rather better off in
the early nineteenth century than they would have been in the 1750s. For
some at least the real burden (rather than the nominal amount) of the
rate must have fallen significantly in the later eighteenth century and the
fact that the consumer revolution developed strongly at the same time

as relief bills spiralled provides notional support for the idea that the potential supply of welfare may have expanded. Moreover, the extension of this theme, as was suggested in chapter three, is that the spatial disparities in the scope and generosity of relief between the north and west and the south and the east reflected at least in part differential 'ability to pay'.

Yet while this simple model might be attractive, several complexities in the negotiation of a 'supply of welfare' manifest themselves. At the aggregate level, some communities had a declining rather than expanding rate base, and for ratepayers in these communities the increasing real burden of relief bills made negotiating a supply of welfare difficult. By the early nineteenth century, ratepayers throughout the rural south were complaining of the burden of poor relief bills. Naturally some of these complaints were overplayed, but a cursory look at the bankruptcy notices in any provincial newspaper after 1800 would show clearly that some ratepayers were under very real pressure in the rural south and east. Rising poor relief bills at the aggregate level may thus not represent in any very direct or consistent way a measure of increasing wealth and ability to pay. Meanwhile, at the level of the individual community, three other influences on the process of negotiating a supply of welfare might be found at work.

First, different overseers had different reputations and levels of commitment to the job, so that while some individuals found it easy to raise a rate others did not have the social authority to compel their neighbours to accept the assessment. Thus from year to year the balance of power in negotiating a supply of welfare would shift, and with it perhaps the meaning of poor law expenditure statistics. Second, the ability to pay did not always equate to a willingness to pay, and defaulting and attempts at avoidance appear to have been common. Thus, in Wimbledon almost every eighteenth-century vestry meeting had to consider what to do about defaulting ratepayers. Richmond in Surrey also had a problem with defaulting ratepayers, but its vestry records demonstrate very well the more common prevarications that ratepayers used. Between 1725 and 1764, there was only one year where a poor rate went completely unchallenged as individuals or groups of local ratepayers called for a revaluation of their property or challenged the expenditure plans of the overseer. This may have been an extreme experience, but work for this book on the surviving Westmorland rate lists between 1750 and 1820 indicated that one in three rate assessments were either challenged or had at least one defaulter. Third, even where the ability to pay was accompanied by no such prevarication, arrears and late payment were common experiences for most overseers and vestries, as diarists such as Thomas Turner of East Hoathley or Robert Sharp of South Cave, who both served as overseers and collecting officers, suggest. Indeed, in places such as Kettering, where in 1823 some 9 per cent of all ratepayers were in arrears, chronic late payment could paralyse the whole relief system. Of course, some of these arrears were accidental. In Kettering, Richmond and most of the Westmorland parishes analysed for this book absentee property-owners were rated and obtaining their contributions was a logistical nightmare. Others used arrears as a form of protest and in Richmond even the local vicar was in substantial arrears with his poor rate contributions.

For these reasons, to assume a fluid and seamless relationship between the supply of and demand for welfare is incorrect. Rates – and therefore the supply of welfare – were a contested issue and the rhetoric of vestry minutes from most communities clearly suggests that the need to be seen to be keeping a grip on the demands made of ratepayers was an important bargaining tool in the negotiation process. Though the poor law running into debt may sometimes reflect short-term emergencies or simply the incompetence of the overseer, there were also times when debt reflected the political limit on raising revenue via the poor rate. The fact that so many parishes consistently failed to balance their books may be some indication of the disparity between the ability and the *willingness* to pay for welfare. Thus, while rising aggregate poor relief bills may in some senses reflect a greater supply of welfare as much as they reflect a greater demand for it, the spatial patterns of relief spending may well have their roots in a differential willingness to pay. We return to these themes in later chapters.

Negotiating a parish policy on relative poverty

As well as ensuring a 'supply' of welfare, overseers also had to set limits to potential demand. One method for doing so was to negotiate entitlement with the poor, and this is the subject of the next section. Another way to limit demand, however, was to generate an agreed parish stance on the point at which the parish would intervene in the descent of individuals and families from independence to total destitution and to make this stance known to potential applicants before they applied. In turn, the nature of this stance has important implications for the level of local expenditure and the relationship between local expenditure and local poverty. More widely, the lessons to be drawn from national relief expenditure totals, and indeed from other poor law statistics, are shaped very much by whether the poor laws provided help only to the totally destitute or, alternatively, whether those who were less poor (relatively poor) or not really poor at all were being caught in the net and receiving allowances.

Welfare historians are divided on this issue, probably reflecting diverse and changeable local practice. Marshall talked of 'only a very considerable measure of poverty, and not utter destitution' as the central criterion for relief eligibility.[33] The Webbs were also sceptical of how much relief lists could tell historians about poverty. They noted that in some areas anybody who applied could get relief, perhaps masking non-poor recipients of regular and irregular payments. Similarly, they concluded that once someone was getting a pension as opposed to irregular payments, it might be very difficult to subsequently shift them from the relief lists, even if their underlying poverty circumstances changed.[34] Of course, this was not the case everywhere. Some vestries and overseers had no qualms about ending pensions. Stone in Staffordshire, for instance. Yet even areas with particularly active vestries and overseers often found it difficult to remove pensioners as opposed to squeezing their allowances in a periodic or progressive manner. Growing relief lists might thus become less and less effective as a proxy for poverty by virtue of the inertia of the administrative system. Features of the poor law system such as the formation of select vestries and a move to publish the names of recipients of welfare in many communities from 1800 onwards could in this sense be regarded as a response to the problem that many people who would not conventionally be defined as poor were in fact receiving relief.

In a theoretical and practical sense this is a difficult debate to call. Vestry minutes suggest that not all who were destitute always got communal relief, but the question of the depth of poverty experienced by those who *did* come on to relief cannot be judged from this source. In the absence of formalised poverty lines marking out absolute and relative poverty, an alternative approach is to make use of the surprisingly large numbers of pauper inventories which appear in parish collections. These suggest that under the old poor law large numbers of communities did not leave it until the last minute to intervene in the process whereby a person became poor.[35] Thus, Peter King has recently used a selection of pauper inventories from Essex to look at the material lives of the poor. He concludes that the southern poor managed to accumulate a substantial battery of consumer goods and that the poor law was instrumental in keeping this material world intact.[36] Inventories for Norfolk parishes, while showing a more varied picture, also suggest that the majority of paupers had a substantial household-effects reper-toire.[37] In wealth terms, then, not even a 'very considerable measure of poverty' was needed in these communities to establish entitlement to relief.

Relatively few of the pauper inventories from Essex or elsewhere contain valuations, and they are not liable to easy quantification except in the sense that one might count the number of items as a proxy for poverty.[38] This feature of the data is unfortunate, making it difficult to draw out the stark disparities in the timing of poor law intervention between and within regions detected using this methodology. We can, however, make a first crude inter-regional comparison by ranking in terms of size the Essex inventories, and an alternative sample of fifty-six pauper inventories assembled for different towns and villages in Lancashire, Westmorland and West Yorkshire.[39] In the Essex sample, Widow King had an inventory of goods taken at her death in July 1798. The inventory, one of the least detailed in the whole sample, contained:

> Corded bottom bedstead, Featherbed, Bolster, 1 pillow, 4 sheets, 2 blan-kets, coverlet, 1 round deal table, 2 chairs, 1 small oak box, 1 gown 2 pet-ticoats, 1 pair stays, 1 pair shoes, 1 pair hose, 4 caps, 2 handkerchiefs, 3 shifts, 2 aprons, 1 bonnet, 1 pillowcase, 1 wheel, 4 plates, pint basin, 6 pieces crockery, 4 pieces tinware, copper tea kettle, 1 trammel, tin kettle with cover, saucepan, 2 wooden dishes, 2 small pans, 1 water pail[40]

For Widow Hayes of the Lancashire township of Rawtenstall at the same date, and in roughly the same position in the alternative hierarchy of inventories as Widow King was in Essex, the list of goods ran: '1 stool, 1 chest, 1 camber, firegrate, old loom, bed, bedding'.[41] Once we discount clothes, the material difference between the two inventories is limited. The real difference between the samples lies in the upper and middling ranks of pauper inventories. Widow Cottam's inventory of 1763 was one of the most detailed of the whole alternative sample, but still only contained:

> one feather bed, one feather bolster, one feather pillow, one pair of blan-kets, one sheet, one cadow, one Thron chair and too gurnishens [cush-ions], one stool, one fireiern, too bedcords, one box, one pair bedstocks, one baskit, too mes tins and too spoons, 1 wheel, 1 reel, 1 pan, 1 sheet, 1 box, 1 shift, 1 bed and bedstead.[42]

In value terms, the inventory of Widow Cottam would probably have amounted to not much more than that of Widow King in Essex, despite the fact that she would come near the bottom of the Essex hierarchy. By contrast, the inventory of Widow Childs, somewhere near the middle in the Essex listing, contained fifty-five items, including an 'old fashioned trunk', while John Stanes (inventory of June 1756) who would be at the upper end of the distribution had items in five separate rooms and a yard, totalling over 150 different categories of goods.[43] Indeed, if we gave an arbitrary value to the goods which appear in the alternative sets of inventories, almost all would fall in the lowest quartile of Essex inventories in wealth terms. Some of this is of course to be expected. Essex and the southeast lay at the heart of what has become known as the consumer revolution, and so the inventories of household goods should have been larger. The key point, however, is that these were by and large the inventories of people receiving poor relief, and the really very stark differences of scale highlighted in this comparison reflects less the relative participation in consumer revolution than differences in the timing of poor law intervention in the process of becoming destitute.

It thus becomes much less clear than it appeared at the start of this chapter what sort of poverty poor law records are actually showing to the welfare historian. This point takes on even more force when we look at variations in inventory size and content within regions and within communities. Norfolk inventories were on balance less voluminous than those in Essex. In Oxfordshire one inventory for Chalfont St Peter ran to just six items, while others in Banbury ran to more than one hundred.[44] In the north, the Westmorland parish of Ravenstonedale could exhibit even bigger variations as early as 1729.[45] Thus, Old Roger Barber had 'Only a great bible' besides his clothes, while Elizabeth Ridding had 'a cupboard, a pan and dishes, a table and odd things, 2 coarse bedds and a pare of bedstocks.'[46] Robert Robinson, on the other hand, had 109 items in his 'pauper inventory', and William Garrett had 100 items. The timing of poor law intervention in the process of becoming poor could also change in some communities. This was certainly the case, for instance, in Leigh (Lancashire) where we have pauper inventories stretching over almost one hundred years. Here, judging by the size of inventories, the poor law apparently moved from intervening early during the late eighteenth century to intervening late by the early nineteenth century. A tailored definition of poverty gave way to a destitution test and eligibility for relief moved from relative to absolute poverty. The 'meaning' of expenditure statistics is thus altered over time, complicating our ability to discern the underlying message on poverty.

In other words, the process of negotiating a parish or township stance on the timing of poor law intervention under the old poor law generates a situation in which expenditure on relieving destitution on the one hand and relieving pressure on conventionally accepted living standards on the other hand contribute in unknowable proportions to aggregate expenditure figures. These were not simply north/south or east/west contrasts, and they mean that we must use considerable caution in linking the numbers on a relief list and payments to them and the scale and intensity of underlying poverty.

And while these are examples drawn from the old poor law, exactly the same issues were faced by the relieving officers of the new poor law. Indeed, differences in the definition of what was 'poor' between areas was a perennial problem for the Poor Law Commission. Thus, while some Hampshire unions instructed their relieving officers to do a weekly tour of the union to seek out need, some Lancashire unions expected workers to try every available means to avoid relief applications.[47] The balance is difficult to draw. Some contemporary commentators certainly thought that the new poor law was subject to a high degree of fraud among those who were not really poor. On the other hand, it is possible that the 'destitution test' became more common under the new poor law, especially in urban areas, so that poor law statistics constitute a more reliable indicator of 'poverty' after 1834. Boot, for instance, explained a gap of six months between unemployment and the claim for poor relief for workers in Manchester in the 1840s in terms of the exhaustion of all other means.[48] Cooke-Taylor also suggested as much when he toured the Lancashire manufacturing districts during the depression of the 1840s, giving accounts of people who had sold the clothes off their own backs and gone without food to avoid what they saw as the ignominy of poor relief.[49] These differences of focus and interpretation are significant, for they suggest that, as with the old poor law material, adopting any sort of uniform or strong link between poor relief statistics and the nature of underlying poverty is an approach fraught with difficulties.

The negotiation of entitlement

As we saw in chapter two, while poor law legislation in 1601 gave parishes and townships a duty to relieve the 'deserving' poor, it also allowed the local administration to define the term 'deserving' and its analogue 'undeserving'. In a practical sense, such power was hardly touched by reform in 1834. Those who got no poor relief during this process of definition were theoretically in this position either because they were not deserving, or because they could not be regarded as poor in the local context. In order to move from the background of poverty to the foreground of poverty as recognised by the relief lists, people presumably had to prove both poverty and deserving poverty.[50] The key point is that the categories of 'deserving' and 'undeserving' or 'entitled' and 'not entitled' were defined during an often long process of information gathering and decision making. This began with a pauper's application for relief and might have a whole range of outcomes. Applicants could be refused, have their applications suspended to allow further investigation, have their requests modified, be granted their requests with strings or simply be granted their request. However we look at it, the *recording* of a relief payment by an official – the event which contributes to the relief expenditure on which we have been concentrating – was the very last part of the process of obtaining relief and there was plenty of scope for people to fall out of the system before this stage was reached. The way in which entitlement was established – and by inference the way in which demand for welfare was controlled – thus has important implications for the lessons about poverty that we can draw from poor law statistics.

Such observations are not new. The wider poor law historiography implicitly notices and disregards many of the consequences of poor relief as a process for estimates of the scale and character of poverty. Some of the reasons for disregarding the process problem will be familiar from chapters two and three, but they are worth restating here. Thus, it was argued by contemporaries, and has subsequently become gospel, that many of the units of administration in the old poor law in particular were small. Here the administration of relief was a face-to-face process with familiar parties, where the overseer would be unlikely to disregard claims. Application and relief were often a seamless web. Even under the new poor law, the story goes, the financing of relief on a parish not a union basis meant that many of those applying for relief would have been familiar to the relieving officer, and the pressure to meet an application correspondingly more pressing after the initial enthusiasm for the spirit of the new poor law waned. The opposite side of the coin is the argument that in large parishes or small but densely populated urban parishes, the overburdened overseer or new poor law relieving officer would actually have lost the ability to investigate applications because there were simply too many people applying. Again, application and relief were a seamless web. In any case, the most optimistic views of the poor law old and new suggest that major groupings amongst the poor (for instance the old, the sick or widows) had attained a 'right' to relief, and hence were unlikely to be turned down except in the most exceptional circumstances related to their character

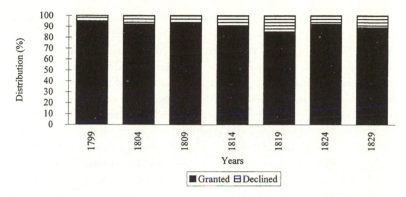

Figure 4.3 Decision making in a sample of southern and eastern vestries

or the particular burden on the ratepayers in that year. Paul Slack claims that, 'It was assumed . . . that the poor were entitled to relief if they required it'.[51] In other words, proving deserving poverty was relatively easy, and the ostensible freedom of definition in the hands of overseers and vestries was strikingly limited in practice.

Certainly we could review cases, spanning regional boundaries, which support all of these points. Thus in the Westmorland parish of Ravenstonedale in 1729: 'The four and twenty did meet and settled the rates or allowances of the poor from the day of this date till Lady Day, as follows (according to former custom).'[52] A relief schedule fixed months in advance provides little evidence of consistent monitoring of the sort which the law and many manuals for poor law officials envisaged. Some places took this one step further and drew up relief tariffs for different types of pauper (the old, sick or widowed) or paupers in different family situations. London, Oxfordshire and Essex parishes can be found applying such tariffs from the 1760s, and the whole idea of a 'tariff' was enshrined in the Speenhamland system. It is certainly the case that poor law administrations willing to draw up tariffs and schedules were unlikely to turn down large numbers of applicants. Even for places which adopted no such scales, the texture of the decision-making process revealed in vestry books could often be favourable to paupers.

Figure 4.3 attempts to quantify the outcome of decision making during the early nineteenth century using material from three southern and eastern (as these terms were defined in chapter one) vestries.[53] Clearly, the theoretical power to judge deservingness did not always translate to harsh judgement on relief applicants. Few people were apparently turned down in these places, and the borderland between 'deserving' and 'undeserving' appears to have been wide and clearly defined. Where applicants were turned down, the nature of the decision-making process was transparent and flexible. In Lyndhurst, for instance, David Woods was turned down because he assaulted the overseer, while in Enfield pension requests were turned down and existing pensioners stripped of pensions where the vestry found out that pensioners were obtaining very substantial sums through work. Part of the explanation for why few people found themselves on the wrong side of the vestry lies in the peculiar traditions of relief in the areas considered here. When faced with a situation where systematic labour-market subsidies through the poor law blurred the distinction between independence and poverty, deserving and undeserving, southern vestries may have had comparatively little freedom in their decision making. However, vestries were equally sympathetic in other places too. In the North Riding town of Richmond, for instance, Hastings found that declined applications were rare, and usually confined to those who were non-resident or who wanted help with medical bills.[54] Similarly, in Westmorland, the town of Kendal turned down just 5 per cent of applicants, while in Orton turning down relief applications was the occasion for considerable agonising.[55] A benevolent decision-making process was thus not simply a feature of a few southern communities.

Such commentary might give us heart that 'background' poverty was slim. However, this is only one part of the story. When the benevolent parishes so popular in current historiography were placed into unions under the new poor law some of them crushed the poor with venom. Under the old poor law, as we have seen, parishes throughout the country had also been willing to farm the poor at rates which hardly guaranteed the barest subsistence, to sell the goods of paupers and to badge pauper clothing. That they might also turn down relief applications should not be overlooked. Figure 4.4 traces the outcome of relief applications for paupers in three Lancashire towns where particularly good vestry books were kept before the Sturges Bourne Acts.[56] We can see that a central core of between 20 and 40 per cent of applicants for relief were always turned down depending upon the year. At the level of individual townships and years, figures could range up to 55 per cent. A few narratives help to illuminate how the borderline between back-ground and foreground, deserving and undeserving, was defined in a decision-making process which was both harsher and longer than the examples underlying figure 4.3. Thus, in Garstang in 1815, Molly Crossley, 'made application for something towards buying coals. At the

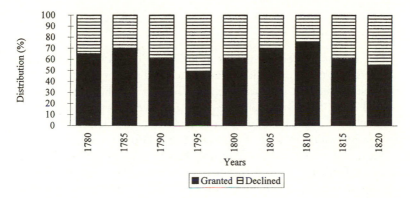

Figure 4.4 Decision making in a sample of northern and western vestries

meeting of the 1st August she said she could go on with 6 shillings allowed her towards her rent. The committee think that she should not so soon trouble the town again after the former promise.'[57] In November of the same year the Garstang vestry noted that, 'Jno Pedder attended and wanted some relief. He admits being in constant employ . . . earning 6s a week plus meat. He has only a wife and 3 children. Resolved that he is to have no further relief.'[58] Even on the most optimistic estimates, this family could not have been generating an income of more than 10 shillings per week. By December 1815 he was out of work altogether but the vestry again refused his application for help. John Gregson's family could earn only half the amount of John Pedder's but when he applied to the vestry in August 1815, 'Jno Gregson is a year and a half rent in arrears (£7 10s 7d) wants it met by the town. To pay his own rent.'[59] In 1817,

> Alice Wakefield, the wife of John Wakefield who has run away with another woman, attended wanting relief. Her goods have been seized hold for rent. She has had a series of ill health which has brought her to her present distress – she has only 1 daughter 16 years of age a weaver at home to support her at present. Resolved nothing to be done. To have a ticket for Brindle [workhouse] if dissatisfied. [60]

There is little evidence of customary treatment of the poor in this case, and it is certain that in other areas these circumstances would have merited generous relief. Then, in 1820,

> Francis Ellison applies for relief – has six children each works with him at his trade – Robt 14 years of age, Fanny 13 years old, Wm 10 years old Ellen 6 years old and Francis 3 years old. Wants 7 pounds 10 shillings for rent.

> Resolved, cannot be agreed to. The Overseer to take Robert, William and Fanny into places.[61]

Having applied for relief, Ellison lost three of his most productive workers, and it is little wonder that he then had to keep coming back to the vestry over the course of the next five years. Other requests were turned down for less material reasons. In December 1820 one of the reasons for William Kendall being denied relief was that he 'keeps 2 or 3 dogs and which are a great annoyance to children going to school.'[62]

More widely, the charge of 'improvident conduct' was a familiar way to block further relief applications in Garstang. Those on relief were also monitored to ensure detection of changed circumstances and to enforce moral codes. The former observation is important, for whereas Enfield vestry acted on pauper entitlements when the changed circumstances of individuals came to their attention, in these vestries there was much more active policing of paupers and their situation. In November 1815, the Garstang vestry considered Peggy Makerfield in the following terms:

> Peggy Makerfield's husband Thos Makerfield is come to the army and is now receiving his pay as a soldier and is at present working. Resolved that Peggy Makerfield's pay of 7 shillings to be stopped while he is in employ and receiving his pay as a soldier, and the overseer to first ascertain what he is earning at Messrs Making.[63]

Peggy Makerfield was a deserted wife, and while she appears to have been treated relatively generously in a Lancashire context while on relief, the vestry gave little thought to the nature of husband and wife relations in this case. In September 1820 Margaret Sturt applied to the vestry,

> wanting 4 shillings per week and have had 2 shillings per week to that time which is considered to be sufficient as there is a garden full of potatoes and other vegetables and rent paid to November 1820.[64]

There is some support here for Midwinter's 'chilly appraisal of misfortune'. Moreover, Garstang was not unique, as similar records from the other townships show. Thus, in May 1793, John Wild applied to the Colne vestry for relief. He was taken into the workhouse and his son was charged for the full cost of relief given. In March 1794,

> The wife of William Hargreaves applied for relief but was refused because she had sold clothing and other things given to her by ye contribution to ye late fund for the benefit of the individual poor.[65]

In January 1795, James Wilson's mother applied for relief but the vestry ordered that she should be secured by her son and his wife. For the township of Halliwell in March 1816,

> James Howarth wife applies for relief, her husband is sick. The overseer has lately paid 3 pounds for rent. Resolved that they shall not have an relief as their family are capable of working.[66]

While sickness was a passport to relief in Kettering or Lyndhurst, it was not here. Others were viewed with a more moralistic eye. The Halliwell vestry complained in May 1790 that Thomas Crompton,

> was this day seen drinking in an alehouse in Bolton. Thomas Crompton told John Makinson that he can get a guinea a week and that he could drink and who has any business with that.[67]

It is no surprise to find Crompton turned down by the vestry when he tried to get a renewal of his allowance. One month after the Crompton incident, Thomas Bradley was turned down for relief because, 'The man has not a good character.'[68]

The lessons of these bleak histories are instructive. Not only were large numbers of people who felt poor enough to apply for aid ignored in poor law figures, but the borderland between background and foreground, deserving and undeserving, was narrow and uncertain. People did not enter the formal recording arena if they were working, if they were deemed capable of exploring other welfare avenues, if they were deserted women or if there was any sort of moral question mark attached to their characters. Even being old, frail or sick did not guarantee help from the poor law in these communities, though it might have in other places or at other times. Moreover, deeper analysis of these sources reveals that when people with almost exactly identical circumstances presented themselves, they were frequently treated in very different ways. None of this is to say that some of the treatment was not generous. Some of the allowances offered by Garstang were more than the entire wages of an adult male in Essex, while the allowances offered by Colne were amongst the meanest in the entire county.

We return to the question of generosity of allowances in chapter six, but the key point at this stage is that these vestries adopted what we might label a harsh decision-making process on the entitlement of the poor. This was not simply a north–south contrast, and harsh vestry decision making can also be detected for communities in other areas. For Stone, Staffordshire, Broadbridge shows how a policy of individual examination after 1791 halved the poor rate and the number of welfare recipients.[69] In Wimbledon the vestry looked like that in Colne, concluding in 1748 that 'Jo Skinner to be allowed no relief for it is the opinion of the vestry that he is capable of doing something for his livelihood'.[70] More examples could be drawn, but enough has been said to demonstrate that there were extremely wide differences in the way in which entitlement was worked out. In some communities almost all of those who applied for relief got it; in other communities a large minority (and in places a majority) of those who felt poor enough to apply were not eventually recognised as poor by the poor law accounts.

Conclusion

At both local and national level, then, the meaning which we should attach to poor law expenditure is not at all clear. Expenditure figures represent the outcome of a multi-layered process of negotiation in which a limited supply of welfare was matched to potentially unlimited demand for it. Custom, politics, personalities and ideologies wove their way through all levels of the negotiation process to generate a complex patchwork of local outcomes. In some places, allowances were given in response to the most desperate of plights while in others poor law resources were expended in response to pressure on conventionally accepted living standards. There appears to have been little spatial, chronological or socio-economic logic to these experiences and so the concrete lessons about the scale of or chronological trends in poverty that can be drawn from poor law statistics are strictly limited. A focus on Kent brings us to the essence of the problem. In 1803, 14 per cent of the 307,624 people of Kent were in receipt of relief. Of these, 9,227 adults and 10,939 children were receiving regular out-relief and 6,337 were receiving relief within workhouses. This left 15,129 people (36 per cent of recipients) getting only occasional relief. At what point in the descent into poverty had the Kentish poor law intervened? What was the difference between those on indoor relief and outdoor relief? Had those in receipt of occasional relief originally asked for regular relief? How many people had been turned down and thus never made it to these statistics? What proportion of the population was really reliant on relief when we account for dependents? How many people were really poor? And how do the answers to all of these questions relate to the answers we would get for rural Sussex right next door? The mere fact that the numbers on relief in Kent increased by 18 per cent between the 1790s and 1803, and that poor law expenditure increased by one-third is uncertain testimony to increasing poverty.

Such views are perhaps too pessimistic. Contemporary commentators provide us with ample evidence that between 1750 and 1850 both the scale of the poverty problem and its intensity increased. More people became more poor over the latter part of our period, and by the late eighteenth century the increasingly visible gulf between rich and poor had begun to force itself upon the conceptions of a middle-class public. Their efforts to justify the gulf and to pass the blame for it on to the failings of the poor themselves provides proof enough that society was becoming more polarised in many ways. What is less certain is the role that the communal welfare system had in addressing this poverty and bridging this gulf. Its statistics tell us something, but what? Can the message be made more precise? And what else do we need to know about the experience of poverty in eighteenth- and nineteenth-century England in order to be able to approach a review of regional solutions with confidence? Questions like this are the subject of chapter five, the final chapter in this section of the book dealing with the analytical framework.

Notes

1 For an exception to this rule, see J. Henderson and R. Wall (eds), *Poor women and children in the European past* (London, Routledge, 1994), pp. 1–28.

2 In Bluntisham, Cambridgeshire, in 1823, the new workhouse master was obliged to sign a contract in which he agreed not to apply for poor relief himself unless unemployed for one month or more. See C. F. Tebbutt, *Bluntisham-cum-Earith, Huntingdonshire: records of a fenland parish* (St Neots, privately published, 1941). See also J. Kennedy, *History of Leyton* (London, privately published, 1894).

3 A. Peat (ed.), *The most dismal times: William Rowbottom's diary 1787–99* (Oldham, Oldham Library Service, 1996), p. 30.

4 See also T. Sokoll, 'Old age in poverty: the record of Essex pauper letters 1780–1834', in T. Hitchcock, P. King and P. Sharpe (eds), *Chronicling poverty: the voices and strategies of the English poor, 1640–1840* (Basingstoke, Macmillan, 1997), pp. 127–54, and J. S. Taylor, 'Voices in the crowd: the Kirkby Lonsdale township letters, 1809–36', in *ibid.*, pp. 109–26.

5 M. Bulmer, *The social survey in historical perspective 1880–1940* (Cambridge, Cambridge University Press, 1991), and G. Himmelfarb, 'Mayhew's poor: a problem of identity', *Victorian Studies*, 14 (1971) 307–20.

6 As a variant of this argument, it is perfectly plausible for a shift in wealth or income distribution to have created a perceived increase in 'poverty'. See J. A. James, 'Personal wealth distribution in late eighteenth century Britain', *Economic History Review*, 41 (1988) 543–65.

7 See R. Jutte, *Poverty and deviance in early modern Europe* (Cambridge, Cambridge University Press, 1994), p. 9.

8 L. Hollen-Lees, *The solidarities of strangers: the English poor laws and the people 1700–1948* (Cambridge, Cambridge University Press, 1998), p. 13.

9 The Board of Trade collected national figures in the 1690s. While individual parish figures do not survive nationally, manuscript returns do appear to have been preserved at local level. Allied with exemptions from the duties on vital event registration which were also payable in the 1690s, these lists may provide a way forward in looking at poverty at the turn of the eighteenth century. My thanks to the reader of the original manuscript of this book for this point.

10 T. Arkell, 'The incidence of poverty in England in the later seventeenth century', *Social History*, 12 (1987) 23–47. Also M. F. Pickles, 'Labour migration in Yorkshire 1670–1743', *Local Population Studies*, 57 (1996) 29–49.

11 W. Newman-Brown, 'The receipt of poor relief and family situation: Aldenham, Herts, 1630–90', in R. M. Smith (ed.), *Land, kinship and life cycle* (Cambridge, Cambridge University Press, 1984), pp. 405–22, and T. Wales, 'Poverty, poor relief and life-cycle: some evidence from seventeenth century Norfolk', in *ibid.*, pp. 351–404. The process of family reconstitution basically involves using parish registers to create a family tree for every traceable person living in a place over a given period.

12 However, see P. Slack, *From reformation to improvement: public welfare in early modern England* (Oxford, Clarendon Press, 1999).

13 But see R. M. Smith, 'Ageing and well being in early modern England: pension trends and gender preferences under the English old poor law 1650–1800', in P. Johnson and P. Thane (eds), *Old age from antiquity to post-modernity* (London, Routledge, 1998), pp. 64–95.

14 See J. Innes, 'The "mixed economy of welfare" in early modern England: assessments of the options from Hale to Malthus (c. 1683–1803)', in M. J. Daunton (ed.), *Charity, self-interest and welfare in the English past* (London, UCL Press, 1996), pp. 139–80. We know rather more about the rising scale of the urban poverty problem in the eighteenth century, than we do about rural and rural industrial experiences. See Slack, *From reformation*.

15 P. Slack, *The English poor law 1531–1782* (Basingstoke, Macmillan, 1992), p. 30.

16 E. A. Wrigley, R. S. Davies, J. E. Oeppen and R. S. Schofield, *English population history from family reconstitution* (Cambridge, Cambridge University Press, 1998).

17 Though see the limited poor law role identified by S. Horrell and J. Humphries, 'Old questions, new data, and alternative perspectives: families' living standards in the industrial revolution', *Journal of Economic History*, 52 (1992) 849–80, and also S. A. King, 'Reconstructing lives: the poor, the poor law and welfare in rural industrial communities', *Social History*, 22 (1997) 318–38.

18 The fact that unpaid officials frequently tried to make a profit out of their office by (over-)charging for dinners, journeys, writing accounts and almost any duty one could think of is well known. Less obvious is that trends in settlement legislation, the changing relationship of magistrate and overseer, and the need to be both informed and vigilant, really did push up administration costs. These rose more or less consistently in most places from the mid-eighteenth century. Thus, in Walthamstow administration costs as a percentage of relief rose from 4 per cent in 1750, to 6 per cent in 1776 and 9 per cent in 1794. See S. J. Barnes, 'Walthamstow in the eighteenth century: vestry minutes, churchwardens and overseers accounts 1710–94', *Walthamstow Antiquarian Society Publications*, 16 (1927). Also, for a particularly good manuscript example of rising administration costs and the tension which this could create among ratepayers can be found in Cumbria Record Office (hereafter CRO) WPR 4/3, 'Overseer accounts for Cartmel Fell 1721–98'. Under the new poor law, administration costs burgeoned even further. By 1844 just 73 per cent of total poor law expenditure was being spent directly on relief to the poor, and there was a further fall to 68 per cent in 1850.

19 See K. Williams, *From pauperism to poverty*, (London, Routledge and Kegan Paul, 1981), on the patchy response to many of the later national returns.

20 See A. Digby, 'Malthus and reform of the English poor law', in M. Turner (ed.), *Malthus and his time* (Basingstoke, Macmillan, 1987), pp. 157–69, and E. A. Wrigley, 'Malthus on the prospects for the labouring poor', *Historical Journal*, 31 (1988) 813–29.

21 T. Sokoll, 'The household position of elderly widows in poverty: evidence from two English communities in the late eighteenth and early nineteenth centuries', in J. Henderson and R. Wall (eds), *Poor women and children in the European past*, (London Routledge, 1994), pp. 207–24.

22 B. Stapleton, 'Inherited poverty and life-cycle poverty: Odiham, Hampshire 1650–1850', *Social History*, 18 (1993) 339–55.

23 F. M. Eden, *The state of the poor: a history of the labouring classes in England with parochial reports*, 3 vols (London, Cass, 1963 reprint).

24 See R. Adair, *Courtship, illegitimacy and marriage in early modern England* (Manchester, Manchester University Press, 1996), and L. Weatherill, *Consumer behaviour and material culture in Britain 1660–1760* (London, Macmillan, 1988).

25 See W. J. Keith, *The rural tradition: William Cobbett, Gilbert White, and other non-fiction prose writers of the English countryside* (Brighton, Harvester, 1975).

26 For mapping of these later statistics, see I. Levitt, 'Poor law and pauperism', in J. Langton and R. J. Morris (eds), *Atlas of industrialising Britain 1780–1914* (London, Macmillan, 1986), p. 161.

27 On urban poverty, see C. Chinn, *Poverty amidst prosperity: the urban poor in England 1834–1914* (Manchester, Manchester University Press, 1995).

28 In May 1816, for instance, the vestry of Garstang in Lancashire resolved to cut all pensions by 40 per cent to reflect falling food prices. See Lancashire Record Office (hereafter LRO) DDX 386/3, 'Vestry records of Garstang'.

29 D. A. Baugh, 'The cost of poor relief in south east England 1790–1834', *Economic History Review*, 28 (1975) 50–68, and R. P. Hastings, *Poverty and the poor laws in the North Riding of Yorkshire, 1780–1837* (York, Borthwick Institute, 1982). Also M. Neuman, *The Speenhamland county: poverty and the poor law in Berkshire 1782–1834* (New York, Garland, 1982).

30 See S. Horrell and J. Humphries, 'Women's labour force participation and the transition to the male breadwinner family, 1790–1865', *Economic History Review*, 38 (1995) 89–117, and S. Horrell and J. Humphries, 'The exploitation of little children: child labor and the family economy in the industrial revolution', *Explorations in Economic History*, 32 (1995) 485–516.

31 K. Mason, *Addingham: from brigantes to bypass* (Settle, Addingham Civic Society, 1996). The existence of such debts could shape the way in which the poor law was administered. In Lancashire for instance, most debts of this sort (which ran for many years) were incurred to cotton-manufacturers who then pressured fellow vestrymen to provide wage subsidies during short-time mill work. This has important implications for what Keith Wrightson has called the politics of the parish. See K. Wrightson, 'The politics of the parish in early modern England', in P. Griffiths, A. Fox and S. Hindle (eds), *The experience of authority in early modern England* (Basingstoke, Macmillan, 1995), pp. 10–46.

32 LRO PR 797, 'Miscellaneous notes'.

33 D. Marshall, *The English poor in the eighteenth century* (New York, Routledge, 1969 reprint), p. 2.

34 S. Webb and B. Webb, *English poor law history part I: the old poor law* (London, Cass, 1963 reprint), p. 164.

35 These were sometimes taken as part of the process by which the poor law had the right to appropriate the household possessions and money of poor people to help reimburse the support given to that person by the community. The poor usually retained a life interest in the goods listed. The paucity of some inventories suggests that even clothing and bits of bedding were worth subjecting to inventory.

36 P. King, 'Pauper inventories and the material lives of the poor in the eighteenth and early nineteenth centuries', in T. Hitchcock, P. King and P. Sharpe (eds), *Chronicling poverty: the words and lives of the English poor 1640–1840* (Basingstoke, Macmillan, 1997), pp. 63–89. Such conclusions sit uneasily with Brown's portrayals of the position of the Essex agricultural labourer and with Sharpe's portrayal of the dimensions of the family economy in the county, but these may in fact refer to the experiences of the marginal rather than the poor defined by receipt of relief. See A. F. J. Brown, *Meagre harvest: the Essex farm workers' struggle against poverty,*

1750–1914 (Chelmsford, Essex Record Office, 1990), and P. Sharpe, *Adapting to capitalism: working women in the English economy, 1700–1800* (Basingstoke, Macmillan, 1997).

37 B. Cornford, 'Inventories of the poor', *Norfolk Archaeology*, 35 (1970–73) 118–25. Also, F. M. Cowe (ed.), *Wimbledon vestry minutes 1736, 1743–1788* (Guildford, Surrey Record Society, 1964), where James Cox had thirty-two items in his inventory.

38 Essex Record Office (hereafter ERO), 'Inventories for Hatfield Broad Oak, 1730–1833' (D/P4). Of the forty-one inventories in this collection, just two contain values. These inventories were transcribed and generously made available to me by Henry French.

39 These inventories for the eighteenth and first two decades of the nineteenth centuries are drawn from a wide range of areas. See CRO WD/MG, 'Metcalfe-Gibson papers', and CRO WPR 4/3, 'Accounts for Cartmel Fell'. Other locations include LRO MBc/637, 'Account of goods belonging to Widow Cottam', LRO PR 3031, 'Poor law accounts of Mitton', Wigan Record Office (hereafter WRO) TR.Ab 5–7, 'Poor law accounts of Abram 1691–1800', and TR.Ab 61–77, 'Miscellaneous accounts 1800–1837', RL RC 352 RAW, 'The poor law accounts of Cowpe, Lenches, Newhallhey and Hall Carr', WYAS, 'Accounts of the overseer, constable and churchwardens, Calverley parish', and F. Pope, *The accounts of the constables and overseers of Parr 1688–1729* (Windle, privately published, 1971).

40 ERO D/P4/18, 1798.

41 RL RC 352 RAW, 'Accounts'.

42 LRO MBc/637, 'Account of goods belonging to Widow Cottam'.

43 ERO D/P4/18, 1756.

44 G. C. Edmonds, 'Accounts of eighteenth-century overseers of the poor of Chalfont St. Peter', *Records of Buckinghamshire*, 18 (1966) 3–23.

45 CRO Uncatalogued, 'The great end book of Ravenstonedale'.

46 Ibid.

47 Hampshire Record Office (hereafter HRO), 25M84/DU 2–10, 'New forest union records'.

48 H. Boot, 'Unemployment and poor law relief in Manchester 1845–50', *Social History*, 15 (1990) 217–28.

49 W. Cooke-Taylor, *Notes on a tour of the manufacturing districts of Lancashire* (New York, Augustus Kelley, 1968 reprint).

50 New analyses of pauper correspondence and other narrative material suggest just how skilled the poor became in shaping the notion of what appeared to be deserving. See, for instance, J. S. Taylor, *Poverty, migration and settlement in the industrial revolution: sojourners' narratives* (Paolo Alto, SPSS, 1989).

51 Slack, *The English*, p. 29.

52 CRO Uncatalogued, 'The great end book of Ravenstonedale'. My thanks to Richard Hoyle for this reference.

53 For data, see S. J. Peyton, *Kettering vestry minutes 1797–1853* (Kettering,

Northamptonshire Records Society, 1933), Greater London Record Office, DRO4, 'Vestry books of Enfield', and HRO, 25M84/PO1–70, 'Poor law documents for Lyndhurst'.

54 Hastings, *Poverty*.
55 CRO WSMB/K/62, 'Assorted poor law papers', and WPR/9/VI, 'Orton vestry minutes 1790–1902', and WPR/1/01, 'Overseer accounts for Orton'.
56 LRO MBCo/7/1, 'Ratepayers minutes for Colne', Bolton Record Office (hereafter BRO) PHA/1/2, 'Vestry minutes of Halliwell', and LRO DDX 386/3, 'Vestry records of Garstang'.
57 LRO DDX 386/3, June 1815.
58 *Ibid.*, November 1815.
59 *Ibid.*, August 1815. This amount represented rent for the current year plus previous arrears.
60 *Ibid.*, February 1817.
61 *Ibid.*, February 1820.
62 *Ibid.*, December 1820.
63 *Ibid.*, November 1815.
64 *Ibid.*, September 1820.
65 LRO MB/Co 7/1, March 1794.
66 BRO PHA/1/2, March 1816.
67 *Ibid.*, May 1790.
68 *Ibid.*, June 1790.
69 S. R. Broadbridge, 'The old poor law in the parish of Stone', *North Staffordshire Journal of Field Studies*, 13 (1973) 11–25.
70 Cowe (ed.), *Wimbledon*.

CHAPTER FIVE

ALTERNATIVE WORLDS OF POVERTY

Overview

The relationship between poor law statistics and 'poverty' can be shown to have been both complex and fluid. Some of those whose allowances contributed to the aggregate relief expenditure on which it is so tempting to focus were in what we might label 'relative poverty', others were completely destitute and yet more may not have been poor at all. Moreover, in most communities there were also other individuals who thought of themselves as poor but who never actually made it through the process by which demand for welfare reached an equilibrium with what was often a restricted supply. None of this means that analysis of poor law statistics is useless. After all, even if we inflate the expenditure figures for, say, Lancashire to account for those who applied but never received relief, the county would still stand out as having the lowest per capita expenditure figures in England. This might have reflected the fact that the county had less poverty than other places, that poverty was of a different type or that ratepayers were unwilling to expand the supply of welfare to cope with demand. Whatever the explanation, poor law expenditure statistics do convey an outline message about the likely experience of being poor in Lancashire. And if we reject the idea that poor law statistics provide some index of poverty what do we put in their place to substantiate the impression of historians such as Geoffrey Taylor, who thought that 'the evidence of acute poverty in the last decades of the old poor law is overpowering'?[1]

As an alternative first step, we might follow contemporary commentators who suggested that anyone dependent upon wages should be regarded as 'poor'. The report which underpinned the 1834 poor law reform, for instance, defined poverty as 'the state of one, who in order to obtain mere subsistence is forced to have recourse to labour'.[2] More recent contributors such as Keith Snell have also equated 'poverty' and 'labouring classes'.[3] The individual stories which pepper this book provide support for such a view, and in some areas it really was the case that most of those without land or independent wealth might end up needing poor relief or charity. The tendency for important industries such as cotton, wool or metalworking to concentrate in a limited spatial area made this more likely by opening up large sections of local and regional populations to the degradations of the trade cycle. We return to this theme later. This wide definition of 'poverty', however, could mean that 90 per cent of the population have to be regarded as 'poor' by the early nineteenth century and we would lose any hope of drawing regional patterns. More importantly, a blanket definition fails to distinguish the *risk* of poverty at any one time or over the life cycle from the *actuality* of poverty at any one time or over the life cycle. It is a description of marginality rather than poverty.

Looking to other potential approaches is not much more satisfactory. Dorothy Marshall believed that all of those potentially subject to the settlement laws should be regarded as in 'poverty'. However, this would notionally burden prosperous urban areas with a greater poverty problem than the many rural communities of, say, Dorset where chronically low wages are often seen to have generated endemic poverty.[4] An alternative approach might be to label the 704,350 members of England's 9,672 friendly societies in 1803 as 'poor' alongside those actually receiving relief. Whether friendly society members would have regarded themselves as 'poor' is an entirely different matter. Many of them would surely have seen membership as an insurance against this very eventuality. A more comfortable definition of poverty might be that favoured by some continental commentators, who see those without savings as 'poor'.[5] However, such an approach mixes up once more the risk and actuality of poverty. In any case, it is of little use prior to the emergence of working-class savings vehicles from the mid-1820s.[6] Given these problems, many would perhaps agree with the solution of Peter Wood, who gives up on definition and measurement altogether, using the scale and intensity of disease to act as a proxy.[7]

How can we obtain a more precise appreciation of the risks and actuality of poverty? What happened to the 'quality of poverty' as well as its quantity? How did structures of causation change? What were the life-cycle contours of poverty and how did they change over time? Did people become more or less likely to pass on their poverty to their children? And how did ordinary people think about the state of being poor? Answers to questions like these can help to create a picture of what role we might expect the poor law to have played in ordinary lives, providing a yardstick against which to measure what actually happened. This chapter thus looks, inevitably crudely, at 'alternative worlds of poverty' – at alternative ways of thinking about scale and trends, at the changing structure of poverty and at contemporary perceptions of the state of being poor.

The scale and trends of 'poverty' revisited

Over a decade ago Tom Arkell pointed to a methodological middle way between the wide definition of poverty implied by the concept of proletarianisation, and the narrow and uncertain definition provided by poor law data. As chapter four showed, he noticed for the seventeenth century that some sources which might throw light on poverty, such as charity returns or lists of those who did not pay taxes, had a wider inclusivity than poor relief accounts, and he suggested that we calculate ranges of poverty using these sources rather than exact figures from poor relief data.[8] Of course, welfare historians have long accepted that 'need' could be defined differently by overseers of the poor and others who had a hand in welfare, for instance the administrators of charity or the organisers of the urban relief funds which periodically sprang up to help the poor from the 1770s. In general, these bodies cast their definition of 'need' widely, and even included those in work.

Yet, if welfare historians have realised the existence and potential of these sources, they have been slow to use them, and equally slow to engage with other sources – such as lists of rate arrears or lists of those whose goods were distrained (forcibly sold to meet debts) – which might help to pin down accurate ranges of poverty at any point in time. That rate arrears might be a useful supplementary indicator of 'poverty' is indicated by the Kettering vestry book. On 16 March 1843 the vestry considered cases of rent arrears in detail. It is worth dwelling on their conclusions at some length, for they show very well the subtle dividing lines between the states of poverty, marginality and comfort in actuality and in the minds of local elites. Thus,

1. Wm Patrick – wife and 2 children, is not able to pay. Sells a few fish but travels many miles and *is much as he can do to keep off the parish himself*. Acquit.
2. Jas Wrigley – wife and 4 small children. In bad health himself and unable to pay. Is recommended to get a lower priced house. Acquit. [. . .]
4. Wm Curtis (late master of the workhouse) states that he lives in Mr Ley's yard and owes one rate 5/10, that he has no employment and is not able to pay. Acquit. [. . .]
7. Jos Lilleyman *evidently ill*. Acquit without hearing. [. . .]

11. Wm Lousby is not able to pay, has a wife very ill and has no regular employment and nothing coming in but his pension. Acquit. [. . .]

14. Anne Coleman has two sisters heavily afflicted, one blind and the other in deep decline and has besides to support her aunt Flemming and begs to be let off the poors rate. Acquit. [. . .]

18. Widow Turner owes 7/6 cannot pay, is 74 years old, had a sum of money left her by a lodger four years ago when *she took herself off the parish books*, but that it is nearly all gone, when she must again come to the parish for relief. Acquit.[9]

None of these people appears to have received poor relief, but the discussion of their situation suggests that they were nonetheless temporarily or permanently 'poor'.[10]

Blessed with sources like this, Arkell's approach may constitute an important way of supplementing the poverty picture obtainable from relief statistics. However, a systematic 'national' or even regional discussion of ranges of poverty using a diverse array of sources is beyond this chapter. The survival of rich records is patchy, and the survival of a range of different sources for the same period and place is even rarer. A convincing statistical sample of communities would require considerable resources to assemble and to manipulate. Even if this were possible, some sources present thorny interpretative problems. Exemption from local taxes like the poor rate provides a case in point. Theoretically, those not receiving relief ought to have been assessed for the poor rate. Yet, as the Kettering rate arrears show some people were considered too poor to pay their assessment while yet more were never assessed in the first place. Potentially these exemption and forgiveness figures provide a useful index of poverty not recognised by the poor law, but what were the criteria for exemption in each community? Were the criteria uniform over time? How did the criteria employed in one place relate to those employed in another? And what scope was there for jiggery-pokery related to local politics, custom or personal relationships to dilute the relationship between exemption and marginality? Questions like these mean that we must tread warily.

Nonetheless, on a small scale we can use a range of sources like the Kettering vestry minutes to reconsider the dimensions of, and trends in, 'poverty', and to begin to rethink the relationship between the information in poor law accounts and the wider world of poverty. Figure 5.1 provides a useful window in this direction. It is based upon four communities[11] in which some or all of a range of sources which might provide indications of the scale of poverty survive side by side for two short periods (1784–89 and 1827–31).[12] The underlying logic and

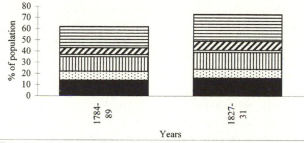

Figure 5.1 Cumulative percentage of the population of four communities ascribed as 'poor' in different sources

methodology require some explanation. Thus, what the chart purports to show is the *cumulative proportion of the population* of these four communities who might have been deemed poor on the basis of their inclusion in a range of sources which offer progressively wider definitions of poverty. It is the outcome of a five-stage process as set out below.

1 A count of the number of people in each source for each place and period.
2 A process of nominal linkage to identify all of those who appear in one source only.
3 The arbitrary ascription of those who appear in more than one source to the category (indicated on the legend of figure 5.1) which seems to best fit the character of their poverty.
4 A count of the final number of people in each source category which is then multiplied by 1.8 to allow for dependents of the individual concerned.
5 The number of people (individuals and their dependents) in each source category across the four communities is divided by the collective actual or estimated populations of the communities to obtain an idea of the percentage of total population encompassed by each source. These are the numbers which are graphed in figure 5.1.

Of course, this sort of analysis has many potential flaws. The graph deals only with outdoor relief, so that if the relative balance of indoor and outdoor relief changed over time this would influence the importance that we assign to poor relief as a measure of poverty. The multipliers to move from individual to family poverty might in reality have needed to be more finely tuned to the potentially differing family circumstances of the people appearing in different sources. The population estimates for the towns may also have been wide of the mark. Moreover, nominal linkage to make sure that people were only counted as appearing in one source is a notoriously difficult and uncertain procedure which can never be error-free. And to apply these admittedly crude and uncertain methods to a wide range of other communities to get a 'national' perspective on the risks and actuality of poverty would be a complex and time-consuming task beyond the abilities of a single historian. Yet, even if we bear in mind a considerable list of potential caveats, figure 5.1 may still hold useful lessons. Let us dwell on three of them.

First, the *range of poverty experiences* was wide. Between 15 and 20 per cent of the aggregate population of these townships were represented in what we might label 'conventional' poverty indicators such as charity and poor relief lists. However, if we adopt the widest possible definition of poverty, including those who were exempt from key local taxes and all of those paying low rents but not receiving either poor relief or charity, it is clear that well over half of the population of these townships in the later eighteenth century and over two thirds by the late 1820s might be characterised as 'poor'.[13] There is clear support here for Geoffrey Taylor's impression that evidence for severe poverty is compelling.

Second, the *magnitude of poverty* grew for these townships between the late eighteenth and early nineteenth centuries. The growth is not particularly dramatic (though it was from an already high base), but then there are good reasons to suppose that the underlying communities would not have expected to share in the large poverty increases that are often seen to be associated with enclosure, rapid urbanisation or industrial decline. Nonetheless, Alan Kidd's suggestion that only one-fifth of ordinary families could expect to escape poverty by the 1830s has considerable resonance.[14]

Third, figure 5.1 confirms that *poor relief data provide a very limited prediction* of levels of poverty, accounting for well under one-fifth of all people who might be described as poor at either date by contemporaries. The underlying data also allow us to go further. They show that the magnitude of poverty was roughly similar in all of the communities considered when we adopt the widest possible definition of 'poverty'. There were minor differences of emphasis in terms of the proportions of the population in the alternative poverty indicators between the different communities – Calverley had more of its population living in 'poverty accommodation' than any of the other three places – but the really significant difference lay in the degree of poverty recognised by the relief system. In Calverley between 1827 and 1831 just 9 per cent of overall 'poverty' was recognised by the poor law whereas in Charing it recognised over 30 per cent of all poverty at the same date.

These conclusions are perhaps tenuous and small-scale, but they are nonetheless significant. If the broad trends to be observed in figure 5.1 were replicated elsewhere, then it is conceivable that poverty, already a central experience in many communities, became ubiquitous in the nineteenth century. If not poverty, then certainly marginality. Poor law statistics pick up a minimal part of this poverty, and what is more, poverty widely defined increases somewhat faster than poverty defined through poor law statistics. Indeed, the abiding impression from figure 5.1 is not how much poverty the poor law engaged with, but how little. Such observations provide support for those who see the communal welfare system as providing only a safety net for a minority of those in need.

Contemporary narratives such as pauper letters provide support for the idea that the poor law recognised only a small part of background poverty. Thus, in April 1824, James Ormerod got his landlady Esther Ellison to write him a note to the overseer of his home parish of Billington in east Lancashire. It said,

> Sir, The Bearer of this James Ormerod is in great distress by reason of his wife is lying in and 2 small children and only one pair of looms to work on and he has lived with me since last September the 11th and has payed me no rent he should have payed me 1s.6d. per week I cannot put off any longer and I hope that you will have the goodness to assist him for I am resolved that he shall not stay any longer with me till he pays me his rent he has no goods that will pay any more than is due.[15]

The sickness of his wife is what apparently pushed Ormerod into a formal application for relief. However, what is clear from this letter is that his whole existence was one of marginality and struggling to make ends meet. His few goods were worth little, and he had presumably coped with the burden of a young family by putting off payment of his rent for six months. The significant thing about his letter, then, is not that he asks for poor relief, but that he does not seem to have asked for it before. On this occasion he received his rent from the township, but his marginality continued as did his attempts to avoid relief. In February 1832, the Blackburn overseer wrote to Billington in the following terms.

> Sir, I write to you relative to the circumstance of James Ormerod a Pauper belonging to your Township, his wife a short time ago got her bed and

since that time has been unable to leave her bed and *must have been removed had she not been relieved by some ladies*, he has now 3 children and can only get by working 5/ a week.[16]

We clearly see charity coming into play here, just as we did in figure 5.1. Meanwhile, a letter in 1827 from the overseer of Burnley makes even more explicit the idea that at individual level poverty outside of that recognised by the poor law could be significant and long-enduring,

> Sir, I am requested by Charlotte Eastwood the widow of the late Richard Eastwood, who called upon you the last summer and you relieved her with 3/, I have to state that she is indebted to her landlord for Rent to the amount of 3.10.0 or thereabouts and if the same is not paid *her goods will be sold*, which will make very little although they are worth much more than the rent. If she is sold up she will be obliged to apply immediately to the overseer to be removed. She is upwards of 62 years of age and *if she had not had good friends at W. Townleys she must have been chargeable to you 12 months ago*. She says if you will send her 2.10.0 the landlord will not make her goods for 6 months to come and she will not trouble you again till after that time.[17]

Yet perhaps the best example of the operation of the spiral of marginality and making do lies in a series of letters sent to James Seed the overseer of Billington by, or on behalf of, an abandoned woman called Barbara Ingham. In October 1824, the overseer of Kendal wrote to the overseer of Billington in the following terms:

> Gentlemen, Barbara Ingham of this place is informed that it is your intention to strip her pension of 4/ a week because her husband has been seen here. This I assure you is very true but he only comes to distress her and her family and goes off again in a few days nobody knows whither – She is very industrious and makes her eldest boy do, and I assure you that *unless it is for the kindness of individuals who employ her* she could not possibly maintain her children – and must inevitably be a charge.[18]

He received a quick reply from James Seed, and penned a response to questions contained in that letter seeking further clarification, as follows:

> Mr James Seed, Barbara Ingham has placed your letter in my hands and in reply to it I have to say from her (and *I know it myself as a fact*) that her husband has been at home at different times for a few days but never brought a single farthing with him for his wife's support, in her own language he came for no other purpose than to distress her, He has said to her that he will not do anything to support her, he left her a fortnight since and she supposed from what she has heard he is skulking around Bury or

118

Burnley but he has declared he will not do anything to support her, he is a very bad fellow and your township ought to punish him – the *poor creature is most industrious and maintains with your 4/ her four small children by washing clothes doing anything for a honest livelihood* and I can assure you she bears a spotless reputation . . . as to your stopping her pension you must do no such thing as it is very little in comparison to the wants of her family.[19]

However, the relief payments were discontinued and there are several other letters setting out her desperate struggles to cobble together a living. The final letter, in May 1831, is perhaps the most fitting addendum to figure 5.1. It says:

Gentlemen, I was called upon to see one Barbara Ingham the Wife of James Ingham who is now laying ill at Dent and in a very poor state and she has been unable to follow *her work* since Christmas 2 *of her children is with her* and she says one is eleven years old and other 9 years old she says that her husband is at Kendal and doing nothing for their support and *she is now with her sister for she had stayed at Kendal till she was near lost*, at present she says that *she is maintained by her friends but they are not able to do so any longer* she therefore applies for relief which I hope you will send without delay or we shall be under the necessity of doing so and putting her under a suspended order your immediate attention to the above will oblige your servant.[20]

A combination of work, splitting the family unit (only two of her four children are 'with her', suggesting the rest were boarded elsewhere) and the charity of friends and kin keep this woman off the relief lists for seven years. She was poor but not as recognised by the communal welfare system. Of course, pauper letters are complex sources and full of ambiguities. However, they confirm what the quantitative sources show us – that by looking at poor law accounts we privilege one group of the poor over and above a larger body of the 'background poor'. In the rest of this chapter, therefore, 'poverty' will be taken to mean a wide definition rather than a narrow one.

The detailed characteristics of the poor on relief are considered in chapters six to eight. In the meantime, the mere observation that poverty (widely *or* narrowly defined) increased, and even that it increased significantly from the late eighteenth century, is only one part of the jigsaw that we need to put together to understand the nature of poverty (and thereby interpret the nature of its relief) in the period before 1850. To hark back to the questions with which we opened this chapter, how did structures of causation change? What were the life-cycle contours of poverty and how did they change over time? Did people become more or less likely to pass on their poverty to their children? And how did the poor think about poverty? These are the foci for the remaining sections.

The aggregate structure of poverty

At any one time, the mass of poor, marginal and less poor people whose aggregate lives underpin figure 5.1 would be in their respective positions for a variety of reasons. Because of *life-cycle* conditions such as widowhood, old age or sickness; because of *structural* problems associated with, for instance, the decline of rural industry;[21] because of *cyclical and seasonal* trends in agriculture or industry; because they had received an unexpected bill or had *budgeted poorly*; or because they were the *casual poor*.[22] For welfare historians interested in the role and character of the poor law and in the wider economy of makeshifts, the structure of poverty at any one time is at least as important as its magnitude. Yet, while individual groups of 'the poor', in particular the aged or those who wrote letters, have come under the microscope in recent years it is still the case that relatively little is known about the poor themselves and why they were 'poor'. Wide generalisations – the able-bodied become *the* poverty problem in the later eighteenth century, the south and east were afflicted with endemic structural poverty, the north had a different structure of poverty to the south and east – substitute for detailed regional analyses.

To some extent while this lack of focus may be disconcerting it is not surprising. The structure of poverty could change rapidly over time or area, making it difficult to characterise at anything but a micro-level. Locating the borderline between 'types' of poverty (even if we have the rich sources of information about the reasons for poverty that are necessary to undertake the classification process) provides an even more thorny problem. The example of handloom weavers illustrates the nature of this problem. Piece rates and employment opportunities for the handloom weaver were under pressure by the early nineteenth century. They rapidly became a reserve labour force for the local mills, weaving the cloth which the mills did not have the capacity to produce in good times, and scratching a living in bad times. In this sense the poverty of groups like the handloom weavers was structural. However, self-exploitation, combined with the fact that the handloom-weaving workforce as a whole was ageing from 1800 because it could not recruit young workers, meant that structural poverty could often be combined with life-cycle poverty (due to age or sickness) or accidental poverty (a failure to budget for the rent, for instance).[23] Even if we choose to ignore tricky declining trades, some of the categories into which we might like to divide the poor and their poverty were distinctly intercorrelated. Cyclical poverty related to the season or to industrial depression could lead naturally on to accidental poverty in the sense of people being unable to budget to meet big bills for coal or clothing, for instance.

These are abstract problems. They can be brought to life vividly by looking again at pauper letters. Thus, Peter Stewart wrote to the overseer of the Lancashire town of Barnacre in April 1822. His letter said:

> Gentlemen, it is with regret and feelings that I cannot express that I send you these few lines to let you know our deplorable situation. It is now nine weeks since I have wrought three weeks work and just as I was beginning to mend, my wife took her trouble [in later letters we find she has TB] and was brought to bed on the 4th of last month and has brought an additional hardship such as must be seen to be believed. We were totally unprepared for any such thing and in my poor state of health and very neare in distraction tried every scheme in honesty to earn some money. But to no purpose; at last a neighbour advised me to go and sell one pair of our looms and not see my wife and children lost. I went and found a man to buy them and give me 1 pound for them and he was so good as to give me three weeks to pay it back again and keep the looms. On Monday 15th the time will be expired and the money is not and more needed now. Gentlemen I appeal to you as husbands and fathers to look to our deplorable condition and prevent the breaking up of a house with 4 little ones under 6 years and 2 months the eldest now.[24]

It is unlikely that Stewart would have been able to write so fluent a letter on his own account, but even allowing for this and for inevitable exaggeration, we can see that he had become poor not for one reason but for several. He was engaged in a dying trade (his looms were cotton handlooms) characterised by structural poverty, he had a large young family, both he and his wife were ill, both were also old, and to cap it all, he was unable to obtain work through honest means because at the time he wrote the central Lancashire textile industry was in a cyclical trough. The whole gamut of potential causes of poverty were rolled together in the immediate experiences of one individual. If all the poor of Barnacre were like Peter Stewart, how would we classify the structure of poverty in the community as a whole? More important, how would we have obtained the information with which to classify Peter Stewart's poverty in the first place if he had not written it down in a letter to the overseer? The answers are, respectively, that we can't and we wouldn't!

Detailed generalisation on the structure of poverty is thus unwise and probably not achievable. This said, however, there *were* wide-ranging changes to the socio-economic fabric of eighteenth- and nineteenth-century England which *ought* to have impacted upon the broad structure of poverty. Many of these developments are themselves the subject of rigorous historiographical debate, and space constraints ensure that we can do no more than offer a thumbnail sketch. We cannot, though, ignore them completely. Several are worth considering in slightly more depth, and they follow on neatly from discussions in chapters one to three about the character of 'highland' versus 'lowland' regions, influences on local administrators in their interpretation of the law and the ways in which welfare historians have sought to explain lower levels of relief in northern England.

First, the development of a vigorous and increasingly regionally concentrated proto-industrial textile and metalware industry from 1750 onwards. The opening up of national and international markets for goods such as cotton and wool textiles stimulated rapid commercial development in the north and midlands. Textile (and metalware) production that had previously been combined with agriculture increasingly took more of the labour power of more people in the proto-industrial heartlands, such that by the early nineteenth century the proletarianisation of the workforce was largely complete outside of bastions of dual occupation production such as west and south Yorkshire. These and other aspects of proto-industrial development have been extensively traced,[25] but regional concentration in early industry, focusing particulary in the north and west as they are defined for the purposes of this book, has two particular implications for our discussion of the structure of poverty. First, the natural corollary of regional concentration was the deindustrialisation of other less well-established rural industrial centres. In effect this meant the gradual (if often overstated) loss of by-employments from the countryside of the south and east. Second, the extension of the opportunities offered to proto-industrial areas by international markets was the grinding cyclical poverty that could be associated with market closure. The subsequent incursion of factories into the northern textile industries enhanced both the risks and the impact of cyclical downturns and created structural underemployment for groups such as the Lancashire handloom weavers or the Leicestershire hosiery workers.

A second general development (already encountered in chapter two) was the curtailment from 1750 of a range of customary and common rights that are often seen to have underpinned the household economies of the marginal and the poor. Thus, Pam suggests that Enfield Chase 'had stood for centuries as a barrier between poverty and disaster', and demonstrated that its enclosure had catastrophic results.[26] In Oxfordshire, individual poor cottagers in the seven villages surrounding the 1,800 acres of common in Otmoor may have been able to make at least 200 shillings per year from various activities associated with the common, but the fifty-year enclosure process running from the late 1770s progressively denuded poor cottagers and squatters of an important plank of their household economies. The result was absolute depopulation once enclosure was finally completed in the late 1820s.[27] Of course there is dispute over who held common rights and how valuable they really were to the poor and marginal.[28] It is also important not to concentrate too heavily on common rights. Peter King has suggested, as we saw in chapter two, that gleaning (the right to take fallen grain from open and enclosed fields after harvest) could provide up to 10 per cent of the average income of poor families in the south and east and that opportunities to practise gleaning were, notwithstanding legal decisions outlawing it, alive and well even in the 1830s.[29] Nonetheless, Humphries provides convincing evidence that the commons allowed women and children to garner resources which in monetary terms might double the income of poor families. The loss of these sorts of opportunities – particularly in the rural south where their disappearance was tied up with peaks in parliamentary enclosure – must thus have had important 'knock-on' effects on the extent and intensity of poverty and perhaps also on its structure.

In turn, we must assess the loss of common rights against the backdrop of a third development in the general socio-economic fabric, viz. a rural – particularly southern and eastern rural – labour market which had been swelled by the loss of by-employments and rapid population growth at the same time as enclosure and other developments in the agrarian economy were pushing up labour productivity and thus lowering the demand for labour, making it more gender-specific, and making it more seasonal.[30] The result was low and sticky wage levels. For labourers on Wiltshire pastoral farms, wages of 6 shillings per week measured over the whole year were common. In Dorset, particularly newly enclosed parts of Dorset in the early nineteenth century, wages of 6–7 shillings per week were normal. And in the east and southeast, even the London hinterlands, agricultural wages were rarely more than 8 shillings per week measured over the whole year. Clearly, these sorts of wage levels could not have kept pace with the inflation of the late eighteenth and early nineteenth century, and there must have been inevitable consequences for both the level and structure of poverty.

We could continue with this sort of general analysis. The key point, however, is that while detailed analysis of structures of poverty might be defeated by problems of sources and definitions, we cannot escape the fact that rents in the socio-economic fabric of England between 1700 and 1850 carried with them substantial generalised poverty implications. Indeed, it is not difficult to conceive a broad hypothetical model of the structure of poverty in the eighteenth and nineteenth centuries that welfare historians might recognise and which we began to hint at in chapter three when talking about the regionality of welfare. Thus, we might suggest that coming into the eighteenth century, a central 'cause' of (especially rural) poverty were life-cycle conditions such as old age (or more particulary an inability to work in old age), widowhood, orphanhood, disability or sickness. The richly detailed 1674 poverty census of Bolton, 'of the aged decayed, blynde lunatick and disabled being past labour as also those fatherless, motherless and infants not able to labour and poor familys overcharged with children'.[31] provides considerable support for this idea. As its preamble suggests, almost all of the people recognised as poor were classified in this way because of life-cycle conditions. The initial page of the survey is worth quoting in its entirety:

Widdow Grundy alias Warr 56 years old
Ann Burges aged 80 years old
Raph Boxwirth, his wife and 3 small children
Margaret Boxwirth 80 years
Gilbert Taylor 80 years
Wm Bowker, 76 years and his wife 70 years
Thomas Clisby 78 years
James Barry his wife and 4 small children
Mary Chisnal, lame
Betty Bray, falling sickness
Lisburne, falling sickness
Elizabeth Haines, so simple as not fit to work or begg
Alice Lomax . . . disabled
James Keay, his wife and 6 children
James Crompton 60 years
Ales Duckworth Lunatick
Dewhurst wiffe 70 years
Richard Haslome his wife and 2 children[32]

Of course, we should beware of reading the lessons of this sort of survey too simplistically. The linen and fustian trades of Lancashire, the wool-cloth trades of the West Country, Norfolk and Essex, the coal trades of the northeast and the iron trades of the Black Country had, even by the late seventeenth century, subjected substantial numbers of people to the vagaries of the trade cycle as a cause of poverty. Structural poverty had also made its mark on the poverty landscape, in the Suffolk woollen industry or the Weald iron trades for instance, by 1700. And there was also a distinctive seasonal influence on patterns of poverty and independence. Thus, the winter frequently brought the coal trade of the northeast to a standstill, regularly plunging miners and their relations into intense poverty for part of the year. In agriculture there was an inevitable low point in activity between December and March, and where this seasonality was played out against the backdrop of enclosure by agreement or changing land usage the effects on the level and intensity of poverty might have been severe. In areas where any or all of these socio-economic conditions prevailed, then it is possible to suggest that while life-cycle conditions were a factor in the overall poverty conundrum they were rarely a sufficient cause. The Bolton census may even demonstrate this point in action; several of those who were relieved were on the list because of large families and while this was nominally a life-cycle condition the primary cause of the poverty these families faced was the insufficiency of household income, and this may have reflected a raft of structural or seasonal problems in the town.

To some extent these difficulties of interpretation are unfathomable. Yet, as chapters six and seven will show, the composition of early eighteenth-century relief lists more generally provides considerable support for the idea that life-cycle conditions may have been both a necessary and sufficient cause of poverty in rural and small-town England. To anticipate some of the conclusions from these chapters, relief lists tended to be dominated by women, the old and children, with 'overburdened' families largely absent from the poverty recognised by the parish welfare system. For these people, the physical breakdown of the family or the breakdown of the earning power of the household economy – life-cycle not structural conditions – was the primary force propelling people from marginality or independence to destitution. And while it may well be true that the majority of old people or widows do not become dependent on the parish in the early eighteenth century, chapters six and seven will argue that this does not mean that they had avoided poverty, merely that they had found alternative ways of addressing that poverty.

Continuing with our hypothetical model, then, it might be reasonable to suggest that this basic structure of poverty remained stable (and relatively uniform on a spatial basis) for the early part of the eighteenth century. Thereafter, the emergence of distinct agricultural regions (crudely a pastoral west, an arable east and a mixed-farming midlands), the stirrings of rapid population growth, a racheting up of the pace of enclosure and the development of a regionally based proto-industrial system may have produced subtle changes in the structure of poverty causation and a more complex spatial picture. Thus, we might trace the emergence of endemic structural poverty amongst rural labourers in the south and east, in which labour oversupply combined with ever more intense seasonality in labour demand because of changes in land organisation and usage to produce wages which were both low and sticky and to undermine the wage-earning economy of rural labour. At the same time, cyclical poverty supplemented with structural poverty amongst well-defined sectors of the working population may have come to dominate the poverty picture in the north and midlands.

Once again, these broad generalisations are much too crude. We have already seen that cyclical fluctuations were experienced well before the mid- to late eighteenth century, while rural counties in the south and east could demonstrate very considerable differences in representative wage levels. Nonetheless, the generalisations do fit with some of the evidence to hand. The so-called crisis of the old poor law after 1790 is widely believed to have coincided with the development of endemic, male-dominated, poverty in the south and east, and those who framed the new poor law had the structurally poor rural southern labourer at the forefront of their minds. For the industrial areas of the north and west, the volume of contemporary commentary on the nature of cyclical poverty is considerable. William Cooke-Taylor, for instance, visited the Lancashire manufacturing districts during the depression of 1842, noting,

> I visited several families of the distressed operatives in Bolton, accompanied by a gentleman well acquainted with the locality . . . the invariable account given in every place was 'no work' and as a consequence 'no food, no furniture and no clothing.'[33]

Of one family he noted that,

> When in good work the united earnings of both [man and wife] averaged about 30s weekly; but for several (I think they said thirteen) weeks they had not been able to earn so many pence. Their furniture had been sold piecemeal to supply pressing necessities, their clothes had been pawned, they hoped for better times, but they felt that their condition was worsening.[34]

This was exactly the sort of poverty that is often seen to have loomed large in the minds of guardians in the north and which made them hostile to the new poor law. On concluding his tour of Bolton, Cooke-Taylor's final comments tell us much about the power of cyclical poverty:

> The misery of Bolton is contagious: it has spread from the operative class to the grades of the middle rank more immediately above them; it ascends higher as it extends wider, threatening to involve all in one common mass of pauperism. [35]

At first blush, then, there are good reasons to expect a change in the aggregate and regional structure of poverty from the mid-eighteenth century. Yet, if we look closely at late eighteenth- and early nineteenth-century poor law records things are more complicated. The pauper letters that we have analysed so far in this chapter, and indeed pauper letters more generally, tend to highlight the essential life-cycle structure of the poverty of the writers. The 1817 census of the poor of Garstang in Lancashire also warns us to tread warily. It provides evidence of wage and family allowances for the endemically poor – people like John Parkinson, his wife and six children or John Etherington the flax dresser, his wife and their five children – yet of the fifty-two heads of household described as poor in this survey just seven (13.5 per cent) were described in terms that might lead us to think that they were people facing anything other than simple life-cycle crises. Children and the aged together comprise 52 per cent of the sample.[36] This despite the fact that 1817 was not a good year for the local calico printworks and that there was a large core of resident handloom weavers in the town.

There is clearly a need to take a more detailed look at the aggregate structure of poverty, and we return to this issue in the following chapters. This discussion has not, however, been in vain. The wide changes that we have seen in the socio-economic fabric of England from 1750 *must* have had an effect on the structure as well as the scale of poverty. If we cannot easily discern this effect in the aggregate structure of causation, then it is likely to have manifested itself in the life-cycle dimensions of poverty,[37] and it is to this theme that we now turn.

Life cycles of poverty

Whatever the notional cause of their poverty, some of those who were poor in a given year would be coming to the end of a period of need, some would be just starting, some would be poor for life, and conceivably pass on their poverty to their children, others would be poor for a short period, or intermittently over a longer time. Some people were never poor. This sort of observation raises important questions. Can we see increasing polarity in society between a poor underclass and a comfortable stratum of the never poor? If there was a poor underclass, did it pass on poverty to the next generation? How much of their lives would the frequently poor actually spend in poverty? How marginal had old people in poverty been before their old age? How often would the sick have been in poverty before a particular period of sickness, and how often would they go on to be poor once they pass out of observation? Addressing issues like these may help to locate the role of the communal welfare system in offering poverty solutions and thus contribute to an unpicking of the circular historiography outlined in chapter three.

Yet despite the recent surge of interest in sojourners' narratives and the life stories of poor people set out in sources like letters and settlement examinations, welfare historians have been slow to engage with the concept of the life cycle. The path-breaking methodological work of Tim Wales on life-cycle poverty in seventeenth-century Norfolk was not followed up in the 1980s, and even my own detailed nominal linkage work failed to conceptualise life cycles as a whole.[38] Failure to develop more sophisticated perspectives on life-cycles of poverty does not reflect a lack of raw material. A number of communities in different parts of England have been subject to family reconstitution. With relatively few exceptions these reconstitutions have been used for demographic analysis rather than being linked to other data from the localities on which they were conducted.[39] However, if the basic demographic life-cycles from some of these reconstitutions can be linked to records which signify individual and family poverty, we should be able to make judgements about whether the frequency and intensity of poverty experiences increased over life-cycles lived out at different times, and also whether it is possible to see the development of an underclass of the endemically poor.

Of course, this simple plan is not as easy as it seems. Family reconstitution is not an uncontested process. It is framed around those who register demographic events, and so the life-cycles of those who register no demographic events (such as single men and women) but whose lives may be important for the study of poverty and welfare are effectively excluded. Even those who do register demographic events tend to do so at long intervals. A complete life cycle might comprise a birth, then a marriage, then the births and deaths of several children and eventually the death of the person concerned. There are substantial gaps between many of these events, when the owner of the life cycle is 'out of observation'. While this may be acceptable in a demographic study, it is more of a drawback when studying poverty life-cycles, where it is important to be able to observe people between, say, the end of their childbearing period and their deaths. An ideal-typical problem would be a situation in which two families headed by John Smith complete their childbearing history in a community but the death of only one John Smith is recorded later in the parish registers. Which one? More importantly from our point of view, which of the John Smiths is it that receives a pension from the parish? We might with good reason prefer the John Smith who dies in the community concerned, but since we do not know when the second John Smith left, we cannot be certain. This apocryphal story demonstrates a further problem with family reconstitution, that in practice even if not in theory it privileges the life-cycles of those who stayed put as against those who moved about.[40]

Even if family reconstitution was a less contested subject, problems would still remain. To create poverty life-cycles from demographic life-cycles, we must have a range of sources to link to them. While the linking of reconstitution evidence and poor law accounts to give life-cycles of relief has recently been used to good effect,[41] establishing life-cycles of 'poverty' requires a greater range of sources. This creates problems of its own. Communities with registers good enough to reconstitute for long periods are relatively rare and thus communities with good parish registers *and* the range of other sources needed to create poverty life-cycles must by necessity be even rarer, and perhaps unrepresentative of most other communities. Moreover, a strategy of reconstructing poverty life-cycles generates very considerable nominal linkage problems. Differences in the depth of nominal information given in sources of different types, the use of aliases (we saw one in the Bolton census of 1672), the lack of a fixed orthography so that spelling of forenames and surnames could vary widely in different sources, and the fact that one never has a fixed reference point to know how many John Smiths were living out their lives in a given place at a given time, are all potentially complex problems which require much ingenuity to overcome. We return to these issues in chapters six to eight.

The key point is that these are not insurmountable problems.[42] Let us consider four reconstitutions where it is also possible to gain access to all or some of the supplementary records (poor law archives, charity accounts, records of voluntary subscriptions, other parish accounts through which we can trace work subsidies to poor people, lists of ratepayers, apprenticeship material, detailed parish registers which signify people as poor, narrative sources, records of rent and rate arrears, cottage rentals, maps of common or waste ground and criminal and other records) that are needed to characterise life cycles of poverty by following individuals through the sources which relate to them. Calverley and Idle lay in the same parish (Calverley) located midway between Leeds and Bradford. Reconstitutions of the communities exist for the period 1680–1830, and for much of the eighteenth century and onwards these were vigorous rural industrial villages in which commercial production of woollen cloth was combined with long traditions of dual-occupation artisanal production. The combined 1801 population of the two places was almost 5,000 people.[43] By contrast, Aynho and Farthinghoe in Northamptonshire were smaller (combined 1801 population: 1,160) and less proximate rural parishes concentrating on mixed arable/pastoral farming by the early nineteenth century. The reconstitutions for these communities run from 1680 to 1820.[44]

Clearly these are not randomly chosen examples, although, as chapter one suggested, they would seem to encapsulate the essential differences in economic structure between the north and west and the east and south as we have defined them for this book. Representative or not, by linking supplementary data to these basic reconstitutions, we can begin to gain some important perspectives on the basic structure of life-cycle poverty at different points in time. Tables 5.1 and 5.2 represent the outcome of a process in which all individuals identified in the respective family reconstitutions (plus others resident in, or passing through, the locality and detected in other ways) between 1680 and 1800 were linked through sources which might be expected to indicate 'poverty'.[45] Thus, anyone appearing in poor law or charity accounts was by definition poor. So was anyone employed by officers of the parish (constables, churchwardens, surveyors of the highway, the overseers of the poor) who went on to be described as poor in more than one other source during the linkage process. Those who rented property with a nominal rental of less than 15s. per year (1700–40), 20s. per year (1740–70), 30s. per year (1770–1800) and 35s per year after 1800 were also described as poor. Anyone accused of theft, living in houses on common or waste land, dispossessed of common rights during enclosure, or described as poor in narrative sources or parish registers, were also deemed to be nominally poor.

This process of nominal linkage is by no means infallible – the fact that several John Smiths identified in a family reconstitution may compete for linkage to a single example of John Smith in a charity account ensures this is so – but what we end up with is a series of demographic life-cycles with the gaps filled in by references to poverty records. Some people were never linked to a poverty source. Not surprisingly, Sir Walter Calverley of Calverley was never seen to be poor. Other life-cycles had the odd reference to 'poverty', or carried intermittent instances of poverty. Perhaps they were apprenticed by the parish when young, needed help from the poor law when they were overcharged with children and then became parish pensioners in old age. Yet more life-cycles were crammed with references to poverty sources, suggesting that the individuals spent much of their lives in a widely defined state of 'poverty'. By making assumptions about what a reference to an individual in a 'poverty source' implies for their family, and more importantly by making crude assumptions about how long a person might have been in poverty when they are defined as poor by their presence in one of these sources, we can begin to make very preliminary observations about the frequency and duration of life-cycle poverty.[46]

Thus, for the townships collectively table 5.1 takes five life-cycle cohorts and records the mean number of contacts between the life-cycles of that cohort and sources indicating 'poverty', and the mean

Table 5.1 Life cycles of poverty in four communities

Period	Life cycles	Mean contacts	Mean duration
1680–99	474	2.3	3.4 years
1700–24	672	2.7	3.9 years
1725–49	764	3.0	4.4 years
1750–74	1,021	4.9	6.0 years
1775–99	1,643	7.1	10.9 years

Notes Only life cycles lasting until the life cycle owners reached 40+ are used here. To overcome the problem of how to measure duration of poverty, I have employed three core assumptions. First, in sources which give a direct indication of need (such as charity or poor law records) I have assumed the person is 'in poverty' as long as they figure in the source. Second, in sources which give a relatively certain indicator of need at a certain point in time (for instance the payment of low rents or residence on waste land) I have assumed that an individual is 'in poverty' for the year in which the source was taken and in the three previous and subsequent years. Finally, in sources which provide transient evidence of poverty, such as criminal records or the records of doles arising from voluntary subscription), I have assumed individuals are 'in poverty' only for the year in which the source was constructed. Where there were contradictory indicators – for instance where a cottage survey of 1750 indicates poverty by payment of low rent and a parish register entry of the same year ascribes a person but a further parish register entry eight years later ascribes the same person as poor – I have chosen to use the source that places people 'in poverty' for longest.

duration of 'poverty'. On the face of it, the results are significant. There was a consistent increase in the number of times that the average life cycle would experience widely defined 'poverty'. Those of the late seventeenth century came into contact with poverty indicators twice on average, while the cohort of life-cycles starting in the later eighteenth century would on average expect to come into contact with poverty indicators almost six times. Moreover, the duration of 'poverty' also increased, rising from just over three years to over ten years between the later seventeenth and the later eighteenth centuries. These observations could be entirely illusory, a function of the assumptions used to calculate duration of poverty on the one hand and increasingly numerous or more comprehensive sources the nearer to the nineteenth century we get, on the other. Certainly it would be unwise to set too much store by table 5.1.

Yet, when the vestry of Aynho in 1809 lamented 'the late increase' in poverty, they were clearly not simply referring to the rise in number of paupers. Rather they were saying something about the intensity of poverty as well. Table 5.2 thus returns to the basic outcomes of the linkage process – the life-cycles and their frequent, infrequent or non-existent contacts with 'poverty' indicators – to try and construct crude typologies of poverty. Again, this process is beset with more or less crude assumptions, but the idea that some life-cycles, certainly by the late eighteenth century, appear to have been heavily pauperised while others never saw poverty on the definitions employed here, make the exercise worthwhile. Thus, what we see in table 5.2 are four categories of life cycle. The *never poor* were those whose life-cycles we can trace but who never appeared in the 'poverty sources' or who appeared only once and then not in sources (such as charity accounts) which identify core poverty experiences. The *sometimes poor* were those who appeared in the poverty sources on up to three occasions but spent less

Table 5.2 Proportion of life cycles in four communities falling into poverty typologies

Period	Life cycles	Never poor	Sometimes poor	Often poor	Always poor
1680–99	474	32	34	22	12
1700–24	672	38	34	20	8
1725–49	794	40	31	18	11
1750–74	1,021	36	30	17	17
1775–99	1,643	26	34	19	21

Notes For the definition of labels, see text.

than five years in poverty, while the *often poor* were those who appeared in the poverty indicators up to six times but spent less than ten years of their life cycles in poverty. The *always poor* appeared more than six times and spent more than ten years of their life cycles in poverty. Such divisions are clearly both crude and arbitrary. However, if we can rely on these categorisations then it is clear that life-cycles as a whole became less poor during the early part of the eighteenth century, notwithstanding experiences such as the demographic crisis of the late 1720s and early 1730s. Falling prices, stagnant rents and generally rising incomes clearly made more life-cycles viable. However, the later eighteenth century was to see a marked turnaround. While substantial numbers of life-cycles in these communities saw little or no poverty, even those which ran through the crisis decade 1796–1806, over one-fifth of life-cycles from the last cohort of the eighteenth century were to experience chronic poverty during their life-cycles as a whole. In other words, the growing polarity between the comfortable and the endemically poor which had come to be recognised by contemporaries was clearly played out on the ground here. What is more, there is evidence that the core of the always poor was one that was increasingly likely to pass on its poverty to its own children. Irrespective of those falling down the social scale, then, it would appear that the chronically poor bred themselves into a more numerous position. This is exactly what Malthus feared and suggests that contrary to the weight of current historiography we do see the development of a distinct underclass of the chronically poor by the nineteenth century. Such observations provide support for the renewed pessimistic characterisations of the communal welfare system prior to 1834, as explored in chapter three.

Though there is absolutely no reason to think that the experiences of these communities were particularly representative, there is a convincing logic to this picture. We can begin to put occupations and social groups against the label 'always poor'. These were the dockworkers and casual labourers of urban England, the itinerant labourers of rural England and the proletarianised weavers of the proto-industrial sector. They inhabit the novels and art of the period, and they come to dominate the fears and the imaginations of nineteenth-century social commentators. Nor do we have to look hard for individuals to fill up our abstract labels. The Duckett family from Banbury provide one of the best examples of endemic and inherited poverty that I have ever come across.[47] The analysis is penetrated by too many assumptions and technical ambiguities to offer wide-ranging theories, but with imagination it could be clear that a substantial and rising poverty burden in the aggregate was underpinned by a rising core of the chronically poor who stood in contradistinction to a substantial number of the increasingly comfortable in any community. This is one of the perspectives to be carried forward to the second part of this book.

Contemporary perceptions of the state of being poor

Yet, before we move on to poverty solutions, there is a further issue to be considered, albeit briefly. For much of this chapter and chapter 4 it has been assumed that the 'poverty' we measure is poverty that would have been recognised as such by contemporaries. This is by no means a safe assumption. Would those in arrears with their rent have regarded themselves as 'in poverty' or would they have regarded themselves as 'coping' which has entirely different connotations? Did the receipt of charity signify poverty to the recipient, the giver and the neighbours of the giver, or did the person have a right to expect charitable aid so that the mere receipt of it would not equate to 'poverty'? Would a person accumulating goods at one stage of the life cycle and selling or pawning them at a later stage of the life cycle have regarded themselves as poor?

Questions like this demand more attention than they can be given here. The vicissitudes of 'public opinion' on poverty in the form of books, pamphlets and letters are now well established, but the perspectives of ordinary people are much less clear.[48] The contention of Woolf that, 'To be poor did not mean being different from others, precisely because poverty was such a normal condition. To be described as poor, on the other hand, was perceived as something distinctive by all parties.'[49] is a useful starting point. It suggests that some of the experiences that historians call 'poverty' might not have been regarded in that way by those living through them, and its extension is that those who were 'poor' would have worked hard to avoid the obvious badges of poverty. There is considerable support for both perspectives.

Take the issue of pawning possessions. Tomkins and Mackay provide convincing evidence that being without items of clothing, furniture or even food was not necessarily considered as poverty. People expected to lend and borrow to cover the temporary material shortfalls of the life cycle, and for many the pawnshop was a regular feature of life even in relatively small villages. Women in particular were likely to pawn household goods and clothing as a way of making ends meet on a weekly basis, retrieving goods once a wage was paid. It was also a way of combating cyclical downturns, as the testimony of Cooke-Taylor reviewed above showed. In an objective sense, we might take pawning as evidence of poverty and need and yet it is far from certain that those pawning would have seen their position in these terms. Indeed, they often talked of their actions in terms of making ends meet rather than in terms of their poverty and need.[50] In objective historical terms, we might also regard the need for a family to sell their material possession built up at earlier stages of the life cycle as 'poverty'. Yet, for the weavers visited by Cooke-Taylor, this was a normal and expected part of every-day life. Significant trade disruptions would occur in Lancashire roughly every five to seven years, prompting a regular cycle of accumulation and dissipation. The weavers of Bolton 'looked forward to better times' by which they meant they could take their clothes out of pawn, buy back their furniture and wait for the next cyclical down-turn. Whether this dance with depression amounted to poverty in the eyes of the weavers is very doubtful indeed.

There is equally strong evidence that people sought to avoid the symbolism of poverty. The prevailing characteristic of most pauper letters, as we have already seen in this chapter, is the extraordinary lengths that people claim to have gone to in order to keep away from dependence on the communal relief system. We can regard their stories as posturing, but we can equally regard them as a true record of the individual and family struggles with various states of need, marginality and making ends meet before they were obliged to accept the 'label of poverty' under the poor law. Peter Stewart, the start of whose letter to the overseer of Barnacre was reviewed earlier, continued his narrative in the following terms:

> If you do not look to this last request that I shall ever make, I shall have no other shift left but see what that we have and keep my wife and chil-dren till she gets better and then she shall come to you. Depend on what I say if I am live till she is well I will never starve them and myself while the law of the land has made a place for her and them, if not for me. I am not fit to maintain myself at present but I shall not come to you. *I shall never undergo another brow beating by a fellow as fierce as if he had a brief to bleed my life away*. I shall die in a ditch first if you think proper to stop this overwhelming torment of destiny.[51]

Clearly, Stewart had come into contact previously with the poor law and found a significant difference between his own perception of poverty and its cure, and that of its administrators. His determination to be free of the label of the poor law was matched by the determina-tion of others not to take on alternative symbols of poverty. The pauper burial was something to be avoided at all costs. So, for some, was living in parish housing. Widow Breakes from Wimbledon, for instance, was told to go into a parish house in 1752, but 'says she will sooner go a-begging about the country than live in a parish house'.[52] Moreover, both the poor and the poor law administrators realised the key symbolism of clothing, the former often rigorously preserving a Sunday best while the latter spent considerable sums on clothing that varied in quality between adequate and elegant. Parish elites also acted to maintain the clothing of the poor on their own account. The Somerset parson William Holland liberally gave out flannel waistcoats and other clothing at his own expense, and he traces what might be styled a voluntary clothing industry in which the wives and daughters of the parish elites provided clothing to both indoor and outdoor paupers.[53] Such evidence suggests strongly that the ubiquitous poor had a distinct conception of what *real* poverty meant. Their definition was apparently tied up with symbolism as much as material circumstances, but the overwhelming aim was to avoid 'real poverty' as opposed to the problems of making ends meet that dominated their everyday lives.

Yet, there is also contrary evidence – evidence of those who turned to the poor law as a court of first rather than last resort, of people who preferred to pawn parish clothing rather than wear it and of those who embraced the workhouse rather than fleeing from it under the new poor law. William Holland encountered 'this scoundrel Porter', who 'will not work tho he can earn much more than anyone, but he wants the parish to maintain him in idleness. I say he must work while he can or starve.'[54] Moreover, as we saw earlier in the book Robert Sharp of South Cave encountered George Dunn, who 'after all his spending and extravagance and running into debt has likewise applied for relief and had some money given him'.[55] Each community had their Porters and their Dunns and each community had people like George Adams:

> He is 86 . . . weak and with a long beard. I gave him some of the sacrament money. God bless you he said I have no one but you and madam [his wife] to look after me. I answered you have your own family, son and daughter, He shook his head and replied . . . 'they are best off who can help themselves"[56]

There were, then, not one but two sorts of contemporary attitudes towards the state of being poor. For one group of the poor, there was a conscious distinction to be made, as Woolf suggested, between being poor and being visibly poor. For another group, however, notions of dependence and independence merged imperceptibly in a life cycle of need which had to be met from whatever sources came along. This group – possibly a growing number by the early nineteenth century – knew no symbolism and used the language of poverty and welfare in much the same way as those who administered the system or commented on it from the middle-class districts of urban England. The role of the communal welfare system in meeting the needs of these two groups is the major focus of the rest of this book.

Notes

1 G. Taylor, *The problem of poverty 1660–1834* (London, Longman, 1969), p. 24.
2 See S. Mencher, 'Introduction to the poor law reports of 1834 and 1909', in R. Lubove (ed.), *Social welfare in transition: selected English documents 1834–1909* (Pittsburgh, Pittsburgh University Press, 1982), p. 52.
3 K. D. M. Snell, *Annals of the labouring poor: social change and agrarian England 1660–1900* (Cambridge, Cambridge University Press, 1985).
4 D. Marshall, *The English poor in the eighteenth century* (New York, Routledge, 1969 reprint). However, see also A. Digby, 'The rural poor law', in D. Fraser (ed.), *The new poor law in the nineteenth century* (Basingstoke, Macmillan, 1976), pp. 149–70.
5 See C. Lis and H. Soly, *Poverty and capitalism in pre-industrial Europe* (Brighton, Harvester, 1979), pp. 151.
6 See P. Johnson, *Saving and spending: the working class economy in Britain 1870–1939* (Oxford, Oxford University Press, 1985), and A. J. Kidd, *State, society and the poor in nineteenth century England* (Basingstoke, Macmillan, 1999), who outline the development of working-class saving institutions.
7 P. Wood, *Poverty and the workhouse in Victorian Britain* (Stroud, Sutton, 1991).
8 T. Arkell, 'The incidence of poverty in England in the later seventeenth century', *Social History*, 12 (1987), 23–47.
9 S. A. Peyton, *Kettering vestry minutes 1797–1853* (Northampton, Northamptonshire Records Society, 1933), pp. 159–60. My italics.
10 Some caution is needed here. In some of these alternative sources people were being defined as poor while in others they were defining themselves as poor.
11 These are Calverley (West Riding), Charing (Kent), Cartmel (Lancashire/Westmorland) and Farthinghoe (Northamptonshire). References are set out in the Bibliography. These communities are not representative of either of the regions identified in chapter one, and they are certainly not randomly selected. My thanks to David Turner for contacting me with regard to the Charing material and for letting me have sight of those documents in his possession.
12 The sources are: outdoor relief lists, charity lists, rent schedules (in which

anyone not already on relief and paying less than 18s. rent per year in the first period and 25s. per year in the second period was deemed poor), lists of those exempt from paying local taxes, lists of those with rate arrears and anyone whose goods were distrained for debts during or in the years surrounding either of the two chronological reference points. Not all communities supported all of the sources. Those exempt from the poor rate also had to be exempted from other taxes or to appear in another source suggesting marginality before they were considered 'poor'.

13 Exclusion from taxes means in this context those explicitly excluded by not being rated. Those nominally rated but never paying and never asked formed a bigger group whose inclusion would push 'poverty' levels on the widest definition to well over 80 per cent.

14 Kidd, *State*.

15 Lancashire Record Office (hereafter LRO) PR2391/8, 'Letter'.

16 LRO PR2391/34, 'Letter'. My italics.

17 LRO PR2391/24, 'Letter', My italics.

18 LRO PR2391/11, 'Letter', My italics.

19 LRO PR2391/12, 'Letter', My italics.

20 LRO PR2391/31, 'Letter', My italics.

21 See P. Sharpe, *Adapting to capitalism: working women in the English economy, 1700–1800* (Basingstoke, Macmillan, 1996), and D. Ashforth, 'Settlement and removal in urban areas: Bradford 1834–71' in M. E. Rose (ed.), *The poor and the city: the English poor law in its urban context 1834–1914* (Leicester, Leicester University Press, 1985), pp. 58–91.

22 There is no inevitable reason why the structure of poverty amongst the poor recognised by the relief system should be the same as the structure of poverty amongst the poor recognised by other sources. However, the detailed reasoning on rate arrears conducted by the Kettering vestry provides convincing evidence that any differences in the structure of poverty amongst those recognised in different combinations of sources is likely to be one of degree rather than order.

23 See J. G. Timmins, *The last shift* (Manchester, Manchester University Press, 1993).

24 LRO PR1349/10, 'Letter'.

25 P. Hudson, 'Proto-industrialisation in England', in S. Ogilvie and M. Cerman (eds), *European proto-industrialisation* (Cambridge, Cambridge University Press, 1996), pp. 49–66.

26 D. Pam, *A parish near London: a history of Enfield volume 1* (Frome, Enfield Preservation Society, 1990), p. 329.

27 S. A. King and J. G. Timmins, *Making sense of the industrial revolution* (Manchester, Manchester University Press, forthcoming), chapter 7.

28 For early work downplaying the value of commons, see J. D. Chambers and G. E. Mingay, *The agricultural revolution 1750–1880* (London, Batsford, 1966). For more pessimistic interpretations, J. M. Neeson, *Commoners: common right, enclosure and social change in England 1700–1820*

(Cambridge, Cambridge University Press, 1993), and J. Humphries, 'Enclosure, common right and women: the proletarianisation of families in the late eighteenth and early nineteenth centuries', *Journal of Economic History*, 50 (1990) 17–42.

29 P. King, 'Customary rights and women's earnings: the importance of gleaning to the rural labouring poor 1750–1850', *Economic History Review*, 44 (1991) p. 468, and P. King, 'Gleaners, farmers and the failure of legal sanctions 1750–1850', *Past and Present*, 125 (1989) 116–50. Also Sharpe, *Adapting*.

30 M. Overton, *Agricultural revolution in England: the transformation of the agrarian economy 1500–1850* (Cambridge, Cambridge University Press, 1996).

31 LRO DDKe 2/6/2, 'Bolton survey 1674'. My thanks to Richard Hoyle for drawing my attention to this reference.

32 *Ibid.*

33 W. Cooke-Taylor, *Notes on a tour in the manufacturing districts of Lancashire* (New York, Augustus Kelley, 1968 reprint), p. 41.

34 *Ibid.*, p. 42.

35 *Ibid.*, p. 44.

36 LRO DDX 386/3, Vestry records of Garstang'.

37 A single life cycle could encompass all forms of poverty (structural, accidental, cyclical, life-pressure) at least once.

38 T. Wales, 'Poverty, poor relief and the life-cycle: some evidence from seventeenth century Norfolk', in R. M. Smith (ed.), *Land, kinship and life-cycle* (Cambridge, Cambridge University Press, 1984), pp. 351–74, and S. A. King, 'Reconstructing lives: the poor, the poor law and welfare in rural industrial communities', *Social History*, 22 (1997), 318–38. Though see L. Botelho, 'Aged and impotent: parish relief of the aged poor in early modern Suffolk', in M. J. Daunton (ed.), *Charity, self-interest and welfare in the English past* (London, UCL Press, 1996), pp. 91–112, and R. M. Smith, 'Charity, self-interest and welfare: reflections from demographic and family history', in *ibid.*, pp. 23–50.

39 E. A. Wrigley, R. S. Davies, J. E. Oeppen and R. S. Schofield, *English population history from family reconstitution 1580–1837* (Cambridge, Cambridge University Press, 1998).

40 For this view, see S. Ruggles, 'Migration, marriage and mortality: correcting sources of bias in English family reconstitution', *Population Studies*, 46 (1992) 507–22.

41 Smith, 'Charity'.

42 See S. Ottoway and S. Williams, 'Reconstructing the life cycle experiences of poverty in the time of the old poor law', *Archives*, 23 (1998) 19–29, and S. A. King, 'Multiple source record linkage in a rural industrial community, 1680–1820', *History and Computing*, 6 (1994) 133–42.

43 The reconstitutions of these townships were conducted as part of a much wider project to reconstruct everyday life in rural industrial townships in

West Yorkshire. See P. Hudson and S. A. King, *Industrialisation, material culture and everyday life* (forthcoming).

44 The reconstitution of Farthinghoe was conducted for this study. That for Aynho was conducted by Mr James Wiley, and I am grateful to him for sharing his data with me.

45 Life cycles starting in the later eighteenth century could conceivably continue to the later nineteenth century. Individuals were selectively followed through sources after 1840.

46 The latter point is very important. If a child is apprenticed by the parish, do we assume that the child was poor at all (the parish had the power to apprentice the children of those who looked like becoming chargeable as well as those who were), and if so was it poor just for the year in which it was apprenticed, for the year previously and the year following, or for the whole term of the apprenticeship? If someone was defined as 'poor' by virtue of low rent payments in one cottage survey, but the next cottage survey does not occur until twenty years later, when the person has died, how long might they be defined as in 'poverty' – the year of the survey, the four years either side? The notes to table 5.1 suggest a solution to these problems.

47 See P. Renold (ed.), *Banbury gaol records* (Banbury, Banbury Historical Society, 1987).

48 See D. Valenze, 'Charity, custom and humanity: changing attitudes to the poor in eighteenth century England', in J. Garnett and C. Matthew (eds), *Revival and religion since 1700: essays for John Walsh* (London, Hambledon, 1993), pp. 59–78.

49 S. Woolf, 'Order, class and the urban poor', in M. L. Bush (ed.), *Social orders and social classes in Europe since 1500* (London, Longman, 1993), pp. 185–98.

50 L. Mackay, 'Why they stole: women in the Old Bailey 1779–1789', *Journal of Social History*, 32 (1999) 623–40, and A. Tomkins, 'Pawnbroking and the survival strategies of the urban poor in 1770s York', in S. A. King and A. Tomkins (eds), *Coping with the crossroads of life: the economy of makeshifts in early modern England* (forthcoming).

51 LRO PR1349/10, 'Letter'. My italics.

52 F. M. Cowe, *Wimbledon vestry minutes 1736, 1743–1788* (Guildford, Surrey Record Society, 1964), p. 24.

53 J. Ayres, *Paupers and pig killers: the diary of William Holland, a Somerset parson 1799–1818* (Stroud, Sutton, 1984).

54 *Ibid.*, pp. 230.

55 J. Crowther and P. Crowther (eds), *The diary of Robert Sharp of South Cave: life in a Yorkshire village 1812–1837* (Oxford, Oxford University Press, 1997), p. 241.

56 Ayres, *Paupers*, p. 272.

CHAPTER SIX

WELFARE IN THE SOUTH AND EAST, 1700–1820

Overview

Chapters four and five have suggested a growing eighteenth- and nineteenth-century 'poverty problem', both at particular times and over the life cycle. There is at least some empirical evidence to support the views of middle-class contemporary commentators who thought that they could witness the emergence of a group of chronically poor people in both towns and rural areas after 1780. Whether such perspectives are accurate or not, there is a clear sense in which marginality became an overwhelming problem by the early 1800s. Were there any regional dimensions to either the structure or the scale of poverty? Hypothetical models flounder on ambiguous evidence. However, important changes to the broad economic and social fabric ought to have had an impact on both the causes and regional scale of poverty after 1750. Certainly, national poor law expenditure statistics suggest that a broadly defined 'south and east' bore the brunt of the developing poverty problem from the later eighteenth century.[1] Evidence of accumulating poverty and marginality in the south and east as they are defined for this book can also be gleaned from other sources. Thus, by the mid-1790s some 41 per cent of the households in the Essex village of Ardleigh were 'poor'.[2] In 1803, 23 per cent of the Wiltshire population were recorded as in receipt of relief, and for the same date Thomas suggests that if we make due allowance for the dependents of paupers in Berkshire and Essex then between one-third and one-half of the county populations were directly dependent on the relief system. For individual towns and parishes, these figures could be very much higher.[3]

As a rule, it is clear that the communal welfare system recognised and treated only some of the poverty, chronic or otherwise. Chapter five suggested a figure of around one-fifth, but also noted (on the basis of admittedly slim evidence) some tendency for the southern and eastern poor law to engage with more local poverty than communities in the

141

north and west. Such ideas are supported by the evidence of aggregate poor law statistics which, when mapped, demonstrate very considerable and consistent differences between numbers on relief and expenditure on them in the south and east compared to a broadly defined north and west. In particular, counties such as Sussex or Wiltshire were in 1803 relieving three times more of their population than was Lancashire. There are competing explanations for this observation, but the implication of the discussion of wage stagnation, declining rural industrial opportunities and increasingly simple household economies in chapter five should be that the southern and eastern poor law had little choice but to give substantial and sustained help both to the impotent poor (the old, sick, widows and children) and increasingly to individuals and families who could not make ends meet through regular work. Moreover, we should also presumably expect the poor law to have become a major, or rather *the* major, plank in the life-cycle welfare strategies of ordinary people during the eighteenth century.

Chapter three suggested that this perspective has become a compelling truism for many welfare historians looking at the southern and eastern old poor law. Even before our period starts, the work of Tim Wales on Norfolk and Newman-Brown on Hertfordshire suggests that the poor law was providing relatively valuable, regular pension payments, as well as irregular top-ups at need, to a considerable range of poor people.[4] Botelho shows that the seventeenth-century experience (of both generosity and the scope of poor law payments) was more variable in Suffolk parishes, where the limited wealth of some places capped the generosity of the poor law, but Slack confirms the importance of the poor law to the welfare patterns of the poor in the south more generally as the seventeenth century closed.[5] At the opposite end of our period, the work of David Thomson reveals, as we have seen, that the poor law might provide in pension terms the equivalent of some four-fifths of the monthly adult male wage in Bedfordshire parishes. Moreover, it might provide these sorts of benefits to something over one-quarter of local adults at any one time. If we take account of the casual monetary and kind payments that most overseers also made and make some allowance for the likely dependents of poor relief recipients, it might be reasonable to suggest that well over one-half of the population in some nineteenth-century Bedfordshire communities were tied into the communal welfare system in the decade of poor law reform.[6] Of course, Thomson was not really talking about the old poor law in his analysis (his empirical data are largely drawn from the 1840s) but it is hard to escape the inference that a chaotic but potentially flexible southern and eastern old poor law system did intervene ever more pow-erfully (and perhaps ever earlier?) in the late eighteenth and early nine-teenth centuries to play an even more central role in the welfare patchworks assembled by poor and marginal people than had been the case earlier.

Such views have not gone without substantial challenge, and even other studies of Bedfordshire parishes in the nineteenth century reveal less certain evidence of generous and widespread poor law handouts.[7] However, Boyer believed that the allowances of the southern and eastern old poor law were so valuable and so widespread that at the end of the old poor law period birth rates were 8.7 per cent higher (because the poor law underwrote the negative consequences of large family size) than they would have been in their absence.[8] Whether we accept this contentious view or not, others have come to equally firm conclusions that the southern and eastern poor law played a central role in the welfare conundrum faced by ordinary people. Dunkley, for instance, suggests that the 1790s mark a sea change in the nature of relief in the south and east, as the pressure of rising prices and an increasingly inter-ventionist magistracy forced an uprating of allowances and a change in the composition of the relief lists from predominantly female and old to predominantly male and younger.[9] Wells also traces a late eighteenth- and early nineteenth-century change of sentiment, suggesting that by 1800 there was widespread acceptance in the south that certain cate-gories of poor people, most notably the elderly, had obtained 'rights' to relief.[10] Emerging evidence on 'parish health care systems' in the south inevitably adds to the idea that the communal welfare system came to provide a wide range of care by the early nineteenth century.[11]

In practice, of course, chapter two has demonstrated that the way in which statute fed through to local practice allowed individual localities considerable leeway in their recognition and treatment of the 'poverty problem'. The result was a rich patchwork of local practices and a situa-tion in which it was rare for parishes and townships to follow a single definitive 'poor law policy'. Against this backdrop it is unwise to be too quick to draw broad regional characterisations, and this chapter aims to take a more detailed look at the character and role of the southern and eastern old poor law. Who did it relieve? What did the poor law pay for and why? Was there a change in the focus of relief over time? How generous was the relief and how benevolent was the relief system? How did southern and eastern communities cope with an intensification of life-cycle poverty? What were the life-cycle dimensions of relief? What was the character of institutional relief? How did those whose poverty and marginality were not recognised (or at least not consistently recognised) by the poor law make ends meet? Such are the questions that underpin this analysis, and in both asking and answering them the book moves from a broad concern with synthesis to an attempt to push forward the boundaries of what we know about the character and role of the old poor law.

Perspectives and problems

Initially, it is important to reiterate comments in chapter three that welfare historians have not been quick to look at the detailed nuts and bolts of poor law accounts and local definitions of entitlement, even in nineteenth-century communities. There is no southern old poor law equivalent for the 1820s and 1830s to David Thomson's work on the 1840s. Broad county studies, particularly covering the period from the 1790s, are relatively common. However, in so far as these focus on local experiences at all they often rely on aggregate statistics or on disjointed parish examples to illustrate the character of the poor law.[12] Those that deal systematically with local experiences over longer periods often remain unpublished.[13] The eighteenth century has been a particular casualty of this lack of empirical focus. Until recently, detailed studies of local eighteenth-century poor law regimes and paupers have been limited in number and spatial coverage leaving the characterisation of the eighteenth-century southern and eastern poor law and welfare networks open to crude and poorly informed generalisation. In fact, it is probably accurate to suggest that we know rather more about the scope and character of the poor law and poor relief in the relatively poorly documented seventeenth century than we do in the relatively richly documented eighteenth and early nineteenth centuries.

To some extent, this failure to explore the nooks and crannies of local material is understandable. A systematic local study, let alone one which aims to make comparisons between localities, involves grappling with several interrelated problems. Most obviously, as we have seen in previous chapters, carving individual poor relief histories out of local poor law records might involve considering tens of thousands of accounting entries. Even with modern computers this is a considerable undertaking. In addition, of course, the information contained in parish accounts inevitably varies considerably over time in both quantity and quality as the yearly rotation of parish officers placed more or less interested and conscientious people into the office of overseer. For some years the names and ages of recipients as well as the purpose of the relief payment might be given. Distinctions might even be made between regular pensioners and those relieved casually. In other years, the poor law accounts may *at best* consist of no more than a list of names and amounts, while for periods when the poor were farmed (see chapter two) or where relief was administered via the workhouse, records will often be entirely missing. Considering an 'average' set of poor law accounts thus imposes unenviable logistical problems. This said, it is nonetheless relatively simple if time-consuming to abstract crude data on issues such as the size and range of pensions at different chronological points. The real problems emerge where we want to go further than this and to ask about life cycles of relief or the age of recipients.

These questions raise complex nominal linkage problems of the sort we have already encountered in previous chapters. Take a hypothetical example of the problems surrounding the creation of poor relief histories. Between 1760 and 1780 someone called Widow Smith receives a pension of 2 shillings from her parish. We can be reasonably certain that the same woman is living and receiving through the twenty-year period, but is Widow Smith the same person as Hannah Smith who received 3 shillings per week between 1755 and 1759? Whether she is or not, does the entry for Hannah Mitchell in 1735 form part of the relief history of Hannah/Widow Smith (given name changes at marriage and remarriage), or should we be looking for someone entirely different to link these payments to? Obtaining age profiles of paupers is no less difficult, involving a process of multiple-source record linkage between poor law records and family reconstitution data. This procedure, as we have seen in previous chapters, generates its own problems and vastly increases the time scale of a local study.[14]

These problems can be overplayed, and the real reason why eighteenth-century poor law accounts have been so little mined is the small return that one seems to obtain for so much effort. Another small-scale local study to confirm or to slightly modify what aggregate statistics already make plain is a considerable disincentive. Yet, some of the more detailed studies which are available to us do more than simply confirm what is already accepted for the south and east. Neuman's study of selected Berkshire parishes, for instance, suggests no simple or inevitable link between low wages, the practice of family and wage support allowances and male-dominated local relief lists. In Bradfield by the early nineteenth century less than 20 per cent of pensioners were males (let alone able-bodied males) and only eight of the thirty-nine people who received irregular relief appear to have been able-bodied men. More widely, Neuman concludes that what is remarkable about 'Speenham-land parishes' in general is not how many able-bodied males there were on the relief lists, but how few.[15] Such perspectives contrast markedly with those offered by Dunkley. Mary Fissell's study of the parishes of Abson and Wick near Bristol also offers an interesting perspective on eighteenth-century welfare. In these two rural parishes around one-quarter of the population could expect to come into contact with the poor law at some stage of the life cycle, similar to the figures suggested by detailed seventeenth-century studies but somewhat lower than the estimates offered in the previous two chapters. However, those who lacked kin (by virtue of in-migration or the out-migration or death of relatives) were disproportionately likely to resort to the community and to be paid more when they did so by what Fissell labels a 'flexible and transparent' poor law system. The simple facts that wages were low and family economies increasingly one-dimensional thus do not in them-selves act as predictors of poverty and dependency as some commenta-tors have assumed.[16]

Against this backdrop, the recent work of welfare historians who have begun to reverse the failure to engage with local eighteenth- and nineteenth-century poor law records deserves detailed analysis. The first results of a large-scale study to link family reconstitution results with poor law records conducted by Richard Adair and Richard Smith are particularly instructive, as we have already seen in chapter three.[17] This work, focusing mainly on the elderly, suggests that at the turn of the eighteenth century the south and east had a poor law system that was both wide in scope and relatively generous. The majority of all old people over the age of 70, and a substantial number of those aged between 65 and 69 (particularly women who appear to have come to the relief system earlier in the life course and stayed within the remit of the relief system for longer than men), received poor law pensions. Along with extra payments at need these pensions gave some of the elderly an income similar to male day wages in agriculture. In turn, the number of elderly pensioners was considerably out of line with the importance of the aged in the wider southern and eastern populations considered. This, and the fact that the elderly accrued around two-fifths of all poor law pension resources, suggests a bias towards relieving the old. In late seventeenth-century Whitchurch, Oxfordshire, almost half of those aged over 60 received a pension before death, comparable levels to those traced by Thomson for Bedfordshire in the 1840s. The average size of the Whitchurch pension during the same period was 1s. 4d. per week, but this general statistic masks the fact that pensions tended to go up with age and time on relief to account for gradual incapacity and growing ill-health. Indeed, Smith suggests that 'by the end of the seventeenth century there had emerged a detectable sentiment that the elderly were entitled to communal support'.[18]

This is powerful imagery, and if anything the period up to 1750 saw a consolidation of this sentiment. The nominal value of pensions in the small number of parishes representing the south and east grew significantly over time, and their real value also increased as prices were stagnant or even fell. For the elderly poor this was their 'golden age' and they accrued one-half of all poor law pension resources. The later eighteenth century was to see reversals. While mean pensions in southern and eastern communities had reached between 1s. and 6d. and 1s. 8d. by the 1760s, thereafter rates stagnated or even fell despite a significant rise in prices. Moreover, the proportion of communal welfare resources accruing to old people collectively declined. Smith warns that these trends might be illusory, the effect of parishes increasingly taking the neediest old people into workhouses and hence no longer paying them large pensions. However, the 1760s has long held a significance in welfare historiography, and it is surely important that both the number of male pensioners and the percentage of resources accruing to them rose over the later eighteenth century in Smith's data.[19] Rising numbers of male pensioners against the backcloth of static pension resources might be read as suggesting a real shift in the focus of relief to married men (as Dunkley contended), and a change in the role of poor relief from *the* central plank of the welfare patchwork assembled by the impotent poor to a *supplementary* component of the welfare patchwork assembled by working families and represented in the relief lists by male householders. Of course, this is only one of a number of potential interpretations, but the Enfield vestry was acutely aware of the changing composition of the pauper host and its significance, concluding in 1806 that,

> It cannot be thought right so to feed . . . the poor at the expense of the parish as to hold out a perpetual premium and reward to the idleness and improvidence of the labouring class . . . a constant source of indignant mortification to all who have the honest pride of independence to see those who have become paupers by . . . their own vices living in luxury compared with their own far earned with the sweat of their brows.[20]

These are important perspectives based upon good empirical evidence of the sort which is so often missing from the current debate over the role and character of communal welfare. They suggest clearly the safety-net role that the English poor laws may have played in the population as a whole before 1800. Yet, they are not uncontested conclusions. Susannah Ottoway, for instance, links full or partial reconstitution data to poor law accounts for eighteenth-century Terling (Essex) and Puddletown (Dorset) to show that the role of the poor law in the welfare patchwork of the elderly *increased* over the period 1700 to 1800 as a whole. In Terling some 10 per cent of old people were dependent on the poor law in 1700, rising to 32 per cent in the 1750s. This figure had almost halved by 1790, but by 1800 some 32 per cent of all elderly people were in contact with the communal welfare system. For Puddletown the rise was more consistent. Just under one-fifth of old people were on the poor law in 1700 and this proportion had risen to over 50 per cent by the late eighteenth century before falling back in the face of the problems of the 1790s. Moreover, while mean pension levels as a whole could often experience considerable periods of stagnation, the pensions of the elderly in Puddletown seem to have increased significantly during the later eighteenth century and in Terling from 1790. The share of the elderly in total relief expenditure remained roughly stable at between 25 and 33 per cent over the century as a whole. Such observations start to suggest potential sub-regional divisions which are explored in more depth in chapter nine

There are important differences between these findings and those of Smith. Dependency levels amongst the elderly were significantly lower in Terling and Puddletown at all points of the eighteenth century than in, say, Whitchurch. And while the place of the elderly poor in the concerns of poor law administrators appears to have been usurped over the course of the eighteenth century by other groups of the poor and marginal in some parts of the south and east, the same does not appear to be true in these communities. That said, even at the peak of their importance, the elderly poor in Terling and Puddletown accrued a smaller percentage of poor law resources than elderly paupers in Whitchurch. Ottoway also offers a very different gloss on pension values, noting that while inflation did eat away at the contribution of the poor law to the welfare of the old when measured against average wages it is important to realise that pensions given to the elderly were generally aimed at their sole use or just the support of a spouse, so that their real value may not have declined as fast as the value of daily wages (which were also stagnant but aimed at family subsistence) in the late eighteenth century. In other words, poor law recipients may actually have become better off.[21]

Differences of emphasis should not surprise us in a poor law system where 'rampant individualism remained the chief character of poor relief'.[22] Indeed, we can learn much that is relevant to the wider debate over the role and character of the poor law from an emerging literature on the relationship between old age and relief. Even amongst the group theoretically most vulnerable to poverty – the elderly – at best only a bare majority received help from the poor law in any of these southern and eastern communities. And while that help could at times be generous there is at least some evidence that old people would by and large have had to supplement their allowances with what Ottoway labels 'self-help'. If this was the case with the elderly, then presumably it was even more so for other groups of regular and casual paupers. Such conclusions provide support for those commentators, encountered in chapter three, who suggest that the poor law was a *welfare safety net* even if one which was capable of both generous and flexible treatment for those genuinely in need. The extent of that safety net must necessarily have widened over the course of the eighteenth century, for the corollary of stagnating or declining help for the elderly against the backdrop of vigorously rising 'real' poor relief bills of the sort outlined in chapter four was more extensive or perhaps more generous aid to other groups of the poor.

The fact of these differences of interpretation is testimony to how little detailed research there has been on the welfare experiences of groups like the able-bodied or the elderly poor. While this situation is now being remedied, it is still true that our characterisation of the old poor law in the south and east collectively depends on detailed published studies of less than twenty communities. Larger-scale studies of counties such as Oxfordshire and Devon provide important overviews, but we are still a long way from being able to draw out definitive spatial patterns. For this reason, the chapter will deal with welfare under the old poor law at the level of the macro-region as a whole, while chapter nine offers more detail on potential sub-regional divisions. Meanwhile, the lack of research on the detailed operation of the poor law is more than matched by our ignorance of alternative welfare networks in the south and east. While it is generally assumed, as chapter five suggested, that alternative welfare avenues in the south and east withered as charity dried up, rural industry declined under the impetus of regional comparative advantage and commons and wastes were eaten up by parliamentary and agreed enclosure, we have already seen that the majority of those who received poor relief, and perhaps even a majority of those who were given pensions, could not have survived by relief alone. Alternative welfare avenues must have been alive and well, and yet they are almost completely ignored by welfare historians.[23] To consider the

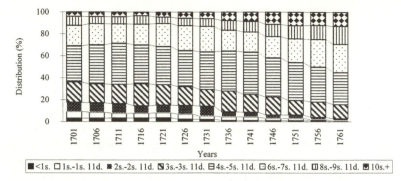

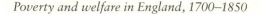

Figure 6.1 The distribution of monthly pensions in fourteen parishes, 1701–61

role and character of the communal welfare system within this general framework of uncertain knowledge, let us start with the vexed, though ultimately crude, question of the generosity of the southern and eastern poor law.

The southern and eastern old poor law, 1700–1820: how generous?[24]

Chapter three considered in some depth the theoretical and practical problems inherent in using the concept of 'generosity' as an umbrella to consider the nature of poor law allowances. Bearing these complications in mind, figure 6.1 represents the scale and distribution of nominal monthly outdoor pension payments in fourteen rural southern and eastern parishes at indicative dates between 1701 and 1761.[25] The poor law authorities in these towns and parishes were clearly willing and able to dispense substantial pensions. In Farthinghoe, Widow Cross and her four children were given a pension of 16s. per month in 1721, while in Charing the biggest pension was 19s. per month given over a seven-month period. In fact the top 10 per cent of individual recipients over all fourteen places appear to have accrued just under 23 per cent of poor law pension resources, and at the level of individual parishes pauper burials or the problem of (expensive) lunatic paupers had the power to fundamentally skew resource distribution to an even smaller minority of welfare recipients in some years. At any one time, however, the majority of pensions were well under these top levels, with the mean for all fourteen parishes over the period as a whole at 6s. 6d. per month and the modal pension at 4s. 7d. per month. The skewed nature of payments and the magnitude of these allowances have considerable resonance in the work of Smith. So do trends in mean payments. There was a clear

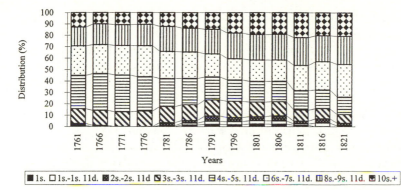

Years

1s. □ 1s.-1s. 11d. 2s.-2s. 11d. 3s.-3s. 11d. 4s.-5s. 11d. □ 6s.-7s. 11d. 8s.-9s. 11d. 10s.+

Figure 6.2 The distribution of pension payments in fourteen parishes, 1761–1821

uprating of poor law pensions over time, and most notably from the 1720s as the number and the value of the smallest strata of poor law pensions fell away and those people receiving more than 2s. per week increased commensurately. Indeed, by the quinquennium 1756–61 the average weekly pension had risen to 1s. 6d. The rise would have been even more noticeable had it not been for periodic economy drives which resulted in the expulsion of pensioners from the claimants list and the reduction of some of the pensions of those who remained.

These absolute figures and trends should not surprise us. Even in 1710 the mean pension payment for Eaton Socon was 5s. per month and Emmison thought that pensions represented the outcome of detailed and sensitive consideration of the needs and family circumstances of the paupers.[26] We might question this rosy picture of flexibility and sensitivity on the part of poor law administrators in the current sample but the point is that pension payments *were* relatively widely distributed around the mean and that pensions of 5–8s. per month *were* relatively common features of the more general relief landscape outside of Eaton Socon. Thus, Hampson suggests that pensions of between 1s. 6d. and 2s. per week were usual in Cambridgeshire before 1750, exactly the same figure as Marshall styled 'normal' for the south prior to 1760.[27]

Figure 6.2 takes the analysis forward, using payment histories from fourteen parishes between 1761 and 1821 (the run-up to the new poor law is considered in chapter eight) to construct a similar distribution of nominal payments.[28] Again, the overseers were willing and able to offer very considerable pensions to some people. Widow Hall of Bluntisham was paid a mean pension of 21s. per month between 1799 and 1801,

James Hall of Charing was given a regular monthly pension of 26s. per month for the first six years of the nineteenth century, and in Duston during the 1770s four pensioners were paid more than 22s. per month. However, there was a fall in the percentage of resources accruing to the top 10 per cent of recipients. More widely, the uprating of pensions clearly visible in the last years of the period 1701–61 stabilised during the 1760s and 1770s when a mean pension of 1s. 8d. per week appears to have been the norm in most parishes. Between 1781 and the early nineteenth century the number of modest pension payments increased noticeably in the face of rising prices and labour oversupply, but the mean weekly pension also experienced a sustained rise, reaching 2s. 4d. by 1821.

Clearly, poor law administrators adopted a three-strand approach to meeting the substantial economic pressures building up from the 1780s, granting more small pensions, uprating the top pensions and pushing more pensioners into higher pension brackets. Again, the mean figures would have been somewhat higher had it not been for increasingly frequent attempts to cut back the size and cost of the pension list in response to spiralling relief bills from the 1780s. In turn, these broad aggregate figures mask some important inter-community differences, more so than in the period up to 1761. In Paxton between 1809 and 1811, for instance, there were an average of twelve pensioners per year and the mean pension was over 3s. per week. In Farthinghoe, there were an average of eight outdoor pensioners at the same date and the mean pension was just 1s. 9d. per week. However, the trends were uniform if the magnitudes were different.

On one level the idea that pensions were relatively buoyant and rising should not surprise us. Snell believed the representative poor law pension in the south and east during the late eighteenth and early nineteenth centuries to be between 2s. 6d. and 3s. per week, while in both Cambridgeshire and Hertfordshire mean pensions of 2–3s. per week seem to have been common by the early nineteenth century.[29] Indeed, Marshall claimed that 'anything under 1/6 or 1/ in the south and midlands must have been very much in the nature of mockery'.[30] Mean pension payments in communities to the north of London also seem to have fallen with the 2–3s. range by 1800, and Ottoway traces a very significant rise in pensions in Puddletown from the 1s. 3d. average up to 1770 to an average of 2s. 3d. in the decade 1790–1800. Yet, the picture is clearly a complex one. Smith's analysis suggests that in late eighteenth-century Whitchurch, the mean pension fell, while in Eaton Socon the payment of wage subsidies to dozens of able-bodied males from at least the 1790s encouraged the payment of standard doles and a contraction of the range of relief payments. In Kent, Barker-Read also suggests a late eighteenth-century stagnation of pension levels.[31]

We still lack sufficient examples to draw sub-regional patterns, but it is clear that by the later eighteenth century there were two distinct relief strategies being employed in the south and the east as it is defined here. In some places, pensions grew strongly in both number and magnitude, while in others they may have grown in number but stagnated in value. The difference of experience was not simply linked to the granting of family or wage allowances, or to any distinction between urban hinterland, pastoral and arable areas, but may have been related to the fact that rising relief bills ran ahead of the greater ability (or perhaps more likely given the conclusions drawn in chapter five, the willingness) of local ratepayers to finance relief in some communities compared to others. Alternatively, the differences may be entirely spurious, a function, as Smith suggests, of different institutional provision in different communities and counties, or they may simply reflect the peculiar short-term situation of the parishes concerned. Perhaps we might also add another potential explanation, with kin-rich communities paying less to fewer people than kin-poor communities. The importance of kinship is explored later in this chapter. Meanwhile, all of this is speculation, but it highlights keenly the need for more work on the nature of the parish pension in the late eighteenth century.

For now, the key question is when (if ever) was the poor law pension in these southern and eastern parishes 'generous', and when was it not? On the face of it the answer is simple, as chapter three began to suggest – the real value of pensions was potentially highest before 1760. If we assume a monthly wage of 26s. for the decade 1730–40, then the mean monthly relief totals drawn from figure 6.1 at the same date would suggest that pensions in isolation provided around 25–30 per cent of the male wage. The top pensions would provide a considerably higher proportion. Allowing for Ottoway's suggestion that pensions were often meant to support individuals rather than families would clearly reinforce the idea that the old poor law in the south was 'generous' in the early eighteenth century. Moreover, since pensions were improving in this period but wages were static and prices falling, it is likely that pensions came to look even more generous by the 1740s and 1750s. And as we have seen previously, this eighteenth-century experience seems to have been based upon a rising trend coming out of the seventeenth century suggesting an ever more central welfare role for the poor law. Not everyone agrees. Hampson concludes that 'The sum of 2s. 6d.

allowed to a blind man by the parish of Histon in 1740 could largely have supported him . . . but the grants of 1s., 1s. 6d. and 2s. made at the same time to various other men must clearly have been insufficient . . . Here in essence therefore was the system of supplementary wage subsidy.'[32] As Ottoway and Thane remind us, the role of the poor law may never have been more than to provide a contribution to welfare, even in the south, but this is an interesting example of how subjective the issue of 'generosity' really is.

Paradoxically, for much of the later eighteenth and early nineteenth centuries the pension may have come to represent a higher proportion of the weekly male wage (pensions rose but the wages of labourers in much of the arable south were static at less than 8s. per week measured over the whole year until after 1801) at the same time as inflation eroded what it could buy. Notwithstanding substantial nominal percentage increases in pensions in the sample of later eighteenth-century parishes, it is clear that inflation increased somewhat faster. On the face of it, then, the relief system might look less generous, as Smith suggested was the case. However, this conflicts with much contemporary public opinion which rued the profligacy of the communal welfare system, and if true must suggest that there was a considerable 'bounce-back' in the nominal value of pensions after the Napoleonic Wars in counties such as Bedfordshire. To some extent a 'bounce-back' can be seen in figure 6.2, but there are several difficulties of interpretation which must be confronted before we can accept that the pension was less valuable after 1770.

1 There is a danger of concentrating too firmly on the size of pension payments in assessing the utility of the parish payment system. Payment *regularity* had a value quite apart from the size of the pension. Wage earning became an increasingly uncertain thing as traditional seasonal underemployment patterns were interspersed with bouts of unemployment generated by increasing labour efficiency, immobility and the decline of female rural occupations from the later eighteenth century. A cursory look at most rural wage books after 1780 demonstrates keenly that wage earning often could not generate stable weekly or monthly income. Wage earners might thus become enmeshed in a cycle of credit and rent arrears in which their creditors would be likely to sell them up in the knowledge that there was no guarantee of future income. For poor pensioners, even if their pensions in isolation were inadequate and their real values declining, their income was at least regular and certain. If we discount periodic and short-lived assaults on the relief lists at times of spiralling cost, for this sample of communities it is clear that

pension adjustments in a downward direction were relatively rare and that the income of pensioners was relatively steady. The poor law might thus act as a notional guarantor in the eyes of creditors and potential creditors. It is no accident, as we will see below, that the poor law pays off debts and rent arrears in southern rural parishes in this lender of last resort function. We should not, then, assume that the mere fact that pensions were eroded by inflation meant that they were not actually and symbolically generous.

2 There is also a danger that we might regard pensions with a short-termism that was not apparent at the time. For all of the southern and eastern communities considered here, once someone was granted a pension, they tended to keep it for a considerable length of time and, whatever the nominal value, this had considerable utility when bargaining for credit or negotiating with children for co-residence. For the Kent parish of Headcorn, the overseer recorded both the family circumstances of those in receipt of pensions and the length of time the pension had been paid. Durations of between two and twenty-seven years were recorded, and by the early nineteenth century the average duration of a pension was seven years.[33] In the parishes used here the average duration of a pension was five years for men and eight years for women, and in common with most other studies there was a clear tendency for pension values to rise with age/time on relief.

3 Knowing about the size and duration of pensions is only part of the process of understanding and characterising the generosity of communal welfare. We also need to know what proportion of total payments were directed towards regular pensions and what proportion of those who were regular pensioners also received non-pension help. In short, we need to know about the 'total welfare' package.

Figures 6.3. to 6.5 begin to untangle this complex web for the eighteenth and early nineteenth centuries. Figure 6.3 traces the proportion of poor law resources devoted to pensions, irregular relief in cash and irregular relief in kind for parishes where the information can be traced relatively consistently.[34] Notwithstanding periodic economy drives in individual parishes, and more concerted economy drives from the 1780s, it is clear that the share of pensions in total poor law resources increased slightly during the four decades up to the 1770s, reaching a peak in 1770 when 64 per cent of resources were devoted to this form of relief. Thereafter, these gains were subjected to considerable pressure as the frequency and magnitude of irregular monetary and kind payments outstripped rising numbers of pensions and rising mean pension values. By 1801 only around one-half of communal welfare resources were

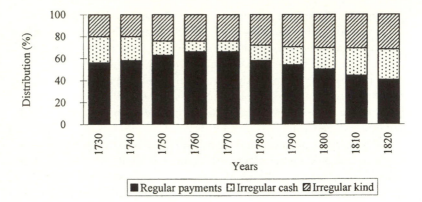

Figure 6.3 The distribution of poor law resources between different types of payment, 1730–1820

devoted to pensions, and this figure was to decline consistently thereafter. Neither the magnitudes nor the trends detected here are out of line with experiences in other places. The Cambridgeshire parish of Linton had channelled one-third of its poor law expenditure to irregular payments in cash and kind in 1731, and this had risen to 42 per cent by 1781 and 51 per cent by 1804.[35] By 1772, only 57 per cent of communal resources in Barking were devoted to pensions.[36] The underlying data showed little by way of meaningful spatial patterns, though this is perhaps not surprising given the experience in the parish of Wychwood where even two adjacent townships (Shipton and Leafield) might spend radically different proportions of communal resources on their pensioners (76 and 55 per cent respectively).[37]

The corollary of declining pension support was more allowances in cash[38] and kind, with the inexorable rise in the proportion of relief paid in kind in particular a reflection of the fact that the poor law in the south and east came to pay for a greater and greater range of goods and services as the wider consumer revolution in this region dragged up acceptable basic standards of life. The review of pauper inventories from Essex in chapter four demonstrated this point forcefully. Figures 6.4 and 6.5 disaggregate the figures for irregular money and kind payments. Reading the two charts together, there is a clear and growing focus on medical and medical related payments, as Williams has suggested for other parishes in the south and east. If we define 'medical relief' to include costs of burial and the costs of nursing, extra food and fuel, and subscriptions to doctors and medical institutions, then just

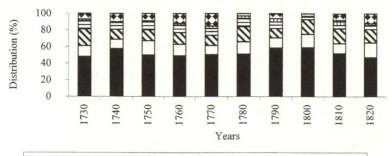

Figure 6.4 The distribution of irregular payments in cash, 1730–1820

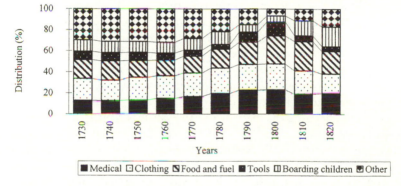

Figure 6.5 The distribution of irregular payments in kind, 1730–1820

under 25 per cent of all irregular payments (whether cash or kind) were linked to medical problems. Similar proportions have been observed in other studies, which also point to a wide variety of medical support. Shipton-under-Wychwood, for instance, sent two of its paupers all the way to Bath for the water treatment, and in large part this helps to explain why 51.7 per cent of its expenditure in kind between 1740 and 1762 was directed towards medical relief.[39] The Enfield vestry purchased a second-hand false leg for one of its paupers, with the vendor noting 'the leg has been worn but little and better than new'.[40] Such expenditure does much to confirm Thomas's view that parishes gave 'sympathetic and humane consideration' to the sick poor, which even extended to their subscribing to hospitals such as the John Radcliffe.[41] This said, medical relief could also act as a cross-subsidy. The Wimbledon vestry in 1751 directed that,

If any pension poor are hearty and able to nurse such as are sick and they refuse when ordered by the officers they shall have their pension taken off. Wid Greenfield allowed 1/6 per week pension for one month on condition she can be serviceable to any poor when sick and if she is attentive to the satisfaction of the officers she shall then be allowed 2/ per week pension during that time.[42]

More widely, overseers were willing to pay rents, buy and distribute food and coals or wood, pay off the debts of paupers and even to pay for paupers to visit relatives at times of dire family need. Above all, they were willing to expend considerable amounts on replacing and repairing clothing, both because paupers tended to be badly clothed when they came to the poor law and because, as chapter five argued, clothing was a visible sign of poverty and of how well the parish cared for its poor. Much historiography covers this issue casually if at all, suggesting that buying second-hand or poor-quality cloth and clothing was the norm. In practice however, clothing could absorb a significant amount of poor law resources, and there is considerable evidence that overseers devoted time and money to obtaining good-quality and sometimes fashionable clothing. In Enfield, clothing cost an average 30s. per adult pauper per year, and in so far as we can calculate an 'average outfit' from the data underlying this part of the analysis it is clear that a figure of 40s. per year was normal. Such figures were considerably more than the average labouring family would have spent on clothing. The vestry at Bluntisham in 1801 approved an order for the overseer to buy William Grounds '2 shirts, a waistcoat lined with flannel and flannel sleeves', and the workhouse master was obliged to agree to the oiling of the shoes of paupers, suggesting that they were of sufficient quality to warrant oiling in the first place.[43] Such clothing certainly had monetary as well as symbolic value – many parish poor law archives contain instances of paupers who had sold or pawned the clothing that they received from the poor law.

Looking at the complete range of welfare payments, then, can we say that the communal relief system in the south and east was generous to individuals? This is crudely put, and we should beware once more of the loaded nature of terminology such as 'generous' or 'not generous'. Large money allowances could be given because the poor law was benevolent and saw it as its duty to maintain a basic acceptable living standard amongst the poor; equally, large money allowances could be given because the poor law simply had no choice in the light of endemic poverty and a limited economy of makeshifts. In both cases the money relief might appear 'generous' but only in the first case was the poor law also benevolent. Against this backdrop it is possible to see three 'types' of poor people and three types of treatment in the underlying records. There were the casual poor who were given occasional doles or longer runs of help because of things like sickness. Their increasing number and the increasing value of payment to them (the mean one-off casual payment had reached over 2s. 4d. by 1801) may explain why the top ten recipients accrue a progressively smaller percentage of poor law resources after 1760 in the sample of communities used earlier. These were the *sometimes poor* of chapter five, and the poor law in the south and east appears to have treated them both generously and benevolently. We can also discern the intermittent and *often* poor, whose occasional casual relief fed through into periodic pensions and then to full pensions over a long period. It is difficult to objectively trace the generosity of their treatment given the length of the periods involved. And then there were the long-term pensioners, the *chronically poor*, many of whom, as Ottoway observes, would only leave the pension list in a coffin. For them, focusing on the pensions is clearly not enough. They would receive help with their rent and medical expenses, occasional food and fuel, and a constant supply of new and mended clothing. They might also have tools purchased for them so that they could make part of their own living. Indeed, pensions were systematically supplemented by between 15–30 per cent (depending on place and period) as a result of the ability of pensioners to call upon the overseers at times of additional need.[44] Thus, while the number of casual paupers and payments to them increased consistently from the 1780s, the proportion of *total* poor law spending accruing to pensioners of all ages fell only slightly during the course of the eighteenth century, reaching 61 per cent by 1790. Only from 1800 was the intricate connection between parish relief and the parish pensioner truly undermined, and it is thus no surprise to see poor relief bills rocketing in this collection of communities from the 1780s. On balance, then, the southern and eastern poor law probably was 'generous'. What is more, it is probably correct to style it as 'benevolent' as well. As we will see in chapter seven, this question of sentiment is an important one.

The question of generosity and sentiment at the level of individual paupers is, however, just one part of the problem of understanding the role and character of the communal relief system in the east and the south. How many poor people were in contact with the relief system? What were the characteristics of those receiving communal benefits? What happened to those who did not want, apply for or get such benefits? These questions are the focus of the later parts of this chapter.

For now, though, it is important to remember that characterising the poor law as generous or not generous, humane or not humane, is only partly a function of looking at outdoor relief lists. We also need to investigate the treatment of the institutional poor.

Institutional care

Initially, it is important to realise that there were important sub-regional differences in the incidence of workhouses and the duration of their use. For some counties, the flirtation with workhouses was insubstantial and brief. In Cambridgeshire, a number of large urban workhouses were built in the 1760s, but in 1776 just fourteen rural parishes had workhouse provision within their own boundaries. Even by 1804 this had risen only to eighteen workhouses serving 127 rural parishes, though it is important to acknowledge that some parishes contracted with workhouses elsewhere to meet their needs.[45] Similarly, there was no extensive workhouse system in Berkshire or Oxfordshire. Indeed, as late as 1815 only 20 per cent of Berkshire parishes had access to a workhouse, their own or that of another parish, while in Oxfordshire at the same date only just over 10 per cent had direct workhouse provision. In other counties, however, workhouses were more numerous. By 1803 even small Huntingdonshire parishes like Earith owned a workhouse alongside the more ubiquitous poorhouses.[46] In Essex, there were 182 workhouse or workhouse-type institutions in existence by 1815, comprising roughly half of all Essex parishes. Meanwhile, in Kent and to a lesser degree in places such as Norfolk, Suffolk, Devon and Sussex, the workhouse was also an integral part of ordinary poor relief and welfare structures. In 1776/77 Kent had 132 workhouses taking 5,799 people.[47] Thereafter the county was to obtain twelve Gilbert unions incorporating almost one-quarter of Kent parishes, and thereby a substantial addition to the workhouse stock. Not all workhouses were functional of course. Many were ramshackle buildings with a tiny and underused capacity. Indeed, the mean capacity in 1776 was less than fifty paupers. Other workhouses, however, were on a much larger scale. The workhouse at Soham in Cambridgeshire could take 200 paupers, while that at Charing in Kent could take 210. The net effect of this patchwork of provision was that in 1803 some 11 per cent of those relieved in the south and east as it is defined here were relieved in an institutional context, rising to 18 per cent by 1813.[48]

The numbers were significant, then, and we must look at the treatment of the institutional poor. However, there are also technical reasons to devote attention to this group. As we saw earlier, Smith has suggested that some of the stagnation in the real value of pensions which might be observed in some southern parishes could be explained by a transfer of the most expensive paupers to the less visible institutional context. Potentially more important, the building of a workhouse also seems to be strongly associated in most places with an upsurge of settlement and removal activity, so that if problem pensioners were not put into the workhouse, they might still disappear from the pension lists by virtue of forced removal. Moreover, whether the most expensive paupers were put into the workhouse or not, a second issue that we must address is the degree to which the institutional poor were a class apart. If paupers could move more or less seamlessly between outdoor and indoor relief, then outdoor relief lists provide a good vehicle for looking at local welfare and characterising the poor law. If, however, the institutional poor were a distinct group, whatever their underlying characteristics their presence undermines the utility of outdoor relief lists of the sort which underpin most local poor law analysis.

Table 6.1 The percentage of the institutional poor in three parishes in various age ranges, 1795–1807

Place	*0–9 yrs*	*10–19 yrs*	*20–39 yrs*	*40–49 yrs*	*50–59 yrs*	*60+ yrs*
Kettering	16	20	18	12	10	22
Farthinghoe	21	20	14	7	14	24
Charing	20	18	12	9	15	26

Notes The ages of nine paupers in the Kettering workhouse were unknown.

With these questions in mind, let us look briefly at some workhouse populations. Table 6.1 records the age distribution of paupers in three workhouses during the late eighteenth and early nineteenth centuries.[49] Clearly, the old and children (most of those in the age group 10–19 were not even teenagers) dominated these workhouse institutions. This is not unexpected. Orphans and other children would often spend time in the workhouse prior to being apprenticed, and we can clearly link workhouse inmates in Farthinghoe to subsequent apprenticeship indentures. Moreover the old people here were by and large very old people. In the Kettering workhouse list, five of those assigned to the age bracket 60+ were actually 70 years old and more. In Farthinghoe, three-quarters of those assigned to this category were over 70. There is clearly a case here for supporting Smith's concern that the potentially most expensive paupers were shifted from the outdoor pension list to institutional care, thereby skewing pension magnitudes downwards. Since eleven of the communities used to trace the value of pension payments earlier in the chapter are known to have had either direct workhouse provision or access to workhouses in surrounding parishes this observation can only add to the impression that allowances were 'generous' under the old poor law in the south and east.

How do we characterise the institutional population in more detail, and how were institutional paupers treated? To answer these questions, we can look in more depth at the Kettering workhouse return for 1799. First, the treatment of the institutional poor. The deliberations of the vestry over the standard of food, clothing and bedding for those in the workhouse suggest very strongly a regime of care rather than punishment. To take just one example of many, the vestry resolved on 8 May 1799 that the workhouse main meal was to consist of 'three days meat, three days pudding, and one day stew if it can be procured otherwise pudding'.[50] This dietary was likely to have been considerably better than that purchased by the average labourer in work and not on relief during the 1790s. Moreover, we should also bear in mind that at well as their board and lodging the poor of the workhouse in Kettering (in return for work where possible) were given weekly cash doles of 2–3s. per week, roughly escalating with age. In short, Kettering devoted considerable resources to the care of the institutionalised poor. This did not mean that standards were consistently good or that the instructions of the vestry were followed. In 1818, a survey of the workhouse found signs of squalor:

> On examination of the sleeping rooms and the bedding the committee find that a considerable quantity of new beds are absolutely necessary – the total number is 48 and as at present there are 95 persons in the house – a very great proportion of the beds are in a very bad state . . . . The master of the workhouse has made a very proper division of the rooms for the separate accommodation of the men, women and children. The sleeping rooms of the latter are clean, wholesome and airy, but those of the men are confined, close and exceedingly unwholesome.[51]

The important thing, however, is that the vestry were quick to follow the directions of the report and instituted new procedures for managing and inspecting the workhouse. This really was an institution of care.

So, what of the character of the institutional poor? The problems of rapidly rising food prices, structural decline of the wool industry and stagnant demand for shoes which took up so much of the time of the vestry in the 1790s are clearly visible in the composition of the institutional poor in Kettering. John Cornfield Junior and Senior were shoemakers, while Robert Stowe was a woollen-weaver. Why able-bodied men like this ended up in the workhouse rather than on outdoor relief as did many of their fellow workers is difficult to understand, but their presence means that the sex distribution of the Kettering workhouse list was roughly even while in workhouse lists for most other places there is a female bias. However, the essential characteristics of the inmates of Kettering workhouse might be taken to represent workhouse populations throughout the south and east at the end of the eighteenth century. Thus, as table 6.1 suggests, a large proportion of inmates were aged or children. Of those people within what one might label the working age groups, four were insane and at least one was afflicted with venereal disease. Clearly, the workhouse was primarily a receptacle for the old and the sick. In this sense, the institutional poor may have looked different from the people on outdoor relief lists only by degree rather than order. Of course this is a difficult conclusion to test. In Kettering and most other places the detail given in workhouse lists is much more substantial than the simple lists of names that constitute the average outdoor relief schedule. What we can do, however, is to contrast the character of workhouse inmates with the character of those who lived in the town poorhouses. A list of 1823[52] details the inhabitants of twenty-four parish houses. If we assume that those who are named as single people (the list appears to say when there was more than one person to a house) were old, then we can see that 9 of the occupants were old, 5 were widows or single people and 11 were families overcharged with children. The difference from the workhouse list of 1799 is clear, but even at this late date over one-half of all of those poor enough to be eligible for parish housing were the traditional life-cycle poor. In Farthinghoe too, there is considerable evidence to suggest that the basic characteristics of the outdoor and indoor paupers were the same. Here, 84-year-old James Powell was relieved with an outdoor pension while his 74-year-old brother was in the workhouse!

Meanwhile, the Kettering data also suggest that going into the workhouse was not a once and for all event. The workhouse list records the deaths of four aged paupers – Jos Marriott (78), John Rowell (66), Frances Althorp (73) and Thomas Smith's wife (71) – suggesting that the old people who were institutionalised had been brought to the workhouse for a reason, probably because they were sick and disabled and near death. In this sense, their tenure on institutional provision was a permanent one, but perhaps not long-term. Other paupers appear to have come and gone. Ann Dorr (22) left the workhouse in September 1799 and her sister Rebecca (20) left at the same time. Mary Mace stayed in the workhouse only one month, while Ann Smith was admitted to the workhouse for as long as it took to cure her of venereal disease. Of the fourteen children of apprenticeable age in 1799, seven of them were to leave the workhouse within two years under the parish apprenticeship scheme. Indeed, perhaps the only permanent and long-term residents of the workhouse were the four insane paupers, whose treatment obliged the vestry to buy manacles and to equip a special room of the workhouse. There is substantial support for the idea that fluid workhouse populations were a more general feature of the welfare landscape. In Wimbledon, for instance, the vestry bargained with those overburdened with children to take the children into the workhouse and support them (with a contribution from the parents) but to leave the parents outside.[53] In Ashwell, the workhouse nominally contained nineteen paupers, but in practice they lived in their own homes and came to this central place to undertake work in return for relief.

This has been a brief discussion, and one which has ignored the great urban workhouses of eighteenth- and nineteenth-century England. However, the Kettering material confirms that southern and eastern outdoor relief lists are a reliable tool for characterising the generosity and humanity of the communal welfare system. Workhouse populations were generally relatively small-scale and if they differed from those on outdoor relief, it was probably by a matter of degree rather than order. More importantly, while some workhouses were tumble-down affairs and represent the conscious repression of paupers, it seems clear that by the later eighteenth century workhouses were part and parcel of the characterisation of the southern and eastern poor law as a relatively flexible and humane institution.

The southern and eastern old poor law, 1700–1820: who was relieved?

To step further than these broad conclusions, we need to know more about the number and characteristics of the poor. Figure 6.6 traces the total numbers on relief (indoor and outdoor) in the sample of parishes from the later eighteenth century used earlier in this chapter. In common with most other places, there was a substantial rise in the total number of people relieved, with those relieved for less than six months outstripping the rise in the number of pensioners.[54] If we make a notional allowance for the families of those recorded in this chart, then by 1810 up to 40 per cent of the collective population of these communities had some contact with the relief system. Chapter five suggested that levels of 'background poverty' were likely to have been somewhat

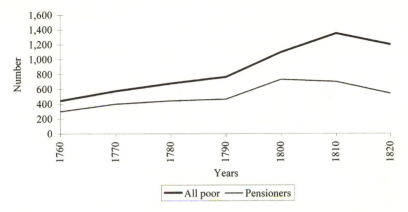

Figure 6.6 Growth in the number of pensioners and all paupers, 1760–1820

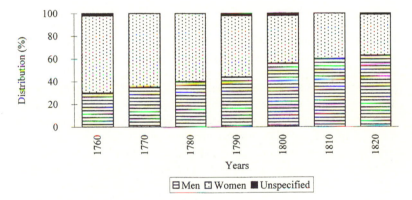

Figure 6.7 The sex distribution of all welfare recipients, 1760–1820

higher than this, but such figures confirm the idea that the southern and eastern poor law did have a relatively wide remit by the later eighteenth and early nineteenth centuries.

Crudely, then, more people were treated more generously. So who were these poor people? The general figures mask some important gender inequalities, as figures 6.7 and 6.8 suggest. On balance, the total recipient list moves from being heavily skewed towards women in 1760, to being heavily skewed towards men in the early nineteenth century. Six of the fourteen communities on whose experiences these figures are based had intermittently operating workhouses with a broadly female

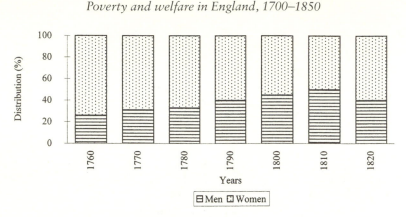

Figure 6.8 The sex distribution of regular pensioners, 1760–1820

inmate population. However, their presence does little to change the impression of the passing of female domination of relief lists.

Such observations fit in well with the views of commentators like Dunkley, who sees the underemployed male and men overburdened with large families coming to dominate the relief list during the so called 'crisis of the old poor law' after 1790. This said, figure 6.8 which traces the gender composition of the pension list in isolation, warns against overgeneralisation. While Smith has detected a sustained decline in the proportion of female pensioners during the later eighteenth century, in these parishes the decline was hardly dramatic. Moreover, if anything there was a resurgence of female pensioners in the nineteenth century. We should not be surprised by these findings. Of the 53 pensioners in Enfield in 1796, just seven were men, let alone able-bodied men.[55] The Wimbledon vestry recorded a consistently female-dominated pension list, as did Barking. It is unwise, therefore, to talk in global terms about a sea change in the composition of the growing body of 'the poor'.

Yet, as figure 6.9 suggests, if we turn away from raw numbers and towards an analysis of the distribution of total resources between different groups of pensioners, the growing importance of men is clearly seen. The fact that women re-establish their numerical position in the relief lists after 1810 does not translate to a similar clawing back of their previous domination of the resources underlying the pension list, even where we make a notional allowance for the likely value of payments to women relieved in an institutional context.

There is clearly something very complicated going on, though it is important not to lose the key point here that the poor law in the south was relieving growing numbers of people with consistently larger

Figure 6.9 The distribution of total pension resources between different groups of pensioners, 1760–1820

nominal payments over the late eighteenth and early nineteenth centuries. What else can we say about the relief recipients? To move further we must link poor relief data with nominal data, and in the absence of the magnificent returns found in places like Ovenden (Halifax) and Erdon (Somerset), this means using family reconstitutions. Figures 6.10–6.12 are thus based upon the links between reconstitution and poor law data in four parishes.[56] In common with the work of Smith, Ottoway and others, not all of those who were poor law recipients, nor even all of those who were pensioners, could be linked here to a demographic life cycle identified in the family reconstitutions. In part this reflects the linkage process. It is by no means clear that family reconstitution as currently practised (and as practised here) accurately identifies all of the life cycles being lived out in an area, or that it does not erroneously conflate life cycles that in reality should be separate.[57] Even if we could rely fully on the process, the fact that parishes even in the south and east were willing to pay out-parish relief to significant numbers of people, some of whom may never have actually been resident in the parish or township, also makes it difficult to achieve comprehensive linkage. Meanwhile, other recipients could be linked only to partial demographic histories as a result of movement into or out of parishes, and where this involves missing baptisms we are unable to obtain definitive age data with which to approach poor law accounts. By implication, our best age data for paupers is that for the least mobile poor, and there is little to suggest either way whether the more mobile poor shared the same characteristics, welfare needs and welfare solutions as their less mobile peers.

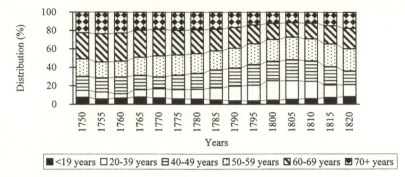

■ <19 years   □ 20-39 years   ⊟ 40-49 years   ▢ 50-59 years   ◪ 60-69 years   ◨ 70+ years

Figure 6.10 The age distribution of total poor law resources, 1750–1820

Linkage problems like these are essentially insoluble, but they do not necessarily detract from our ability to learn much about the role and character of the communal welfare system from this linkage process.[58] Figure 6.10 suggests the age groupings of those on relief (casual and pension) for the period 1750–1820. The focus on older recipients at the mid-eighteenth century is clear. Pensioners who also accrued casual relief in kind or cash are a large part of the explanation for this experience. However, many of the casual poor in these villages were also relatively elderly, with medical relief for old people figuring significantly in the underlying data. The 1780s and 1790s saw important changes in this broad age structure of benefit. Both pension claimants and the casual poor became younger, and this observation applies to men and women equally. The relative importance of the very old was particularly harshly squeezed, though it is possible that some undetected change in the composition of institutional pauperism is at work here.

By 1820 the elderly, and (bearing in mind the lessons to be drawn from figure 6.9) elderly men in particular, were reclaiming their place in the relief landscape. Indeed, the outstanding thing about this chart is the skewing of resources to the elderly when we consider the period as a whole. Of course, such conclusions tell us little without a formal analysis of the prevailing age structure, but a crude estimation from the family reconstitution suggests that while those over 60 constituted around 11 per cent of the background population in these villages this group accrued almost two-fifths of total poor law resources between 1750 and 1820. Moreover, there is little evidence that systematic wage and family subsidies were inexorably drawing ever more men and ever younger men on to the relief lists except in the worst years of agricultural depression such as 1784 or 1796. Figure 6.11 reinforces this picture,

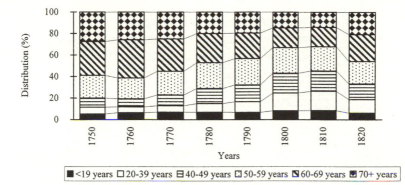

Figure 6.11 The age distribution of pension payments, 1750–1820

demonstrating that while the Napoleonic War period placed a greater emphasis on younger pensioners, the elderly pensioner group reasserted their control over the relief lists by the 1820s.

What lessons can we draw from this series of charts? Peter King claimed that 'By the beginning of the nineteenth century the poor relief system in many parishes can perhaps best be characterised as a rough and ready welfare state in miniature.'[59] The data employed here do not allow us to go so far, but it is nonetheless clear that the southern and eastern poor law did react to changes in the landscape of need and that it did spread its welfare net widely. Moreover, the communal welfare system seems to have been focused particularly on the needs of the elderly for much of the eighteenth and nineteenth centuries. The old, and indeed many of the casual poor who increased in number so rapidly in the later eighteenth century, were also treated with what one might confidently style generosity *and* benevolence. Yet, the picture is more complicated than these simple generalisations allow. In particular, we might make two observations.

The first springs out of figure 6.12, which traces the age at which relief recipients first came into contact with the relief system between 1750 and 1799, distinguishing between those who were kin-rich and those who were kin-poor.[60] Unsurprisingly, there is a broad late middle- and old-age flavour to this chart, but there are also two other characteristics to observe. Thus, of those who were kin-rich 20–25 per cent made their first contact with the relief system before the age of 50. These were a mixture of the chronic life-cycle poor identified in chapter five (who were often rich in kin, also endemically poor), the accidental poor (those, for instance, who were forced by sickness to go to the parish) and

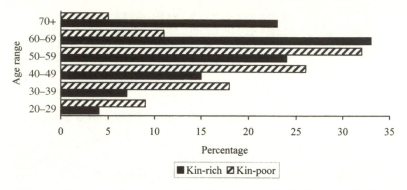

Figure 6.12 Age at first contact with the communal relief systems for the kin-rich and kin-poor

those for whom the poor law intervened early in the descent into poverty in order to keep a material world intact. The more significant group, however, are the kin-poor, who both started relief earlier than those with rich kinship networks on which to draw and tended to stay on relief somewhat longer than the latter group once they had been granted it. If more able-bodied men find their way on to the pension lists over time, it is perhaps less because they were able-bodied than because they were kin-poor.

All of this said, however, the second observation that might be made is that while the communal relief system may have had a wide remit and may have devoted considerable resources to the care of the poor, at no point did the southern and eastern welfare system relieve the majority of the elderly, let alone any other group. Moreover, for most people outside the top 10 per cent of recipients, at no time did the system offer a complete welfare package. It is thus clear that even in the south and east there must have been a range of alternative welfare mechanisms which both kept people off relief and supplemented their income when they did have to turn to the parish. This, albeit too briefly, is the subject of the next section.

Alternative welfare structures

The shape of the wider economy of makeshifts in the south and east is a complex problem. Chapter five suggested convincing reasons to think that the eighteenth century should have seen a progressive narrowing of the life-cycle options for securing alternative welfare avenues. Yet, while it is possible that for some people the total welfare package under the old poor law became more central over time, it was rarely 'enough'. How, then, did the southern and eastern poor 'cope'?

In one sense, the outlines of the alternative welfare patchwork are well known – charity, kinship, taking in lodgers, work, remarriage for widows and widowers, begging, crime and petty dealing were all options open to some southern labouring families. However, finding evidence on these individual strands has often proved problematic, and slotting them together to obtain an overview of the economy of make-shifts for any community has proved impossible in current welfare historiography. This chapter will be able to do little to take the debate forward, but let us consider some of the issues involved.

Figure 6.12 clearly implicated kinship as a major determinant of the timing and scale of relief at individual level, just as Fissell has suggested for Abson and Wick.[61] To use the words of Frank Prochaska, 'running out of relatives was a short cut to the workhouse'.[62] In terms of disjointed and individual instances, it is easy to gain an impression of what having and not having kin meant in the welfare conundrum. Most diary and autobiography writers demonstrate a clear awareness of the value of kin in securing welfare. Indeed, where kinship was not to be found locally or where it did not fulfil an adequate welfare role, it might be manufactured through marriage. The Somerset parson William Holland noted the case of

> Old Savage Ware, past 70, married to Jane Long, about sixty . . . they were married out of the poor house . . . the day afterwards they marched to a house of Ware's at Tyren. Ware, tho old, is a very laborious hearty workman. His children did not behave well to him and so he married.[63]

There is evidence here of both kinship and work as important factors in overall welfare patterns. Nor should we forget that poor law authorities themselves were sometimes eager to bring the kinship network of poor people on board in the relief process. While there has been a tendency in recent literature to downplay the degree to which parishes turned to the law as instituted in 1601 to force kin to look after pauperised relatives, this does not mean that relatives offered no help. Some were unable of course, constrained by their own poverty or life-cycle position, but even the poorest families could offer emotional support if not financial aid. Others might take in pauperised relatives of their own accord or, if they were young single people, stay in the household of a poor relative or parent for much longer than they might otherwise have done. Yet, most support was probably offered with the communal welfare system acting as facilitator. In Ashwell, this facilitation took the form of a visit from the overseer with an order from the vestry to contribute a certain sum every week on pain of distraint of goods. The law of 1601 was not used here, but as we can see there were other means to achieve the same end.[64] In Kettering the facilitation was via a refusal to pay rents. In 1820, the vestry noted:

> It is a common practice with persons who have their rent paid by the parish to allow their grown up sons and daughters to remain with them, paying a very small sum for their board and lodging, and in all such cases the vestry think it only reasonable that by withholding payment of the rents, the children should be compelled to assist the parents.[65]

In most cases, however, the administrators of the local relief system were rather more constructive and conciliatory, as chapter three started to suggest. Thus, it was common to relieve people even if they had kin locally resident, and even if the poor person was actually living with kin members.[66] However, these allowances were rarely anywhere near subsistence-level, obliging kin to give what material help they could. Hollen-Lees portrays perceived obligations in terms of a set of concentric circles, in which the claims of the nuclear family were felt most strongly and the claims of siblings and grandchildren and a range of other distant kin were felt least strongly. This is a convenient way of understanding complex kinship relations, but it does little justice to the help that families offered to a wide range of kin during the eighteenth and nineteenth centuries.[67]

Other aspects of the economy of makeshifts are equally open to general commentary. The poor benefited from periodic collections by parish elites, particularly at times of high unemployment or high food prices. In January 1794 a collection was taken from the leading citizens of Bury St Edmunds, Suffolk, to provide relief for 3,600 poor people. This must be measured against a regular relief list for the same month which contained just 160 names. Between this date and February 1799 a total of £2,400 was raised and distributed, albeit in food rather than money payments. The last distribution, in February 1799, recognised 2,200 poor people, at a time when the poor law was regularly relieving just 159. Given that the relief from such collections lasted for a series of months (between two and three normally) rather than being one-off payments, the contribution to overall welfare may have been significant and the presence of the fund may have helped to keep some people off relief altogether at these times of economic stress. In other words, the sometimes poor may have been under-represented in the poor law accounts of Bury St Edmunds.[68]

However, as Stapleton makes clear, it was formal charitable activity which offered most continuous support, both to those on relief and, more usually, to those seeking to avoid it.[69] The resources of charity in the south and east considered as a whole were considerable, but inequitably distributed on a spatial basis. As Smith makes clear, small rural parishes such as Whitchurch in Oxfordshire had limited or non-existent charitable resources, and this is a feature that might be duplicated across large numbers of the very small parishes in the south and east as it is defined for this book.[70] By contrast, the large urban areas, even if we discount London, could draw upon very substantial accumulated charitable resources. There was also middle ground. By 1710, Enfield had a charitable income from bequests and rents accruing from property purchased with previous benefactions sufficient to maintain its entire poor. Not until 1734 did the needs of poor people outstrip growth in the value of existing charitable resources and their augmentation with new bequests. And not until well into the nineteenth century did charity cease to make a very considerable contribution to keeping people out of the relief system.[71] The eighteenth-century charitable resources of Aynho and Farthinghoe were also substantial, yielding the equivalent of 40 per cent of communal expenditure on poverty before the 1770s, directed primarily at the old and other groups who were at risk of dependence upon the communal welfare system. In general, however, the common theme on the subject of charity in the south and east is the way in which the scale of accumulated charitable resources and new charitable benefactions was far outstripped by the level of background need amongst ordinary labouring people as the eighteenth century progressed. National charity enquiries by Gilbert in 1787 and Brougham in 1817 allow us to take an overview. Thus, where we exclude London and its immediate hinterlands from the analysis, charitable income for the south and east as it is defined here amounted to 45 per cent of total poor law spending in the macro-region at around the same date. By 1817 this figure had fallen to well under 20 per cent, and in the more rural parts of the macro-region, such as Hampshire, Oxfordshire or Norfolk, charitable income made almost no dent in poor law spending by the opening decades of the nineteenth century.

We could turn to other important strands of the economy of makeshifts. Friendly societies, for instance. Nationally, 26,000 friendly societies were enroled after 1793, with a heavy concentration of membership in the industrial districts. Counties such as Hertfordshire, Sussex, Kent and Dorset all had under 5 per cent of their population as friendly-society members, and of those towns with the highest density of friendly-society members per head of population identified by Gorsky, not one falls within the south and east as it is defined here.[72] This is not to say the friendly-society membership was unimportant. Fuller provides evidence that Wiltshire friendly societies paid an average of 7s. per week to their members who were in need during the period between 1770 and 1850, far beyond the resources which they would have been able to obtain via the relief system.[73] The Potters Friendly Society in Dorset likewise paid around 7s. per week to members who were sick.

However, if we accept Gorsky's characterisation of the reasons for the broad spatial discontinuity between the counties of the south and east and those of the north and west, then we can potentially learn much about both the limitations of alternative welfare avenues and the role of the relief system. He argues that high densities of membership were connected less to occupational and wage structures, and much more to levels of urban development and aggregate poor relief spending. Migrants in particular were prone to turn to friendly-society membership in larger urban areas where their kinship and other networks were least dense and in those areas where the support of the communal welfare system was least marked. In other words, friendly-societies acted as a substitute for the two major planks of the welfare spectrum – kin and friends, and the communal relief system. By implication, then, the less dense friendly-society networks of the south represent less urbanisation but also more focus on these two props to welfare.[74]

This is not to say that a whole range of opportunistic but ultimately unquantifiable openings for securing welfare were missed by families in the south and east. These might take the form of the formation of neighbourhood borrowing and lending networks, or, as we saw in the pauper letters used in the last chapter, it might involve informal charity on the part of prominent families. In some places the ways of keeping off relief or of supplementing it could take on a very innovative flavour. In 1808, for instance, the Kettering vestry decided to clean up the streets but, 'to accommodate as much as possible those poor people who have been accustomed to lay manure in the street and to sell the same, public notices shall be given . . . to sell or remove it.'[75]

Conclusion

This chapter has barely scratched the surface in terms of the questions that could be asked of the poor law data used here. How many of those on long-term relief passed on their dependence to children? Did allowances increase with age or time on relief? What was the demography of poor people? How do results from these communities compare with other published and unpublished work from welfare historians on the south and east? How many people were turned down in the process of equating demand for and supply of welfare in these communities? Did rising relief bills constitute an increasing burden on ratepayers, or was the supply of welfare elastic? How did the poor regard their brushes with the poor law in these communities? Such questions are largely beyond the scope and space of this book, but the analysis that has been conducted throws up some interesting and important conclusions which are worth summarising.

Thus, there is little indication that in the south and the east the poor 'had become a distinctive species, a sect apart'.[76] Nor is there convincing evidence for Hollen-Lees' contention that the poor were systematically marginalised in the last three decades of the old poor law.[77] Expanding relief lists and the changing age and sex composition of the recipients suggest that the communal welfare system in the south and the east *was* a flexible institution. Its remit expanded during the later eighteenth century to cope with the stresses and strains that the Napoleonic Wars placed upon family economies. Relief lists became more male-dominated and by the early nineteenth century it is clear that the poor law was recognising a substantial core of the 'background poverty' that we know to have existed. In part this must reflect a relatively weak, and weakening, economy of makeshifts in the south after 1750, but it is important to realise that the communal welfare system appears to have recognised and treated *all* of the classes of poor people identified in chapter five. Moreover, in some places and for some people the communal relief system was also a generous and benevolent institution once we take account of the total care package on offer. The aged poor – particularly aged males on long-term pensions – seem to have been treated with respect and compassion. And the southern and eastern old poor law *was* very much a system. There is little evidence in the foregoing discussion of any systematic sub-regional patterns in either eligibility for, or in the generosity of, relief, though chapter nine returns to this general theme by adding in the results of published and unpublished research by other welfare historians.

Yet nor must we forget that this was, as Lees and Thane suggest, a residual system. Poor law administrators did not usually leave it until the last minute to intervene in the descent into poverty, and they do seem to have had much more compassion and sensitivity than the terms 'residual' or 'safety net' can convey, but ultimately, the majority of people who might be deemed poor had either no relationship with communal welfare or a very intermittent one. The majority of old people were never dependent on communal relief, and many of those who did become dependent did so at late stages of old age. Nor did the vast majority of the able-bodied ever become dependent on relief, though there were chronological peaks of temporary relief which are largely explained by the more frequent and more generous treatment of this group. This despite the fact, as chapter five showed, that many of them were frequently or often poor. In short, the southern and eastern poor law was a relatively central plank in the welfare system, but it was by no means the only one. Vestries, overseers and the poor themselves expected to see other avenues explored before communal relief was applied for, and even those people that chapter five has labelled chronically or always poor were often only intermittently dependent on the communal welfare system. The Kettering ratepayer who took herself off relief when a lodger left her some money tells us much about the essential character of this system – about the woman who takes in a lodger to make ends meet and then, as we might expect given the discussion of chapter five on the symbolism of poverty, jettisons the shackles of the poor law when possible. So, a residual system certainly, but a potentially generous, benevolent and wide-ranging system as well. As we will see, such a characterisation differs somewhat from the practice and sentiment that might be detected in the north and west.

Notes

1 On the household economy in these areas, see S. Horrell and J. Humphries, 'The exploitation of little children: child labor and the family economy in the industrial revolution', *Explorations in Economic History*, 32 (1995) 485–516, and S. Horrell and J. Humphries, 'Old questions, new data and alternative perspectives: families' living standards in the industrial revolution', *Journal of Economic History*, 52 (1992) 849–80.

2 See T. Sokoll, 'The pauper household small and simple? The evidence from listings of inhabitants and pauper lists in early modern England', *Ethnologia Europaea*, 27 (1985) 25–42.

3 E. G. Thomas, 'The treatment of poverty in Berkshire, Essex and Oxfordshire 1723–1840' (unpublished Ph.D. thesis, University of London, 1971).

4 T. Wales, 'Poverty, poor relief and the life-cycle: some evidence from seventeenth century Norfolk', in R. M. Smith (ed.), *Land, kinship and life-cycle* (Cambridge, Cambridge University Press, 1984), pp. 351–74, and W. Newman-Brown, 'The receipt of poor relief and family situation:

Aldenham, Herts, 1630–90', in *ibid*., pp. 405–22. The contemporary term 'pension' will be much used in this and subsequent chapters. In the context of this book, the term is taken to mean a regular weekly or monthly payment which lasted for at least six months.

5 L. Botelho, 'Aged and impotent: parish relief of the aged poor in early modern Suffolk', in M. J. Daunton (ed.) *Charity, self-interest and welfare in the English past* (London, UCL Press, 1996), pp. 91–112, and P. Slack, *From reformation to improvement: public welfare in early modern England* (Oxford, Clarendon Press, 1999).

6 See D. Thomson, 'The welfare of the elderly in the past: a family or community responsibility?', in M. Pelling and R. M. Smith (eds), *Life, death and the elderly: historical perspectives* (London, Routledge, 1991), pp. 194–221.

7 S. Williams, 'Poor relief and medical provision in Bedfordshire: the social, economic and demographic context 1750–1850' (unpublished Ph.D. thesis, University of Cambridge, 1999).

8 G. R. Boyer, 'Malthus was right after all: poor relief and the birth rate in southeastern England', *Journal of Political Economy*, 97 (1989) 93–114.

9 P. Dunkley, 'Paternalism, the magistracy and poor relief in England, 1795–1834', *International Review of Social History*, 24 (1979) 371–97 (385).

10 R. Wells, 'Migration, the law and parochial policy in eighteenth and early nineteenth century southern England', *Southern History*, 15 (1993) 86–139.

11 E. G. Thomas, 'The old poor law and medicine', *Medical History*, 24 (1980) 1–19, and Williams, 'Poor relief'. For an excellent Oxfordshire discussion, see J. Howard-Drake, 'The poor of Shipton under Wychwood parish 1740–62', *Wychwoods History Society Journal*, 5 (1989) 4–44.

12 For one of the best and most wide-ranging, see E. M. Hampson, *The treatment of poverty in Cambridgeshire, 1597–1834* (Cambridge, Cambridge University Press, 1934).

13 See G. Body, 'The administration of the poor law in Dorset 1760–1834, with special reference to agrarian distress' (unpublished Ph.D. thesis, University of Southampton, 1968).

14 See S. Ottoway and S. Williams, 'Reconstructing the life-cycle experience of poverty in the time of the old poor law', *Archives*, 23 (1998) 19–29.

15 M. Neuman, *The Speenhamland county: poverty and the poor laws in Berkshire 1782–1834* (New York, Garland, 1982).

16 M. E. Fissell, 'The sick and drooping poor in eighteenth century Bristol and its region', *Social History of Medicine*, 2 (1989) 49–81.

17 R. M. Smith, 'Ageing and well-being in early modern England: pension trends and gender preferences under the English old poor law 1650–1800', in P. Johnson and P. Thane (eds), *Old age from antiquity to post-modernity* (London, Routledge, 1998), pp. 64–95.

18 *Ibid*., p. 82.

19 See D. Marshall, *The English poor in the eighteenth century* (New York, Routledge, 1969 reprint), pp. 101–4.

20 D. Pam, *A parish near London: a history of Enfield volume I*, (Enfield, Enfield Preservation Society, 1990), p. 327.
21 S. R. Ottoway, 'Providing for the elderly in eighteenth century England', *Continuity and Change*, 13 (1998) 391–418, and S. R. Ottoway, 'The decline of life: aspects of ageing in eighteenth century England' (unpublished Ph.D. thesis, Brown University, 1997).
22 M. Crowther, 'Family responsibility and state responsibility in Britain before the welfare state', *Historical Journal*, 25 (1982) 131–45.
23 For exceptions, see B. Stapleton, 'Inherited poverty and life-cycle poverty: Odiham, Hampshire, 1650–1850', *Social History*, 18 (1993) 339–55, and Ottoway, 'The decline'.
24 This chapter focuses largely though not exclusively on communities with under 4,000 people in 1801. In part this reflects the numerical superiority of small rural parishes in the south and east, and in part the added logistical problems of collecting and working with data from the larger urban areas. It is hoped to remedy this omission (duplicated for the north and west) in later work.
25 The parishes were Chalfont St Peter, Chipping Camden, Richmond, Aynho, Farthinghoe, Paxton, Bluntisham, Charing, Lyndhurst, Ashwell, Downham, Drayton, Bradfield and Broomfield. References can be found in the Bibliography. This collection under-represents town hinterlands, coastal parishes, rural industrial areas and parishes towards the western boundaries of the south and east as they are defined here. Not all places had continuous poor law records throughout the period 1700–61, and where periods of farming coincided with reference dates in any place, the parish is temporarily excluded from the analysis.
26 F. G. Emmison, *The relief of the poor at Eaton Socon, 1706–1834* (Bedford, Bedfordshire Record Society, 1933).
27 Hampson, *The treatment*, Marshall, *English*. In Smith, 'Ageing', Devon parishes in the early eighteenth century were somewhat meaner than those elsewhere in the south.
28 The parishes, most of them mainly agricultural, were Charing, Bluntisham, Linton, Ashwell, Farthinghoe, Thatcham, Wakes Colne, Wye, Old Duston, Bottisham, Woodford, Drayton, Bradfield and Paxton. Full references are given in the Bibliography. As with the previous sample, not all parishes had poor law books spanning the whole period. Missing information because of this or because of farming and use of workhouses meant that not all parishes figured in the returns for all years.
29 K. D. M. Snell, *Annals of the labouring poor: social change and agrarian England 1660–1900* (Cambridge, Cambridge University Press, 1985), Hampson, *The treatment*.
30 Marshall, *English*, p. 101.
31 M. Barker-Read, 'The treatment of the aged poor in five selected west Kent parishes from settlement to Speenhamland 1662–1797' (unpublished Ph.D. thesis, Open University, 1988).

32 Hampson, *The treatment*, pp. 189.

33 B. Keith-Lucas, *Parish affairs: the government of Kent under George III* (Ashford, Kent County Library Service, 1986).

34 The parishes were Charing, Farthinghoe, Broomfield, Bluntisham, Chalfont and Drayton. Full references can be found in the Bibliography.

35 Hampson, *The treatment*, p. 182.

36 J. E. Oxley, *Barking vestry minutes and other parish documents* (Colchester, Essex Records Society, 1955).

37 J. Howard-Drake, 'The poor'.

38 An average 18 per cent of total poor law spending was on irregular cash payments during the later eighteenth century. This is somewhat higher than in other places for which information is available, and may in part be a reflection of the tendency for the parishes which underpin this analysis to lie near to main roads and thus to have a significant casual-poor problem.

39 Howard-Drake, 'The poor'.

40 Pam, *Enfield*, p. 190.

41 E. G. Thomas, 'The old poor law and medicine', *Medical History*, 24 (1980) 1–19.

42 F. M. Cowe (ed.), *Wimbledon vestry minutes 1736, 1743–1788* (Guildford, Surrey Record Society, 1964), p. 22.

43 C. F. Tebbutt, *Bluntisham-cum-Earith, Huntingdonshire: records of a fenland parish* (St Neots, privately published, 1941).

44 There is no allowance in this analysis for cross-subsidy in the parish accounts.

45 Hampson, *The treatment*.

46 Tebbutt, *Bluntisham*.

47 The fact that Kent parishes tended to be small also meant that they showed a disproportionate tendency to come together to provide workhouse accommodation. See Keith-Lucas, *Parish affairs*.

48 However, Norfolk, Suffolk, Essex, Kent and Sussex accounted for well over one-half of the paupers in workhouses between 1803 and 1813.

49 The data are drawn from Kettering, Farthinghoe and Charing.

50 S. A. Peyton, *Kettering vestry minutes 1797–1853* (Northampton, Northamptonshire Records Society, 1933), p. 2. For the Enfield workhouse dietary, see Pam, *Enfield*, 327.

51 Peyton, *Kettering*, p. 52.

52 *Ibid.*, p. 92.

53 Cowe, *Wimbledon*, p. 41.

54 We might contrast these figures with those offered by K. Williams, *From pauperism to poverty* (London, Routledge and Kegan Paul, 1981), which suggest that 31 per cent of individuals were relieved occasionally.

55 Pam, *Enfield*.

56 The reconstitutions were of Farthinghoe, Aynho, Ashwell and Paxton. For details on the former two studies, see chapter five. The latter two were conducted for the purposes of this book. It should be stressed that these were

small communities. Collectively their 1801 populations amount to somewhat less than 2,000 people. Given this and a spatial distribution which is skewed away from the west and the south of the region as it is defined here, the communities are by no means representative.

57 S. A. King, 'Multiple source record linkage in a rural industrial community 1680–1820', *History and Computing*, 6 (1994) 133–42.

58 For those without definitive or implied age data, I have applied guestimates based upon length of time in observation and the size of relief payments.

59 P. King, 'Pauper inventories and the material lives of the poor in the eighteenth and early nineteenth centuries', in T. Hitchcock, P. King and P. Sharpe (eds), *Chronicling poverty: the voices and strategies of the English poor 1640–1840* (Basingstoke, Macmillan, 1997), pp. 155–91 (10).

60 Kin-rich means individuals who were linked by blood or marriage to at least two other people in their locality. Kin-poor means those who were linked to no other people by blood or marriage in their locality.

61 Fissell, 'The sick'.

62 F. K. Prochaska, 'Philanthropy', in F. M. L. Thompson (ed.), *The Cambridge Social History of Britain 1750–1850* (Cambridge, Cambridge University Press, 1990), pp. 357–93 (363).

63 J. Ayres, *Paupers and pig killers: the diary of William Holland, a Somerset parson 1799–1818* (Stroud, Sutton, 1984), p. 229.

64 B. Davey, *Ashwell 1830–1914: the decline of a village community* (Leicester, Leicester University Press, 1980), p. 39.

65 Peyton, *Kettering*, p. 87.

66 T. Sokoll, 'The household position of elderly widows in poverty: evidence from two English communities in the late eighteenth and early nineteenth centuries', in J. Henderson and R. Wall (eds), *Poor women and children in the European past* (London, Routledge, 1994), pp. 207–24.

67 L. Hollen-Lees, *The solidarities of strangers: the English poor laws and the people 1700–1948* (Cambridge, Cambridge University Press, 1998), p. 171.

68 J. Fiske (ed.), *The Oakes diaries: business, politics and the family in Bury St Edmunds, 1778–1800* (Woodbridge, Boydell Press, 1990).

69 B. Stapleton, 'Inherited poverty'.

70 Smith, 'Ageing'.

71 Pam, *Enfield*.

72 M. Gorsky, 'The growth and distribution of English friendly societies in the early nineteenth century', *Economic History Review*, 51 (1998) 489–511.

73 M. D. Fuller, *West Country friendly societies* (Reading, Oakwood Press, 1964).

74 Gorsky, 'The growth'.

75 Peyton, *Kettering*, p. 25.

76 Marshall, *English*, p. 46.

77 Hollen-Lees, *The solidarities*.

CHAPTER SEVEN

WELFARE IN THE NORTH AND WEST, 1700–1820

Overview

On the basis of limited evidence, chapters four and five suggested that levels of poverty, widely defined, were similar in the north and south and that in both regions we can see a developing late eighteenth- and early nineteenth-century life-cycle poverty problem. The details of this perspective require more fine-tuning, but the empirical evidence for substantial levels of poverty in northern and western towns and villages both before and after 1700 is persuasive. The 1672 survey of the poor of Bolton to which we referred in chapters two and five listed 740 paupers and their dependents.[1] In other words, perhaps 40 per cent of the local population were considered poor at that date. By the 1730s William Grimshaw was able to point to overwhelming poverty amongst the 'lesser class' in Haworth,[2] and Geoffrey Hornby remarked on the evident link between rising crime and rising poverty in Lancashire at roughly the same date.[3] The decline of the mining industry in Whickham during the eighteenth century left 43 per cent of households dependent on the parish in 1715, and 36 per cent by 1743.[4] By the late eighteenth century some communities certainly had a serious and long-run poverty problem. In Tysoe, Warwickshire, between 1783 and 1792, 35 out of 113 burials were of paupers while in Addingham during the same period, one-half of all those buried were classified as poor.[5]

There is evidence that poverty was less severe in some parts of the north and west as it is defined here. We noted in chapter four, for instance, Hastings' idea that outside the lead dales the North Riding did not have a real poverty problem.[6] However, such observations tell only part of the complete story. The North Riding as a whole, and many of its individual communities, recorded a net loss of population in the later eighteenth century. Its poor moved elsewhere in a process analogous to the attempts by southern poor law administrators in the nineteenth century to reduce their poverty problem by shipping paupers off to the new world.[7] In any case, by the opening decade of the nineteenth century, while just 8 per cent of the North Riding population were dependent upon relief, almost one-third of many town and village populations were included in the disbursements from public subscriptions to meet pressing needs associated with war and rising prices. Such influences had taken their toll on other places too. By the second decade of the nineteenth century, three Lancashire censuses of the poor (Ashton and Haydock in 1816, Tottington in 1817 and Garstang in 1817) suggest, with appropriate multipliers, that between one-quarter and two-fifths of local populations may have been 'in poverty' as recognised by local elites. Richard Hodgkinson, the estate steward to Lord Lilford on his Lancashire estates put the figure for poverty amongst rural labourers somewhat higher, estimating that in 1814 nearly half of all households had insufficient income to make ends meet.[8]

Yet, while these poverty experiences may have been substantial, they were not apparently as severe as the figures for the south and east. This seeming disparity may reflect the fact that chapter five erroneously saw a common widely defined poverty problem in the north and west and the south and east, but more likely it reflects the fact that the full extent of poverty in the north and west cannot be gauged using these sorts of snapshot. As we saw in chapters three and five there may be a case for suggesting that poverty in the north in particular, but also in large parts of the west and midlands, was by the later eighteenth century of a different type to the endemic structural poverty that characterised the south and the east. Rural industrial development during the eighteenth century put increasingly large numbers of people at risk of trade-cycle fluctuations, and when these came serious poverty could rip through rural areas. The co-existence of rural industry alongside the development of factories and centralised workshops from the later eighteenth century merely added to this problem. Nor were rural areas immune to industrial fluctuations. The West Riding drew heavily on the farmers of Nottinghamshire and the North Riding, as well as the cheese makers of Cheshire, and when the woollen industry faced market downturns so levels of destitution in these rural areas faithfully tracked those of the area around Leeds. North Lancashire and south Westmorland are also prime examples of areas which although not directly in the firing line of the trade cycle saw poverty increase substantially when industrial depression did come. Over a life cycle or a period of time individual instances of need associated with cyclical fluctuations could add up to significant periods spent in poverty, but snapshots of the sort which we have been taking will miss this 'extra' stratum of poverty experience in the north and west.

Meanwhile, the important question is what role the communal welfare system played in addressing such poverty? Chapter five drew a marked division between two northern and two southern communities, suggesting that the former recognised only around 10 per cent of local poverty widely defined. Clearly, these communities are not representative of the 'north and the west', but as we have noted on at least three occasions, mapping poor relief statistics for the early nineteenth century certainly suggests that the poor law relieved fewer people and did so with lower nominal allowances than counties in the south and the east. In 1803 Lancashire had 6.7 per cent of its population on the relief lists, the West Riding and Durham 9.3 per cent, Staffordshire 9.1 per cent and Northumberland 8.8 per cent. Such experiences were not uniform in the north and west as it is defined here. In Gloucestershire, 15 per cent of the 1803 population were on relief, while in Somerset and Devon the figure was 12 per cent and in Warwickshire 13 per cent. These figures are somewhat below the 20 per cent plus dependency figures which chapter four found in some of the 'home counties', but similar to those in counties at the lower end of the distribution in the 'south and east'. Moreover, in individual places, dependence on relief could be very much more substantial. By 1801 around 25 per cent of the population of Powick, for instance, were on relief and the vestry were obliged to extend the rate base, effectively narrowing the gap between paupers and ratepayers.[9]

These observations may point to a problem with the drawing of regional boundaries – an issue addressed more fully below and in chapter nine – but it is also important to bear in mind an important caveat on the subject of spatial variation. Concentrating on bald figures risks missing the important issue of the sentiment of relief policy in the north and west. Thus, while James Taylor concludes that 'Paternal attitudes towards the poor prevailed in many parts of Devon well into the nineteenth century' it is not clear that this is what Smith's analysis of Devon poor law accounts for the eighteenth century shows.[10] Even if Taylor is right, it is doubtful that the same paternalism could be traced for Westmorland, Staffordshire or Lancashire. Indeed, of Lancashire, Midwinter has noted that 'In short, the old poor law in Lancashire was a more vivid advertisement of what the poor law commissioners planned to do than of the faults they so sternly denounced.[11] Moreover, while Gloucestershire nominally had well over 10 per cent of its population dependent on relief in 1803, Ripley concludes of relief experiences in Gloucester itself that 'The performance of the Corporation suggests that under-provision was regarded as tolerable in many years'.[12] The 'sentiment' of the poor law in the north and west may thus have been 'harsh' whatever the nominal figures involved. We return to this issue in subsequent sections. In the meantime, the key point is that while we can certainly point to sub-regional variation, over the region as a whole it is undeniably true that fewer people were relieved than in the south and the east. At the level of individual parishes this may have reflected constraints on the ability to pay, but in an aggregate context such experiences were not a reflection of affordability. In 1821/22 Sussex with a rate base of £915,348 (and static) paid out £275,000 to the poor but Lancashire with a rate base of £3,087,777 (and growing rapidly) gave allowances valued at just £261,730.[13] If the northern and western communal welfare system paid out less to fewer people, therefore, it was either because it did not have to or because its administrators chose not to be more benevolent.

The inference to be read from these observations is that the north and the west had a different sort of communal welfare system to that which we observed in chapter six. Whether this is true is the subject of the rest of this chapter. Initially, though, the evidence from chapters four and five is that the communal welfare system in the north and west turned down large numbers who felt poor enough to apply and intervened late in the descent of families towards complete destitution. Given the accumulated wisdom of the last six chapters, such a conclusion should not perhaps surprise us. A different sort of poverty problem – one that could yield moderate relief bills and pauper totals in most years but then periodically push relief bills and dependence up to levels rarely seen in the south and east – called for a different set of poverty solutions and a different role for the communal welfare system. Moreover, as chapter three demonstrated, most commentators have suggested that there were more avenues for the poor to remain off relief (though still in poverty) in the north and west than there were in the south and east. Charity, common land and petty work opportunities are usually assumed, following Eden, to have survived longest as realistic alternative welfare avenues in the north and the west, allowing the welfare system to adopt a residual function. Presumably the experience of the Lancashire township of Longton best portrays the situation which many general commentators have assumed. Here in 1820/21 the overseers paid the loom hire charges (amounting to £16 or 10–12s. per weaver) of twenty-eight people who might otherwise have been fully or partially dependent on relief.[14] Similarly, in Brampton, North Riding, the vestry regularly paid the rent of loom shops and lent out textile equipment, while in the Lancashire township of Cowpe the vestry in March 1818 actually hired their own mechanic to keep the looms of the poor and marginal in good order and thus allow them to contribute substantially to their own welfare.[15] The role of the poor law in this sense was to act as a facilitator rather than as a central provider of welfare.

But how reliable are these perspectives? Was relief really small-scale and supplementary in the north and west? Do the aggregate poor law statistics portray a real spatial division in numbers relieved and attitudes towards poverty? And if relief was supplementary and entitlement was narrowly defined, was this because the poor law chose not to do more? Even more than in the south and east, broad characterisations of the northern and western poor law are based upon a slim empirical base. Detailed county surveys of poor relief are rare for the region, and also relatively elderly.[16] Systematic local studies have been even more noticeable by their absence, and indeed the whole fabric of poor law and poor-law-related research is weaker in the north and west than in the south and the east. This chapter will rectify some of the lack of empirical focus in an attempt to draw a broad and tentative picture of the character and role of the communal welfare system in the north and the west. Who did it relieve? What did the poor law pay for and why? Was there a change in the focus of relief over time? How generous was relief in a variety of different township contexts? What was the sentiment behind relief giving? How did communities cope with the inexorable increase in background poverty which was revealed in chapter five? What were the life-cycle dimensions of relief? What was the character of institutional relief? How did those whose poverty and marginality were not recognised by the poor law make ends meet? Such are the questions that underpin this analysis, though as with chapter six they represent only the tip of an analytical iceberg in respect of the data that follow.

Perspectives and problems

Not surprisingly, untangling the issue of the role of the communal welfare system in the north and west is no less complicated than it was for the south and the east. Poor law accounts pose the same nominal logistical problems as they do elsewhere, but there are added complications. First, the tendency for communities in the north and the west to turn to 'farming' for longer and rather more frequently as a way of controlling their poor relief bills than communities in the south has cut

185

a swathe through poor law documentation. Farming was a common occurrence in counties such as the North Riding and Shropshire, and above all in Cumbria where *every* parish appears to have experimented with farming the poor. Working with interrupted poor law documentation for places like this involves some imagination. Second, the north and west also pose additional logistical problems for the welfare historian. The large size of many parishes and the fact that individual townships within parishes often took control of their own poor relief and rating mean that 'parochial policy' let alone 'regional policy' has to be distilled from a complex array of poor law documentation. There were 546 bodies which dispensed some form of official poor relief in the North Riding alone by 1800, and 446 in Lancashire. Against this backdrop, it is no surprise that broad county studies have been so infrequent.

A third complication centres on the practice of 'out-parish relief'. While Wells claims that it was relatively common for southern and eastern parishes to pay relief to people settled in their parish but resident elsewhere, this practice in the north and west was of an altogether different order. In Stokeseley (North Yorkshire) by 1815 one-half of all pensioners were non-resident, while in Cowpe (Lancashire) between 1806 and 1820 one-third of all recipients of poor law help were resident outside the township.[17] Moreover, Broadbridge suggests that in Stone (Staffordshire) the parish was dealing with 60 or more parishes and paying over £200 in out-parish relief by 1820.[18] On the face of it, these practices need not be too damaging to our attempts at characterising poor law policy if the relief of the person concerned is consistently recorded in the poor law accounts of their home parish. However, this was not always the case. The overseer of Mitton (Lancashire) sent lump sums to agents in places where there were particular concentrations of Mitton poor, but in the poor law accounts recorded only the lump-sum payments to the agents rather than the individual payments to the poor who were supposed to receive that money.[19] To the unwary, some poor law payments might thus seem very generous! Moreover, this is not the only problem that out-parish relief poses, as chapter three reminded us. If we want to link poor law accounts with family reconstitution records, then it is possible that large numbers of pensioners and other recipients would have continuous poor relief histories but incomplete or nonexistent demographic life cycles because the processes of marriage, birth and death were largely played out elsewhere.

Even if manipulating the data were easier, however, there are three much more subtle ways in which out-parish relief can influence the characterisation we apply to the communal welfare system in the north and the west:

1 As we can see from pauper letters, the relief process conducted at a distance was a matter of negotiation between the poor person who stated their needs and the overseer of the home parish who often sent less than was requested, or indeed nothing at all. Such was the experience of William Taylor who wrote to the overseer of the Lancashire township of Barnacre in January 1823:

> Sir, I have received yours on the 6th instant and was sorry that I could not send by return of post. I had the money to borrow from the landlord to receive the letter the charge of postage was 1s 9d. We are very thankful for your kindness in sending the £5, but our rent is £5 5s. but the landlord was so good as to look over the 5s. and the 2s. we borrowed for the letter so there remains 7s. to him unpaid.[20]

In most instances, the outcome of the process of negotiation was relief at a basic level compared to what the pauper would have received at home. Where out-parish and in-parish paupers are not consistently delineated in the poor law accounts, then a simple percentage distribution of relief payments might give an uneven perspective on the nature of communal policy.

2 Out-parish relief poses accounting problems in addition to those already reviewed. Two in particular stand out. First, where a poor person was receiving out-parish relief from their home parish, there was no reason at all why they should appear as poor in the books of the overseer of the reception parish. If we are interested in the generosity of poor law treatment to *all* local paupers, then this becomes a problem. Second, pauper letters and letters between overseers suggest that out-parish paupers were often relieved with small payments by the overseer of the reception parish well before they applied to their parish of settlement, and sometimes even while they were receiving relief from that parish of settlement. In accounting terms, these payments might show up as small pensions to the poor in the parish of reception (even though their overall payment from the two places combined was likely to be much higher) and larger (though still understated) payments in the books of the settlement parish. Neither situation would reflect the real circumstances of the pauper.

3 Finally, whatever the allowances which seem to be given under the out-parish system, it is clear that many overseers prevaricated on the sending of relief, leading paupers to write more and more urgent letters. Stephen Garnett of Kirkby Lonsdale may be a famous example of this

genre, but he was not the only one, and nor was he the worst.[21] Whatever the relief eventually given, the sentiment may have been harsh.

The final and perhaps most important additional complication with northern and western poor law records is simply the range of experience which can be observed.[22] As chapter two suggested, and as chapter six has shown for the south of England, the diversity of poor law practice over space and time could be very considerable. However, this is even more the case in the north and west as it has been defined here. In his study of communal relief in the North Riding, Hastings suggested that 'At Richmond those refused were mostly seeking medical relief or were non resident. Elsewhere townships seem to have cared for even the least deserving of their poor.'[23] Robert Sharp of South Cave (East Riding), located in the 'south and east' for this study, expressed similar sentiments about the wide remit of the poor law, lamenting the fact that the overseers of the town were a soft touch for even the most profligate of the poor.[24] In this sense, the North Riding might look more 'south and east' than 'north and west'. The same applies to Shropshire, or at least parts of it. Yet, these counties are in the north and west for the purposes of this study, alongside undeniably harsh poor law regimes such as that of Lancashire. This is a potentially serious problem, but one that pales into insignificance when compared with variations in the poor law regimes of communities within counties. While there is not the space here to provide a definitive picture, it seems clear from the research underpinning this book that the spectrum of intra-county variation in generosity and scope of relief was very much wider than in the south and the east. Witness Lancashire, where Garstang paid weekly allowances to many paupers which were somewhat above the entire male wage of families in the south and east at the same time as Whalley was telling its paupers that they would have to subsist on meagre private charity because no poor rate was going to be raised to meet their growing needs.

Does this mean that the spatial limits of the north and west are incorrectly drawn? Jewell suggests a more refined characterisation of 'the north', involving the classification of a far north (Cumberland, Westmorland, Durham and Northumberland), a middle north (Lancashire and Yorkshire) and a near north (Nottinghamshire, Derbyshire, Staffordshire and Cheshire), which might be more appropriate. Presumably we could also make a distinction between a near west (Gloucestershire, Worcestershire, Herefordshire) and a far west (Cornwall and the parts of Somerset and Devon not included in the south and east as defined here).[25] These issues are addressed further in chapter nine, but for now it is important to acknowledge that this broad macro-region does have more unity than these initial sceptical comments allow. The differences between counties and communities within the broad regional framework that I have offered may in large part be a function of the lack of a spectrum of detailed local work comparable to the south and the east. This chapter goes a little way to setting the limits of the spectrum of experience and smoothing what appear as stark spatial disparities. Moreover, even if spatial disparities remain, we should remember that they were unstable. To return to the example of Garstang, between 1815 and 1820 the town gave incredibly generous allowances. George Wakefield's wife, for instance, was given 6s. per week because her husband was failing to send money from Milnthorpe and the vestry noted that this person 'must be looked after by the overseer'. Yet, by November 1822 the vestry was making savage cuts to entitlement and to pension values for those who kept them, moving from one of the most generous Lancashire communities to one of the least by 1830. This very instability tells us something about the character and role of the communal welfare system in the north and west.

In the meantime, the lessons of this discussion of sources and approaches are clear – it is important to be both cautious and sensitive when grappling with the poor law archives of the north and west. This said, some important studies have begun to redress the lack of detailed work on the northern and western poor law and to suggest a broad framework for deeper analysis. In other work, I have looked at eighteenth-century poor law accounts for the rural industrial township of Calverley near Leeds. This study suggested that in terms of the scale of allowances, the communal welfare system fulfilled only the barest residual function. Pensions were invariably low. Amounts of under 1s. per week were the norm even during the inflation and cyclical problems that dominated the later part of the eighteenth century. Indeed, as most parishes in the south and east were raising the scale of their regular allowances in the late 1790s, Calverley was reducing its allowances. Nor was entitlement wide. The vast majority of old people could expect no help from the poor law even at the extremes of old age, and there was compelling evidence that pauper incomes from the poor law were very volatile indeed compared to the south. While the mean duration of pensions was over five years in most southern and eastern communities, in Calverley it was less than three, and there was no systematic tendency for the money value of the pension to rise with age or time on relief. In turn, what help the poor law did offer appears to have been concentrated upon those with least kin and people who were first generation in-migrants; natives were relatively unlikely to either apply for or obtain relief, and I suggested that this reflected the fact that kinship support at times of poverty was the mainstay of the relief strategies of a large body of the background poor.[26] There are good reasons to think that the sort of dual-occupation artisan culture which underpinned life in Calverley during the eighteenth and early nineteenth centuries might generate a distinctive communal welfare system. Certainly Ottoway's study of the magnificent poor law records of Ovenden, a chapelry of Halifax where the 'putting-out' of woollen cloth dominated the economic structure, suggests subtle differences from Calverley in the treatment of elderly paupers over their life cycle, even if it concurs that allowances were on balance meagre.[27]

Rural industrial townships in general may constitute a special case, but Richard Smith has ranged rather more widely in the north and west as it is defined here, looking at pension magnitudes in several communities and linking reconstitution data and poor law accounts for the parish of Worsfield in Shropshire and the mining community of Whitkirk in the West Riding. His conclusions are instructive. Coming into the eighteenth century, pension magnitudes in the north were around fivepence per week, less than half the normal figure for the south, and only a third or less of the value of pensions in the most generous of southern and eastern parishes. During the early part of the eighteenth century the mean figure climbed to perhaps 11d., compared to the 1s. 6d. mean in Whitchurch, and hence there was some improvement relative to the south and the east. Such improvement was illusory, however. Modal pension values in eighteenth-century southern communities appear to have been around 1s. per week, but modal values in the northern and western communities appear to have been around 6d. per week, or just half of those offered in the south. A few recipients of large pensions were thus skewing the distribution in the north.[28]

By the later eighteenth century pensions appear to have stagnated at between 10d. and 1s. per week if we ignore Woodplumpton in Lancashire which appears to have offered extremely generous relief after 1750. The same stagnation was observed for the south, but the level of pensions was very different, with Whitchurch offering its pensioners a mean allowance of 1s. 8d. by the later eighteenth century. In short there were persistent divisions between communities of the south and east and those of the north and west in the generosity of relief. There were also differences in the underlying life-cycle experiences. The reconstitution and poor law linkage for Worsfield suggested that the communal welfare system was heavily tied into the relief of older people, with almost three-quarters of all pension resources accruing to those over the age of 61. Using differently constructed data on the age at which paupers first came into the relief system, I have suggested a similar skewing in Calverley.[29] In the south and east the evidence suggested that younger men with families increasingly made an impact on both the pension and casual poor lists.

On balance, then, the broad implications of the maps presented in chapter four would seem to be correct. Notwithstanding sub-regional differences, northern and western communities do seem to have relieved fewer people, and the representative allowances do seem meagre when balanced against southern experiences. Moreover, there is at least some evidence of a harsher sentiment underlying these policies. The rest of this chapter will provide more data to try to fill in some of the spatial gaps and to draw wider and sounder conclusions. First, then, the issue of relief generosity.

The northern and western old poor law, 1700–1820: how generous?

Previous chapters provide a stark warning on the difficulties of using labels like 'generosity'. For communities in the north and west it is particularly important to bear these warnings in mind, even if we do need to ask similar questions of different spatial data for comparability purposes. Thus, the issue of yardsticks against which to measure relief payments is a critical one given important differences between the north and west and the south and east with regard to acceptable standards of dress, housing and diet. These were highlighted by Frederick Morton Eden in the 1790s. Crudely put, the northern diet was coarser, the clothing needs of the northern labouring poor simpler, the housing conditions of northern families somewhat worse, and their general consumption standards lower than their counterparts in the south and east. In short, 1s.would buy less of the acceptable basic standard of living in the south than in the north, much as £1 would do today. One way around this thorny problem would be to try to establish the cost of a minimum standard of living in different counties and regions, but this strategy has yet to be realised.

Meanwhile, there are also other problems with assessing 'generosity' which were less often faced by southern communities. Responses to cyclical fluctuations are a case in point. Some disruptions could be short-lived and by the time the poor law had accumulated the resources

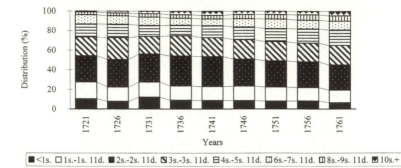

Figure 7.1 The distribution of monthly pension payments in fourteen communities, 1721–61

to respond to them the need may have passed while in the meantime the 'poor' would have been given small pensions. Do we characterise this as a conscious attempt to impose harsh treatment or a logistical problem which prevented a more humane appraisal of need? Longer-term depressions were more serious and pushed up poverty at the same time as the ability of ratepayers to pay for the communal welfare system went down and the number of voluntary collections amongst local elites went up.[30] Almost without exception the poor law paid meagre allowances to those caught in trade-cycle poverty, but was this because they could do no more? Or was this a harsh decision-making regime? These issues, and the implications of out-parish relief for our characterisation of generosity, suggest that we must tread warily in what follows.

Figure 7.1 depicts the distribution of monthly pension magnitudes in fourteen northern and western communities between 1721 and 1761.[31] As in the south, some people were treated generously. Widow James of Leigh was awarded a pension of 9s. per month for the whole of the period 1731–33, while in Chorlton Old James Savage was given 10s. per month during his illness. However, the mean and modal pensions were very low indeed at 2s. 8d. per month and 2s. 1d. per month respectively in the 1720s. On balance there was a modest but sustained uprating of pensions over time which gathered pace towards 1750, roughly mirroring the situation in the southern and eastern communities reviewed in chapter six. Indeed, by 1755, the mean pension was 3s. 2d. per month, representing an 18 per cent increase over levels in the 1720s. However, we should not be blinded by the aggregate figures here. The rise was almost wholly generated by the modest growth of pensions in just a few of the larger or more isolated communities. Troutbeck, for instance, had a mean pension (financed from charitable income rather than a poor rate) which rose from 11d. in the late seventeenth century to 1s. 3d. between 1731 and 1741. By the latter decade, the small number of men on relief were accruing pensions approaching 2s. per week. However, in a numerical sense the experience of Ravenstonedale was most representative. Of the 13 pensions set by the vestry in 1729, the average was 8d. per week and only three pensions were 1s. or more. Thereafter the rates were consistently pared, the vestry noting in December 1730 that 'the four and twenty did meet sooner than ordinary to settle the poor rates chiefly because the price of corn being lowered since the last settlement and have ordered the rates as follows (if something extraordinary do not intervene) till Michelmas next'. The effect of this declaration was a decline in mean pensions and a number of people losing pensions to be given relief 'at discretion'.[32] The contrast with the experience of southern and eastern communities is a powerful one. Here, falling prices and static wages were accompanied, as we have seen, by substantial rises in mean pension values and while it was common for southern parish authorities to launch economy drives after 1723, there were few as severe or as sustained as those to be found in places like Ravenstonedale.

Not all communities in this broadly defined north and west had similar experiences. Rushton believes that in Durham parishes the eighteenth century built on a rising seventeenth-century pension trend. By 1720 the average was 4s. 4d. per month, still below mean southern levels, but well in advance of those for this sample.[33] Moreover, as Smith points out, between 1722 and 1730 Worsfield had mean and modal monthly pensions around the 4s. mark. Some Warwickshire parishes were also much more generous than the central trends in figure 7.1 indicate, and more generous even than the Warwickshire parish in our sample. Tysoe, for instance, had a mean pension of 6s. 6d. per month by 1730, directly comparable to levels in Whitchurch and Terling. However, these were exceptions and for each exception we could quote a counter-example. In Rossendale (Lancashire), for instance, no township paid more than an average 1s. 9d. pension in the first half of the eighteenth century, while in Tong (West Riding) mean pensions fell consistently between 1721 and 1761. A wide survey of parish accounts conducted for this book in an initial attempt to pin down the study areas indicated that parishes with low nominal allowances outnumbered the Troutbeck's by over three to one, suggesting a wider unity in the region as a whole from the early eighteenth century. We return to these themes in chapter nine.

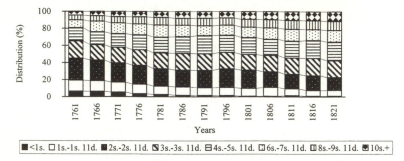

■<1s. □1s.-1s. 11d. ■2s.-2s. 11d. ◥3s.-3s. 11d. ⊟4s.-5s. 11d. ▨6s.-7s. 11d. ▥8s.-9s. 11d. ▨10s.+

Figure 7.2 The distribution of monthly pension payments in fourteen communities, 1761–1821

Figure 7.2 takes the analysis forward, tracing the distribution of pension amounts in fourteen townships between the mid-eighteenth and early nineteenth centuries.[34] As before, some of these communities could be very generous to individual paupers. The accounts for Lund towards the end of the period covered by figure 7.2 provide an excellent example. Between 12 June and 2 August 1816, John Bonney was paid 23s. during an illness, all of it in cash rather than kind. Clearly both he and his wider kinship group were endemically poor. Between 27 November 1817 and 20 January 1818, John Bonney was paid 15s. 6d., while his brother Thomas was paid 18s. 6d. plus 23s. for the funeral of one of his children.[35] Moreover, for the townships collectively there was a rise in the proportion of resources accruing to the top 10 per cent of recipients, in direct contrast to the fall that we see in southern areas. By the early nineteenth century well over one-quarter of all resources were accruing to this select group of poor people. The Lund material shows how this was played out on the ground, with Mary Battersby receiving 8s. per week in 1819 while several other pensioners were, like Margaret Grayson, receiving 1s. a week or less. We return to the issue of why poor law administrators came to treat people like Battersby on such favourable terms later in this chapter.

Meanwhile, the central message of figure 7.2 is that mean and modal pensions remained low in this sample of communities, though on a rising trend. By the 1770s the mean pension had reached 3s. 9d. per month. Thereafter the generalised stagnation which Smith has elaborated can clearly be seen, and in the 1790s there is evidence of a fall in mean pension levels. This contrasts with the end of century pension rises identified in the south. The nineteenth century was to bring a sustained uprating of pensions, with the mean reaching almost 5s. per

month by the 1810s. However, this effect was disproportionately generated by a small increase in the number of people accruing the most
generous range of pensions and a rise in the value of those pensions at
the top end. The central consideration is that if we look to the modal
pensions offered by Whitchurch and Terling in the later eighteenth
century the generality of allowances seem very meagre indeed in these
northern and western communities.

Once again, not all northern communities, nor indeed all components of this sample, had such restrained experiences. Troutbeck breaks
the mould. Here between 1780 and 1800 the average weekly poor law
pension was 2s. 6d. for men and 1s. 6d.–2s. for women, roughly in line
with the allowances offered by Whitchurch in Oxfordshire. Indeed,
Parsons concludes that the old poor law had 'a real appreciation of the
comfort and contentment of these old men' who dominated the top end
of the relief scale.[36] By 1820 in Mitton, the average pension touched 3s.
per week. Tysoe, Warwickshire, had an average pension of 2s. 6d. per
week by 1778, and in the remote Cumbrian community of Eskdale, pensions varied between 1s. and 3s. 6d. per week, with an average of 2s.
7d.[37] However, we should not be lulled by the exceptions. Troutbeck
might be balanced by Whickham, where men found it almost impossible to get relief and had to rely on charity, and where after 1760 persistent attempts to restrict the size of pensions and the rules for
entitlement reflected a 'hard faced determination to restrict narrowly
the recognition of need'.[38] Indeed, Wrightson and Levine go further,
claiming that, 'the system of relief came to alienate some of the poor
profoundly, for it had become a threat to what little independence they
retained and to their closest personal ties'.[39] The vestries of Wyke and
Kildwick in West Yorkshire did not wait for their poor to become alien-
ated. They simply slashed their relief lists in the 1770s and restricted
entitlement so much that by the 1820s the numbers relieved had still not
returned to their 1770 level.

Just as in the south and the east, then, we can see two types of community responses to rising levels of poverty, both recognised and
unrecognised by the poor law. In places like Troutbeck both entitlement
and magnitudes expanded, whereas in places like Calverley, both
remained restricted. Such divisions are not easy to explain. The socio-
economic composition of communities has no predictive value, and nor
paradoxically does the degree of kinship, which was as strong in
Troutbeck as in Calverley. Rather, there seems to be some tendency for
poor relief to be higher in more isolated communities (whatever their
socio-economic composition) and higher in places least affected by

nonconformity but most dominated by large landowning families.[40] Such suggestions require more empirical investigation, and we return to them in chapter nine. However, the key point is that it was the communities paying meagre allowances that numerically dominated the sample for the north and the west. What does this imply for our perceptions of 'generosity' and 'benevolence'?

Of course, these questions are too crude, but as with pensions in the south and east, we must place magnitudes and trends against the backdrop of falling prices and stagnant wages in the early eighteenth century. The fact that pension payments were often to support individuals rather than families, and that living costs were invariably lower in the north and west than elsewhere even in the 1740s, must also be factored into our assessment of the generosity of payments. In this sense, the simple fact that pension magnitudes were meagre cannot on its own be taken to imply a lack of generosity on the part of overseers during the early part of the eighteenth century. Indeed, the fact that nominal payments were on a rising trend may well suggest *increasing generosity*. But how generous?

Let us consider two yardsticks against which to measure 'generosity'. First, that of wage levels. Data for Calverley in the 1740s suggest that a fully employed wage labourer might earn around 7s. per week, so that the mean pension probably equated to no more than around 10 per cent of the average wage. Of course, this assumes full employment but even if we make a notional allowance for unemployment it is unlikely that the mean pension would equate to more than 15 per cent of the individual income of labourers before 1750, whether nominal pension payments were increasing or not. The second yardstick arises out of more detailed research on Calverley and constitutes a rough estimate of minimum living standards in the 1750s, incorporating house rental, allowances for use of waste ground and monetary valuations of clothing standards.[41] Balancing pensions against this measure suggests that, for a pensioner living alone, the pension in isolation would provide just over 20 per cent of the minimum acceptable living standard in 1750.[42] In short, while it is certain that poor law allowances in the north and west were more generous in 1750 than they had been in 1720, at best they provided a small welfare supplement. There is little evidence here that the poor law was becoming more central to the lives of more people as it was undoubtedly becoming to some poor people in the south and east even at this early date. Moreover, while in the south and east payment regularity and the guarantee of a long-term pension had an added value in itself, in this sample such luxuries were rarer. As the example of Ravenstonedale outlined above shows, getting and keeping a pension could be an uncertain affair and the ubiquity of this experience in the communities underlying figures 7.1 and 7.2 is reflected in mean pension durations of under three years before 1750.

Pension magnitudes continued to rise between 1760 and 1780, but so did wages and, if the example of Calverley is representative, so did rents and minimum standards for the domestic environment. By 1790 it seems certain that pensions amounted to well under 10 per cent of mean weekly wages in many of the northern and western areas analysed here. This is no real index of generosity, but even if we relate the mean pension levels illustrated in figure 7.2 to the wages of southern agricultural labourers in the 1790s the allowances seem parsimonious. Commentators on the plight of nineteenth-century handloom weavers provide us with perhaps a more sensitive indicator of generosity. In their surveys of the 1820s and 1830s they calculated that the minimum income needed to sustain life was 2s. 6d. per family member, though this figure rose to 3s. 2d. for those living alone on the basis of the old maxim that two can live as cheaply as one. Relating mean northern and western pensions to the latter figure suggests that they provided just over a third of the absolute basic subsistence level recognised by contemporaries.[43] Had we applied a similar analysis to the south and the east, then it is clear that pension allowances would have provided all or most of the minimum subsistence level.

This is perhaps not a valid comparison, but it nonetheless indicates strongly that the northern and western poor law did little to alleviate the inevitable poverty problems of the 1790s and 1800s. People like Mary Battersby in Lund are an exception to this rule. Indeed, if we turn briefly to Calverley pensioners in the five years 1780–84 it is possible to see figure 7.2 depressingly played out in real life. Of the twenty-three distinct pensioners in this period, the majority were aged; almost two-fifths of them were over 70. The average pension for this group was just 9d. per week, nowhere near enough to meet the cottage rents of the pensioners and increasingly falling behind rising prices in the town during the 1780s and 1790s. Had these pensioners been in the south they would have been considerably better treated, even if we allow for differences in acceptable living standards that the poor law had to address. In sum, pensions were generally meagre, and they became less adequate over time.

As we know from our analysis of southern and eastern communities, however, 'generosity' is not just about pensions. What proportion of resources were devoted to these miserable pensions at different points

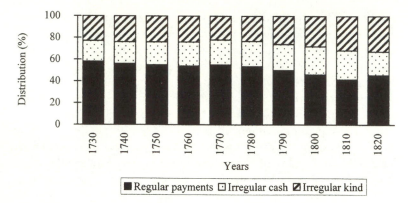

Figure 7.3 The distribution of poor law resources between different types of payment, 1730–1820

in time? How do trends relate to southern and eastern communities? In what form were the rest of local poor law resources dispensed? What was the net effect on the welfare income of individual pensioners and the casual poor? Figures 7.3 to 7.5 begin to address these sorts of issues. Figure 7.3 traces the proportion of resources devoted to regular payments and to irregular payments in cash and kind in seven communities for which the information can be more or less consistently traced.[44] While the proportion of resources spent on pensions could vary radically between communities in individual years, just as was the case in the south, we can make some general observations. Thus, by 1740, 56 per cent of all resources were devoted to pensions in these northern communities compared to 59 per cent in the south and the east. However, if these magnitudes are similar, they were part of very different mid- to late eighteenth-century trends. In the south and east the proportion of resources devoted to pensions climbed significantly until 1770 whereas in these seven northern and western communities there was a slight but definite fall. From the 1780s, both regions share a downward trend, but the decline is nowhere near as sharp in the north and west as in the south and east. Nonetheless, in both regions by 1810 pensions account for not much more than two-fifths of all poor law resources. These observations have significant implications for our characterisation of the generosity of relief, for at the very time pension values seem to be falling behind needs, other forms of expenditure were in any case growing more rapidly. Even more than in the south and east, then, we need to know about the irregular payments doled out by overseers.

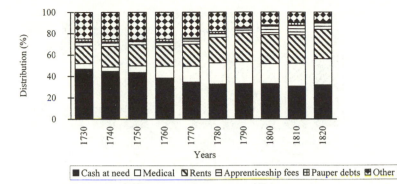

Figure 7.4 The distribution of irregular payments in cash, 1730–1820

Figures 7.4 and 7.5 illustrate the focus of irregular payments in cash and kind. The poor law was clearly intervening in all of the areas familiar from the discussion of the south and east, but there were marked differences of emphasis which may reflect either the ideology and sentiment of the relief system or the nature of the underlying poverty. Three points in particular might be highlighted. First, it is clear that the northern and western communal welfare system became heavily involved in the payments of rents during the latter part of the eighteenth century, with rents accounting for almost one-third of cash payments by 1820. This is a minimal estimate since many of those payments described as 'other' may actually have been for rents. Such figures equate to perhaps 10–12 per cent of total relief expenditure by the early nineteenth century. These observations should not surprise us. Hastings felt that rent payments accounted for between 10–20 per cent of total poor law spending in most North Riding parishes by 1800, while in Lund by the 1820s, rent payments might absorb up to 50 per cent of total poor law resources in some years.

On the face of it, this experience tells us much about the poverty that the poor law had to cope with and the wider role of communal welfare. Crudely, we might style the poor law as a firefighter, reacting to the sudden pressing and substantial needs that poor people were not able to meet through other welfare avenues. This may be a useful characterisation, but we should not assume that the communal welfare system always intervened with good grace. Take the example of the Lancashire township of Longton again. Here in 1820/21 the overseer paid the rents on fifty-six cottages. However, the schedule of payments also records substantial accrued rent arrears and while in the south and east overseers

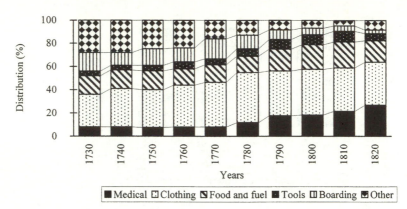

Figure 7.5 The distribution of irregular payments in kind, 1730–1820

were often willing to pay rent arrears, in Longton the overseer left them on record for the poor themselves to pay 'because they should'.[45] If the northern and western welfare system was reactive, therefore, it was reactive in a minimalist way.

The second observation lies in the importance of medical spending. This was considerably below the 'normal' figures for the south in the early part of the period, but then increased substantially from the mid-eighteenth century onwards. By the early 1800s almost one-third of resources in cash and kind were being devoted to medical and medical-related expenditure, well ahead of the average for the southern and eastern communities in chapter six. To some extent this is not surprising. There is a broad rural industrial bias to the data underpinning these charts and the declining public and private health that rural industry invariably brought with it clearly fed through to the nature of poor law expenditure. However, there are also much less inevitable differences between north and south and east and west in the makeup of medical expenditure. For instance, the response to medical problems in the north and west was more through the granting of cash doles, and while this might take the form of the odd sixpence, by and large medical payments in cash were between 1s. and 1s. 6d. per payment. Such figures were somewhat in advance of the resources devoted to pensioners on a monthly basis. This may reflect the fact that illness prevented earning of any sort, obliging the poor law to temporarily step in to the welfare and income patchwork in a more substantial way than was normal. Alternatively, it may represent a backdoor supplement to low pension values.

However we explain a greater tendency to adopt cash responses to medical problems, its corollary is that the northern and western poor law appears to have spent less on doctors, less on medicine and less on nursing care than communities in the south and east. Thus, while Thomas found that 30 per cent of Oxfordshire parishes and 20 per cent of Berkshire parishes subscribed to the John Radcliffe hospital in Oxford, Tomkins has suggested that it took three decades for parishes surrounding the Salop infirmary to start subscribing in any numbers.[46] There were also other subtle differences in the composition of medical relief, with northern overseers much more likely than their southern and eastern counterparts to give clothing and dietary supplements as a response to medical needs. These observations notwithstanding, however, it is important to realise that overseers in most communities set distinct limits to the extent of their involvement in medical problems. One brief example epitomises this and highlights differences with the south and east. While as chapter six showed, Shipton in Oxfordshire sent two of its paupers to Bath for the waters, in Leigh there was a public subscription to send paupers to Bath, to which the poor law authorities made a small contribution. The culture of expectation surrounding communal relief may thus have looked very different to that in the south and east, a theme to which we return in chapter nine.

The final observation is that a more substantial element of relief in kind went on clothing than appears to have been the case in the south and the east. By the 1790s, well over one-third of all relief in kind was being directed towards clothing. There are clearly a number of ways of reading this situation – that the poor law was a generous provider of basic necessities or perhaps that the poor law authorities did not trust paupers to purchase clothes and hence gave low pensions supplemented with clothing allowances. However, we must be careful about bringing clothing into the question of whether or not the poor law was generous. Most obviously in Parr and Calverley, but also in most of the other parishes underpinning this analysis, those providing cloth or clothing were the overseers themselves or their relatives. While such practices were not unknown in the south, as chapter six showed, there was an inexorable tendency for those supplying the poor law in the north and west to have some connection with the system already. The importance of clothing, then, can tell us only limited amounts about the generosity and benevolence or otherwise of the communal welfare system.

There is potentially much more to be said about these charts, but the key question is whether an understanding of the total relief picture paints a different gloss on our appreciation of the character of the communal welfare system in the north and west. Let us turn first to the regular pensioners. As with the south and east, it is clearly inappropriate in assessing the generosity of the communal welfare system to concentrate solely on pension payments. Pensioners in all of the individual communities received additional benefits from casual funds, most notably clothing and rental payments. What is more, the frequency and the value of these casual payments increased over time, as one might expect on the basis of figure 7.3. Thus, pensioners in the 1750s could expect to supplement their incomes by perhaps 8–10 per cent through these additional allowances, whereas by the early 1800s this figure fluctuated between 10 and 18 per cent. Moreover, the small number of people who received the very high pensions that we see emerging from the late eighteenth century did not benefit from supplementary allowances by anywhere as much as pensioners on lower monthly sums, so that the skewing of *total resources* to the top 10 per cent of recipients is nowhere near as marked as it becomes in terms of monetary pension resources only. The net result of such casual payments to pensioners is that while, compared to the south and east, the proportion of resources devoted to pensions is relatively low at all points before the early nineteenth century, the total proportion of resources accruing to pensioners remains stable at 50–60 per cent until well into the nineteenth century. This said, of course, the value of the total care package offered to individual pensioners was probably still less than half that in southern and eastern communities by the 1790s. Set against mean wages or probable levels of acceptable living standards, the total relief package to most pensioners in the north and west can have been no more than the barest supplement to alternative ways of making ends meet. In this sense, it is also important to note that the ability of pensioners to hold on to that care package was often uncertain. Even in 'generous' Troutbeck, as we saw in chapter two, a series of rapid policy changes meant that the income situation of regular pensioners was very uncertain. While they may have had pensions of between 2s. and 3s. per week when on outdoor relief, the regular poor in contact with the welfare system for a decade would perhaps have spent only limited time receiving their own allowances as opposed to being in a workhouse, boarded with households in the community or at the tender mercies of a farmer. This was not, then, a benevolent system, whatever the level of nominal allowances.

What of the casual poor? How well or badly were they treated? The implication of figure 7.3, notwithstanding the fact that pensioners also accrued casual payments, is that the number of casual poor increased noticeably in the late eighteenth and early nineteenth centuries, a point which is reinforced by figure 7.6 below. Rent payments and sickness allowances appear to have figured significantly in the landscape of pay-ments to these casual poor, and it is certainly the case, as we have sug-gested, that compared to the level of regular pension payments one-off allowances in these forms could be considerable. However, we have insufficient evidence to discern whether this constitutes a generous and flexible response to urgent need. As chapter four suggested, some of those who received casual payments may have applied before and been turned down, or they may have applied for a regular pension and been given a one-off payment instead. A surprising number of casual allowances to the non-pension poor when entered in the overseers accounts of communities such as Leigh carry the annotation 'by order', suggesting that the relief was only afforded on the intervention of a magistrate. Even where a casual payment was given willingly, its purpose may have been only to slightly arrest the headlong descent of the recipient into destitution. Certainly, reading decades of poor law accounts suggests that overseers in many of these northern and western communities could have done more and could have acted earlier to prevent later catastrophe. The example of Richard Ainsworth of Cowpe will have to stand for many that could have been quoted. In 1810 he was given a cash allowance for part of his rent but refused a regular allowance. He applied again in 1811, but was again simply given a cash allowance towards rent. In 1812, his landlord distrained his goods for rent arrears and the overseer went to the subsequent sale to buy furni-ture and household goods for recycling to other paupers. Only at this point was a small regular pension offered. The meaning of even quite large casual payments is thus uncertain.

The northern and western poor law was thus far from 'generous' to most of those who received relief even where, as in the communities that underpin this analysis, we substantially control for the statistical vagaries of out-parish relief. Spiralling late eighteenth-century poor relief bills in the individual communities which underpin this analysis reflected a complex mixture of small increases in the money value of the inadequate pensions accruing to most regular recipients, the emergence of a top stratum of regular recipients who did rather well from the poor law, modest increases in the monetary cost of casual payments, an increasing frequency of casual payments and considerable increases in all classes of paupers. Rising local costs did *not* by and large reflect the development of a nominally more generous or benevolent communal welfare system. These experiences may be consistent with a situation in which the closure of other potential welfare avenues forced more and more people into contact with the poor law at low levels. Alternatively, they may reflect conscious attempts by myriad local officials to enforce a culture of self-reliance on an increasingly poor population. Or what we see may reflect complex underlying change in demographic, kinship and residential structures. In order to explain the observations of the last section and to pin down the character and role of the communal welfare system in the north and the west, we need to know more about the poor themselves rather than the allowances they received. We can start with the institutional poor.

Institutional care

In 1803, Lancashire, the West Riding, Cornwall, Northumberland, Nottinghamshire, Herefordshire and Westmorland relieved just 11.5 per cent of their permanent paupers in an institutional context, and 15.5 per cent of the total relief spending of these areas was on the institutional poor. These were similar to figures for the south, but there was much less in the way of sub-regional divisions. The North Riding had 35 workhouses in 1776 (combined capacity of almost 1,000), but the only ones of any size and used regularly were those for the towns of Whitby, Scarborough and Malton. Of the rest, no less than 13 were in the lead dales. In Cumberland and Westmorland, even by 1832 there were only 24 workhouses, and 12 of these had a capacity of less than thirty people. Indeed, only 2 workhouses serving incorporations (Kirkby Lonsdale and Milnthorpe) and the workhouses of Workington, Kendal and Whitehaven were of any real size. Meanwhile, excluding the workhouses attached to incorporations by private acts and those attached to Gilbert unions, only forty-one places used workhouses in Shropshire by the early nineteenth century. For many communities, the flirtation with workhouses was brief. Parr in Lancashire opened a work-house with the nearby township of Windle in 1733, but by 1743 the whole scheme had been abandoned. Calverley obtained a workhouse as part of the conditions of the sale of the Manor to Thomas Thornhill in 1755, but while it remained a nominal part of the communal welfare system until 1834, only in particular years did the overseers revive the institution in a practical sense. Similarly, Cartmel obtained its first workhouse in 1735, but its operation can be traced irregularly. Divisions, such as they were in the north, tended to be between urban and rural areas. Birmingham relieved 14.5 per cent of its paupers in the workhouse by 1815 and Leeds in 1800 some 19 per cent.[47] By 1795,

Kendal was relieving one-half of its paupers in an institutional context, and Milnthorpe almost two-thirds.[48] A large part of the 15.5 per cent of spending which went on workhouse inmates in a swathe of northern and western counties thus reflects the spending priorities of broadly urban areas, a considerable contrast to the south where in some counties even very rural areas were spending considerable amounts on workhouses and their inmates.

Table 7.1 The percentage of the institutional poor in three parishes in various age ranges, 1795–1809

Place	0–9 yrs	10–19yrs	20–39yrs	40–49yrs	50–59yrs	60+yrs
Calverley	29	18	16	15	7	15
Horsforth	23	21	14	15	10	17
Leigh	20	26	10	17	11	16

Source See text.

These observations notwithstanding, it is still important (for all of the reasons outlined in chapter six) to understand who workhouse inmates were and how they differed from the wider poor population. Table 7.1 provides an initial view, tracing the age distribution of paupers in three workhouses for which returns survive between 1795 and 1808.[49] A heavy focus on children is the most obvious feature of all three workhouse listings. Just under one-half of inmates over the sample as a whole were under 20 and almost all of them were below the age of 14. Workhouse returns not used here convey the same message. In Kendal in 1795, 64 out of 137 workhouse inmates were children, and even by 1830 children were the most common residents in Kirkby Lonsdale workhouse.[50] The contrast with the south and east is interesting. Only 37 per cent of all workhouse inmates in Kettering, Farthinghoe and Charing were under the age of 20. Equally significant is that the aged appear to have been a less important presence in these northern workhouses than they were in the south and east. Only one-quarter of inmates in the sample as a whole were aged over 50, though as in the south and east the very old appear to have been overrepresented in the workhouse population. Clearly, then, the old were either maintaining their independence longer than in the south and east or else the poor law authorities were consciously avoiding taking them into the workhouse. Such a state of affairs sits easily with assumptions that a variety of earning opportunities in northern communities allowed the old to work for longer and thus to avoid full dependence on the community. The extension of these observations is that those in the working age groups were more heavily represented in the workhouse population than was the case in the south and the east. Were these the able-bodied paupers who have figured in so much of the historiographical literature? Or were they the sick and the insane? Whoever they were, how were the institutional poor treated and how does this influence our characterisation of the poor law?

To answer questions like these, we can look in more depth at the Calverley workhouse return for the relief year 1807–8. As with the Kettering workhouse, the evidence that the communal welfare system provided institutional paupers with better dress, food and standards of warmth than could be obtained outside the institution is compelling. While no dietaries survive, bills presented to the overseers between 1805 and 1809 include beer, mutton, offal, beef, bacon, biscuits, vegetables and the raw material for making bread. Given rising wheat and other prices from the 1790s onwards, it is doubtful that ordinary rural artisans could have afforded such a diverse diet, though the fact that many grew some of their own crops in this township makes any definitive statement impossible. What is more certain is that clothing standards were considerably better than those amongst the general population. While the accounts are complex, it is clear that the workhouse master spent almost 50s. on clothing for each pauper who entered the house, and a further 15s. per pauper per year on maintaining the clothing of the indoor poor. These sums would have been beyond even moderately prosperous clothiers in the early nineteenth century. Moreover, there are also other odd references which suggest that the overseers looked to the comfort of at least some of the institutional poor. In 1809, for instance, they accepted a donation of a carpet for the quarters of the old in the workhouse and then provided matching funding to get curtains.

For those in extreme old age and decrepitude, then, it is clear that the workhouse offered an acknowledgement of the right to care. But what were the characteristics of the other inmates, and what was the sentiment of the poor law as far as they were concerned? As table 7.1 suggests, the concentration on children was a more general experience. However, this crude analysis masks more than it reveals. In Calverley we can link family reconstitution data with the return of 1808 and in doing so highlight three interesting points about the child population, and by inference something important about the wider function of the workhouse for the adults we find within its walls. Well over one-third of the children who appear in the workhouse population in 1808 were orphans. Moreover, almost another third were the children of widows, and their mothers were also in the workhouse. Finally, of the remaining unaccounted for children one-half were illegitimates who were also in the workhouse with their mothers.

In short almost the whole child population of the workhouse can be explained away as casualties of the demographic system in the town. That they should appear in the workhouse rather than being boarded out with other township families or being given outdoor relief might suggest that the overseer saw the workhouse as a way of capping costs. The observation that women vulnerable to poverty ended up in the workhouse with their children adds weight to this picture. Of the 7 women who became widows between 1800 and 1808 and probably had small children, 3 were in the workhouse in 1808, 3 had apparently left the township at that date and just 1 was making ends meet on a small outdoor pension. Younger and potentially more expensive widows were thus under-represented in the outdoor relief lists. So were the mothers of illegitimate children. Such observations lend strong credence to Smith's idea that mean pensions in some places may be deflated by a tendency to use workhouses as a receptacle for the most expensive poor. Whether this conclusion affects the lessons to be drawn from figures 7.1 and 7.2, given the relatively small scale and very patchy nature of workhouse provision, is doubtful, but the fact that overseers were willing to force able-bodied women in particular into workhouses is an important signpost to the fact that the workhouse in the north was not so clearly the institution of care that it appears to have been in southern and eastern communities.

Meanwhile, it follows from these observations that the vast majority of adult workhouse inmates were female. Indeed, of the six males over 20 years old in the workhouse in 1808, three appear to have been insane and the others were in the most advanced states of old age. Such feminisation of the workhouse population was less marked in the small number of southern and eastern workhouse populations considered in chapter six. It is clear also that the turnover of the workhouse populations was different. In Kettering, long-term residence was uncommon – the old went to the workhouse to die, children before apprenticeship and the only really long-term residents were the insane. Calverley workhouse too was a place where the very old went to die. All of those old people resident in 1808 were dead by 1810. However, many of the orphan children and young widows appear to have had a longer tenure. In an otherwise comprehensive collection of parish documentation apprenticeship indentures for poor children are small in number, suggesting that apprenticeship was unlikely to provide a way out of the workhouse for orphan children.[51] Once children were in the workhouse, then, they were probably there for a long time. The situation was not much better for young widows and their children. While the intervention of a relative with the offer of money or housing might have been one way to re-establish independence, remarriage was perhaps the only other way to get out of the workhouse. It is surely significant that all of the young widows resident in the workhouse in 1808 subsequently remarried and that in at least one instance the overseers paid for the ring and the service. Thus, while we saw evidence in chapter six that the workhouse could be a temporary safe haven, this was not the case in Calverley. Indeed, for young widows and the bearers of illegitimate children, the workhouse had the capacity to become just as much a prison as it was for the insane poor.[52]

There is much more work to be done on northern workhouse populations, which seem in this small sample to meet all of the objectives set by the new poor law – careful and sensitive treatment of the most vulnerable (in this case those in advanced old age) and the punishment and confinement of the errant or the problematic. How representative were these experiences? Was it usual to have low turnover in the workhouse population in the north and west? How should the composition of the workhouse population influence our characterisation of the northern and western communal relief system? These are the questions which require more work. For the purposes of this analysis, however, it is clear that the character of the workhouse population may have differed significantly from those on the wider relief lists, and that the very presence of a workhouse might be grounds for regarding some of the policies of local administrators as harsh and unyielding. This said, the really important thing for our understanding of the character of communal welfare is not the treatment of the small number of indoor poor, but the composition of the much larger body of the outdoor poor.

The northern and western old poor law: who was relieved?

As a precursor to asking who was relieved, we need to know how many. Figure 7.6 traces the numbers (indoor and outdoor) on relief in a sample of northern and western communities from the mid-eighteenth century. The total number of recipients experienced strong growth between 1790 and 1810, and this experience was common to all of the townships under the microscope here. However, the rising number of casual poor did not outstrip the rising number of pensioners as forcefully as appears to have happened in the south and east.[53] If we make a notional

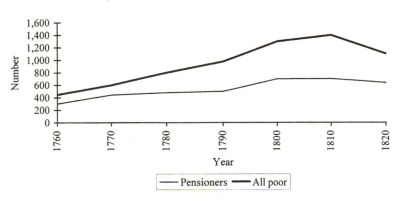

Figure 7.6 Growth in the numbers of pensioners and paupers, 1760–1820

allowance for the families of these recipients, then it is likely that the poor law in northern and western communities dealt with between one-fifth and one-quarter of the population. This is somewhat below the two-fifths to one-half which was taken to be representative of the south and east in the last chapter. Given rising background levels of poverty as highlighted in chapters four and five, there is thus little support for the idea that the poor law either had a wide remit or was coming to play a more central role in the strategies of more people. The question is, exactly who *was* the communal welfare system engaging with?

Figures 7.7 and 7.8 address the issue of the gender distribution of poor law recipients and poor law resources.[54] As in the communities taken to represent the south and the east, the gender distribution of the total recipient list is initially heavily skewed towards women at the mid-eighteenth-century, reflecting the dominance of life-cycle strain in the causation of poverty. However, while there is a later eighteenth-century trend for men to figure more prominently in the overall relief list, it is neither so strong nor so permanent as the same trend that was observed for the south and east. This is surprising given the feminised workhouse populations that seem to have been common in northern and western communities and suggests a very considerable difference indeed with the south and east. As we might expect, the years 1790 to 1810 stand out as a period in which men made substantial numerical gains in the recipient population, reflecting the fact that they outnumbered women as casual recipients. By the 1820s, however, women had begun to reassert their place on the relief lists. This said, we must be aware that general trends mask substantial differences between communities in the gender composition of the total relief list. In Powick by 1801, 72 out of 119

Figure 7.7 The sex distribution of all welfare recipients, 1760–1820

relief recipients were men, and in Calverley just one-half of all recipients were women by 1808, contrasting with the workhouse list for the same year and suggesting that the workhouse population really was a class apart from those on outdoor relief. Yet, in Lund by 1820–21, 60 per cent of all recipients were female and in Sutton Bonnington some 75 per cent. Similar differences can be observed in the wider literature. In Tysoe, Warwickshire, the relief list in 1778 entirely comprised women and by 1820 it was dominated by men being paid allowances for 'lost time'.[55] In Whickham, by contrast, men were effectively excluded from the relief lists and obliged to rely on charity.

Pension lists were more stable over time and area, and as figure 7.8 shows they confirm the broad focus of the relief system on the welfare of women, and also confirm the trends in the male–female ratio which appeared to emerge from figure 7.7. The contrast with similar data from the south and east is a powerful one and it suggests that groups which we might label the 'traditional' poor – widows, children and the disabled – continued to have a central place in the communal relief culture of the north and the west in a way that was passing in the south and east by the late eighteenth century. Indeed, if we turn briefly to the poor law accounts of Cowpe, we can exemplify this conclusion very well. Situated on the Lancashire–Yorkshire border, in a steep valley, and having a high proportion of its population engaged in weaving, bleaching and other activities, if the poor law was going to provide anywhere in the north the family allowances, labour market subsidies and widening entitlement characteristic of some parts of the south and east, it should have been here. However, the accounts for 1806 suggest very

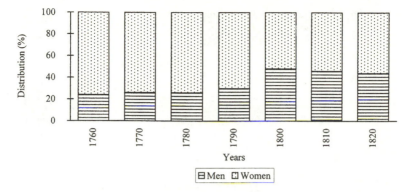

Figure 7.8 The sex distribution of regular pensioners, 1760–1820

clearly the fallback role that the poor law was consigned to play. Of the 24 genuine recipients of pensions during this year (i.e. correcting for out-parish relief), 14 were women and children, 2 were disabled (1 blind and the other 'simple' – though this can only be seen from later entries in the accounts) and 8 were men. After almost ten years of rapidly rising prices and fluctuating industrial fortunes, there were just 8 men on regular relief. Of these, 6 were over the age of 70. Moreover, of the 9 people relieved occasionally in 1806, just 3 were men. The profile of poor law accounts in most southern and eastern communities by the early nineteenth century would have looked rather different from this.

Figure 7.9 reinforces this message well, detailing the gender distribution of resources rather than recipients. The tendency for men, particularly in the mid- to late eighteenth century, to receive the lowest mean pensions is clear from a comparison between this chart and figure 7.8; and while the 1790s and early nineteenth century see male recipients climbing up the scale relative to women, this is not a permanent fixture of the relief landscape. Unlike the south, the central theme is the way in which the distribution of resources to women and children remains the cornerstone of outdoor relief policy. Such conclusions would be reinforced were we to take account of the composition effect of workhouse provision. To say more about recipients like these we must once again turn to the linkage of poor law accounts and family reconstitution data. Figures 7.10–7.12, therefore, make use of reconstitution data available for five northern and western communities between the late eighteenth and early nineteenth centuries.[56]

The problems inherent in this sort of analysis have been reviewed in chapter six, but again considering northern and western communities

Figure 7.9 The distribution of total pension resources between different groups of pensioners, 1760–1820

means surmounting extra obstacles. The communities with which this chapter engages had relatively mobile populations and this, allied with problems over the identification of out-parish relief, means that linkage between life-cycles of poor relief and life-cycles found in family reconstitution was less successful than in the communities of the south and east. Some 37 per cent of those who had a relief life cycle did not have a demographic life cycle. Figure 7.10 traces the age groups of those who received relief between 1750 and 1820. In 1750, the similarities with the picture for the south and east are profound. Well over 50 per cent of total poor law resources accrued to those over the age of 60. However, while in the south there was a substantial fall in the importance of old people and a rise in the percentage of resources accruing to those under 50 in the problem years of the late eighteenth and early nineteenth centuries, the same was not true of these northern and western communities. Between 1795 and 1805 the proportion of resources devoted to recipients in their forties rose significantly, but the proportion of resources devoted to the old and very old remained at well over 50 per cent in all of the years considered here. By implication, the increasing number of casual paupers apparent in figure 7.6 must have been relatively elderly. Given that there is reason to think that the age structure of the communities underpinning this analysis was more youthful than those which we examined for the south and east, this is a significant finding. It means that poor law administrators very definitely favoured old people in their allocation of resources, though those resources were still inadequate to provide a total welfare package for even the very old,

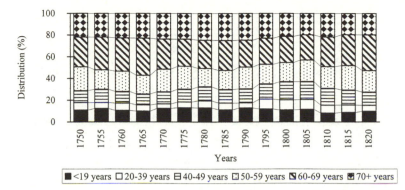

Figure 7.10 The age distribution of total poor law resources, 1750–1820

as we have seen. What is more, given the lessons of previous charts, it is clear that the communal welfare system in the north and west must have particularly favoured old women, where that in the south disproportionately favoured old men.

Figure 7.11, tracing the age distribution of pension resources, reinforces this picture and highlights more contrasts with the south and east. Between 1750 and 1770, 57 per cent of pension payments went to those over 60 years of age, roughly similar to the south and east. However, while the proportion of pension resources accruing to this group fell consistently between the 1760s and 1820s in the south and the east, in the north and west the proportion remained roughly stable at 54 per cent. This reinforces the point that many of those who were awarded casual payments were also old, but also gives little indication that the communal welfare system moved decisively to meet the needs of families during the crisis years between 1790 and 1810. This said, the observations that we have already encountered with regard to institutional paupers should act as a warning. If more of our communities in the north and west turned to using workhouses during the later eighteenth century, and if those workhouses shared the same broad function as the workhouse in Calverley, a broad band of relatively expensive female paupers and their children might be missing from this graph for the lower age groups. This potential problem is essentially unfathomable, but as Smith's analysis of Worsfield in Shropshire for the later eighteenth century indicates, it was not unheard of for communities to devote more than 70 per cent of their pension resources to those aged over 60.

What, then, do all of these charts add up to? The northern and

213

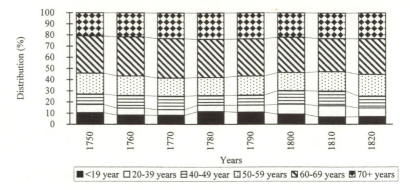

Figure 7.11 The age distribution of pension payments, 1750–1820

western poor law looked different from that in the south certainly. Where we compare like communities, in most years the total welfare package offered to paupers in the north was in value terms less than half that offered in the south and east. This does not inevitably mean that the poor law in the north and west was ungenerous, since we also have to account for lower costs of living and lower living standards in the north and west. However, it seems likely that when measured against any reasonable yardstick, northern relief values were meagre. What is more, there is strong evidence that such meagre payments were accompanied by the sort of harsh sentiment rarely seen in the south on any concerted basis. The emergence of a small group of recipients who swallow up relatively large proportions of local welfare budgets by the later eighteenth century means that not all paupers were embroiled in this harsh regime. Whether these people are a figment of statistics – a function of people who might previously have appeared in workhouses increasingly appearing on outdoor relief lists – or a real group of paupers requires more research. So does the question of why poor law administrators might have been prone to favour a small stratum of their local poor above all the rest.

Figure 7.12 may provide part of the answer, suggesting that, as in the south, those who were kin-poor came to the communal relief system early and stayed on it longer than the kin-rich. It is conceivable, then, that the emergence of a core of people who were treated relatively generously could reflect a precipitous drop in kinship options for some people during the late eighteenth century. This is not as outlandish as it seems. Greater mobility in northern counties after 1770 is now well established, and given the broad proto-industrial bias underlying the

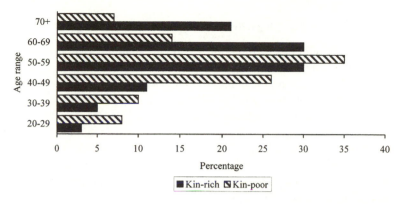

Welfare in the north and west, 1700–1820

Figure 7.12 Age at first contact with the communal relief system for the kin-rich and kin-poor

sample used here, rising death rates may also have compromised the kinship options especially of marginal people. In particular, work on Calverley suggests that those who were orphans, notably those who were the orphans of first-generation migrant parents, showed a definite tendency to become chronically poor in later life, and to have more of that poverty recognised by the poor law than was usual amongst others of their specific birth cohorts.

Yet, there is a danger of missing the main points here. These are threefold, and simply stated. First, the poor law relieved relatively few people at relatively ungenerous levels. Second, it is not adequate to portray the communal welfare system in the north and west as providing a safety net. There were essentially harsh sentiments underpinning this system and the poor law gave meagre relief because it did not choose to rather than because it could not afford to or did not need to. In this sense, it was something less than a welfare safety net; to borrow the words of an earlier chapter, the communal welfare system in the north and west was a threadbare and much mended canvas riven with barely disguised holes through which large numbers fell. Finally, while there was a broad skewing of resources and recognition of entitlement to the elderly, at no point did more than 30–35 per cent of those over 60 depend on the poor law for pensions. The upshot of these observations is that those on relief must necessarily have had a very dense set of alternative welfare strategies, while those who never turned to the welfare system but were undoubtedly poor in the terms set out in chapter five, must have been equally active in guaranteeing their welfare in other ways.

Alternative welfare structures

In a chapter and book of this length, it is clearly impractical to explore the point in time and life-cycle economy of makeshifts in real depth. Such analysis will have to be undertaken in other work.[57] This said, the broad outlines of the mass of alternative coping strategies are well known and worth considering. In 1803, Lancashire, the West Riding, Gloucestershire, Staffordshire, Cornwall, Nottinghamshire and Northumberland had 260,336 friendly-society members, or 37 per cent of the total of friendly-society members in the entire country. By 1815 the absolute number had expanded to 330,172, just keeping pace with the rising populations of these counties. Very roughly, friendly society-members outnumbered the paupers relieved in this collection of counties by just under 2:1 in 1803, and outnumbered permanent paupers by over 3:1. On the face of it, then, membership of a friendly society was one way in which the 60–70 per cent of those in poverty or at risk of poverty widely defined could avoid dependence. Such conclusions are, of course, too strong. The fact that friendly-society membership was most dense in larger urban areas is now well established, so that in the small towns and rural areas with which this book is concerned the friendly society may have been less important.

Cumberland and Westmorland provide a good example of this problem. In 1815, the two counties had eighty friendly societies, but thirty-eight were based in Whitehaven and Kendal. Notwithstanding the fact that such societies might draw in members from dozens of miles away, it would be wrong to overstate the potential of friendly societies for preventing poverty in the counties as a whole. Paradoxically, however, the two counties also provide evidence of the potential of this avenue. Thus a friendly society was started in the small and isolated community of Lamplugh in 1788. By 1798 it paid out 7s. per week to the sick, and by 1825 this sum had risen to 8s., or only just under the average male weekly wage for the area. The population of the town in 1801 was just 601.[58] Examples such as this and the numerous rural friendly societies to be found in north and west Lancashire suggest that they could be a first port of call at times of need occasioned by sickness even in communities like those dealt with here. In November 1820, for instance, the vestry of Garstang noted the case of William Shoemaker: 'His family consists of himself, his wife and 5 children. He has 7s. per week out of club and two of the children bring in 5s. per week.' It also recorded four other instances of men and women whose primary income was from friendly-society benefits.[59] Little wonder, then, that

Walsh sees a strong negative correlation between the density of friendly-society membership and the scale of relief bills in Shropshire as a whole, though which came first is a thorny question, as Gorsky reminds us.[60]

Many northern communities, and indeed most of those considered in this chapter, also had charitable resources at their disposal. Much of this had been accrued over a couple of hundred years, but, unlike many communities in the south and east, individuals were still making very considerable benefactions for the benefit of the poor in the north and the west by the early nineteenth century. In Mitton, for instance, William Parkinson left £200 to the churchwardens, the interest on which was to be distributed annually to the poor of Mitton.[61] In Foulshaw, Cumberland, £300 worth of bequests were accrued in the later eighteenth century, the interest on which paid for food doles in 1800; these were then translated into small regular cash doles of 3d. per week. While this sum may seem small, it was given to many more poor people than were recognised by the township relief system, and it amounted to just under one-quarter of the mean regular weekly pension in the 1790s.[62] Meanwhile, in Cartmel almost £1,000 was bequeathed to the poor between 1760 and 1810, building upon a rich tradition of charitable giving in the town over the preceding one hundred years. By 1820, the interest on charitable investments was providing a sum equal to three-quarters of annual poor relief spending on regular pensions, and this money was distributed to poor people both recognised and unrecognised by the poor law system. We could go on with these sorts of local examples.

More widely, though, charitable resources could have a substantial countywide impact. In Cumberland and Westmorland, for instance, the capital value of charities operating in 1817 was £200,000, yielding charity income of £8,376. This amounted to just over one-fifth of total yearly spending on the regular poor, and while some of this charity money had to be spent on certain types of pauper and certain types of relief (such as clothing), we should not make the mistake of thinking that charity was an insignificant part of the welfare patchwork. The figures for Lancashire are even more stark. It has been estimated that charitable income in 1787 stood at roughly 70 per cent of total poor law spending, and while again some of this spending was encumbered (those bequeathing money were peculiarly likely to do so for educational purposes in Lancashire), the contribution to total welfare was significant.[63] Against this backdrop, it is also important to remember the very considerable sums raised in ad hoc collections in northern areas during the later eighteenth and early nineteenth centuries. One estimate suggests that some £450,000 was raised through collections and related activities such as charity balls between 1795 and 1811 alone. Indeed, in places such as Halifax or Burnley such collections were the main response to poverty occasioned by wars and trade cycles, the poor law itself in these places barely registering these events.[64]

Other areas of the welfare patchwork also stand out. Thus, while Ottoway found little evidence that families were forced by the law to offer supplementary or substitute care for her parishes in the south, the evidence that northern families were key elements in the welfare process, forced or voluntary, is persuasive.[65] Poor law administrators in places like Garstang bargained with relatives to take on paupers, particularly the elderly poor, paying small allowances to facilitate co-residence. More generally, the pauper letters that we have examined in the last few chapters suggest that applicants had at least tried to gain help from kin before they had recourse to the communal welfare system. Indeed, the importance of kin to the welfare process appears to have been confirmed by figure 7.12, which suggested persuasively that those without kin came to the poor law soonest and had a much greater risk of becoming chronically or always poor in the terms defined by chapter five.

In some instances, of course, kinship help could merge imperceptibly with another, perhaps the most, important strand of the alternative welfare patchwork – work. Thus, in 1816, the overseer of Cowpe loaned £6 to Robert Ashworth to buy looms and 'his brother David Ashworth [has] given a promissory note to pay lawful interest for the same'.[66] This tells us much about the northern and western poor law; in the south the loan may have been a gift, and even if it was not, the likelihood of having to pay interest would perhaps have been slim. However, the episode also tells us rather more about the culture of self-reliance and work which permeated the issue of poverty and welfare in the north. An example from Holm provides evidence of such sentiments in action. The vestry recorded the case of Jane Rogers who, 'Subsists on the bounty of the neighbours but would never take money. Her whole apparel, hats and shoes excepted, she knitted on wooden pins, of the wool she gathered on the commons and spun herself.'[67] As welfare commentators have been keen to point out, the fact that there was a market for the products of the Ashworth looms and the fact that the commons had not been enclosed in Holm meant that northern and western paupers of this sort had potential coping strategies that the poor in the south and the east did not. This is true, but the existence of these avenues against the backdrop of a relief system that relieved relatively few people and then in meagre fashion does not mean that the northern poor were doing any more than scraping a basic living in the face of intense poverty. Nor does it mean that real and substantial differences in the cultures of poverty and communal welfare between the north and west and the south and east were absent.

We return to these issues in chapter nine. In the meantime, we could also point to a whole range of other supplementary opportunities. James Taylor notes a letter from an out-parish pauper back to the over-seer of Kirkby Lonsdale which pleads 'for I cannot get one penny of trust as I am not known in this town'.[68] Credit could thus be one response to poverty and marginality in the micawberish hope that something would turn up before the debts had to be paid. Pawning goods, petty selling, and providing goods and services to the poor law were also supplementary welfare opportunities. So was taking in lodgers. If we tie up entries in the 1787 census of Westmorland for Crosby Ravensworth with contemporaneous charity accounts, we can see that four of the eleven people who received benefits from charity in 1787 had also taken in lodgers as a way of making ends meet.[69] The linking of sources in this manner provides the way forward in under-standing the point-in-time and life-cycle dimensions of the economy of makeshifts in the north and west. Unfortunately, there is not the space here to undertake this sort of analysis, but as a way of exemplifying the complex welfare networks within which people were tied, we can link poor law and charity accounts for the Lancashire township of Mitton.[70]

Thus, in the relief year 1820/21 there were twenty-three people in the poor law accounts and twenty-eight on two separate charity lists. Ten people were to be found on both the poor law and charity lists. This sug-gests two things. First, that the local charities recognised a rather larger body of local poverty than did the overseer. Second, that at least as many people who were receiving communal relief were probably using charity to remain outside the clutches of the communal welfare system (eighteen people were to be found only on the charity lists) while over a third of those who were on relief were supplementing their income from charitable sources. Of course, the total expenditure of the poor law dwarfed the outgoings of the charities, but a few brief case studies might illustrate how significant charitable income could be. Thus, Mary Noblet received a pension of 2s. per week when her husband died midway through 1820, but she also received an 8s. lump sum (the equiv-alent of almost one month's relief) from Parkinson's charity. Neither Alice Sanderson nor her husband received regular relief, but in 1820 the husband went to the poor law for help with the rent while Alice went to

Parkinson's charity and obtained 5s. This was roughly equivalent to five weeks of pension. Richard Carter had a pension of 1s. 6d. in 1820, but he obtained 17s. from the Parkinson and Hawksworth charities in the town. This was worth well over ten weeks of pension. Finally, poor people like William Jarvis were subsisting entirely without poor law help, and the 4s. that he regularly obtained from the Parkinson charity may have made the difference between dependence and independence.

Of course, much more could be said about this data, and about the wider economy of makeshifts. The key question, though, is the one with which we started. How do we characterise the old poor law in the north and west?

Conclusion

This analysis has had to contend with ambiguous data, the volatility of poor law practice over time in any given community and, above all, complex spatial variations within the arbitrarily defined 'north and west'. Yet, we can and we should draw general conclusions for the whole region. The communal welfare system looked different to that in the south and the east. Some of the ways it looked different are well known – fewer people relieved, lower relief levels, more payment in kind – and they have lead welfare historians to suggest that the residual/safety net function of poor relief is most clearly seen in the north in particular. By implication, if the north and the south differed, it was by a matter of degree rather than order. No surprise then that commentators such as Taylor have been emboldened to make sweeping positive statements about the character and role of the English welfare system. He concludes that, 'Apart from the humane feelings many parish officers quite certainly possessed, the law as it in fact worked meant a measure of charity was economical . . . The cruelty and stupidity of the few . . . should not obscure the plodding competence of the many',[71] and goes further to suggest that 'only those who view British history in vacua can remain blinkered critics of that welfare system'.[72] As chapter six suggested, Taylor may well be right for the south, but what does our evidence show for the north and west?

It shows a threadbare and creaking relief system, dominated by the traditional paupers who had begun to disappear from the 1750s in the south. It shows a considerable number of background poor obliged to make a bare living using other welfare avenues. It shows a welfare system which recognised the problem of lack of kin but by implication required kin to look after relatives if at all possible. Above all it shows us a harsh poor law system in which the sentiments behind the relief practice were consistently unlike anything we find in the south and east as they are defined for this book. When faced with rising late eighteenth-century poor relief bills the vestry in Stone opened a workhouse and instituted a policy of individual examination. The cutback to relief entitlement was so severe and so prolonged that the number on the 1788 relief list was not matched again until the 1830s despite a 75 per cent rise in population in the town.[73] However we look at it this was harsh decision making, and its corollary is that many poor people must have fallen through the threadbare canvas that welfare historians have come to call the safety net.

But there is also another more important point to be made. What is significant is not that poor people fell though the net, but that they were meant to and that they expected to. By reading all of the evidence and reading its hidden as well as explicit messages we can see that the north was permeated by a culture of self-reliance on the part of poor law administrators and a culture of making do on the part of the potentially poor. Volatile poor law practice, meagre allowances, uncertain and shifting entitlement and the downright obstructive attitude of many local welfare officials drummed into generations of poor and potentially poor people the message that there was no such thing as a right to relief. The poor law helped certain well-defined groups of people, and the help it offered was supplementary and late. The poor, both those recognised and unrecognised by the relief system, thus had to adopt complex mechanisms for coping with the lack of even a basic safety net. Welfare historians have generally seen the existence of these alternative welfare avenues as a positive thing; more than in the south and east they enabled the poor to survive outside the poor law or at least to supplement its tender mercies. But surely we could read the situation in another way? With large numbers of the needy identified in chapter five drifting past the communal welfare system, competition for a place in the alternative welfare avenues was strong, and for many their lack of access to the poor law may well have placed them into grinding poverty even worse than the sort experienced by the agricultural labourers of the south who have so dominated welfare historiography. For the poor themselves, a southern culture of dependency may have been rather more advantageous than a northern culture of making do.

Such ideas will have to be explored in other work, but what I think that this analysis shows is that the southern/eastern and northern/western poor laws were different by *both* order and degree. There were at least two systems of welfare practice and sentiment evolving during the eighteenth and nineteenth centuries to cope with the changing and growing point-in-time and life-cycle poverty problems exposed so visibly in the first part of this book. Chapter nine explores more fully the sub-regional dynamics which may modify such a contention. However, this was the basic culture and practical superstructure upon which the new poor law was imposed. How did it fare?

Notes

1 Lancashire Record Office (hereafter LRO) DDKe 2/6/2, Bolton survey Bolton, 1674'. I am grateful to Richard Hoyle for this reference.
2 F. Baker (ed.), *William Grimshaw, 1708–1763* (Haworth, Epworth Press, 1963).
3 LRO DDX/320/2/1, 'Justicing memoranda book of Geoffrey Hornby of Preston 1723–31'.
4 K. Wrightson and D. Levine, *The making of an industrial society: Whickham 1560–1765* (Oxford, Oxford University Press, 1991), pp. 379–80.
5 A. W. Ashby, *One hundred years of poor law administration in a Warwickshire village* (Oxford, Oxford Economic Studies, 1926), and K. Mason, *Addingham: from brigantes to bypass* (Addingham, Addingham Civic Society, 1996).
6 R. P. Hastings, *Poverty and the poor law in the North Riding of Yorkshire, 1780–1837* (York, Borthwick Institute, 1982).
7 See G. Howells, 'For I was tired of England sir: English pauper emigrant strategies 1834–60', *Social History*, 23 (1998) 181–94, and E. Richards, 'How did poor people emigrate from the British Isles to Australia in the nineteenth century?', *Journal of British Studies*, 32 (1993) 250–79.
8 F. Wood and K. Wood (eds), *A Lancashire gentleman: the letters and journals of Richard Hodgkinson 1763–1847* (Stroud, Sutton, 1992).
9 J. A. Johnston, 'The parish registers and poor law records of Powick, 1663–1841', *Transactions of the Worcestershire Archaeological Society*, 9 (1984) 55–66.
10 J. S. Taylor, *Poverty, migration and settlement in the industrial revolution: sojourners' narratives* (Paolo Alto, SPSS, 1989), p. 4, and R. M. Smith, 'Ageing and well being in early modern England: pension trends and gender preferences under the English old poor law 1650–1800', in P. Johnson and P. Thane (eds), *Old age from antiquity to post-modernity* (London, Routledge, 1998), pp. 64–95 and especially tables 4.8 and 4.9.
11 E. C. Midwinter, *Social administration in Lancashire, 1830–1860* (Manchester, Manchester University Press, 1969), p. 14.
12 P. Ripley, 'Poverty in Gloucester and its alleviation 1690–1740', *Transactions of the Bristol and Gloucester Archaeological Society*, 103 (1985) 185–99.
13 See K. Williams, *From pauperism to poverty* (London, Routledge and Kegan Paul, 1981).

14 LRO DDHe 83/54, 'Cottage rents paid'.
15 Hastings, *Poverty*, p. 12, and Rawtenstall Library, 'The poor law accounts'.
16 Though see the brief studies of Hastings, *Poverty*, and P. Rushton, 'The poor law, the parish and the community in north-east England 1600–1800', *Northern History*, 25 (1989) 135–52. Also, for the end of the old poor law period, M. E. Rose, 'The administration of the poor law in the West Riding, 1820–1855' (unpublished Ph.D. thesis, University of Oxford, 1965).
17 Hastings, *Poverty*, p. 28. For Cowpe, see Rawtenstall Library RC 352 RAW, 'The poor law accounts of Cowpe'.
18 S. R. Broadbridge, 'The old poor law in the parish of Stone', *North Staffordshire Journal of Field Studies*, 13 (1973) 11–25.
19 LRO PR3031/10/1, 'Poor law accounts'.
20 LRO PR 1349, 'Miscellaneous letters'.
21 J. S. Taylor, 'Voices in the crowd: the Kirkby Lonsdale township letters, 1809–36', in T. Hitchcock, P. King and P. Sharpe (eds), *Chronicling poverty: the voices and strategies of the English poor 1640–1840* (Basingstoke, Macmillan, 1997), pp. 109–26.
22 I could find little support for J. S. Taylor, 'The impact of pauper settlement 1691–1834', *Past and Present* 73 (1976), pp. 42–74, who claims that the considerable inter-parochial correspondence on settlement probably stimulated uniformity of practice.
23 Hastings, *Poverty*, p. 32.
24 J. Crowther and P. Crowther (eds), *The diary of Robert Sharp of South Cave: life in a Yorkshire village 1812–1837* (Oxford, Oxford University Press, 1997).
25 H. Jewell, *The north–south divide: the origins of northern consciousness in England* (Manchester, Manchester University Press, 1994).
26 S. A. King, 'Reconstructing lives: the poor, the poor law and welfare in rural industrial communities', *Social History*, 22 (1997) 318–38.
27 S. R. Ottoway, 'The decline of life: aspects of ageing in eighteenth century England' (unpublished Ph.D. thesis, Brown University, 1997).
28 The exception was Worsfield where the median, mode and mean pension was 1s. per week.
29 Smith, 'Ageing'. King, 'Reconstructing'.
30 See P. Shapley, 'Voluntary charities in nineteenth century Manchester' (unpublished Ph.D. thesis, Manchester Metropolitan University, 1995), and M. Whittle, 'The changing face of charity in a nineteenth century provincial town' (unpublished Ph.D. thesis, Lancaster University, 1990).
31 The communities were Calverley, Addingham, Parr, Butlers Marston, Wenlock, Leigh, Troutbeck, Bleasby, Sutton Bonnington, Chorlton-upon-Medlock, Cartmel, Morland, Chipping Sodbury and Ravenstonedale. Full references are given in the Bibliography. Counties such as Derbyshire have no representation here, and the conclusions to be drawn from figure 7.1 must thus be read with caution. Not all the communities had data for the whole period. Short gaps in poor law accounts which encompass the chronological

reference points have been filled by substituting the nearest complete yearly account to the date concerned.

32 Cumbria Record Office, Uncatalogued, 'The Great End Book of Ravenstonedale'.

33 Rushton, 'The poor law'.

34 The townships were Troutbeck, Calverley, Stokesley, Powick, Lund, Holm, Great Strickland, Leigh, Addingham, Mitton, Butlers Marston, Sutton Bonnington, Horsforth and Cartmel. References are given in the Bibliography. Not all places had records covering the whole period continuously. Gaps in the records for individual communities were treated as in the last sample. The communities either denote out-parish relief or else give good reason to suspect that this was not likely to be a serious problem.

35 Lund account book. I am grateful to Martin Ramsbottom for allowing me access to this book. The accounts in this case are the most difficult set I have come across, since the overseer paid paupers by the week, month, quarter or year more or less at random.

36 M. A. Parsons, 'Poor relief in Troutbeck 1640–1836', *Transactions of the Cumberland and Westmorland Antiquarian and Archaeological Society*, 155 (1995) 169–86.

37 Ashby, *One hundred*, and M. Hall, 'Poor relief in Eskdale in the early 1800s', *Transactions of the Cumberland and Westmorland Antiquarian and Archaeological Society*, 152 (1992) 205–12.

38 Wrightson and Levine, *Whickham*, p. 381.

39 *Ibid*.

40 There were often unseen relationships between religious charity and neighbourliness and the communal welfare system which worked to deflate mean allowance figures. For an important case study which strays into the territory of chapter eight, see R. Watson, 'Poverty in north east Lancashire in 1843: evidence from Quaker charity records', *Local Population Studies*, 55 (1995) 28–44. The Quaker charity was active from at least 1819.

41 For more on this, see P. Hudson and S. A. King, *Industrialisation, material culture and everyday life* (forthcoming).

42 In this equation, while nominal pensions were rising against food and clothing prices they actually fell behind rent increases.

43 For more on these figures, see S. A. King and J. G. Timmins, *Making sense of the industrial revolution* (Manchester, Manchester University Press, forthcoming).

44 The communities are Calverley, Parr, Sutton Bonnington, Mitton, Wenlock, Leigh and Butlers Marston. Full references are given in the Bibliography.

45 LRO DDHe/83/54, 'Cottage rents paid'.

46 E. G. Thomas, 'The treatment of poverty in Berkshire, Essex and Oxfordshire 1723–1840', (unpublished Ph.D. thesis, University of London, 1971), and A. Tomkins, 'Paupers and the infirmary in mid-eighteenth-century Shrewsbury', *Medical History*, 43 (1999) 208–27.

47 See P. Anderson, 'The Leeds workhouse under the old poor law 1726–1834', *Publications of the Thoreseby Society*, 56 (1979) 75–113.

48 See C. Bouch and G. Jones, *A short economic and social history of the Lake counties 1500–1830* (Manchester, Manchester University Press, 1961).

49 The returns were for Calverley (1808), Horsforth (1802) and Leigh (1797). References are given in the Bibliography.

50 Bouch and Jones, *A short*. Also CRO WDX/382, 'Inmates of Kirkby Lonsdale workhouse in 1830'.

51 Indeed, there is a sense in which the chronic life-cycle poor identified in chapter five had their northern human embodiment in these orphans, as we will see later in the chapter.

52 See also L. D. Smith, 'The pauper lunatic problem in the west midlands 1815–1850', *Midland History*, 21 (1996) 101–18.

53 In 1803, Lancashire, the West Riding, Cornwall, Northumberland, Nottinghamshire, Herefordshire and Westmorland collectively relieved 40,148 casual paupers and 66,401 permanent indoor and outdoor paupers, suggesting that 38 per cent of the pauper total were casual. However, the 1803 returns to parliament are clearly flawed and there is no guarantee that those relieved permanently as pensioners and those relieved as casuals were different people.

54 These charts consider adult paupers only. 'Unspecified' relates to instances where just a surname is given or where a forename, such as Frances, might indicate either sex.

55 Ashby, *One hundred*.

56 The communities are Calverley, Farsley, Cowpe, Middleton and Sutton Bonnington. The reconstitution of Calverley and Farsley was carried out for the purposes of a joint research project with Professor Pat Hudson. See Hudson and King, *Industrialisation*. The reconstitutions of Cowpe and Middleton were conducted for a project investigating the shape of the economy of makeshifts in the early modern north. Sutton Bonnington was reconstructed by James Mayes and I am grateful to him for allowing me to use his reconstitution. Not all places have continuous poor law accounts. Full references can be found in the Bibliography.

57 S. A. King, 'Making the most of opportunity: the economy of makeshifts in the early modern north', in S. A. King and A. Tomkins (eds), *Coping with the crossroads of life: the economy of makeshifts in early modern England* (forthcoming).

58 R. F. Dickinson, 'The friendly society of the inhabitants of the parish of Lamplugh and its neighbourhood', *Transactions of the Cumberland and Westmorland Antiquarian and Archaeological Society*, 96 (1965) 418–31.

59 LRO DDX 386/3, Vestry record of Garstang.

60 V. Walsh, 'Poor law administration in Shropshire 1820–1885' (unpublished Ph.D. thesis, University of Pennsylvania, 1970), and M. Gorsky, 'The growth and distribution of English friendly societies in the early nineteenth century', *Economic History Review*, 51 (1998) 489–511.

61 LRO PR3031/11/1, 'Mitton overseer accounts'.
62 CRO WD/D/D6/68, 'Donations to the poor in Foulshaw'.
63 J. Mannion, *A northern tour* (Leeds, Black, 1838).
64 *Ibid.*
65 Ottoway, 'The decline'.
66 Rawtenstall Library RC 352RAW, 'The poor law accounts of Cowpe'.
67 CRO WD/H01.1, 'Old poor law accounts 1721–1774'.
68 Taylor, 'Voices in the crowd,' p. 153.
69 L. Ashcroft (ed.), *Vital statistics: the Westmorland census of 1787* (Berwick, Curwen Archives Trust, 1992), and CRO WPC/12, 'Charity account book 1751–1840'.
70 LRO PR3031/10/1, 'Poor law accounts of Mitton', and PR3031/8/1, 'Hawksworth and Parkinson charities'.
71 Taylor, *Poverty*, p. 105.
72 *Ibid.*, p. 173.
73 Broadbridge, 'The old poor Law'.

CHAPTER EIGHT

WELFARE UNDER THE NEW POOR LAW, 1821–50

Overview

Chapters six and seven have provided preliminary evidence of a considerable and enduring regionality in the English welfare system under the old poor law. Whatever gloss we paint on this regionality and the underlying individual experiences of poverty, marginality and welfare, the fact of substantial regional divisions is undeniable. It was upon this quicksand that the new poor law of 1834 was built. Chapters two and three have offered a broad overview of the 'what' and the 'why' of the new poor law and the intention of this chapter is not to afford a narrative history of its development or its personalities. It is, however, worth recapping the perspectives offered in chapters two and three. Broadly, the report into the state of the old poor law in 1832 characterised it as a ramshackle system of local welfare initiatives that bore only a limited resemblance to what the state thought was happening. Generous allowances encouraged idleness and immorality, undermining the desirable self-help ethic which should have lain at the heart of welfare. The result was spiralling relief bills and a vicious circle of poverty.[1]

The (eventual and contested) outcome of the report was a legislative initiative that sought to impose new systems of administration on the welfare landscape, to shift the focus of welfare policy (though not welfare finance) away from the locality, and to impose an explicit needs test and standard levels of care (the principles of the workhouse test and less eligibility respectively) on a collection of localities where neither had existed before. A temporary central body (the Poor Law Commission) appointed a raft of assistant commissioners whose job it was to mark out the new poor law unions on the ground in a process which rippled northwards and westwards from the south and the east. By 1840 this process was largely complete and there were 587 poor law unions, each nominally controlled by an elected Board of Guardians who had core responsibilities to the poor, to ratepayers and to the state. These responsibilities were monitored and enforced by functionaries as diverse as union auditors and Poor Law Commission inspectors.

Of course, the processes of change were by no means as smooth as they have been portrayed here. The Commission itself was in a parlous state after its initial five-year mandate expired in 1839. It had to survive on one-year extensions of its role until 1842 when, in the face of political opposition, a further five-year term was granted. In the meantime the resources available to the Commission, which had always been too small for the task in hand, were pared further. On the ground too there were problems. Assistant commissioners responsible for organising unions frequently found themselves in conflict with local elites, and the intemperate reaction of some northern and midland poor law authorities to even the suggestion of unionisation are now well known.[2] Even where there was less dispute, there could be a considerable gap between the formation of the union and the Board of Guardians taking control of the relief process. In Oldham the gap was almost six years.[3] Nonetheless, the obstacles should not be overstated. The Webbs thought that in rural southern England, the starting point for the unionisation of parishes, leading elites were 'pleased to be relieved of their disagreeable tasks; and most people were glad to adopt anything that promised reform'.[4] Our analysis of the south and east in chapter six suggests no such despair, but the really important thing about the implementation of the new poor law, in name at least, was not how much conflict and opposition it generated, but how little.

Certainly by the early 1840s, the Commission was at a stage where it could set about its central task – that of curtailing outdoor relief and trying to impose standard responses to unstable poverty and welfare conditions at local level. The Outdoor Relief Prohibitory Order introduced in 1844 was weakly drafted and allowed parishes to continue outdoor relief to able-bodied people in cases of urgent (particularly medical) need, but by 1847 it was in force in 396 unions. Most of the remainder enforced different grades of order – such as the Outdoor Relief Test Order which imposed a work test on prospective recipients. Meanwhile, however, the Commission and its orders and inspectors were disengaged from the issue of outdoor relief to those who were not able-bodied, which was left very much at the discretion of individual unions.[5]

On the ground, the poor in receipt of relief, the poor who were not in receipt of relief and other local residents would have noticed elections to the Board of Guardians (though they would have seen very few real election contests) and they may subsequently have noticed, in newspaper reports of the activities of guardians, a chronic absenteeism amongst those elected. They would have seen parish houses sold, and in the south and east of England they would have seen the closure of ramshackle parish workhouses and the building of much larger institutions to serve the whole union. By 1850, the number of workhouses in the south and east as it is defined here had fallen from a peak of around 2,150 in 1830 to just 750, while mean capacity had grown more than tenfold.[6] Paupers may have noticed less change aside from the workhouse. Surprisingly large numbers of Boards of Guardians failed to sit as a board, instead devolving day-to-day responsibility to local committees. The immediate personalities that paupers engaged with may thus have changed little.

We return to these themes below, but the key question is what have welfare historians noticed about the process of the new poor law? On its immediate consequences there is relative consensus. The initial results of the 1834 act were to be seen in aggregate spending, which, notwithstanding the costs of local reform and rebuilding of the poor law fabric, witnessed a profound fall. The detailed figures were charted in chapter four, but it is worth repeating them here. In 1820 the relief bill stood at £7.3 million, by 1830 the bill had already fallen to £6.82 million, and by 1840 the figure was just £4.6 million. When we realise that this fall was disproportionately generated by southern rural communities, given the sloth with which the north took up the 1834 act, then it becomes even more significant than it looks at first blush. In places such as Uckfield in Sussex, these national trends translated into a halving of poor relief expenditure compared to the last years of the old poor law. Numbers in receipt of relief also fell radically in individual unions. How far we may in any case have expected reduced dependency on the communal relief system given generally rising living standards after 1830 is difficult to say. Certainly the inference to be drawn from chapter five is that there was a more substantial life-cycle and point-in-time poverty problem by the 1830s than there had ever been before, and the unrest in rural communities of the south and east during the 1830s must have been at least in part a reflection of endemic need amongst rural labourers. Thus, on the face of it, the downward trend in expenditure and the tightening up of entitlement apparent after 1834 may have reflected an even smaller role for the poor law in the relief of background poverty than had been the case previously. Ideas like this are explored below, but Hollen-Lees's characterisation of the period after 1834 as 'Residualism refined' is initially appealing.[7]

Yet, while these figures are apparently stark, chapter three suggested that welfare historians still disagree radically on how we should characterise the medium- and long-term impact of the new poor law on the welfare framework as it was played out at local level. It is these competing perceptions and the issue of how we decide between them that form the focus of this chapter. Initially however, and at risk of repetition, it is worth distilling some more of the lessons from chapters two and three so that the different positions are in sharp focus. Thus, on the one hand there are those commentators who portray the new poor law as a damp squib. In conception and legal reality the new poor law was an unsteady compromise addressing an inappropriately defined problem with inadequately designed solutions. It was staffed in its central component by an odd collection of idealists and administrators with little grasp of local traditions, cultures and experiences. In a practical sense its enduring feature was the continuance of local diversity, traditional personnel, often the traditional built fabric and, before too long, traditional policies. Indeed, by the end of our period there were fewer workhouse inmates as a percentage of the total pauper population in our regions than there had been in 1803, while relief to the able-bodied may have been more common than ever, albeit disguised.[8]

Others, though, have seen a more radical change in the character of local relief structures and sentiments towards the poor, pointing to the crushing of able-bodied out-relief, the fall or stagnation of allowance values and the stigmatisation of the poor. Barker and Harris, for instance, contrasted the coarseness of the old poor law with 'the moral disapproval, the stinginess, the mechanical regulation of the later new poor law' and suggested that under the old poor law 'the boundary moreover between pauperism and independence was less strict, and the stigma less cruel'.[9] The workhouse has been a particular focus for those who regard the poor as having succeeded in its deterrent ambitions and thus as having instigated radical change in the welfare culture. This is perhaps hardly surprising in the light of comments from the town clerk of Banbury in April 1836 that 'if the gaol should be thought insufficient we have a large building in the town lately used as a workhouse, which might be converted into a very commodious prison'![10] There was also a more intimate connection between the new poor law and the criminal law. The Banbury gaol records suggest strongly that the number of prosecutions for offences connected to the poor law spiralled in the 1830s. James Master and James Robinson were prosecuted for 'an assault on the relieving officer at Wardington' in 1835, whereas Joseph Savage had been put in the stocks for assaulting the overseer under the old poor law. Charges of misconduct in the union workhouse became relatively common, as did prosecutions for leaving the workhouse without the permission of the master. In January 1837, for instance, the gaoler recorded the case of 'Three men charged with leaving the union workhouse without leave and taking their clothes with them belonging to the workhouse.' The next day he noted their fate with some surprise, 'The above three taken before the magistrates and committed for three months. A hefty punishment.'[11] In short, the criminal law was being used to enforce the local discipline of the poor law in ways that had not been the case before. Such ideas provide important support for those who see the new poor law as auguring fundamental changes in the structure of welfare and the experience of being poor. Poverty, we might say, had moved from being an accepted and expected part of local life, to being something that had a cause and could thus be attacked.[12]

Alternatively, chapter three suggested that there were also more positive views which call for the new poor law to be judged by appropriate yardsticks. Karel Williams, for instance, suggests that all that changed after 1834, and indeed all that was meant to change after 1834 was the treatment of the able-bodied. The Webbs agree, though they put a rather different gloss on the performance of the new poor law as a whole. They suggest that the commissioners 'threw altogether into the background the requirements of the large numbers of sick, insane, crippled, blind, infirm, aged persons or orphan children, without resources . . . the continuance of outdoor relief to them as a general system was . . . explicitly suggested'.[13] For these groups, eligibility in the eyes of the communal relief system may actually have improved in some areas after 1834, while more generally the new poor law still provided at least a basic safety net for those in need. Indeed, in some places and to some groups of the poor, the post-1834 welfare system offered much more than basic allowances. As chapter three noted, the work of David Thomson on the elderly in Bedfordshire has suggested that new poor law pensions could be relatively generous in both nominal money terms and compared to yardsticks such as wages.[14] And as chapter six suggested, such attitudes towards the welfare of the old would chime neatly with practices under the old poor law in this region. Moreover, there were also other positive aspects to the relief system. The Commission acted as a repository for best practice, and it was sensitive to the peculiarities of individual localities, seeking 'not to eradicate local differences, but to make them more manageable'.[15]

Reconciling these three radically different positions is no easy task, especially given the fact that reading the narratives of paupers, poor law administrators and local worthies provides evidence for any and all of the perspectives. Two additional problems make our task harder:

1 What indicators do we use to identify the role and character of the new poor law? Stated national aims? The changing parameters of some local practice? Spending? The experience of being poor? Whether the 1834 legislation managed to iron out the massive regional divisions in entitlement and welfare generosity that we saw under the new poor law? This is no easy question, as one brief example can show. Thus, the fact that spending fell precipitously after 1834 could be read as a reflection of savage cost cutting by (especially southern and eastern) local administrations suddenly freed from the shackles of magistrates. In this sense, the falling relief bill would have had harsh and enduring consequences for the endemically poor. Yet, what was significant and what was not in the sphere of cost cutting? Poor law authorities had always been prone to volatile poor relief strategies, and massive enduring cutbacks were a feature of the welfare system of Eaton Socon, Stone and Ravenstonedale well before the new poor law ever came along. What made the period after 1834 so different? We return to the question of realistic indicators in the next section.

2 Our lack of detailed local information. On the face of it we seem to know plenty about the new poor law. Felix Driver and Anne Digby have demonstrated persuasively that the basic fabric of the poor law – the workhouse and its related buildings – was gradually replaced or regenerated up to 1850. The latter has also suggested that even before the end of the period covered by this book the workhouse had become an institution delivering care to the life-cycle casualties of nineteenth-century England, much as it appears to have been in some areas under the old poor law.[16] Meanwhile, extensive work on those at the opposite end of the poor law experience – the guardians – has shown us that the new poor law could become a focus for division and dispute in ways which we rarely appreciate by looking at indicators such as relief expenditure. Boards of Guardians split on a range of religious, social, political and other grounds were much more representative of the poor law than were boards acting with a concerted unity of purpose to crush the poor.[17] And then of course we have the broad county studies. Brundage, for instance, has looked at the twelve Northamptonshire unions, pointing to significant reductions in expenditure in the late 1830s and tying this to a decline in the nominal value of welfare payments rather than savage cuts to the length of the relief lists which he labels 'The most dramatic encounter between rich and poor under the new poor law'.[18] Dunkley and McCord have engaged with wide-ranging material in the northeast, Thompson with unions in Leicestershire and Digby with the new poor law in Norfolk.[19]

To restate, then, we seem to know a lot about the new poor law. Yet in practice key components of the necessary historiography are missing. The detailed deconstruction of welfare practice and experiences of being poor in individual unions remains relatively uncommon, at least compared to the material on the old poor law. We know plenty about the workhouse and its poor, but comparatively little about the outdoor poor who dominated the pauper host. The generosity of payment remains in the background of most general studies, and the issue of how regular and irregular relief combined at individual level to generate a total welfare package has been largely ignored. While commentators such as Walsh have tried to analyse the old and new poor laws as a continuous process, the nature of the transition between the two systems from the standpoint of paupers remains poorly observed.[20] And the issue of what happened to the broad regional dimensions of welfare practice after 1834 has lain consistently dormant. Thus, while Kidd regrets the tendency to generalise from local studies in poor law history, the whole point is that we do not have enough local studies to begin reconciling the very different views of welfare historians on the character of welfare under the new poor law.[21]

Clearly, this chapter can only scratch the surface of this issue. Given the logistics of distilling new poor law policy from vast sets of union records, the chapter does not have the underlying data range which underpinned the discussion of the old poor law. Indeed, strictly speaking the two case studies used here can tell us only limited amounts about regional and sub-regional differences in the practice and sentiment of the communal welfare system. That said, regional comparison is only one of the aims of this chapter; equally as important it aims to show what can be done with new poor law records and to trace the connection between the old poor law and the new. With these limited ambitions in mind the chapter will attempt to consider the local and regional impact of the 1834 legislation in more depth. Who was relieved under the new poor law? How generous was relief? What form did relief take? How was entitlement constructed and reconstructed? How did a new national system interact with existing local and regional diversity of welfare practice and the prevailing welfare culture? These are the core issues that underpin this analysis.

Problems and perspectives

It is tempting to launch straight into detailed local analysis, but part of the process of establishing the role and character of the new poor law in itself and in relation to the old poor law is, as Karel Williams suggests, to construct an outline of how much *could* have changed rather than looking just at how much *did* change. Some of the constraints to change are familiar – the small number of assistant commissioners, the lack of compulsory powers, and the active opposition of some northern and midland poor law authorities all mean that truly radical change from the old poor law should not be anticipated. However, there were also more pressing but less obvious problems which might influence our thinking.

1 The sheer rapidity of development and the size of the units that resulted. In Durham, 280 parishes were consolidated into 14 unions in a process lasting just three months. Shropshire had 212 parishes concentrated into 13 unions over an equally short space of time. In Lancashire, the unionisation process took much longer but there were wide variations in the size of the 29 unions eventually created, with the smallest union incorporating 4 townships or parishes and the largest some 29. It is easy to run off these figures, but what did they mean on the ground? On 31 January 1837, Richard Hodgkinson, estate steward to Lord Lilford 'met Mr Buchanan, clerk to the magistrates, coming to me with the package he had just received from the commissioners'. He was disconcerted by the instructions within,

> I have now to observe that Culcheth and Lowton are parts of the parish of Winwick, why they are put into Leigh Union we have no means of knowing. It is the general wish and has been the general expectation that Leigh parish wd form a board of itself. This wish the inhabitants had no opportunity of expressing as no Commissioner has been among us . . . How 8 townships extending over a space of ground nearly 8 miles in diameter and containing a population of more than 24,000 souls can be brought in one short fortnight to act consistently upon any uniform plan, I am at a loss to know.[22]

Everybody else was at a loss too. The rushed nature of the unionisation process is clear for all to see and mistakes and miscalculations were inevitable.

Even if assistant commissioners divided up the relief landscape so as to put rural parishes with rural parishes and urban parishes with urban parishes within the union structure, deep and enduring local divisions would have to be played out at union level well before the union could be expected to function. In Lancashire, for instance, the Ormskirk union was riven by conflict between its rural parishes for over a decade from 1837, while the Chorlton union saw six townships added and four removed between 1837 and 1849. In similar fashion, where the assistant commissioners managed (as they all too often did in the north) to put urban and rural parishes together in the same union there was a cultural and practical clash to be played out. In practical terms, urban parishes often had a more substantial poverty problem than rural parishes in the same union, and sometimes very different mechanisms for coping with that poverty. Such divisions could generate terminal stresses and strains on the basic fabric of the union. Manchester union was a case in point. Convened in January 1841, the union contained eleven townships in addition to Manchester itself. The effect of the formation of the union was to *raise* the poor rate (compared to that in the individual townships prior to unionisation), and by 1848 it had reached 6s. 8d. in the pound. For the rural parishes tied into the union this was a (Manchester-inspired) massive rise, and the union finally broke up in 1850.[23] Once again, even where there was no ill will towards it, waiting for the new poor law and then dealing with its immediate logistical impact brought considerable turmoil to local poor relief strategies. Discerning the true character of the relief system thus becomes problematic.

2 The issue of staffing the new poor law given its rapid sweep over the English administrative landscape. There was no body of trained poor law staff waiting to fill the positions that the reform of 1834 necessitated. Clerks, relieving officers, workhouse masters, workhouse nurses and others inevitably had to be recruited from the staff of the old poor law and from a variety of other sources. They then had to be trained and to learn their jobs. Robert Sharp the schoolmaster of South Cave in the East Riding suggests that this was no easy process. He had to give lessons to the new auditor for the Beverley union![24] Once trained, new poor law staff then had to learn how to balance their two conflicting roles – duty to the guardians, and by inference ratepayers, on the one hand but their need to care for the poor on the other. Again, this was no easy lesson to learn and some imbalance was inevitable. The simple fact that there was an overhang of personnel or indeed that standards of care went down in the initial years after the 1834 reform should really not surprise us and should not be used as a yardstick with which to characterise the new poor law in relation to the old. The more relevant issue is how many of these staff would still have been in place five or ten years after the initial reform.

3 Local attitudes. While the new poor law brought the centralised state into the locality in ways and with a frequency which would have appeared radical to some contemporaries, essentially it left (by accident or design) very much power in the hands of local officials and the people who elected them. Some of these local officials were extremely hostile

both to the new poor law and to the whole (and much wider) process of changing central and local relations. This is hardly surprising in a situation where the prevailing experience in localities over the previous 150 years had been a distant government without the power, will or need to change traditional relations between centre and locality. Indeed, most textbooks point very forcibly to the way in which new poor law riots, refusals to co-operate, and general obstruction and bumbling were tools used to great effect in Lancashire, Yorkshire and parts of the midlands in prolonging the unionisation process and stifling radical changes to local activity once unionisation had taken place. Yet downright hostility was not the real problem the new poor law faced. Rather there was a more serious initial incredulity which took some time to break down. The sentiment of Robert Sharp is typical of the concerns which we can see expressed in a whole range of narrative sources. He noted in June 1836, 'Talk of Irish oppression indeed when every parish in England is prevented from conducting their own affairs.'[25] In practice, energy and resources were taken up in smoothing and mitigating the experience of lost jobs and lost authority and it is important not to judge an initial lack of action out of context in trying to discern the character and role of the new poor law.

4 The new poor law faced a problem of immediate legitimacy. The fact that the 1834 act was a compromise would have been well known at local level. Perhaps more important, however, was that unionisation took place against the backdrop of the survival of other means of addressing issues of poverty and welfare. In Lancashire, for instance, the slow process of unionisation (it started in 1837 and was not effectively completed until 1847) was accompanied by the survival of the Caton union formed under Gilbert's Act. Policy here diverged significantly from policy in surrounding new poor law unions.[26] Similar observations could be made of most counties. In Hampshire, for instance, parishes were divided into twenty-three unions, but Alverstoke, Headley, Farnborough, Southampton and the Isle of Wight retained their incorporated status. There can be little doubt that the unions around these sorts of incorporations had one eye on the law and their own past experience, but also an eye on what was going on next door. This, and the fact that the law itself remained an ambiguous guide to what should happen at local level, means that there would inevitably be some settling-down period before it becomes possible to distil the essence of the character of the new poor law.

The lessons from this brief analysis are complex, but it seems clear that if we want to uncover the essential character of the new poor law as it was played out at local level, we should avoid focusing on the immediate new poor law period and placing too much store on aggregate numbers, and we should not be beguiled by the prescriptions of the law or the changing outline character of local administration. Instead, we should place the new poor law firmly in the context of old poor law practice and engage with the sentiment of relief giving and the range of experiences amongst individual paupers at local level after 1834. Above all, we should judge the new poor law in light of the view that not much could have changed, so anything that did may have been 'significant'.

These are the strategies employed in the next section. Before we move on, however, it is important to realise that national poor law statistics and some recent overviews of welfare history provide us with a framework of what to expect. It is important to briefly explore this framework. Thus, we have already seen that during the 1830s and 1840s, both aggregate spending and the number of people in receipt of relief fell. More detailed perspectives are also available. Karel Williams, for instance, has suggested that the mean outdoor dole per pauper in 1840 was just 1s. 1d., falling to under 1s. in 1843 and then stagnating at around 1s. for the rest of the 1840s. Such figures are well below those found for the old poor law in either region.[27] By 1850, national statistics also suggest that almost 90 per cent of those receiving relief were doing so outside the workhouse and that in most years less than 18 per cent of total expenditure was on indoor paupers. The latter figure matches almost exactly the 15–16 per cent of spending directed towards workhouse care by communities in the south and east and north and west during the early nineteenth century. We can also find out much about the composition of the pauper host. In 1850, 40 per cent of those receiving relief were adult females, 40 per cent were children and just 20 per cent were adult men, so that two-thirds of all adult recipients were women on the national stage. The broad characteristics of the entire body of relief recipients will be familiar from chapters six and seven. In 1851, the aged and infirm accounted for 42 per cent of all recipients, while 'fatherless families' accounted for 25 per cent of all recipients. Widows with dependent children formed the largest part of the latter category, and a growing part. In 1840 this group had comprised 13 per cent of all paupers, but by 1821 they accounted for almost 21 per cent. Indeed, by 1851, it is likely that almost 40 per cent of all widows between the ages of 20 and 45 were on outdoor relief.

This perspective could be developed rather more, but we can see subtle differences between these statistics and the lessons to be drawn from chapters six and seven on issues such as the gender composition of relief, the importance of children and the generosity of payments. It is little wonder in this sense that recent attempts to take an overview of the new poor law have characterised 1834 as instigating a process of dis-entitlement and the rolling back of welfare. Alan Kidd, for instance, suggests that 'The contraction in state welfare . . . can be dated to the poor law reform of 1834 and was in sharp contrast to the more pater-nalistic and comparatively generous philanthropy which underpinned much public provision under the poor law in the eighteenth century.'[28] Chapters six and seven add caveats to this idea, but it is one shared by Hollen-Lees. She suggests that the elderly were by far and away the most sympathetically treated of recipients under the new poor law, and traces a broad range of outdoor pension values, from 3s. per week in Bedfordshire to 1s. 6d., per week in Atcham near Shrewsbury. Even the top levels of pensions paid to the elderly poor, however, could only provide around two-fifths of the welfare afforded by the prevailing adult male wage. For other groups the experience of the communal welfare system was even less favourable. Hollen-Lees suggests that those under 60 years of age received between 1s. and 2s. per week per capita and that these rates were stagnant after 1834 despite rising wages and back-ground living standards. As a best guess, it seems that the relief system could only have provided a family of five with a maximum of 42 per cent of the living standard of a similar family in work. What is more, 'Who you were and where you were mattered, but not a lot', suggesting that regional divisions of the sort that we traced under the old poor law are not to be seen under the new.[29] This particular issue will recur later in the chapter, but for now the general consensus of recent work is that the new poor law saw reduced entitlement, reduced generosity and harsher sentiments.

Going further than this general picture involves engaging with detailed new poor law data. However, this is not as simple as it sounds. Many of the problems familiar from chapters six and seven have reso-nance here. Thus, the very rapidity of the process of unionisation often means that late old poor law and early new poor law records are sparse. Where the records do survive, and more especially after 1840, they can be voluminous and tedious. The new poor law history of Bolton must be written from 500 or more ledgers and other pieces of documentation. And that documentation can be just as treacherous as overseers' accounts under the old poor law. Even in well-documented unions, nominal information on the poor who receive outdoor relief is often missing, making it difficult to look at the complexities of entitlement. Where nominal information is found, interpretative problems arising from practices such as out-parish relief are as potentially powerful as they were with old poor law documentation. Thus, in 1845 some 111 parishes had agreements with Bradford township to pay out-parish relief to their paupers there, and 117 parishes had similar arrangements with Leeds township. William Day also noted the ubiquity of out-parish relief throughout Shropshire and lamented the way in which such practices could compromise any overview of the Shropshire poor law.[30]

It is also important to realise that, as under the old poor law, what we see recorded in the accounts of new poor law unions is the end of the process of establishing entitlement and matching the (still often contested) supply of poor relief with demand for it. Some of those who felt poor enough to apply initially might be turned down, others might of their own accord drop out at some point between application and the decision to grant relief, and yet more may have had their relief disguised so that they never appear in the mainstream poor law records as opposed to highway or churchwarden accounts. Having more information on these background poor, and more information on how their requests were constrained by an unwillingness or an inability to pay more, might throw a rather different gloss on our appreciation of local relief strategies. Hollen-Lees, for instance, has analysed settlement examinations conducted on those applying to unions for relief in six provincial towns, and she finds that younger married men were a very significant component of those applying for relief in any year but a small proportion of those actually granted relief. The disparity is significant for our characterisation of the sentiment behind local administration, and problems like this mean we must tread carefully.[31]

The new poor law and welfare – a regional structure?

This section uses records from two diametrically opposed unions, in terms of both location and socio-economic structure, to try and make sense of the competing perspectives on the new poor law. Bolton was a large union in Lancashire created in 1838. It had 82,000 residents, just over half in the town of Bolton itself and the rest in several rural and semi-rural townships. The New Forest union in southwest Hampshire could not be more different. Established in 1835, the union encompassed all or part of eight rural and forest parishes, with the community of Lyndhurst at the centre, and contained just one-tenth of the population of Bolton union in 1841. In effect, then, these unions represent either end of the socio-economic spectrum over which the new poor law washed in the 1830s. By tracing their experiences, we can perhaps provide a framework within which to locate other detailed local studies. More importantly, the individual parishes which formed these unions closely represent the practice and sentiment of welfare under the old poor law in the regions to which they belong. By comparing the individual parish experiences of entitlement and generosity in the 1820s and 1830s with the union experiences of the same variables, we should be able to discern the consequences that the new poor law had for welfare within broad regional boundaries and, by contrasting those experiences, to make tentative suggestions about how the new poor law influenced the regional disparities which gave the old poor law its essential flavour.[32]

In the parishes that were to become the New Forest union, pension and other data exist for the period between 1827 and the formation of the union in 1835. Figure 8.1 takes the distribution of pension payments for Lyndhurst, and contrasts them with the outdoor pensions granted by the Board of Guardians in 1841, once the initial teething troubles of the new poor law had passed. To some extent these figures are misleading. Between 1827 and 1831 the vestry in Lyndhurst adopted a series of standard doles to different types of recipients with no consideration of their underlying circumstances. Only from 1832 were pension values free to rise and fall according to perceived need and the supply of welfare resources. Then pension values were uprated significantly. By 1834, the mean pension stood at around 2s. 9d. per week, or perhaps one-quarter of the adult male wage in the area at the time. The new poor law was to generate substantial change in this picture. The trend for the lowest levels of allowance to disappear from the relief landscape continued, but there was a skimming of the number of people receiving top pensions and a rise in the 4–8s. category of pension payments and thus a fall in the mean outdoor pension. Brundage observed a similar cut in the scale of outdoor payments for unions in Northamptonshire and the experience might be taken to represent a new-found harshness amongst the guardians.[33]

However, three factors make this assumption more problematic than initially it seems. First, the New Forest economy may well have been more buoyant by the 1840s than it had been in the 1820s or 1830s. If so, it might have been reasonable to expect a fall in the number of pensions and their value, and even a redistribution of pension values, whatever the stipulations of the new poor law. Whether the economy improved or not, it is certainly the case that out-migration from many areas of Hampshire, including this one, had increased by the 1840s. In so far as the bulk of out-migration was by the young, the effect of this increased

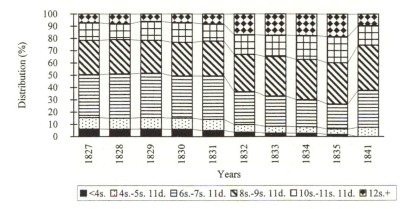

Figure 8.1 Distribution of monthly pension payments in the New Forest area, 1827–41

mobility may have been to cut the kinship options of those who were already poor and marginal and thus to have forced them into greater dependency on communal relief. The question is where in figure 8.1 we would expect to see the effects of this experience manifested? If the lessons of chapters six and seven are correct, then those on the top rungs of the pension ladder were likely to be the old and the kin-poor, people who had no kin to lose or for whom kinship had become an irrelevance. The effects of out-migration were unlikely to be seen here, then, but rather more likely to show themselves in a greater emphasis on lower-level pensions going to people who had previously used kinship to keep away from relief. This is precisely what we see in figure 8.1.

The second influence affecting our interpretation of figure 8.1 is the workhouse. What was really new about the new poor law in the New Forest area was that it pushed the workhouse for the first time on any substantial or concerted basis into the relief equation. By 1841, 77 per cent of union funds were allocated to outdoor relief and the rest to fund the workhouse. If we strip costs such as administration, interest payments and other expenditure that did not benefit the poor from the total expenditure equation, then 81 per cent of available funds went towards outdoor relief and 19 per cent to fund indoor relief. These figures are not much above the average for the whole south and east region from 1813 onwards, and certainly do not stand out as high or low in Hampshire as a whole. Nonetheless, they represent a considerable local policy departure, and it is quite feasible for the workhouse to have filtered off the potentially most expensive pauper groups from the outdoor relief lists, contributing to both a reduction in the number of outdoor paupers and a reduction in mean allowances when compared to the old poor law period.

In this sense it is unfortunate that workhouse admission and discharge registers do not survive for the union. Nonetheless, by comparing the composition of the outdoor relief lists in the 1830s and the 1840s, it is possible to make some speculative comments. Thus, while (ostensibly) younger widows and their children were relatively common on the relief lists of the 1830s, they had largely disappeared from the listing of pensioners in 1841. Moreover, while the listings of the 1830s do not provide age data, it is clear that very old men in particular are missing from the 1841 list. In the national statistics reviewed above, both groups were significant contributors to the pauper host. Thus, although we can offer no definitive statement, it seems likely that the workhouse population was over-represented by old men, young widows, children and, presumably, the younger men with families who appeared on the outdoor relief lists of the 1830s but are almost entirely missing by 1841.[34] If this is true, then we would perhaps expect pension distributions to change under the new poor law, and the very fact that they do cannot be taken as prima facie evidence of increased harshness.

The final problem is that we must not consider the size of pensions in isolation, as chapters six and seven have pointed out. The key question is the distribution of resources between pensions and other allowances that were given to the regular and irregular poor. In both the south and east and north and west by the 1820s, the proportion of resources devoted to pension payments had fallen to well under one-half, with the rest devoted towards irregular payments in cash and kind. In Lyndhurst by the 1830s, for instance, just 40 per cent of all resources were devoted to pension payments, and the overseers offered rent subsidies, clothing, food, fuel and medical relief to regular pensioners and the intermittent poor. On average, pensioners could expect to supplement their pension incomes by up to 32 per cent in some years through these sorts of irregular payments. The situation is more complex by the early 1840s. The rules of the new poor law defined what was and was not acceptable expenditure,[35] and it is unclear whether the New Forest union workhouse had a casual ward to offer relief, clothing and medical help to those who also received monetary relief. However, neither payment in kind nor irregular cash allowances *had* to cease in 1834, and the New Forest union continued to offer supplements to regular pensions. What is more, these continued to be substantial. In aggregate it seems that a pensioner might be able to increase the value of their

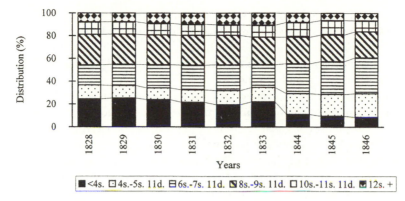

Figure 8.2 Distribution of pension payments in Bolton, 1828–46

pensions by at least one-fifth through casual payments at need. The big difference compared to the old poor law was that these payments were more likely to have been in cash rather than kind, reflecting the fact that the New Forest union lost the buying and distribution infrastructures that had been built up by individual overseers under the old poor law. Overall, then, many pensioners may well have seen stagnation rather than decline in their total welfare package.

Much more could be said about the data for the New Forest union. However, it seems clear that once we allow for the statistical effect of workhouse provision and a raft of supplementary payments, the really significant thing about figure 8.1 is not how much impact the poor law had on the outdoor relief situation, but how little. Moreover, while the absolute number of relief recipients did fall, compared both to the old poor law and over time after unionisation, it is still the case that between 1841 and 1848 up to 40 per cent of the union population had come into contact directly or indirectly with the relief system. The central role that the southern poor law seemed to play in the welfare patchwork of many people by the 1820s can thus been seen to have continued under the new poor law, just as David Thomson suggested. Of course, the New Forest union is just one small part of the area that we have labelled the south and east but it provides enough evidence for us to speculate that the new poor law may have concretised regional experience rather than undermining it.

What of Bolton? Figure 8.2 contrasts the distribution of outdoor pensions in the last years of the old poor for several of the communities that were to form part of the Bolton union with a set of detailed out-relief lists for all of the constituent parishes of the union between 1844 and 1846.[36] An 1842 Poor Law Amendment Bill had allowed unions to establish district relief committees and Bolton union quickly took advantage of this provision to appoint committees consisting of local guardians, parish overseers and a range of local business people and philanthropists. It is the registers of these committees which form the bedrock of this analysis. Three features of figure 8.2 are immediately obvious:

1 Chapter seven suggested that there was a trend in a wide sample of old poor law parishes in the north and west for the lowest pension values to fall out of the relief strategy employed by local administrators. A similar trend can be seen in the Bolton data in the last years of the old poor law. Thus, while figure 7.2 suggested that over 40 per cent of all pension payments were under 4s. per month by 1821, in the townships that were to go on and form Bolton union the figure was well under 30 per cent by 1832. The rise thereafter may be illusory, the result of temporary small-scale help to handloom weavers in the crisis of that year, and is in any case the only blip in an otherwise continuous story of decline.

2 During the last years of the old poor law, communities in the Bolton area appear to have had higher-value pensions than the northern and western communities analysed in the last chapter. Only 28 per cent of pensions in these places in 1821 were 6s. per month or more, whereas in figure 8.2 by the early 1830s up to 40 per cent of pensions were above this level. The mean pension in 1830 thus stood at 9s. 3d. per month, somewhat in advance of the figure which was normal for rural townships in the north and west less than a decade earlier. To some extent this difference is to be explained by the passage of time – even in 1821 the mean pension values outlined in chapter seven were on a rising trend and we would have expected some growth in the intervening decade. However, some of the difference was also real, a reflection of the differing socio-economic composition of the two samples. Pensions in the urban areas of the north and their immediate hinterlands had traditionally been higher than in rural and rural industrial areas.

3 The advent of the new poor law would seem to have introduced wide-ranging changes to the structure of pensions. While the data for the last years of the old poor law represented in figure 8.2 cover a different spatial area to the union, introducing some uncertainty as to the relationship between the two sub-periods considered here, there would seem to have been a definite rollback in the generosity of pensions under the new poor law. The very lowest pension values continued to pass into memory, but there was a consolidation of the importance of the 4–8s.

pension category compared to the situation under the old poor law, and a fall in mean pension values. To some extent this is not unexpected. The sample of townships used to generate 'the old poor law experience' was more urban than the union as a whole, where the relative generosity of Bolton was set against the traditional parsimony of rural and semi-rural parishes surrounding the town. Nonetheless, this compositional effect cannot explain all that we see. Between 1839 and 1840, outdoor relief rates for the whole union were set at between 1s. 6d. (for children) and 3s. (for the elderly) per week. These were generous allowances by historic standards, and even compared to other unions in Lancashire. However, the advent of district committees brought both a downrating of general pensions and significant spatial variation in allowance values. By 1844 the standard pension in Bolton was 2s. per week (and falling), but in some of the rural townships it was just 11d. to 1s. per week, reminiscent of late eighteenth-century levels of relief.[37] Harshness indeed, and harshness that could be seen in both the urban and rural parts of the union.

As with the New Forest data, we should not initially read too much into these experiences. Falling mean pension values may have been partly a reflection of the gradual passing of some of the longer-term consequences of the cotton depression of 1842. As we saw earlier in this book, Cooke-Taylor identified Bolton as an area of particular suffering in 1842, with whole districts unemployed and all household comforts disposed of in a bid to avoid poor relief. It is inconceivable that the new poor law in Bolton would not have had to cope with some of the aftermath of that depression in terms of recurring sickness, orphaned children and fragile domestic environments, and as families re-established secure independence in the 1840s we should see some adjustment to pension distributions. Alternatively falling mean pension values might be partly a function of the removal policy of the union, which after 1838 seems to have targeted the Irish, families with young children and young widows, thus taking part of a significant group of outdoor paupers out of the underlying data for figure 8.2.

However, it is less clear in Bolton than it was in the New Forest that the changing composition of the outdoor relief lists can help to explain changes in perceived generosity. Many of the townships that were subsequently to form Bolton union had their own workhouses or had used the workhouses of other places well before the new poor law. A group of paupers was thus not suddenly taken from the relief lists as was the case in the New Forest. Indeed, it may be the case that former institutional paupers were *added* to the outdoor relief lists as the union closed the former parish workhouses but did not build its own central institution. By 1841 Bolton union gave relief to 7,984 outdoor paupers and at the same time it had three workhouses inherited from the old poor law and not subsequently closed down, with a joint capacity of just 453. Even if the workhouses had been filled to capacity, they could have accounted for no more than 5 per cent of the total number of those receiving relief in the union. In practice, though, they were not full. Bolton workhouse in 1841 had just 209 inmates, including 71 children under the age of 14, 39 old and sick people, and 99 people between the ages of 14 and 60. There is little ostensible evidence that the most expensive people were being streamed away from the outdoor relief lists. Indeed, the proportions of paupers in these different categories look very much like the proportions suggested for late eighteenth- and early nineteenth-century workhouse populations in the northern and western communities analysed in chapter seven. More detailed information is available for 1843, when a survey of the workhouse facilities of Bolton union drew attention to the appalling structural condition of the workhouses and lamented the vermin, squalor and vice that could be found inside their doors. In this year, 41 per cent of inmates were children, 11 per cent were mothers to some of these children, 18 per cent were aged over 60 and 30 per cent were able-bodied or sick. Thus, while the structure of workhouse populations may partly explain why the aggregate generosity of pension payments differs between the New Forest and Bolton in the first place, changing workhouse composition does not explain away the fall in mean pension values under the new poor law. There is, then, a real downrating of pensions to be explained here, more so than in the New Forest.

Of course, it is important to see these pensions alongside the irregular payments which might have supplemented them. In common with the rural and rural industrial townships analysed in chapter seven, less than half of all resources were expended on pension payments in this sample by the late 1820s. For the new poor law period it is extremely difficult to deconstruct voluminous and disjointed accounts to gain an impression of the relative expenditure on pensions, irregular cash allowances, irregular allowances in kind, administration and the workhouse. However, for the year 1843, when we have more information than usual on the workhouse, it seems that around 53 per cent of net expenditure on the poor was devoted to pensions. In short, the distribution of casual payments has the potential to significantly amend our reading of the distribution of pensions, just as it did in the New Forest.

The relative balance of irregular payments in cash and kind changes perceptibly under the new poor law, as we would expect given that things like medical aid in kind were supposed to be co-ordinated centrally and provided via the workhouse. By the mid-1840s Bolton was paying just 7 per cent of all outdoor relief in kind, somewhat below the figures suggested in chapter seven for a range of communities under the old poor law, and the broad focus of relief in kind had become the provision of clothing.[38] On the other hand, irregular cash payments became more common. In 1841 the union paid £754 in rents, and this had risen to £900 by 1844. Bolton also continued to set people up in trade, spending nearly £200 on this welfare initiative in 1846. Cash doles at times of sickness, however, had become the biggest component of irregular expenditure.

It is difficult to pin down these general observations with real pauper experiences given the volume and patchiness of the information, but as a best guess it would seem that regular pensioners could supplement their pension by around 10–15 per cent through their ability to accrue extra allowances at need. As we saw earlier, the figures were higher in the New Forest union, where a greater proportion of resources appear to have been focused on the pensioner population. By the mid-1840s, then, it is likely that mean pensions in Bolton union, even for groups like the elderly, would have reached nowhere near one-fifth of the adult male wage in southeast Lancashire. Even less could they have got near family incomes. And even if some of the fall in mean pensions represents the statistical effect of removal policy, this cannot explain the trends apparent in figure 8.2. Moreover, read alongside declining numbers receiving relief of all sorts both compared to the old poor law period and in the aftermath of unionisation in the late 1830s, these trends do suggest harsh sentiments on the part of local administrators.

Yet, were these experiences out of line with what we might expect of a regional welfare system which had a long tradition of being harsh in both sentiment and practice? As chapter seven showed, many places in the north and west had a long history of stripping back relief lists and pension values much more harshly and on a more sustained basis than is apparent in figure 8.2. Surely, in Bolton union, local relief committees, volatile relief magnitudes and the expectation of harsh decision making on their applications must have made things seem like 'business as usual' to the poor in the 1840s. In fact, there is considerable support here for Midwinter's observation that 'all in all, the more Lancashire's poor law changed, the more it stayed the same'.[39] A preliminary conclusion might well be that the new poor law reinforced rather than undermined the regional welfare systems identified in chapters six and seven.

Who was relieved?

What happened to entitlement under the new poor law, and can we see regional characteristics being hardened in this area too? Consider the New Forest union first. Here, the union returns for 1841 allow us to classify the outdoor poor by age group and thus to look at the age distribution of the totality of poor law resources, as we were able to do using family reconstitution records for the south and the east in chapter six. The results of the exercise are instructive. Some 49 percent of all welfare payments in 1841 accrued to those in the age group 20–59, roughly in line with the figure that emerges from the analysis of rural townships in the south and east prior to 1834. The elderly by contrast took around 38 per cent of total resources, and while this is an advance on their position in the last years of the old poor law, it is less than spectacular under a new poor law committed to hounding the young and able-bodied. Moreover, the position of the elderly was to deteriorate by 1848. The union returns in December of this year indicate that exactly 50 per cent of those who received outdoor relief during the course of the year had been in the age group 20–59.

There was rather more change compared to the old poor law in the gender composition of recipients. In common with the other parishes of the south and east considered in chapter six, those which were to subsequently form the New Forest union had maintained a relief list which was broadly male-dominated right up to 1835. By 1831, just over two-thirds of all relief recipients were male. As we might expect given the discussion of national figures in the last section, things were to change once the union was formed and its initial birth pains had subsided. By the early 1840s, 51 per cent of all outdoor relief recipients were female; ostensibly a significant gain. However, we have already seen that the workhouse may have removed large numbers of men from the outdoor relief lists, and even if this figure is more than statistical trickery, the key question is why was it not higher? In common with administrators throughout the south the guardians and relieving officers of the New Forest Union suddenly discovered immense amounts of sickness and disability in their male pauper populations and these labels were used to justify the continued granting of pensions and casual payments. Clearly, the basic sentiments of the new poor law administrators matched those under the old poor law in these communities, and perhaps, if we can have confidence in the representativeness of places like Bedfordshire and Northamptonshire, in the whole region.

The entitlement criteria employed in Bolton are less directly comparable to the experiences of those communities which underpinned the analysis of chapter seven. Even if they were, the records are less yielding than those for the New Forest. However, partial returns for 1843 allow us to take a more detailed look at entitlement for several of the communities locked into Bolton union. In this year, just 35 per cent of the total poor law resources of these townships was devoted to those in the age group 20–59, and the concentration of poor law resources on the old and very old so obvious in figure 7.10 clearly fed through to the new poor law. The tendency for children to absorb a greater proportion of poor law resources in northern and western communities than they did in the south and east is also clearly visible in the data for these disparate townships. None of this should surprise us – the townships considered were amongst the most rural in Bolton union and we would perhaps expect them more than the town itself to focus resources on to the elderly poor. Yet, there were also other and wider continuities with old poor law practices. A gender breakdown of relief recipients in 1847 for several of the township indicates that the female-centred relief lists which emerged from an analysis of the northern and western data up to 1820 persisted into the era of the new poor law. Some 69 per cent of all adult paupers were female in 1847, and this figure was to remain roughly stable up to and past the end of the period covered by this book. In terms of entitlement, then, the broad-brush regionality of the old poor law appears to have been hardly changed by the blood and thunder of the new poor law.

These two case studies are insufficient and in any case too brief to draw definitive conclusions about the impact of the new poor law on the nature of entitlement to relief, the generosity of relief, the sentiment of the poor law and its administrators in the localities, and the regional structure of welfare. Yet, what they seem to show is that what we might label regional sentiments and relief cultures were largely unaffected by the new poor law if we ignore the immediate aftermath of the administrative and legal changes put in place between 1834 and about 1838. Of course, practice could vary widely within and between counties – Alan Kidd's 'organised diversity of practice' – but on the face of it there is little support here for the idea of a fundamental discontinuity in 1834 of the sort which has been popular in recent overviews of the welfare system.

There is also a wider continuity between the old and the new poor law. In neither the south and east nor the north and west did most pensions, even when supplemented with continuing casual relief in cash or kind, provide enough to live on. Hollen-Lees suggests that pensions may have provided up to two-fifths of male wages in some parts of the south, and David Thomson suggests an even higher figure for Bedfordshire. In the New Forest these dizzy heights were unlikely to have been reached while in the north and west the value of pensions measured in these terms barely left the ground. Nor at any point did the majority of local populations obtain relief, and even amongst groups such as the elderly or widows, many more remained off relief than were ever dependent upon it. The same conclusions could have been drawn in the context of the old poor law. Thus, while the nature of the economy of makeshifts may have changed between 1740 and 1840, it was still central to the point-in-time and life-cycle welfare experiences of those who were poor but not receiving relief and those who were poor and getting an allowance from their union. It is no surprise at all, then, to find Rex Watson suggesting that of 440 households in Marsden, Lancashire, deemed poor enough by the Quakers to be given charity in 1843, just 143 were also receiving parish relief.[40] Nor is it any surprise to read in Banbury gaol records the case of,

> Thomas and Dulstone committed for stealing 6 pairs of worsted slippers from a shop. The prisoners, who were in a very wretched condition, stated they committed the offence for the special purpose of getting taken to prison as they were in a state of starvation.[41]

The nineteenth-century economy of makeshifts has been considered in great depth elsewhere and does not need further elaboration here.[42] The fact that we continue to talk about it at all is testimony to the basic role and character of the poor law old and new.

Conclusion

We started with three very distinct positions on how we should characterise the new poor law and its impact upon the nuts and bolts of local relief strategies. Clearly, more local work will need to be done before we can draw wide and definitive conclusions. However, what this brief analysis does suggest is that all three positions could be right. Fundamental continuities in personnel, types of allowances and the gender distribution of relief are there for all to see. So are discontinuities in the form of declining mean pension values, the tendency to place the most expensive (and therefore most vulnerable) paupers into the workhouse and the culture of investigation that the formation of unions inevitably brought. And Karel Williams is certainly right to suggest that welfare historians have often spent much of their time talking past one another because they have an inadequate appreciation of the aims of national legislation and use a raft of different measures to approach the same question. Even David Thomson is right to suggest that the poor law in places could be extremely generous to the old.

Yet we could equally say that all three positions are essentially false. They arise because welfare historians have concentrated on the symbolism of the 1830s and seen two welfare systems in this decade separated by the year 1834. In so doing, they have missed the key issue, which is not whether the new poor law restricts entitlement and reduces allowances, but whether it alters the enduring regional patterns in welfare culture that we can see developing from at least 1600 onwards. I do not think it does, and in this sense welfare historians are surely wrong to think in terms of two poor laws which clashed in the 1830s. Should they not instead be concentrating their energies on identifying the boundaries of the coalescing regional welfare systems which had always given England at least two and maybe more 'poor laws'?

Notes

1 For an overview, see D. Englander, *Poverty and poor law reform in 19th century Britain, 1834–1914* (London, Longman, 1998).

2 See N. Edsall, *The anti poor law movement 1833–44* (Manchester, Manchester University Press, 1971), and M. E. Rose, 'The anti-poor law movement in the north of England', *Northern History*, 1 (1966) 41–73.

3 E. C. Midwinter, *Social administration in Lancashire 1830–1860* (Manchester, Manchester University Press, 1969).

4 S. Webb and B. Webb, *English poor law history part II: the last hundred years* (London, Cass, 1963 reprint), p. 113.

5 See A. J. Kidd, *State, society and the poor in nineteenth century England* (Basingstoke, Macmillan, 1999).

6 F. Driver, *Power and pauperism: the workhouse system 1834–1884* (Cambridge, Cambridge University Press, 1993).

7 L. Hollen-Lees, *The solidarities of strangers: the English poor laws and the people 1700–1948* (Cambridge, Cambridge University Press, 1998).

8 See A. Digby, 'The rural poor law', in D. Fraser (ed.), *The new poor law in the nineteenth century* (Basingstoke, Macmillan, 1976), pp. 149–70. On relief to the able-bodied, J. V. Mosley, 'Poor law administration in England and Wales, 1834–1850, with special reference to the problem of able bodied pauperism' (unpublished Ph.D. thesis, University of London, 1975).

9 T. C. Barker and J. R. Harris, *A Merseyside town in the industrial revolution: St Helens 1750–1900* (London, Cass, 1993 reprint), p. 148.

10 P. Renold (ed.), *Banbury gaol records* (Banbury, Banbury Historical Society, 1987).

11 *Ibid.*
12 On changing conceptions of the poor, see Hollen-Lees, *Solidarities.*
13 Webb and Webb, *English*, p. 64.
14 See D. Thomson, 'The welfare of the elderly in the past: a family or community responsibility?', in M. Pelling and R. M. Smith (eds), *Life, death and the elderly: historical perspectives* (London, Routledge, 1991), pp. 194–221. Also Hollen-Lees, *Solidarities*, and W. Apfel and P. Dunkley, 'English rural society and the new poor law: Bedfordshire 1834–47', *Social History*, 10 (1985) 41–69.
15 Driver, *Power.*
16 Driver, *Power*, and A. Digby, *Pauper palaces* (London, Routledge, 1978).
17 See, for instance, D. Ashforth, 'The urban poor law', in D. Fraser, *The new poor law in the nineteenth century* (Basingstoke, Macmillan, 1976), pp. 128–48.
18 A. Brundage, 'The English poor law of 1834 and the cohesion of agricultural society', *Agricultural History Review*, 11 (1974) 405–17 (409).
19 P. Dunkley, 'The hungry forties and the poor law: a case study', *Historical Journal*, 17 (1974) 329–46, and N. McCord, 'The 1834 poor law amendment act on Tyneside', *International Review of Social History*, 14 (1969) 1–23. Also Digby, *Pauper*, and K. Thompson, 'The Leicester poor law union 1836–1871' (unpublished Ph.D. thesis, University of Leicester, 1988).
20 V. J. Walsh, 'Old and new poor laws in Shropshire 1820–1870', *Midland History*, 2 (1974) 225–43.
21 Kidd, *State*, p. 30.
22 F. Wood and K. Wood (eds), *A Lancashire gentleman: the letters and journals of Richard Hodgkinson 1763–1847* (Stroud, Sutton, 1992), p. 387. For a detailed anatomisation of the union formation process which suggests a greater sense of ownership than we see here, see B. Song, 'Continuity and change in English rural society: the formation of poor law unions in Oxford', *English Historical Review*, 114 (1999) 314–38.
23 A. Redford, *The history of local government in Manchester: borough and city* (London, Longman, 1940), pp. 122–8. Also, on the problems of putting rich and poor communities together, see P. Wood, *Poverty and the workhouse in Victorian Britain* (Stroud, Sutton, 1991), p. 86.
24 J. Crowther and P. Crowther (eds), *The diary of Robert Sharp of South Cave: life in a Yorkshire village 1812–1837* (Oxford, Oxford University Press, 1997), p. 857.
25 *Ibid.*, p. 855.
26 C. Workman, 'The effect of Gilbert's act on poor law administration in north Lancashire: Caton union 1800–1841' (unpublished Diploma thesis, University of Liverpool, 1989).
27 K. Williams, *From pauperism to poverty* (London, Routledge and Kegan Paul, 1981). These figures are misleading. They are generated by dividing yearly expenditure on relief by the average number of paupers on relief. This assumes that those who received relief did so throughout the year, makes no

distinction between types of payment and fails to allow for the fact that different regions could be going in different directions in terms of mean pensions.

28 Kidd, *State*, p. 4.
29 Lees, *Solidarities*, p. 186.
30 R. A. Lewis, 'William Day and the poor law commissioners', *University of Birmingham Historical Journal*, 9 (1964) 163–96.
31 Hollen-Lees, *Solidarities*.
32 Full references to primary material is given in the Bibliography.
33 Brundage, 'The English'. These are absolute and not per capita pension values. Thus, if a family of five received 5s. per week, I have taken this as a grant of 5s., as it would have appeared in old poor law accounts, rather than five grants of 1s.
34 Nationally elderly people accounted for 20 per cent of all indoor paupers in 1851, and children just 13 per cent. The figures must necessarily have been higher in the New Forest. For comparative material, see M. Caplan, 'The poor law in Nottinghamshire 1836–71', *Transactions of the Thororton Society*, 74 (1970) 82–98.
35 Though the Poor Law Board did not issue their Outdoor Relief Regulation Order – stipulating that one-half of outdoor relief to the able-bodied and one-third of that to the sick and other outdoor paupers should be in kind, and that unions were not to buy tools – until 1852.
36 In Bolton union, as elsewhere in the north, there were substantial disputes between the townships which were brought together at the end of 1838. Not surprisingly there was dispute between the two urban townships (Great and Little Bolton) and the other more rural townships which had a less significant poverty problem and rather different relief traditions. However, rural townships themselves were also in constant dispute, with Lostock refusing the contribute to the common fund during the first six years of the existence of the union. On disputes more generally in Lancashire, see R. Boyson, 'The history of poor law administration in north east Lancashire 1834–1871' (unpublished M.A. thesis, Manchester University, 1960).
37 For similar values in Atcham, see Hollen-Lees, *Solidarities*.
38 Boyson, 'The history', p. 194, suggests that around 7 per cent of all out-relief was in kind in Clitheroe by the early 1840s.
39 Midwinter, *Social*, p. 61.
40 R. Watson, 'Poverty in north-east Lancashire in 1843: evidence from Quaker charity records', *Local Population Studies*, 55 (1995) 28–44.
41 Renold, *Banbury*, p. 67.
42 Kidd, *State*.

CHAPTER NINE

CONCLUSION: OLD AND NEW PERSPECTIVES IN WELFARE HISTORY

There are a number of complex and interlinked lessons to be distilled from this analysis. On the issue of the scale, causes and experiences of poverty, the book opened with Mary Dewhurst's warning that in nineteenth-century England, all were susceptible to poverty. Chapter five demonstrated that she was basically right. We can observe a spiralling eighteenth- and nineteenth-century poverty problem which could leave well over two-thirds of people in many communities by the late 1820s 'in poverty'. Robert Sharp of South Cave was right as well, observing that in nineteenth-century England 'luxury and want now rule with wide sway'.[1] On the ground this sentiment manifested itself in an increasingly wide divide between those who were never poor or sometimes poor and those who were often or always poor. In particular, we can see an underclass of poor people emerging from the mid-eighteenth century onwards who would spend much of their lifetimes in poverty and who were likely to pass on that poverty to their own children and to share their poverty with brothers, sisters and friends.

Mary Dewhurst was part of this underclass. Her brother flitted on to and off the out-relief lists in his parish of settlement, and was eventually buried by the parish which then claimed his wearing apparel and residual furniture to defray the costs of relief during his lifetime. Mary's sister, Ann, was also a writer of letters. She wrote to the overseer of Billington from the town of Preston in October 1825 with the following message:

> Overseer of Billington. Sir as you have Relieved Ann Dewhurst with 1s 6d per week I have sent you a few lines to let you know that the last time I wrote you sent me 5s which did me great kindness. I desired in the last letter that you would Relieve me with 2s per week and now I am indeed forced to tell you that if you can not relieve me 2s per week I must be removed in a cart to your parish for true *I have borrowed and got into debt*

254

so that I cannot carry on any longer. I desire that you would be so Charitable as to allow me 6d per week more and *some money to bye into my Baskit*. I could remain in my situation and I would return you many thanks for so doing so I desire that you as soon as possible will let the said Peter Worden. I know that he must relieve me with 2s per week and some money for my Baskit and I should be greatly Obliged for your goodness So I am your most affectionate Servant Ann Dewhurst.[2]

The letter is a complex mixture of threats and attempts to play on the heartstrings of the overseer, but it provides us with two clues as to the cause of her poverty. She had borrowed money and she had a casual job, hawking from a basket. Other reasons for chronic poverty might be gleaned from this book – illness, lack of kin, particularly being an orphan, the decline of some types of employment and the disappearance of access to common land. All of these things could start or perpetuate the decline of individuals and families into a spiral of intense poverty which resulted in their becoming a part of the marginal society of the poor.

Others had a more intermittent relationship with destitution. Richard Mason, the overseer of Blackburn, wrote to James Seed, the overseer of Billington, on 15 August 1825 in the following terms:

> It is the request of James and Nanny Ormerod that I write to the overseer of Billington to inform him that Nanny has been very poorly for a month and four days so that *she has not been able to wait of herself* and is poorly yet and the hope you will have the goodness to relieve them at this time as they are very ill of at present and are sorry that they have to trouble you but it is necessity that makes them apply to you and they hope you will help them at this time as *they hope not to be regular paupers but will be able to do for themselves* if Nanny gets better, James would have come over but it is not convenient for him but Ann Pye will attend your meeting on thursday instead of her father.[3]

The Ormerods saw illness as a temporary setback to an otherwise viable family economy and like many of the poor who we encountered in chapter five, they were apparently loathe to adopt the trappings of poverty by applying for relief. Yet, as the growing amount of poor law spending on medical relief during the eighteenth and nineteenth centuries indicates, there were many more people like the Ormerods for whom illness meant temporary dependence on the communal welfare system.

However, it was above all old age that could generate chronic long-term need and marginality for those not anyway caught in the culture of endemic poverty characteristic of the underclass. The story of Walter

Keeling from Hull demonstrates this point very well. Between December 1784 and March 1798 he wrote seven letters to the overseers of his home parish, outlining a litany of problems associated with his old age and family circumstances. His letter of November 1795, at which time he was around 60, tells us much:

> Mr Turner Sir I have meade bould to rite to once again as my wife hase been verrey badley this maney years Not able to help hir self and me getting old and lame in my leg and side Where my bowels was lett out at Mr Crookes At Marton which is verrey trobelsom to me Now I am old sir if you and the Gentleman overseers Would be so kind as to send me one ginney to pay my rent which is due the 11th day of this month it will be so kind as wee pay 4 shilings for forteen pond of flore here if you will be so kind t send this I shall be for ever oblidge to you as I have had nothing from you this maney years I shall never troble you no more as my sone is just out of his prentis ship which he has sarved 7 years which is verrey good lad and sir if you will be so kind.[4]

Old age, lameness (he was an ex-soldier) and his wife's illness explain the application and these factors suggest just how precarious life could be in eighteenth- and nineteenth-century England. The letter also suggests that he did not see the communal welfare system as the key to his long-term welfare. Rather, the implication is that his son, just out of apprenticeship, would fulfil his legal and moral duty to look after his sick and aged parents.

Was Keeling right to believe that his son would offer help? How many of the ever growing number of poor in eighteenth- and nineteenth-century England would have turned to the communal welfare system temporarily or in a longer-term fashion, and how many, like Keeling or the Ormerods, would have relied on other welfare avenues to avoid the poor laws old and new for as long as they could? If they applied for relief, would they get it? If they got it, how generous would it have been? How long would they have kept relief once they got it? Did some groups of poor people obtain moral 'rights' to relief even if the law did not grant them such rights? What form would help from the communal welfare system come in? How did the poor and local ratepayers view the poor law and the poor? Did the poor have a legitimacy problem in their own community? And was there any regional dimension to the answers for any of these questions? The foregoing analysis has engaged with issues like these and we can offer some key lessons by way of synthesis. Five in particular stand out.

First, there *was* a distinct spatial flavour to the character and role of the old and new poor laws. Aggregate statistics suggest that by the opening decades of the nineteenth century the rural counties and market towns of the south and east had put in place a wide definition of entitlement and the communal welfare system granted more substantial nominal allowances to more people than did communities in the north and west. Detailed analysis of poor law accounts in the two 'macro-regions' strongly supports this conclusion, suggesting that the southern and eastern old poor law in particular may have intervened early in the descent of individuals and families into poverty, may have recognised relative as well as absolute poverty and on balance probably turned down relatively few people. By contrast, communities in the north and west had a narrower definition of entitlement and devoted fewer resources to the communal welfare framework, not because they had insufficient money or there was no demand for welfare, but because they chose not to.

Second, and following on from these observations, detailed analysis of poor law accounts suggests that the total care package offered to poor people by the communal welfare system in the south tended to be substantially higher than the package offered to regular and casual paupers in the north and west. By the end of the eighteenth century, regular allowances of at least 2–3s. per week were common in southern and eastern communities, and regular pensioners could expect to supplement their pension income by an average of 30 per cent through irregular payments in cash and kind. Even the advent of the new poor law in the south and east apparently failed to eliminate this basic characteristic of the relief system. Whether this means that the southern and eastern poor laws were 'generous' or not is a subjective matter plagued by our inability to reconstruct appropriate yardsticks. However, it is important to bear in mind that measured in terms of the basic male wage, the poor law pension and its supplements might offer up to half of the income available to a man in full-time work to support his family in the south and east. Moreover, notwithstanding periodic cutbacks these allowances were by and large given with good grace – as well as being flexible, the southern and eastern old poor law was benevolent.

The contrast with communities in the north and west, even where we allow for a few sub-regional differences (to which we return shortly) is profound. Here, aggregate allowances of under 2s. per week were almost universal and while pensioners might be able to make up their income through supplementary payments in cash and kind as in the south, the net addition appears to have been only between 10 and 20 per cent. Moreover, allowances were not given in good grace, as the example of Ravenstonedale in chapter seven suggested. The circumstances of paupers were often investigated in depth and the process of giving relief was a policed and monitored one. This does not, of course, mean that the poor law in the north and west was ungenerous. Lower standards of living in these areas must inevitably have fed through to lower allowance values. This said, when measured against a range of indicators, the analysis here has found the northern and western pension wanting.

Third, there appear to have been considerable and enduring gender differences in the composition of outdoor and indoor relief lists in different regions. Crudely, from a common position in the early eighteenth century where women experiencing life-cycle crises dominated the relief lists, the experiences of the south and east and the north and west diverge. In the south and east both pension and casual allowance relief lists tend to become increasingly male-dominated, so that by the second or third decade of the nineteenth century men accounted for at least two-thirds of all recipients of allowances. The gender composition of the pension list in isolation changed less markedly, but even here men, and younger men in particular, came to have an impact. The picture in the northern and western macro-region is not so clearly uniform; nonetheless, on balance it seems clear that neither the composition of the 'all allowances' list nor the pension list moved rapidly, decisively or permanently in favour of males. Over the period as a whole, the northern and western poor law demonstrated a deep concern with the plight of women, and elderly women in particular.

Fourth, notwithstanding generous treatment and relatively wide entitlement in the south and east in most places and at most times, the majority of any vulnerable group – the old, widows or children, for instance – were not dependent on the communal welfare system. For those who did obtain relief, most welfare historians accept – and this book confirms – that the total welfare package was rarely enough to guarantee subsistence. The poor and the marginal would thus have had to engage in a complex strategy of 'making do' in order to avoid dependence on the community in the first place or to supplement the relief given if they did become dependent. The communal welfare system was thus, as Hollen-Lees suggests, residual. It is unfortunate in this sense that so little systematic work has been done of the alternative avenues for making ends meet.

Finally, the book argues that against the backdrop of a common poverty problem we can see two distinct cultures of welfare developing in the eighteenth and nineteenth centuries. Crudely, we might balance a harsh north and west against a more relaxed and inclusive south and east – a culture of making do against a culture of dependency. The two were part of the same notional system, and yet they formed their own distinct welfare regimes, which were different in both order and degree. Of course, the spatial boundaries for this study were crudely drawn, but the question for welfare historians is should they be drawn differently or should they not be drawn at all? Is the 'English poor law' a red herring? Rather than having a standard national safety net is it not the case that some regions offered a relatively comprehensive regional state of welfare while others, like the northwest, had a welfare system which never did, and never set out to, fulfil the function of a safety net? Did England have several poor law systems and not one?

These questions take us neatly to the issues that the book has only hinted at – the nature of smaller-scale spatial divisions and the explanatory framework for the spatial dimensions of welfare that we have been tracing. In the sense that this book is a starting rather than a finishing point, these are issues that should be taken up by others. However, there are some useful speculations that might be made. First, on the issue of sub-regional development. As chapters six and seven began to suggest, while it is possible to make a case for the broad macro-regions having their own 'unity' in terms of the nature and role of the communal welfare system, in practice there are always exceptions to the rule. While the south and east was essentially 'rural', it conflates the welfare experiences of communities where landholding was concentrated and the poor law was financed and controlled by a few major landowners (closed parishes) and those of others where landholding was so disjointed (open parishes) that almost no one was in charge of the communal welfare system. The rural areas of the north and west as they have been defined for this book were also riven with open and closed parishes. These parish types looked different from each other in socio-economic and maybe also in poor law terms. There were also other important divisions. Parishes in the hinterland of London looked different in socio-economic terms from communities far away from main transport arteries. River communities looked different from railway communities. Rural industrial communities looked very different in economic, social and cultural terms from either rural or urban communities. Urban communities often looked very different from each other. Counties and communities with a substantial aristocratic inheritance may also have looked and felt different from communities and counties where aristocrats were less well represented. We could go on with these observations, but if we accept the broad contention that the nature and role of the poor law is at least indirectly related to socio-economic backdrop there are good reasons to expect more subtle spatial differences in the entitlement of poor people, in the nominal value of money allowances and in the sentiment of the poor law than we have allowed so far in this book.

Chapters six and seven have already begun to suggest some of these complexities. In the south and east during the later eighteenth century it is possible to see two community typologies and two responses to a growing poverty problem. One where pensions grew strongly in number and magnitude and the other where the number on relief grew but the level of pensions stagnated or fell. There were also substantial differences in the level of pensions as well as trend in the south and east, with variations in mean pensions between a low of 1s. 4d. per week and a high of 5s. per week in 1801. For areas that were placed in the north and west during the course of this book, there were equally important sub-regional divisions. Gloucestershire and Shropshire, for instance, looked very much like the counties of the midlands in terms of the percentage of the population falling within the ambit of the poor law in 1803. Rushton characterises the northeast as a relatively generous and wide-ranging communal welfare system, and this contrasts strongly with that in Lancashire, which was neither. In West Yorkshire, relief lists remained dominated by women until well into the nineteenth century, whereas in Worcestershire men came to dominate many relief lists completely by the later eighteenth century. We could go on, but even this rapid overview of the lessons of previous chapters suggests that there were complex and often contradictory intra- and inter-county differences in the role and character of both the old and new poor laws within the macro-regions which form the units of analysis for this book. Chapters six to eight identified little by way of systematic sub-regional patterns. The key question is whether this perspective is true or whether there are in fact more subtle and more useful lines to draw on the welfare map of England in the eighteenth and nineteenth centuries.

Unfortunately we are still a long way from having the databases to map intra- and inter-county variations on any definitive basis, let alone explaining them. Yet, in the absence of such material for the foreseeable future, we can offer some initial speculations. By combining the data used in this book with published and unpublished community studies which throw light on the operation of the communal welfare system under the old poor law (for which we have most information), we can begin to obtain a rather more dense spatial coverage than has been possible so far. Map 9.1 shows the location of the detailed community studies that are available in totem.[5] The contrast with map 1.1 is

Map 9.1 Major studies of poor law systems used to frame sub-regional analysis

significant, and the areas which lacked coverage in this map can largely be brought within the fold of an extended analysis, though some areas, the Lincolnshire wolds for instance, remain very much under-researched and offer scope for future research projects. What lessons can we draw from a detailed reading of the individual studies which underpin this map?

There is not the space here to attempt a systematic analysis and I have not attempted to quantify chronological trends in nominal pension values or any of the other indicators used in chapters six to eight in order to characterise the sub-regions identified in the rest of this chapter. Rather, I can offer an impressionistic and provocative view of English welfare history for others to explore. Thus map 9.2 suggests that we can carve our macro-regions up into several sub-regions, each with distinct experiences of issues such as entitlement, nominal relief

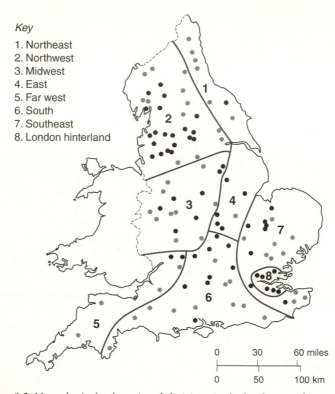

Key
1. Northeast
2. Northwest
3. Midwest
4. East
5. Far west
6. South
7. Southeast
8. London hinterland

0   30   60 miles

0   50   100 km

Map 9.2 Hypothetical sub-regional divisions in the landscape of communal welfare
Source These are impressionistic boundaries drawn on the basis of the findings of the poor law collections and secondary studies of communities indicated on the map.

levels and the sentiment of relief giving. The first of them – a broadly defined 'northwest' – ties together west Yorkshire, Cumberland, Westmorland, Lancashire, and parts of north Yorkshire, Cheshire, Durham and Northumberland. Here the poor law system might be best styled as ramshackle and ultimately parsimonious in both poor law payments and the sentiments of administrators. Communities which break the mould and were generous and recognised need widely (such as Troutbeck or Woodplumpton) stand out because they are so unusual. Moreover, often part of the reason that certain communities stand out is because generous charitable provision took some of the moral pressure off the administrators of communal welfare to enforce self-reliance and the work ethic. By the turn of the nineteenth century, allowances in this sub-region were slim at between 11d. and 1s. 3d. per week on average, and the recognition of entitlement was narrow. Here, female-dominated relief lists were a reality even in the first decades of the nineteenth century, allowances were often unstable because of frequent and prolonged assaults on the length and cost of the relief list in most communities, and the culture and rhetoric of self-reliance was strong notwithstanding what in many cases could be severe poverty.

Meanwhile, the rest of Durham, Northumberland and north Yorkshire, along with east Yorkshire can be grouped together in a second sub-region, one that we might broadly label the 'northeast'. As we have seen elsewhere in this book, commentators such as Dunkley, Hopkin and Rushton have suggested that the poor law in these counties was relatively generous and notions of entitlement relatively flexible. Here mean pensions of 1s. 8d. per week were common by the early nineteenth century and there is persuasive evidence that application and relief were linked by only a short and transparent process of decision making. We have seen Robert Sharp of South Cave lamenting this fact frequently at various points in the foregoing chapters. This said, while these allowances might have been significantly higher than those for the 'northwest', they were also significantly below the levels of early nineteenth-century pensions suggested for the south and east macro-region in chapter six. Moreover, we can still detect an emphasis on self-reliance in the narratives – letters, vestry records, diaries – that surround the poor law decision making process. The words of Robert Sharp of South Cave will have to stand for the sentiments of dozens of narratives that could be considered with more space. The life and death of John Dunlin from South Cave perhaps best sums up the role of the relief system in this sub-region:

> John Dunlin died this day . . . he has long been a pauper, but well respected as he was no imposter . . . he had 2s. per week from the parish but he had good friends who took care that he wanted nothing, when he was ill the overseer asked him if he wanted any thing, but he replied he had plenty of everything and was not in want, indeed, he seemed hurt at being asked if he could be assisted.[6]

While 2s. per week was a relatively generous allowance, it was attended by the rhetoric of self-reliance, a feature that is conspicuously missing from some of the other sub-regions that are considered below.

Our third sub-region might be styled the 'midwest', comprising Shropshire, Staffordshire, Worcestershire, Herefordshire, and parts of Cheshire, Derbyshire and Warwickshire. These essentially pastoral counties appear to have had a strong unity of poor law experience. In this sub-region, allowances moved from the lower end of the distribution for the whole of the north and west in the early eighteenth century to amongst the most generous by 1800. Indeed, by 1801 mean pensions appear to have fluctuated in a narrow band between 1s. 5d. and 1s. 10d., well above the levels for the northwest, but significantly lower than the averages traced in chapter six for the south and east macro-region as a whole. Entitlement was also fluid, with relief lists changing their gender and age composition frequently, though women were heavily favoured when the eighteenth and nineteenth centuries are considered as a whole. The fourth sub-region – broadly the 'east' – incorporating Lincolnshire, Nottinghamshire, Leicestershire, Huntingdonshire, Northamptonshire and part of Warwickshire has limited empirical coverage and in this light I have not tried to characterise its welfare structures here. In the light of more evidence, the boundaries of this area may well shrink or it might merge imperceptibly with the regions that surround it.

The other three potential sub-regions are rather better covered with detailed empirical studies. The 'far west' incorporates parts of Gloucestershire, Somerset and Devon, and all of Cornwall, and in many respects it looks in poor law terms like the northwest. Mean pensions in these counties fluctuated within the range 1s. 2d. and 1s. 6d. by the early nineteenth century, and entitlement was narrow and inflexible. Like the northwest, women continued to dominate the relief lists of most communities, and the evidence from vestry books in the area points to a long and complex decision-making process once poor people had applied to the communal welfare system. The language of self-reliance is also to be found here in abundance, the vestry of Barnstaple noting in 1806, for instance, that 'Widow Parry has a garden full of vegetables. Resolved that her allowance be withdrawn.' The contrast with sub-region six, the classic rural 'south', should be obvious from chapter six. Aggregate statistics from the start of the nineteenth century show the counties of Dorset, Sussex, Wiltshire, Hampshire, Bedfordshire, Oxfordshire, Berkshire and Buckinghamshire spending large amounts on large numbers of paupers, a feature which is confirmed by detailed analysis of poor law records. Such analysis also confirms that generous allowances and a wide notion of entitlement were also a relatively uniform phenomenon across the sub-region as a whole. Here, mean pension levels of 2s. 4d. per week were common by the opening decades of the nineteenth century, and what is more these allowances appear to have been given in benevolent fashion by local administrators. There was little of the rhetoric of self-reliance that we see in the 'northwest' or the 'far west' to be observed in these communities outside periods of severe economic stress and rapidly rising poor relief bills such as the 1790s.

The seventh sub-region, incorporating Norfolk, Cambridgeshire, Suffolk and parts of Essex, Hertfordshire, Bedfordshire and Surrey and broadly labelled the 'south east', had even more generous allowance structures. Here, mean pensions fluctuated between 2s. 6d. and almost 4s., with an average nearer 3s. per week. These levels should not surprise us. As chapter four suggested, communities in Essex appear to have intervened early in the descent of individuals and families to destitution, and in general Essex parishes paid generous allowances when we use county wage levels in agriculture as a yardstick against which to judge them. Relief lists in this sub-region more generally grew inexorably over the course of the eighteenth century, partly reflecting the cutting back of alternative welfare avenues but partly also a reflection of the fact that entitlement was wide and the criteria for proving deservingness relatively easy. More significantly, the sex and age composition of these relief lists changed considerably between the mid-eighteenth and early nineteenth centuries, with young men coming to replace old women as major recipients of the generous welfare structures. Finally, the eighth sub-region might be labelled 'London hinterland' and incorporates parts of all the counties bordering on the metropolis. Communities falling within this boundary appear to have had generous pensions but also restricted entitlement. Mean pensions of up to 3s. per week were common in these communities by the late eighteenth century. However, there was a broad focus of poor law resources not on pensions and pensioners, but on casual payments. This may be associated with the presence of such communities on the arterial transport routes and the related problem of the casual poor, but it may equally reflect the sorts of poverty that these by and large heavily commercialised communities had to deal with. Overall, though, the old, and especially old women, fared best from the welfare system in this sub-region.

Of course, even these sub-regions had their own spectrum of experiences of relief generosity or entitlement, as was suggested earlier. The contrasting welfare experiences of open and closed parishes or, in Shropshire, the difference between pastoral and coalfield districts were significant. So were the differences between urbanising and rural communities. Indeed, with many more detailed local studies it might be possible to write a more sophisticated sub-regional history of the poor law and welfare based upon socio-economic community typologies. For now, though, these speculative and impressionistic divisions will have to suffice. What they suggest is that the English welfare system celebrated by Solar and many other welfare historians was built up from a number of interlinked but nonetheless very different spatial parts. We can with some confidence trace two macro-regions – two regional states of welfare – but with imagination we might be able to trace seven or eight different and more or less unified regional welfare systems in which generosity, entitlement and the sentiment of relief were different by order and degree. In fact, it is possible to suggest a crude model in which the poor law transforms itself from a relatively comprehensive state of welfare in the south and southeast, through a welfare safety net function in the northeast and the midwest, to a ramshackle and inadequate collection of welfare strategies in the far west and northwest. I make no claims for these divisions and their reality on the ground, but the question is less whether they are right or wrong – others can draw different boundaries with richer data – but whether they should be drawn in the first place. Here lies the crux of this book, for my perspective is that complex local diversity can yield wider patterns of welfare experience which ought to inform our characterisation of the nature and role of the English poor laws.

In many respects, of course, observing regional and sub-regional differences is only one part of the story – we also need to explain them. This chapter thus ends by offering some initial attempts at putting explanation behind the observation of the broad macro-regional patterns outlined in chapters six to eight. Some welfare historians have already grappled with the underlying explanations for the spatial peculiarities of the relief system when considering the results of mapping early nineteenth-century aggregate returns to parliament, and we reviewed some of these suggestions in chapter three. If the north and west broadly defined did offer care packages that were in many cases less than half the value of relief packages in the south and east, if the north and west was characterised by relief lists which retained a broad female and elderly focus while relief lists in the south and east became longer, more male-dominated and younger, and if the sentiment of relief giving was harsh in the north and more benevolent in the south, what are the range of explanations that we might deploy? I can offer no definitive conclusions; one book can only do so much. However, some of the conventional explanations have only limited explanatory power when set against the backdrop of the detailed observations offered here. There were certainly important socio-economic differences between (and within) the two macro-regions used as a framework for analysis here. However, the crude model in which an endemically poor rural south and a north and west in which trade cycle and structural poverty were major concerns calling for different welfare solutions does not sit easily with the conclusions of chapter five. It suggested that 'poverty' widely defined was as severe in both macro-regions. At the level of individual communities in the north and west it is certainly true that the poor law might have a firefighting function at times of trade downturn. Equally, it is true, at the level of the individual community, that in the south and east there may have been little perceived choice but to pay generous allowances. At the level of the macro-region, however, attempts to relate socio-economic structures, poverty type and welfare solutions meet with little success.

Nor are other potential explanations more appropriate. I could find little evidence that communities in the north and west were somehow less able to afford to pay generous allowances to growing relief lists than communities in the south and east. Indeed, exactly the opposite may have been true by the later eighteenth century, with the south less able to afford its poor relief system than the north. There may be a little more mileage in the idea that what we see in these broad spatial contrasts is the difference between shallow and deep makeshift economies. In other work I suggest that the north and west did indeed have a multi-strand family economy which was not closed down to anything like the degree or at anything like the rate of that in the rural south and east. However, this is not really a valid contrast. The key question is how many people would have turned to the economy of makeshifts and what aggregate returns it could yield. As I have tried to suggest in different parts of this book, and as I have shown in more depth elsewhere, the parsimony of the northern and western poor law pushes large numbers along these alternative welfare avenues and thus the returns from them grow progressively weaker, leaving the northern and western poor with a lower level of total welfare than their counterparts in the south and east. Of course, some elements of the economy of makeshifts will never be identified in this sort of construct, but it seems to me unlikely that the richness of the economy of makeshifts in the north and west can make any more than a minor contribution to explaining the spatial patterns observed in this book. Indeed, I might turn the whole issue on its head and suggest that a rich economy of makeshifts might have been a response to rather than an explanation of restricted entitlement and generosity.

There are a range of further alternative explanations which might be explored. However, as I have suggested at various points in this book, my favoured explanation is that spatial differences in the nominal value of allowances, entitlement and sentiment reflect very different welfare cultures on the part of both the poor and the poor law administrators in the two macro-regions. Crudely put, the small, face-to-face parishes which characterised many of the counties in the south and east confronted a situation in which custom and a consensual decision-making process created a raft of 'welfare junkies' whose first response when faced with life-cycle stress was to turn to the poor law, and a raft of poor law administrators who perceived that they had no choice but to expand the supply of welfare to meet demand. Yet in the larger parishes of the north and west it might be possible to see a culture of self-reliance and making do which meant that the potentially poor came to the communal welfare system as a last resort and were expected to come to the communal welfare system as a last resort by poor law administrators.

These are really very crude generalisations that mask more than they reveal. Ideally we need to set them against a more detailed appreciation of the narratives of paupers and administrators that the relief process generates and against a detailed discussion of the nature of regional culture in England. However, let us speculate a little further for effect and to end this book. While the contentions are crude, they are also suggestive. The two areas where the rhetoric of self-reliance was most closely observed, the northwest and the southwest, were also those areas with a complex religious history and arguably the most distinctive and potentially puritanical cultures. The north and the west more generally also saw the poor law introduced most patchily and most slowly, so that the transition from self-reliance or reliance on alternative welfare avenues was gradual and almost imperceptible. In Cumberland and Westmorland the survey conducted for this book suggests that at least twenty-one parishes were failing to raise a poor rate as late as 1785, despite demonstrable local need. And in all of the counties from Westmorland to Cornwall and Cumberland to the North Riding charity was continuing to make a very significant addition to the resources of the communal welfare system as late as 1787. By contrast the south and the east saw the rapid dilution of charitable resources, and the transition between older welfare cultures and the communal welfare culture was faster and more complete. Every parish in Cambridgeshire was raising a rate by 1723, and every parish in Dorset even earlier than this. The collective memory in these areas may thus have been very short and the analogy to current-day welfare junkies not so far off the mark.

This is speculation and impression. Ultimately, the aim of this book has not been to draw out a detailed sub-regional picture or to discuss intra-county variations. This requires more, and more detailed, local work. Its aim is to observe the spatial patterns and to bring them to life. These speculations are simply icing on the cake. What seems to me undeniable is that there *were* very substantial spatial differences in entitlement, relief generosity and relief sentiment which are not adequately explained by any of the existing approaches to poor law history. Welfare historians may choose to draw the lines differently, but the point is that the lines *should* be drawn because they encourage us to move away from thinking about *the* English poor law system, to thinking about English poor law *systems* and regional states of welfare.

Notes

1 J. Crowther and P. Crowther (eds), *The diary of Robert Sharp of South Cave: life in a Yorkshire village 1812–1837* (Oxford, Oxford University Press, 1997), p. 122.
2 Lancashire Record Office PR2391/19, 'Letter'. My italics.
3 Ibid., PR2391/18, 'Letter'. My italics.
4 Staffordshire Record Office, D24/A/PO/2902, 'Letter'. I am grateful to Alannah Tomkins for furnishing me with the typescript of this letter.
5 These studies, from Richard Smith, Robert Thompson, Peter Rushton, Robert Hastings, Vick Walsh and others, are listed fully in the Bibliography.
6 Crowther and Crowther (eds), *The diary*, pp. 206–7.

APPENDIX ONE

PLACES

Data collection for this project has been ongoing since 1987. The references for the communities listed below are to be found in the Bibliography. Some of the material which was originally in private hands when initially consulted has now been deposited with county record offices and local studies libraries. One set of poor law documentation that was in private hands in 1990 – that for Duston and Farthinghoe – was stolen in that year. The owner's transcript of this material is available at Oxford Brookes University Library.

The individual communities do not, as map 1.1 suggests, constitute a systematic or random sample. They represent places with good record survival, and there are a number of record sets which were drawn to my attention in response to an advertisement for help in looking at the poor law records of several counties. In this respect, my thanks are due to Dorothy Sware, Jim Dein, Brian Perkins, Charlotte Ripple, James Manley, Sarah Cartwright, William Dodd, Catherine Pullen, Helen Sambern and Tony Barnes. Within the broader sample, counties like West Yorkshire, Lancashire and Westmorland are over-represented, while counties such as Lincolnshire, Cornwall and Suffolk have no representatives at all. To some extent, the work of other people on local poor law accounts makes good these gaps and the wider spread of community perspectives is detailed in the text. Nonetheless, significant gaps remain and it is sensible to regard this analysis as providing no more than a very basic outline of the regionality and sub-regionality of communal welfare provision.

The communities used substantially in this study were:

Addingham (West Yorkshire)
Ashwell (Hertfordshire)
Aynho (Northamptonshire)
Bleasby (Nottinghamshire)
Bluntisham (Cambridgeshire)
Bolton (Lancashire)
Bottisham (Cambridgeshire)
Bradfield (Berkshire)
Bridgnorth (Shropshire)

Broomfield (Kent)
Butlers Marston (Warwickshire)
Calverley (West Yorkshire)
Cartmel (Cumbria)
Chalfont (Buckinghamshire)
Charing (Kent)
Chipping Camden (Gloucestershire)
Chipping Sodbury (Gloucestershire)
Chorlton (Lancashire)

Colne (Lancashire)
Cowpe (Lancashire)
Dartford (Kent)
Downham (Norfolk)
Drayton (Leicestershire)
Duston (Northamptonshire)
Enfield (Greater London)
Farsley (West Yorkshire)
Farthinghoe
  (Northamptonshire)
Garstang (Lancashire)
Great Strickland (Cumbria)
Halliwell (Lancashire)
Hanwood (Nottinghamshire)
Holme (Cumbria)
Horsforth (West Yorkshire)
Idle (West Yorkshire)
Kettering (Northamptonshire)
Leigh (Lancashire)
Linton (Cambridgeshire)
Longton (Lancashire)
Lund (Lancashire)

Lyndhurst (Hampshire)
Middleton (North Yorkshire)
Morland (Cumbria)
Mitton (Lancashire)
Oldbury (Wiltshire)
Parr (Lancashire)
Parver (North Yorkshire)
Paxton (Cambridgeshire)
Powick (Worcestershire)
Ravenstonedale (Cumbria)
Richmond (Surrey)
Stokesley (North Yorkshire)
Stone (Staffordshire)
Sutton Bonnington
  (Nottinghamshire)
Thatcham (Berkshire)
Troutbeck (Cumbria)
Wakes Colne (Essex)
Wenlock (Shropshire)
Wimbledon (London)
Woodford (Gloucestershire)
Wye (Kent)

A LEGAL CHRONOLOGY OF
THE POOR LAWS

1531, 22 Hen. VIII, c. 12. Recognised that the impotent poor needed to be provided for; directed justices to give them licences to beg. Repealed in 1624 by 21 Jas. I, c. 28.

1536, 27 Hen. VIII, c. 25. Responsibility for the poor was placed on parish and borough officers – to be funded by the gathering of alms with boxes every Sunday, holiday and festival day – so that the impotent poor should be fully provided for.

1563, 5 Eliz., c. 2. All servants travelling from one place to another were to have a testimonial from their late master, or the officers of a parish, testifying to their cause and destination.

1563, 5 Eliz., c. 3. Compulsory weekly contributions for poor relief were to be made by householders according to their ability to pay.

1572, 14 Eliz., c. 5. Aged poor, impotent and decayed persons who had been born within each division of the county, or had resided there for three years, were to be sought out and registered. The Act was to be administered locally, and unpaid overseers could be appointed to help constables and churchwardens. Vagrants were defined as a group containing all masterless men not owning land, as well as tinkers, pedlars and minstrels. The Act ordained whipping and boring through the ear as punishment for a first offence – a third offence carried the death penalty. Punishment was reduced to whipping only in 1593 (35 Eliz., c. 4).

1576, 18 Eliz., c. 2. Any woman with an illegitimate child, actually or likely to become chargeable, to be examined by two justices as to the circumstances. Justices could require the mother or reputed father to make weekly or monthly payments to the overseers.

1576, 8 Eliz., c. 3. Allowed for provision of stocks of hemp, flax and iron for the able-bodied poor to work with.

1597–98, 39 Eliz. An act for the relief of the poor. Required the appointment of an overseer in every parish, with the duty of providing for the poor without means to maintain themselves. Overseers were to submit a full account of their activities and finances to two justices at the end of the year. Justices were empowered to levy a rate on one parish in aid of another. Convenient houses of habitation or dwelling were to be provided for the impotent poor – more than one family could be placed in the same house or cottage.

1601, 43 Eliz. Churchwardens and overseers were empowered to bind any children (from the age of 7) whose parents they judged not able to maintain them, to be apprentices where they thought fit, until male children reached the age of 24 and female children reached the age of 21 or were married, whichever was soonest. Long servitude of boys continued to 1778 (18 Geo. III, c. 47), although the limit had been reduced to 7 years or the age of 21 in London in 1767 (7 Geo. III c. 39). Parishes were to relieve the lame, impotent, old, blind, etc., being poor and not able to work, and to provide work for the unemployed.

1609–10, 7 Jas. I, c. 4. Giving birth to an illegitimate child was not a civil offence unless the child become chargeable on the parish; fornication (i.e. intercourse outside marriage) was still an offence punishable by the church courts.

1662, 3 & 14 Chas. II. Law of Settlement and Removal. Overseers were given the right to remove by justice's warrant any person or persons coming to settle themselves in any tenement under the yearly value of £10, if they judged them likely to be chargeable to the parish. The poor were to be removed within forty days to the parish where he or they were last legally settled either as a native, sojourner, householder, apprentice or servant for the space of forty days at least. Persons not renting a £10 tenement, or qualifying in any other ways for a settlement in a new parish were required to carry a certificate from the minister and a churchwarden or overseer. In the six northern parishes, Cheshire and Derbyshire, each township, chapelry or constablewick could appoint its own overseers. Parish officials were given powers to seize goods of absconding fathers of bastards.

1691, 3 Wm. & Mary, c. 2. Required that the names of those who received relief were to be enrolled in a book which was accessible to the parishioners. Vestries were to purge the list of the poor receiving regular or permanent doles every Easter. No relief was to be given, except in emergency, without the authority of a justice.

1691, 3 Wm. & Mary, c. 11. Act of Settlement. Indentured apprentices acquired a settlement in the parish in which they served. Servants hired for a complete year were granted settlement, provided they were unmarried.

1696 , 7 & 8 Wm. III, c. 32. Bristol Local Act – the first 'union' workhouse.

1697–98, 8 & 9 Wm. III, c. 11. Act for regulation and administration of the poor. Introduced a uniform procedure for granting of certificates – with the consent of a majority of churchwardens and overseers and the approval of two justices; labourers and their families could seek work in other parishes. Once a parish had received a certificate no removal was possible until the person actually became chargeable. A parishioner refusing to accept an apprentice from the overseers was to forfeit the sum of £10. Those in receipt of relief were to be 'badged'.

1713, 12 Anne, c. 18. Apprentices or hired servants of a person themselves residing by certificate were prohibited from gaining a settlement.

1716, 13 Anne, c. 26. Rogues and vagabonds were defined – to be taken before a justice and examined as to their place of settlement, their depositions to be filed among the records of the quarter sessions. Vagrants were to be returned to place of settlement – taken to the next house of correction on a direct route home and handed over for transfer to the next one, etc. Soldiers and mariners licensed by testimonial under the hand of a justice were specifically excluded.

1723, 9 Geo. I, c. 7. Workhouse Test Act. Gave legal powers for individual parishes to establish a workhouse (powers had already been given to 'unions' of parishes by a number of local acts); relief could be withheld from any person refusing to enter the workhouse. No settlement was permitted just by virtue of paying the highway rate. The Act also allowed 'farming out' the maintenance of the poor at a fixed rate to a contractor. No pauper was to apply to a justice for relief unless already refused by the overseer.

1730, 3 Geo. II, c. 29. Overseers removing certificated persons were to be reimbursed for reasonable charges by the receiving parish – the overseer was to accompany the person to the parish of settlement. Charges to be approved by justices of the county from which removal was made.

1733, 6 Geo. II, c. 13. The mother of an illegitimate child could not appear before justices for examination until one month after the child was born.

1740, 13 Geo. II, c. 24. Repealed all previous vagrancy laws and attempted to deal with vagrants in one statute.

1744, 17 Geo. II, c. 3. Churchwardens were to give public notice in church or chapel of any rate for relief of the poor.

1744, 17 Geo. II, c. 5. All rates levied for poor relief were to be entered in a book for public inspection.

1746, 19 Geo. II, c. 19. An apprentice could appeal to the justices against his master's ill treatment.

1778, 18 Geo. III, c. 47. Completion of apprenticeships for boys was reduced to 7 years, or the attainment of 21 years of age outside London. No parish apprentice was to be bound for a premium of less than £4.2.0 throughout England.

1782, 22 Geo. III, c. 83. Gilbert's Act. Parishes were given the right to form 'unions' for the better management of the poor, with a common workhouse. Responsibility rested with elected gentlemen to supervise the overseers. Overseers were able to supplement wages of labourers from the poor rate in times of dearth.

1819, 59 Geo. III, c. 12. Parishes were allowed to acquire up to 20 acres of land for cultivation by the poor; and allowed to form select vestries.

1834, 4 & 5 Wm. IV, c. 76. Poor Law Amendment Act.

BIBLIOGRAPHY

Primary sources

Cumbria Record Office (CRO)
WD/BIG/1/64/36, 'Plan of encroachments', WPR 4/3, 'Overseer accounts for Cartmel Fell 1721–98', WPR/89, 'Poor law accounts for Cartmel 1761–1832', WPR/14, 'Accounts', WSMB/K/62, 'Assorted poor law papers', WPR/9/VI, 'Orton vestry minutes 1790–1902', WPR/1/01, 'Overseer accounts for Orton', WD/MG, 'Metcalfe-Gibson papers', Uncatalogued, 'The great end book of Ravenstonedale', WPC 8, 'Overseers accounts of Ravenstonedale, 1763–1886', WPC/5/2, 'Overseers accounts for Milnthorpe 1741–1823', WDX/382, 'Inmates of Kirkby Lonsdale workhouse in 1830', WD/D/D6/68, 'Donations to the poor in Foulshaw', WD/H01.1, 'Old poor law accounts 1721–1774', WPC/12, 'Charity account book 1751–1840', WPR40, 'Books of the overseer of the poor of Middleton 1662–1840', WPR 62, 'Troutbeck poor law accounts 1640–1857', WD/TE/24, 'Poor law accounts for Troutbeck', Browne MSS, WPR/17, 'Morland poor law'.

Hampshire Record Office (HRO)
25M84/PO1–70, 'Poor law documents for Lyndhurst', 25M84/DU 1–20, 'New forest union records', 103M94, 'Old poor law records for Lyndhurst'.

Lancashire Record Office (LRO)
PR2391, 'Miscellaneous letters', DDKe 2/6/2, 'Bolton survey 1674', DDX 386/3, 'Vestry records of Garstang', DDGa/17/88–9, 'Correspondence regarding trespassing', DDHe/82/18, 'Correspondence regarding the taking of game by unqualified persons, 1804', DDHe/79/104a, 'Memorandum regarding trespassing in Hesketh fisheries, 1821', DDIn/45/14, 'Report on town cottages, Birkdale 1815', DDIn/46/37, 'Lease', MBCo/7/1, 'Ratepayers minutes for Colne', PR797, 'Miscellaneous notes', MBc/637, 'Account of goods belonging to Widow Cottam', PR3031, 'Poor law accounts of Mitton', PR1349/10, 'Letter', DDX/320/2/1, 'Justicing memoranda book of Geoffrey Hornby of Preston 1723–31', DDHe 83/54, 'Cottage rents paid', PR 797, 'Miscellaneous notes', PR 1349, 'Miscellaneous letters'.

Calverley 84, 'Poor law accounts', Horsforth 1–24, 'Poor law records', 49D90, 'Addingham parish council records', '48D90, 'Addingham church records', plus other Addingham poor law material and accounts in different collections.

Other record offices

Berkshire Record Office, 'Poor law accounts of Thatcham and Bradfield'.

Bolton Archive Service, 'Vestry minutes of Halliwell and Bolton Union records' (GBO).

Cambridgeshire Record Office, 'Poor law accounts of Bottisham, Linton and Bluntisham'.

Essex Record Office, 'Inventories for Hatfield Broad Oak', 1730–1833 (D/P4), 'Poor law accounts for Wakes Colne'.

Greater London Record Office, 'Vestry books of Enfield'.

Kent County Record Office, 'Poor law accounts of Dartford, Broomfield and Wye'.

Leicestershire Record Office, 'Poor law accounts for Drayton'.

North Yorkshire Record Office, 'Poor law accounts of Stokesley and Parver'.

Northampton Record Office, 'Vestry minutes of Farthinghoe', The Cartwright Collection.

Nottingham Record Office, 'Poor law accounts for Bleasby and Sutton Bonnington'.

Shropshire Record Office, 'Accounts of Wenlock', 'Poor law accounts of Bridgnorth'.

Staffordshire Record Office, 'Poor law accounts and other material for Stone'.

Warwickshire Record Office, 'Poor law accounts of Butlers Marston'.

Wigan Record Office, 'Poor law accounts of Abram 1691–1800, Leigh and Parr'.

Wiltshire Record Office, 'Poor law accounts of Oldbury'.

Worcestershire Record Office, 'Poor law accounts for Powick'.

Other repositories

Ashwell Village Museum, 'Poor law accounts of Ashwell'.

Chalfont vestry (when examined in 1987), 'Poor law accounts'.

Gloucestershire Archive Service, 'Poor law accounts of Chipping Sodbury, Chipping Camden and Woodford'.

Rawtenstall Library, 'The poor law accounts of Cowpe, Lenches, Newhallhey and Hall Carr', The Whitehead collection.

Richmond Public Library, 'Vestry minutes for Richmond'.

St Helens Library, 'Poor law accounts of Parr'.

Wye church, 'Poor law accounts'.

Manchester Central Library, 'Chorlton overseers accounts', 'Poor rate assessments' (L/75/81) and 'Parish records' (L75/8).

Bibliography

Records in private hands

Bridgnorth, Parver and Wye – Bob Simpson, University of Birmingham.

Charing – David Turner, Kentish Historical Society.

Chipping Sodbury and Woodford (in 1989) – William Males, Sodbury Civic Society.

Downham – Mike Giles, planning officer for Norfolk County Council.

Farthinghoe and Old Duston – Peter Rule. Owner transcripts are available for consultation at Oxford Brookes University Library. However, see also entry for Northamptonshire Record Office above.

Lund (Lancashire) – Martin Ramsbottom. A copy of the poor law accounts is available for consultation at Oxford Brookes University Library.

Sutton Bonnington – Transcripts of the original poor law books with James Mayes.

Printed or edited primary sources

Ashcroft, L., *Vital statistics: the Westmorland census of 1787* (Berwick, Curwen Archive Trust, 1992).

Aspinall, A., and E. A. Smith (eds), *English historical documents 1783–1832* (London, Eyre and Spottiswoode, 1969), pp. 414–15.

Ayres, J., *Paupers and pig killers: the diary of William Holland, a Somerset parson 1799–1818* (Stroud, Sutton, 1984).

Baker, F., (ed.), *William Grimshaw, 1708–1763* (Haworth, Epworth Press, 1963).

Coats, A. W,. (ed.), *Poverty in the Victorian age* (Farnborough, Allen and Unwin, 1973).

Cooke-Taylor, W., *Notes on a tour of the manufacturing districts of Lancashire* (New York, Augustus Kelley, 1968 reprint).

Cowe, F. M., (ed.), *Wimbledon vestry minutes 1736, 1743–1788* (Guildford, Surrey Record Society, 1964).

Crowther, J., and P. Crowther (eds), *The diary of Robert Sharp of South Cave: life in a Yorkshire village 1812–1837* (Oxford, Oxford University Press, 1997).

Fiske, J., (ed.), *The Oakes diaries: business, politics and the family in Bury St Edmunds, 1778–1800* (Woodbridge, Boydell Press, 1990).

Mackenzie, W., *The overseer handbook* (London, Peterworth, 1820).

Oxley, J. E., *Barking vestry minutes and other parish documents* (Colchester, Essex Records Society, 1955).

Peat A., (ed.), *The most dismal times: William Rowbottom's diary 1787–99* (Oldham, Oldham Library Service, 1996).

Peyton, S. A., *Kettering vestry minutes 1797–1853* (Northampton, Northamptonshire Records Society, 1933).

Pope, F., *The accounts of the constables and overseers of Parr 1688–1729* (Windle, privately published, 1971).

Renold P., (ed.), *Banbury gaol records* (Banbury, Banbury Historical Society, 1987).

Tebbutt, C. F., *Bluntisham-cum-Earith, Huntingdonshire: records of a fenland parish* (St Neots, privately published, 1941).

Wilkins, H. J., *The poor book of Westbury on Trym* (London, Calender, 1910).

Wood, F., and K. Wood (eds), *A Lancashire gentleman: the letters and journals of Richard Hodgkinson 1763–1847* (Stroud, Sutton, 1992).

Secondary sources

Adair, R. *Courtship, illegitimacy and marriage in early modern England* (Manchester, Manchester University Press, 1996).

Adair, R., J. Melling and B. Forsythe, 'Migration, family structure and pauper lunacy in Victorian England: admissions to the Devon county pauper lunatic asylum 1845–1900', *Continuity and Change*, 12 (1997) 373–402.

Anderson, P., 'The Leeds workhouse under the old poor law 1726–1834', *Publications of the Thoreseby Society*, 56 (1979) 75–113.

Apfel, W., and P. Dunkley, 'English rural society and the new poor law: Bedfordshire 1834–47', *Social History*, 10 (1985) 41–69.

Arkell, T., 'The incidence of poverty in England in the later seventeenth century', *Social History*, 12 (1987) 23–47.

Ashby, A. W., *One hundred years of poor law administration in a Warwickshire village* (Oxford, Oxford Economic Studies, 1926).

Ashforth, D., 'The urban poor law', in D. Fraser (ed.), *The new poor law in the nineteenth century* (Basingstoke, Macmillan, 1976), pp. 128–48.

'Settlement and removal in urban areas: Bradford 1834–71', in M. E. Rose (ed.), *The poor and the city: the English poor law in its urban context 1834–1914* (Leicester, Leicester University Press, 1985), pp. 58–91.

Barker, H., and E. Chalus (eds), *Gender in eighteenth century England: roles, representations and responsibilities* (London, Longman, 1997).

Barker, T. C., and J. R. Harris, *A Merseyside town in the industrial revolution: St Helens 1750–1900* (London, Cass, 1993 reprint).

Barnes, S. J., 'Walthamstow in the eighteenth century: vestry minutes, church-wardens and overseers accounts 1710–94', *Walthamstow Antiquarian Society Publications*, 16 (1927).

Baugh, D. A., 'The cost of poor relief in south east England 1790–1834', *Economic History Review*, 28 (1975) 50–68.

'Poverty, protestantism, and political economy: English attitudes toward the poor, 1600–1800', in S. B. Baxter (ed.), *England's rise to greatness, 1600–1763* (Berkeley, University of California Press, 1983), pp. 63–108.

Baxter S. B., (ed.), *England's rise to greatness, 1600–1763* (Berkeley, University of California Press, 1983).

Blaug, M., 'The myth of the old poor law and the making of the new', *Journal of Economic History*, 23 (1963) 151–84.

Bonfield, L., 'Was there a "third age" in the pre-industrial English past? Some evidence from the law', in J. M. Eckelaar and D. Pearl (eds), *An ageing world: dilemmas and challenges for law and social policy* (Oxford, Oxford University Press, 1989), p. 50.

Bonfield, L., R. M. Smith and K. Wrightson (eds), *The world we have gained* (Oxford, Oxford University Press, 1986).

Boot, H., 'Unemployment and poor law relief in Manchester 1845–50', *Social History*, 15 (1990) 217–28.

Botelho, L., 'Aged and impotent: parish relief of the aged poor in early modern Suffolk', in M. J. Daunton (ed.), *Charity, self-interest and welfare in the English past* (London, UCL Press, 1996), pp. 91–112.

Bouch, C., and G. Jones, *A short economic and social history of the Lake counties 1500–1830* (Manchester, Manchester University Press, 1961).

Boyer, G. R., 'Malthus was right after all: poor relief and the birth rate in southeastern England', *Journal of Political Economy*, 97 (1989) 93–114.

Braddick, M., 'State formation and social change in early modern England: a problem stated and approaches suggested', *Social History*, 16 (1991) 1–17.

Brewer, J., and E. Hellmuth (eds), *Rethinking leviathan: the eighteenth century state in Britain and Germany* (Oxford, Oxford University Press, 1999).

Broadbridge, S. R., 'The old poor law in the parish of Stone', *North Staffordshire Journal of Field Studies*, 13 (1973) 11–25.

Brown, A. F. J., *Meagre harvest: the Essex farm workers' struggle against poverty, 1750–1914* (Chelmsford, Essex Record Office, 1990).

Brundage, A., 'The English poor law of 1834 and the cohesion of agricultural society', *Agricultural History Review*, 11 (1974) 405–17.
The making of the new poor law: the politics of inquiry, enactment and implementation (London, Hutchinson, 1978).

Bulmer, M., *The social survey in historical perspective 1880–1940* (Cambridge, Cambridge University Press, 1991).

Bush, M. L. (ed.), *Social orders and social classes in Europe since 1500* (London, Longman, 1993).

Caplan, M., 'The poor law in Nottinghamshire 1836–71', *Transactions of the Thororton Society*, 74 (1970) 82–98.
'The new poor law and the struggle for union chargeability', *International Review of Social History*, 23 (1978) 267–300.

Chambers, J. D., and G. E. Mingay, *The agricultural revolution 1750–1880* (London, Batsford, 1966).

Checkland, S. G., and E. O. Checkland (eds), *The poor law report of 1834* (London, Penguin, 1974).

Chinn, C., *Poverty amidst prosperity: the urban poor in England 1834–1914* (Manchester, Manchester University Press, 1995).

Christian, G., (ed.), *James Hawker's journal: a Victorian poacher* (Oxford, Oxford University Press, 1961).

Coats, A. W., 'Economic thought and poor law policy in the eighteenth century', *Economic History Review*, 13 (1961) 34–78.
'The relief of poverty, attitudes to labour and economic change in England 1660–1782', *International Review of Social History*, 21 (1978) 98–121.

Connors, R., 'Poor women, the parish and the politics of poverty', in H. Barker and E. Chalus (eds), *Gender in eighteenth century England: roles, representa-*

tions and responsibilities (London, Longman, 1997), pp. 126–47.

Cordery, S., 'Friendly societies and the discourse of respectability in Britain 1825–1875', *Journal of British Studies*, 34 (1995) 35–58.

Cornford, B., 'Inventories of the poor', *Norfolk Archaeology*, 35 (1970–73) 118–25.

Cowherd, R. G., 'The humanitarian reform of the English poor laws from 1782–1815', *Proceedings of the American Philosophical Society*, 104 (1960) 328–42.

Political economists and the English poor laws (Athens, Ohio, Ohio University Press, 1977).

Crompton, F., *Workhouse children* (Stroud, Sutton, 1997).

Crowther, J., and P. Crowther (eds), *The diary of Robert Sharp of South Cave: life in a Yorkshire village 1812–1837* (Oxford, Oxford University Press, 1997).

Crowther, M., *The workhouse system: the history of an English social institution* (London, Methuen, 1981).

'Family responsibility and state responsibility in Britain before the welfare state', *Historical Journal*, 25 (1982) 131–45.

Cunningham, H., and J. Innes (eds), *Charity, philanthropy and reform from the 1690s to 1850* (Basingstoke, Macmillan, 1998).

Daunton, M. J., *Progress and poverty: an economic and social history of Britain 1700–1850* (Oxford, Oxford University Press, 1995).

(ed.), *Charity, self-interest and welfare in the English past* (London, UCL Press, 1996).

Davey, B., *Ashwell 1830–1914: the decline of a village community* (Leicester, Leicester University Press, 1980).

Davison, L., T. Hitchcock, T. Keirn and R. B. Shoemaker (eds), *Stilling the grumbling hive: the response to social and economic problems in England, 1689–1750* (Stroud, Sutton, 1992).

Dickinson, R. F., 'The friendly society of the inhabitants of the parish of Lamplugh and its neighbourhood', *Transactions of the Cumberland and Westmorland Antiquarian and Archaeological Society*, 96 (1965) 418–31.

Digby, A., 'The rural poor law', in D. Fraser (ed.), *The new poor law in the nineteenth century* (Basingstoke, Macmillan, 1976), pp. 149–70.

Pauper palaces (London, Routledge, 1978).

'Malthus and reform of the English poor law', in M. Turner (ed.), *Malthus and his time* (Basingstoke, Macmillan, 1987), pp. 157–69.

Making a medical living: doctors and patients in the English market for medicine, 1720–1911 (Cambridge, Cambridge University Press, 1997).

Digby, A., S. A. King and R. M., Smith (eds), *Poverty, poor relief and welfare in England from the seventeenth to twentieth centuries* (Cambridge, Cambridge University Press, forthcoming).

Driver, F., *Power and pauperism: the workhouse system 1834–1884* (Cambridge, Cambridge University Press, 1993).

Dunkley, P., 'The hungry forties and the new poor law: a case study', *Historical Journal*, 17 (1974) 329–46.

'Paternalism, the magistracy and poor relief in England, 1795–1834', *International Review of Social History*, 24 (1979) 371–97.

The crisis of the old poor law in England, 1795–1834: an interpretive essay (New York, Garland, 1982).

Eastwood, D., 'The republic in the village: parish and poor at Bampton 1780–1834', *Journal of Regional and Local Studies*, 12 (1992) 18–28.

'Rethinking the debates on the poor law in early nineteenth century England', *Utilitas*, 6 (1994) 97–116.

Governing rural England: tradition and transformation in local government 1780–1840 (Oxford, Oxford University Press, 1994).

Government and community in the English provinces, 1700–1870 (Basingstoke, Macmillan, 1997).

Eccles, A., 'Vagrancy in later eighteenth century Westmorland: a social profile', *Transactions of the Cumberland and Westmorland Antiquarian and Archaeological Society*, 189 (1989) 249–62.

Eden, F. M., *The state of the poor: a history of the labouring classes in England with parochial reports*, 3 vols (London, Cass, 1963 reprint).

Edmonds, G. C., 'Accounts of eighteenth-century overseers of the poor of Chalfont St. Peter', *Records of Buckinghamshire*, 18 (1966) 3–23.

Edsall, N., *The anti poor law movement 1833–44* (Manchester, Manchester University Press, 1971).

Eekelaar, J. M., and D. Pearl (eds), *An ageing world: dilemmas and challenges for law and social policy* (Oxford, Oxford University Press, 1989).

Ely, J. W., 'The eighteenth century poor laws in the West Riding of Yorkshire', *American Journal of Legal History*, 30 (1986) 1–24.

Emmison, F. G., *The relief of the poor at Eaton Socon, 1706–1834* (Bedford, Bedfordshire Record Society, 1933).

Englander, D., *Poverty and poor law reform in 19th century Britain, 1834–1914* (London, Longman, 1998).

Finlay, R. A. P., *Population and metropolis* (Cambridge, Cambridge University Press, 1981)

Finlayson, F. G., *Citizen, state and social welfare in Britain 1830–1914* (Oxford, Clarendon Press, 1994).

Fissell, M. E., 'The sick and drooping poor in eighteenth century Bristol and its region', *Social History of Medicine*, 2 (1989) 49–81.

'Charity universal? Institutions and moral reform in eighteenth century Bristol' in L. Davison, T. Hitchcock, T. Keirn and R. B. Shoemaker (eds), *Stilling the grumbling hive: the response to social and economic problems in England, 1689–1750* (Stroud, Sutton, 1992), pp. 121–44.

Fraser, D., *The evolution of the British welfare state* (Basingstoke, Macmillan, 1973).

'The poor law as a political institution', in D. Fraser (ed.), *The new poor law in the nineteenth century* (Basingstoke, Macmillan, 1976), pp. 111–27.

'Poor law politics in Leeds 1833–55', *Publications of the Thoresby Society*, 15 (1977) 23–49.

Fuller, M. D., *West Country friendly societies* (Reading, Oakwood Press, 1964).

Garnett, J., and C. Matthew (eds), *Revival and religion since 1700: essays for John Walsh* (London, Hambledon, 1993).

George, M. D., *London life in the eighteenth century* (London, Kegan Paul, 1930).

Gilbert, K., *Life in a Hampshire village: the history of Ashley* (Winchester, Pica Press, 1992).

Goose, N., 'Workhouse populations in the mid nineteenth century: the case of Hertfordshire', *Local Population Studies*, 62 (1999) 52–69.

Gorsky, M., 'The growth and distribution of English friendly societies in the early nineteenth century', *Economic History Review*, 51 (1998) 489–511.

Green, D. R., *From artisans to paupers: economic change and poverty in London 1790–1870* (Aldershot, Scolar Press, 1995).

Green, P. G., 'Charity, morality and social control: clerical attitudes in the diocese of Chester, 1715–1795', *Transactions of the Historic Society of Lancashire and Cheshire*, 141 (1992) 207–33.

Griffiths, P., A. Fox and S. Hindle (eds), *The experience of authority in early modern England* (Basingstoke, Macmillan, 1996).

Hall, M., 'Poor relief in Eskdale in the early 1800s', *Transactions of the Cumberland and Westmorland Antiquarian and Archaeological Society*, 152 (1992) 205–12.

Hamlin, C., *Public health and social justice in the age of Chadwick: Britain 1800–1854* (Cambridge, Cambridge University Press, 1998).

Hampson, E. M., *The treatment of poverty in Cambridgeshire, 1597–1834* (Cambridge, Cambridge University Press, 1934).

Harling, P., 'The power of persuasion: central authority, local bureaucracy and the new poor law', *English Historical Review*, 107 (1992) 30–53.

Harris, J. R. (ed.), *Liverpool and Merseyside* (London, Allen and Unwin, 1968).

Hastings, R. P., *Poverty and the poor law in the North Riding of Yorkshire 1780–1837* (York, Borthwick Institute, 1982).

Hearder, H., and H. R. Koyn (eds), *British government and administration: studies presented to S. B. Chrimes* (Cardiff, University of Wales Press, 1974).

Hellmuth, E., (ed.), *The transformation of political culture in late eighteenth century England and Germany* (Oxford, Berg, 1990).

Henderson, J., and R. Wall (eds), *Poor women and children in the European past* (London, Routledge, 1994).

Henriques, U., 'How cruel was the Victorian poor law?', *Historical Journal*, 11 (1968) 365–71.

'Jeremy Bentham and the machinery of social reform', in H. Hearder and H. R. Koyn (eds), *British government and administration: studies presented to S. B. Chrimes* (Cardiff, University of Wales Press, 1974), pp. 68–79.

Himmelfarb, G., 'Mayhew's poor: a problem of identity', *Victorian Studies*, 14 (1971) 307–20.

The idea of poverty: England in the early industrial age (London, Faber, 1984).

Hindle, G. B., *Provision for the relief of the poor in Manchester 1754–1826* (Manchester, Manchester University Press, 1975).

Hitchcock, T. V., 'Paupers and preachers: the SPCK and the parochial workhouse movement', in L. Davison, T. Hitchcock, T. Keirn and R. B. Shoemaker (eds), *Stilling the grumbling hive: the response to social and economic problems in England, 1689–1750* (Stroud, Sutton, 1992), pp. 145–66.

Hitchcock, T., P. King and P., Sharpe (eds), *Chronicling poverty: the voices and strategies of the English poor, 1640–1840* (Basingstoke, Macmillan, 1997).

Hodgkinson, R. G., 'Poor law medical officers of England 1834–1871', *Journal of the History of Medicine*, 11 (1965) 229–38.

The origins of the National Health Service: the medical services of the new poor law 1834–1871 (London, Wellcome Institute, 1967).

Hobsbawn, E. J., and G. Rudé, *Captain Swing* (London, Penguin, 1969 reprint).

Hollen-Lees, L., *Poverty and pauperism in nineteenth-century London* (Leicester, Leicester University Press, 1988).

'The survival of the unfit: welfare policies and family maintenance in nineteenth century London', in P. Mandler (ed.), *The uses of charity: the poor on relief in the nineteenth century metropolis* (Cambridge, Cambridge University Press, 1990), pp. 68–91.

The solidarities of strangers: the English poor laws and the people, 1700–1948 (Cambridge, Cambridge University Press, 1998).

Hoppit, J. (ed.), *Failed legislation 1660–1800* (London, Hambledon Press, 1997).

Horne, T. A., *Property rights and poverty: political argument in Britain 1605–1834* (London, Ohio University Press, 1990).

Horrell, S., and J. Humphries, 'Old questions, new data and alternative perspectives: families' living standards in the industrial revolution', *Journal of Economic History*, 52 (1992) 849–80.

'Women's labour force participation and the transition to the male breadwinner family, 1790–1865', *Economic History Review*, 38 (1995) 89–117.

'The exploitation of little children: child labor and the family economy in the industrial revolution', *Explorations in Economic History*, 32 (1995) 485–516.

Howard-Drake, J., 'The poor of Shipton under Wychwood parish 1740–62', *Wychwood History Society Journal*, 5 (1989) 4–44.

Howells, G., 'For I was tired of England sir: English pauper emigrant strategies 1834–60', *Social History*, 23 (1998) 181–94.

Hudson, P., 'Proto-industrialisation in England', in S. Ogilvie and M. Cerman (eds), *European proto-industrialisation* (Cambridge, Cambridge University Press, 1996), pp. 49–66.

Hudson, P., and S. A. King, *Industrialisation, material culture and everyday life* (forthcoming).

Hufton, O., *The poor of eighteenth century France 1750–89* (Oxford, Oxford University Press, 1974).

Humphries, J., 'Enclosure, common right and women: the proletarianisation of families in the late eighteenth and early nineteenth centuries', *Journal of Economic History*, 50 (1990) 17–42.

Hunt, E. H., 'Paupers and pensioners past and present', *Ageing and Society*, 9 (1990) 407–30.

Imray, J., *The charity of Richard Whittington* (London, London University Press, 1968).

Innes, J., 'Prisons for the poor: English bridewells 1555–1800', in F. Snyder and D. Hay (eds), *Labour, law and crime: an historical perspective* (London, Longman, 1987), pp. 42–122.

'Parliament and the shaping of eighteenth-century English social policy', *Transactions of the Royal Historical Society*, 40 (1990) 63–92.

'Politics and morals: the reformation of manners movement in later eighteenth century England', in E. Hellmuth (ed.), *The transformation of political culture in late eighteenth century England and Germany* (Oxford, Berg, 1990), pp. 57–118.

'The "mixed economy of welfare" in early modern England: assessments of the options from Hale to Malthus (c. 1683–1803)', in M. J. Daunton (ed.), *Charity, self-interest and welfare in the English past* (London, UCL Press, 1996), pp. 139–80.

'The state and the poor: eighteenth century England in European perspective', in J. Brewer and E. Hellmuth (eds), *Rethinking leviathan: the eighteenth century state in Britain and Germany* (Oxford, Oxford University Press, 1999), pp. 225–80.

James, J. A., 'Personal wealth distribution in late eighteenth century Britain', *Economic History Review*, 41 (1988) 543–65.

Jewell, H., *The north-south divide: the origins of northern consciousness in England* (Manchester, Manchester University Press, 1994).

Johnson, P., *Saving and spending: the working class economy in Britain 1870–1939* (Oxford, Oxford University Press, 1985).

Johnson, P., and P. Thane (eds), *Old age from antiquity to post modernity* (London, Routledge, 1998).

Johnston, J. A., 'The parish registers and poor law records of Powick, 1663–1841', *Transactions of the Worcestershire Archaeological Society*, 9 (1984) 55–66.

Jones, G., *History of the law of charity 1532–1827* (Cambridge, Cambridge University Press, 1969).

Jutte, R., *Poverty and deviance in early modern Europe* (Cambridge, Cambridge University Press, 1994).

Keith, W. J., *The rural tradition: William Cobbett, Gilbert White, and other non-fiction prose writers of the English countryside* (Brighton, Harvester, 1975).

Keith-Lucas, B., *Parish affairs: the government of Kent under George III* (Ashford, Kent County Library Service, 1986).

Kennedy, J., *History of Leyton* (London, privately published, 1894).

Kent, J., 'The centre and the localities: state formation and parish government in England 1640–1740', *Historical Journal*, 38 (1995) 363–404.

Kidd, A. J., 'Historians or polemicists? How the Webbs wrote their history of the English poor laws', *Economic History Review*, 50 (1987) 400–17.

State, society and the poor in nineteenth century England (Basingstoke, Macmillan, 1999).

King, P., 'Gleaners, farmers and the failure of legal sanctions 1750–1850', *Past and Present*, 125 (1989) 116–50.

'Customary rights and women's earnings: the importance of gleaning to the rural labouring poor 1750–1850', *Economic History Review*, 44 (1991) 461–76.

'Legal change, customary right and social conflict in late eighteenth century England: the origins of the great gleaning case of 1788', *Law and History Review*, 10 (1992) 1–31.

'Pauper inventories and the material lives of the poor in the eighteenth and early nineteenth centuries', in T. Hitchcock, P. King and P. Sharpe (eds), *Chronicling poverty: the words and lives of the English poor 1640–1840* (Basingstoke, Macmillan, 1997), pp. 155–91.

King, S. A., 'Multiple source record linkage in a rural industrial community, 1680–1820', *History and Computing*, 6 (1994) 133–42.

'Reconstructing lives: the poor, the poor law and welfare in rural industrial communities', *Social History*, 22 (1997) 318–38.

'Power representation and the self: problems with sources for record linkage', *Local Historian*, 24 (1997) 1–11.

'Dying with style: infant death and its context in a rural industrial community', *Social History of Medicine*, 10 (1997) 3–24.

'A model of vision and benevolence: Mary Haslam and the Bolton poor law union 1880–1914' in A. Digby, S. A. King and R. M. Smith (eds), *Poverty, poor relief and welfare in England from the seventeenth to twentieth centuries* (Cambridge, Cambridge University Press, forthcoming).

'Making the most of opportunity: the economy of makeshifts in the early modern north', in S. A. King and A. Tomkins (eds), *Coping with the crossroads of life: the economy of makeshifts in early modern England* (forthcoming).

King, S. A., and J. G., Timmins, *Making sense of the industrial revolution* (Manchester, Manchester University Press, forthcoming).

Kussmaul, A., *Servants in Husbandry* (Cambridge, Cambridge University Press, 1981).

Landau, N., 'The laws of settlement and surveillance of immigration in eighteenth-century Kent', *Continuity and Change*, 3 (1988) 391–420.

'The regulation of immigration, economic structures and definitions of the poor in eighteenth century England', *Historical Journal*, 33 (1990) 541–72.

'The eighteenth-century context of the laws of settlement', *Continuity and Change*, 6 (1991) 417–39.

'Who was subjected to the laws of settlement? Procedure under the settlement laws in eighteenth-century England', *Agricultural History Review*, 43 (1996) 139–59.

Langton, J., and R. J. Morris (eds), *Atlas of industrialising Britain 1780–1914* (London, Macmillan, 1986).

Laquer, T., 'Bodies, death and pauper funerals', *Representations*, 1 (1983) 109–31.

Laybourn, K., *The evolution of British social policy and the welfare state 1800–1993* (Keele, Keele University Press, 1995).

Levitt, I., 'Poor law and pauperism', in J. Langton and R. J. Morris (eds), *Atlas of industrialising Britain 1780–1914* (London, Macmillan, 1986).

Lewis, R. A., 'William Day and the poor law commissioners', *University of Birmingham Historical Journal*, 9 (1964) 163–96.

Lis, C., and H. Soly, *Poverty and capitalism in pre-industrial Europe* (Brighton, Harvester Press, 1979).

Loudon, I., 'I'd rather have been a parish surgeon than a union one', *Bulletin of the Society for the Social History of Medicine*, 38 (1986) 68–73.

Lubove, R. (ed.), *Social welfare in transition: selected English documents 1834–1909* (Pittsburgh, University of Pittsburgh Press, 1982).

McClure, R. K., *Coram's children: the London foundling hospital in the eighteenth century* (New Haven, Yale University Press, 1981).

McCord, N., 'The 1834 poor law amendment act on Tyneside', *International Review of Social History*, 14 (1969) 1–23.

'The poor law and philanthropy', in D. Fraser (ed.), *The new poor law in the nineteenth century*, (Basingstoke, Macmillan, 1976), pp. 87–110.

MacKay, L., 'Why they stole: women in the Old Bailey 1779–1789', *Journal of Social History* 32 (1999) 623–40.

Mandler, P., 'The making of the new poor law redivivus', *Past and Present*, 117 (1987) 131–57.

'Tories and paupers: Christian political economy and the making of the new poor law', *Historical Journal*, 33 (1990) 81–103.

(ed.), *The uses of charity: the poor on relief in the nineteenth century metropolis* (Cambridge, Cambridge University Press, 1990).

Mannion, J., *A northern tour* (Leeds, Black, 1838).

Marshall, D., *The English poor in the eighteenth century* (New York, Routledge, 1969 reprint).

Marshall, J. D., 'The nottinghamshire reformers and their contribution to the new poor law', *Economic History Review*, 13 (1960/61) 382–96.

The old poor law 1795–1834 (Basingstoke, Macmillan, 1973).

Martin, E. W., (ed.), *Comparative developments in social welfare* (London, Croom Helm, 1978).

'From parish to union: poor law administration 1601–1865', in E. W. Martin (ed.), *Comparative developments in social welfare* (London, Croom Helm, 1978), pp. 25–56.

Mason, K., *Addingham: from brigantes to bypass* (Settle, Addingham Civic Society, 1996).

Mencher, S., 'Introduction to the poor law reports of 1834 and 1909', in R. Lubove (ed.), *Social welfare in transition: selected English documents 1834–1909* (Pittsburgh, University of Pittsburgh Press, 1982).

Midwinter, E. C., 'State intervention at the local level: the new poor law in Lancashire', *Historical Journal*, 10 (1967) 322–43.

286

Social administration in Lancashire 1830–1860 (Manchester, Manchester University Press, 1969).

Mitchison, R., *Coping with destitution: poverty and relief in western Europe* (Toronto, Toronto University Press, 1991).

Mommsen W. J., (ed.), *The emergence of the welfare state in Britain and Germany, 1850–1950* (London, Longman, 1981).

Munsche, P., *Gentlemen and poachers: the English game laws 1671–1831* (Cambridge, Cambridge University Press, 1981).

Neeson, J. M., *Commoners: common right, enclosure and social change in England 1700–1820* (Cambridge, Cambridge University Press, 1993).

Neuman, M., *The Speenhamland county: poverty and the poor laws in Berkshire 1782–1834* (New York, Garland, 1982).

Newman, A. N. (ed.), *The parliamentary diary of Sir Edward Knatchbull 1722–1730* (London, Royal Historical Society, 1963).

Newman-Brown, W., 'The receipt of poor relief and family situation: Aldenham, Herts, 1630–90', in R. M. Smith (ed.), *Land, kinship and life cycle* (Cambridge, Cambridge University Press, 1984), pp. 405–22.

Ogilvie, S., and M. Cerman (eds), *European proto-industrialisation* (Cambridge, Cambridge University Press, 1996).

Ottoway, S. R., 'Providing for the elderly in eighteenth century England', *Continuity and Change*, 13 (1998) 391–418.

Ottoway, S., and S. Williams, 'Reconstructing the life cycle experiences of poverty in the time of the old poor law', *Archives*, 23 (1998) 19–29.

Overton, M., *Agricultural revolution in England: the transformation of the agrarian economy 1500–1850* (Cambridge, Cambridge University Press, 1996).

Oxley, G., 'The permanent poor in south west Lancashire under the old poor law', in J. R. Harris (ed.), *Liverpool and Merseyside* (London, Allen and Unwin, 1968), pp. 16–49.

Poor relief in England and Wales 1601–1834 (Newton Abbot, David and Charles, 1974).

Pam, D., *A parish near London: a history of Enfield volume 1* (Frome, Enfield Preservation Society, 1990).

Parsons, M. A., 'Poor relief in Troutbeck 1640–1836', *Transactions of the Cumberland and Westmorland Antiquarian and Archaeological Society*, 155 (1995) 169–86.

Payne, A., *Portrait of a parish* (Kineton, Roundwood Press, 1968).

Pelling, M., and R. M. Smith (eds), *Life, death and the elderly: historical perspectives* (London, Routledge, 1991).

Pickles, M. F., 'Labour migration in Yorkshire 1670–1743', *Local Population Studies*, 57 (1996) 29–49.

Prochaska, F. K., *Women and philanthropy in C19th England* (Oxford, Oxford University Press, 1980).

'Philanthropy', in F. M. L. Thompson (ed.), *The Cambridge Social History of Britain 1750–1850* (Cambridge, Cambridge University Press, 1990), pp. 357–93.

Redford, A., *The history of local government in Manchester: borough and city* (London, Longman, 1940).

Richards, E., 'How did poor people emigrate from the British Isles to Australia in the nineteenth century?', *Journal of British Studies*, 32 (1993) 250–79.

Ripley, P., 'Poverty in Gloucester and its alleviation 1690–1740', *Transactions of the Bristol and Gloucester Archaeological Society*, 103 (1985) 185–99.

Roberts, D., 'How cruel was the Victorian poor law?', *Historical Journal*, 6 (1963) 97–107.

Roberts, M. J. D., 'Head versus heart? Voluntary associations and charity organisation in England 1700–1850', in H. Cunningham and J. Innes (eds), *Charity, philanthropy and reform from the 1690s to 1850* (Basingstoke, Macmillan, 1998), pp. 66–86.

Rogers, A., *The state of the poor: a history of the labouring classes in England with parochial reports by Sir Frederick Morton Eden* (London, Routledge, 1928 reprint).

Rose, L., *Rogues and vagabonds: the vagrant underworld in Britain 1815–1985* (London, Routledge, 1988).

Rose, M. E., 'The anti-poor law movement in the north of England', *Northern History*, 1 (1966) 41–73.

'The crisis of poor relief in England, 1850–90', in W. J. Mommsen (ed.), *The emergence of the welfare state in Britain and Germany, 1850–1950* (London, Longman, 1981), pp. 64–93.

The relief of poverty 1834–1914 (Basingstoke, Macmillan, 1986 reprint).

(ed.), *The poor and the city: the English poor law in its urban context 1834–1914* (Leicester, Leicester University Press, 1988).

Rose, S. O., 'Widowhood and poverty in nineteenth century Nottinghamshire', in J. Henderson and R. Wall, *Poor women and children in the European past* (London, Routledge, 1994), pp. 269–91.

Ruggles, S., 'Migration, marriage and mortality: correcting sources of bias in English family reconstitution', *Population Studies*, 46 (1992) 507–22.

Rushton, P., 'The poor law, the parish and the community in north-east England 1600–1800', *Northern History*, 25 (1989) 135–52.

Sharpe, P., 'Poor children as apprentices in Colyton, 1798–1830', *Continuity and Change*, 6 (1991) 253–70.

'The bowels of compation: a labouring family and the law c. 1790–1834', in T. Hitchcock, P. King and P. Sharpe (eds), *Chronicling poverty: the voices and strategies of the English poor 1640–1840* (Basingstoke, Macmillan, 1997), pp. 87–108.

Adapting to capitalism: working women in the English economy, 1700–1800 (Basingstoke, Macmillan, 1996).

Sheppard, F. H. W., *Local government in St. Marylebone, 1688–1835* (London, Athlone Press, 1958).

Slack, P., 'Books of orders: the making of English social policy 1577–1631', *Transactions of the Royal Historical Society*, 30 (1980) 1–23.

Poverty and policy in Tudor and Stuart England (Basingstoke, Macmillan,

1988).

The English poor law 1531–1782 (Basingstoke, Macmillan, 1992).

From reformation to improvement: public welfare in early modern England (Oxford, Clarendon Press, 1999).

Smith, L. D., 'The pauper lunatic problem in the west midlands 1815–1850', *Midland History*, 21 (1996) 101–18.

Smith, R. M., (ed.), *Land, kinship and life cycle* (Cambridge, Cambridge University Press, 1984).

'Charity, self-interest and welfare: reflections from demographic and family history', in M. J. Daunton (ed.), *Charity, self-interest and welfare in the English past* (London, UCL Press, 1996), pp. 23–50.

'Ageing and well being in early modern England: pension trends and gender preferences under the English old poor law 1650–1800', in P. Johnson and P. Thane (eds), *Old age from antiquity to post-modernity* (London, Routledge, 1998), pp. 64–95.

Snell, K. D. M., *Annals of the labouring poor: social change and agrarian England 1660–1900* (Cambridge, Cambridge University Press, 1985).

'Pauper settlement and the right to poor relief in England and Wales', *Continuity and Change*, 6 (1991) 375–415.

Snyder, F., and D. Hay (eds), *Labour, law and crime: an historical perspective* (London, Longman, 1987).

Sokoll, T., 'The pauper household small and simple? The evidence from listings of inhabitants and pauper lists of early modern England reassessed', *Ethnologia Europaea*, 27 (1985) 25–42.

Household and family among the poor: the case of two Essex communities in the late eighteenth and early nineteenth centuries (Bochum, Verlaag, 1993).

'The household position of elderly widows in poverty: evidence from two English communities in the late eighteenth and early nineteenth centuries', in J. Henderson and R. Wall (eds), *Poor women and children in the European past* (London, Routledge, 1994), pp. 207–24.

'Old age in poverty: the record of Essex pauper letters 1780–1834', in T. Hitchcock, P. King and P. Sharpe *Chronicling poverty: the voices and strategies of the English poor, 1640–1840* (Basingstoke, Macmillan, 1997), pp. 127–54.

Solar, P., 'Poor relief and English economic development before the industrial revolution', *Economic History Review*, 48 (1995) 1–22.

Song, B., 'Continuity and change in English rural society: the formation of poor law unions in Oxford', *English Historical Review*, 114 (1999) 314–38.

Stapleton, B., 'Inherited poverty and life-cycle poverty: Odiham, Hampshire 1650–1850', *Social History*, 18 (1993) 339–55.

Tanner, A., 'The casual poor and the city of London poor law union 1837–1869', *Historical Journal*, 42 (1999) 183–206.

Taylor, G., *The problem of poverty 1660–1834* (London, Longman, 1969).

Taylor, J. S., 'The impact of pauper settlement 1691–1834', *Past and Present*, 73 (1976) 42–74.

'The unreformed workhouse, 1776–1834', in E. W. Martin (ed.), *Comparative developments in social welfare* (London, Croom Helm, 1978), pp. 57–84.

Poverty, migration and settlement in the industrial revolution: sojourners' narratives (Palo Alto, SPSS, 1989).

'A different kind of Speenhamland: nonresident relief in the industrial revolution', *Journal of British Studies*, 30 (1991) 183–208.

'Voices in the crowd: the Kirby Lonsdale township letters, 1809–36', in T. Hitchcock, P. King and P. Sharpe (eds), *Chronicling poverty: the voices and strategies of the English poor, 1640–1840* (Basingstoke, Macmillan, 1997), pp. 109–26.

Thane, P., *The origins of British social policy* (London, Croom Helm, 1978).

'Government and society in England and Wales 1750–1914', in F. M. L. Thompson, *The Cambridge social history of Britain 1750–1950* (Cambridge, Cambridge University Press, 1990).

'Old people and their families in the English past', in M. J. Daunton (ed.), *Charity, self-interest and welfare in the English past* (London, UCL Press, 1996), pp. 113–38.

Thomas, E. G., 'The old poor law and medicine', *Medical History*, 24 (1980) 1–19.

Thompson, F. M. L., *The Cambridge social history of Britain 1750–1950* (Cambridge, Cambridge University Press, 1990).

Thomson, D., 'The decline of social security: falling state support for the elderly since early Victorian times', *Ageing and Society*, 4 (1984) 451–82.

'Welfare and the historians', in L. Bonfield, R. M. Smith and K. Wrightson (eds), *The world we have gained* (Oxford, Oxford University Press, 1986), pp. 355–78.

'The elderly in an urban-industrial society: England 1750 to the present', in J. M. Eekelaar and D. Pearl (eds), *An ageing world: dilemmas and challenges for law and social policy* (Oxford, Oxford University Press, 1989), pp. 55–60.

'The welfare of the elderly in the past: a family or community responsibility?', in M. Pelling and R. M. Smith (eds), *Life, death and the elderly: historical perspectives* (London, Routledge, 1991), pp. 194–221.

Timmins, J. G., *The last shift* (Manchester, Manchester University Press, 1993).

Tomkins, A., 'Paupers and the infirmary in mid-eighteenth-century Shrewsbury', *Medical History*, 43 (1999) 208–27.

'Pawnbroking and the survival strategies of the urban poor in 1770s York', in S. A. King and A. Tomkins (eds), *Coping with the crossroads of life: the economy of makeshifts in early modern England* (forthcoming).

Turner, M., (ed.), *Malthus and his time* (Basingstoke, Macmillan, 1987).

Valenze, D., 'Charity, custom and humanity: changing attitudes to the poor in eighteenth century England', in J. Garnett and C. Matthew (eds), *Revival and religion since 1700: essays for John Walsh* (London, Hambledon, 1993), pp. 59–78.

Wales, T., 'Poverty, poor relief and life-cycle: some evidence from seventeenth century Norfolk', in R. M. Smith (ed.), *Land, kinship and life cycle* (Cambridge, Cambridge University Press, 1984), pp. 351–404.

Wall, R., 'Some implications of the earnings, income and expenditure patterns of married women in populations in the past', in J. Henderson and R. Wall (eds), *Poor women and children in the European past* (London, Routledge, 1994), pp. 312–35.

Walsh, V. J., 'Old and new poor laws in Shropshire 1820–1870', *Midland History*, 2 (1974), 225–43.

Watson, R., 'Poverty in north-east Lancashire in 1843: evidence from Quaker charity records', *Local Population Studies*, 55 (1995) 28–44.

Weatherill, L., *Consumer behaviour and material culture in Britain 1660–1760* (London, Macmillan, 1988).

Webb, S., and B. Webb, *English poor law history part I: the old poor law* (London, Cass, 1963 reprint).
English poor law history part II: the last hundred years (London, Cass, 1963 reprint).

Wells, R., 'Migration, the law and parochial policy in eighteenth and early nineteenth century southern England', *Southern History*, 15 (1993) 86–139.

Williams, K., *From pauperism to poverty* (London, Routledge and Kegan Paul, 1981).

Wood, P., *Poverty and the workhouse in Victorian Britain* (Stroud, Sutton, 1991).

Woodward, J., *To do the sick no harm: a study of the British voluntary hospital system to 1875* (London, Routledge, 1974).

Woolf, S., 'Order, class and the urban poor', in M. L. Bush (ed.), *Social orders and social classes in Europe since 1500* (London, Longman, 1993), pp. 185–98.

Wright, D., and A. Digby (eds), *From idiocy to mental deficiency: historical perspectives on people with learning disabilities* (London, Routledge, 1996).

Wrightson, K., 'The politics of the parish in early modern England', in P. Griffiths, A. Fox and S. Hindle (eds), *The experience of authority in early modern England* (Basingstoke, Macmillan, 1996).

Wrightson K., and D. Levine, *The making of an industrial society: Whickham 1560–1765* (Oxford, Oxford University Press, 1991).

Wrigley, E. A., 'Malthus on the prospects for the labouring poor', *Historical Journal*, 31 (1988) 813–29.

Wrigley, E. A., R. S. Davies, J. E. Oeppen and R. S. Schofield, *English population history from family reconstitution* (Cambridge, Cambridge University Press, 1998).

Unpublished work

Barker-Read, M., 'The treatment of the aged poor in five selected west Kent parishes from settlement to Speenhamland 1662–1797' (unpublished Ph.D. thesis, Open University, 1988).

Body, G., 'The administration of the poor law in Dorset 1760–1834, with special reference to agrarian distress' (unpublished Ph.D. thesis, University of Southampton, 1968).

Boyson, R., 'The history of poor law administration in north east Lancashire 1834–1871' (unpublished M.A. thesis, Manchester University, 1960).

King, S., 'Grinding out poverty histories: linking poor law records in Wales', unpublished paper, available at the Oxford Brookes University Library.

Mosley, J. V., 'Poor law administration in England and Wales, 1834–1850, with special reference to the problem of able bodied pauperism' (unpublished Ph.D. thesis, University of London, 1975).

Newman, A. E., 'The old poor law in east Kent, 1606–1834: a social and demographic analysis' (unpublished Ph.D. thesis, University of Kent, 1979).

Ottoway, S. R., 'The decline of life: aspects of ageing in eighteenth century England' (unpublished Ph.D. thesis, Brown University, 1997).

Rose, M. E., 'The administration of the poor law in the West Riding, 1820–1855' (unpublished Ph.D. thesis, University of Oxford, 1965).

Shapley, P., 'Voluntary charities in nineteenth century Manchester' (unpublished Ph.D. thesis, Manchester Metropolitan University, 1995).

Shaw, J. M., 'The development of the local poor law acts, 1696–1833, with particular reference to the incorporated hundreds of east anglia' (unpublished Ph.D. thesis, University of East Anglia, 1989).

Tanner, A., 'The city of London poor law union 1837–1869' (unpublished Ph.D. thesis, University of London, 1995).

Taylor, J. S., 'Poverty in rural Devon 1785–1840' (unpublished Ph.D. thesis, Stanford University, 1966).

Thomas, E. G., 'The treatment of poverty in Berkshire, Essex and Oxfordshire 1723–1840' (unpublished Ph.D. thesis, University of London, 1971).

Thompson, K., 'The Leicester poor law union 1836–1871' (unpublished Ph.D. thesis, University of Leicester, 1988).

Thomson, D., 'Provision for the elderly in England 1830–1908' (unpublished Ph.D. thesis, University of Cambridge, 1980).

Tomkins, A., 'The experience of urban poverty: a comparison of Oxford and Shrewsbury 1740–70' (unpublished D.Phil. thesis, University of Oxford, 1994).

Walsh, V. J., 'Poor law administration in Shropshire 1820–1885' (unpublished Ph.D. thesis, University of Pennsylvania, 1970).

Whittle, M., 'The changing face of charity in a nineteenth century provincial town' (unpublished Ph.D. thesis, Lancaster University, 1990).

Williams, S., 'Poor relief and medical provision in Bedfordshire: the social, economic and demographic context 1750–1850' (unpublished Ph.D. thesis, University of Cambridge, 1999).

Workman, C., 'The effect of Gilbert's act on poor law administration in north Lancashire: Caton union 1800–1841' (Unpublished dissertation for the Diploma in Local History, University of Liverpool, 1989).

INDEX